THE HISTORY OF NEBRASKA LAW

Ohio University Press Series on Law, Society, and Politics in the Midwest

Series Editor: Paul Finkelman

The History of Ohio Law, edited by Michael Les Benedict and John F. Winkler

Frontiers of Freedom: Cincinnati's Black Community, 1802–1868, by Nikki M. Taylor

A Place of Recourse: A History of the U.S. District Court for the Southern District of Ohio, 1803–2003, by Roberta Sue Alexander

The Black Laws: Race and the Legal Process in Early Ohio, by Stephen Middleton

The History of Indiana Law, edited by David J. Bodenhamer and Hon. Randall T. Shepard

The History of Michigan Law, edited by Paul Finkelman and Martin J. Hershock

The Rescue of Joshua Glover: A Fugitive Slave, the Constitution, and the Coming of the Civil War, by H. Robert Baker

The History of Nebraska Law, edited by Alan G. Gless

THE HISTORY OF NEBRASKA LAW

Edited by Alan G. Gless

With a foreword by Hon. John V. Hendry,

Chief Justice, Nebraska Supreme Court

Ohio University Press Athens

Ohio University Press, Athens, Ohio 45701
www.ohioswallow.com

Portions of chapter 12 appeared in slightly different form in *International Society of Barristers Quarterly* 17, no. 2 (1982): 259–66, and are reprinted here with permission from the International Society of Barristers.
Portions of chapter 15 appeared in slightly different form in *Nebraska Lawyer* (August 2000): 18–22, and are reprinted here with permission from the Nebraska State Bar Association.

Printed in the United States of America
Ohio University Press books are printed on acid-free paper ∞ ™

15 14 13 12 11 10 09 08 5 4 3 2 1

Library of Congress Cataloging-in-Publication Data

The history of Nebraska law / edited by Alan G. Gless ; with a foreword by John V. Hendry. — 1st ed.
p. cm. — (Ohio University Press series on law, society, and politics in the midwest)
Includes bibliographical references and index.
ISBN 978-0-8214-1787-4 (cloth : alk. paper)
1. Law—Nebraska—History. I. Gless, Alan G.
KFN78.H57 2008
349.782—dc22

2008016771

To Karel and Kathleen

CONTENTS

ILLUSTRATIONS

Maps

Tables

FOREWORD

Two statues stand outside the National Archives Building in Washington, D.C. One bears the inscription "Study the Past," the other, "What Is Past Is Prologue." What these two inscriptions present is a recognition of history's critical role in understanding where we are today and helping us determine where we should be tomorrow.

The History of Nebraska Law brings together in one volume a broad range of Nebraska's legal history. In reviewing the topics presented, I was immediately reminded of a number of cases that were argued and decided by Nebraska's Supreme Court during my eight years as its chief justice. These included issues examining the common law of Nebraska, the evolution of Nebraska's statutory scheme of criminal law, land use regulation as it relates to livestock, water law, and public employment labor disputes and the role of the Commission of Industrial Relations. In looking back on these cases, it would have been useful to have had available *The History of Nebraska Law* to assist in understanding "where we are today" and considering "where we should be tomorrow."

The History of Nebraska Law provides an interesting and rich study of Nebraska law. I am pleased to recommend it to anyone searching to find the past, present, or future of Nebraska's law.

John V. Hendry

Chief Justice, Nebraska Supreme Court

October 1, 1998 to October 2, 2006

ACKNOWLEDGMENTS

Producing a book written by multiple contributing authors requires a small army, every member of which deserves thanks. I don't mean to skip anyone in this set of acknowledgments, but I don't even know the names of some of the people who worked on this book at Ohio University Press. Obviously, the contributing authors all deserve thanks. The small band of anonymous reviewers whose identities will remain undisclosed deserves public thanks, too.

Some folks must be identified, such as Professor Stephen Kalish, of the Nebraska College of Law, now retired, who encouraged me to accept Paul Finkelman's invitation to edit this volume; Dean Steven L. Willborn, of the Nebraska College of Law, and retired Chief Justice John V. Hendry, of the Nebraska Supreme Court, who offered moral support along the way; and Sheila Beins, who tolerated with grace my long periods of mental absence. Nebraska Wesleyan University history professor Ronald C. Naugle, now retired, assisted with advice and shared freely information that I couldn't have found elsewhere, and I thank him. Sandy Placzek and Kris Lauber at the Schmid Law Library of the University of Nebraska College of Law also provided invaluable assistance, as did Brenda K. George, one of the newest members of the Nebraska bar.

Gillian Berchowitz and Paul Finkelman, who taught this hands-on course entitled volume editing 101, answered all of their subneophyte volume editor's ceaseless, clue-free questions; they deserve special thanks. I must have tried their patience, yet neither ever showed it. To Rick Huard, Ohio University Press project editor, I extend my heaviest thanks.

INTRODUCTION

Readers might ask what legitimate place can Nebraska claim in a series devoted to the study of midwestern legal history and the culture and politics of law in the Midwest? That's a reasonable enough question. Series editor Paul Finkelman initially inquired of me whether I, a lifelong Nebraskan, considered Nebraska a midwestern state. I responded that it depends. It depends upon the canons of the discipline of which one inquires and upon whether the inquirer refers to the entire state of Nebraska, to eastern Nebraska, or to western Nebraska. Geographers think of Nebraska as a Great Plains state.[1] Research and reference librarians catalog Nebraska as a midwestern state.[2] It also may depend upon the perceptions of the Nebraskans of whom one inquires. As Warren Hofstra posits, "Perception is as important as political boundaries or the distribution of cultural traits in defining region."[3] While Wyoming may call itself the place where the West begins, a description Nebraska formerly claimed, the West most certainly does begin in central Nebraska at the hundredth meridian, if not farther to the east. Unlike states that merely think of themselves as the center of everything American, Nebraska actually lies at the center of the coterminous United States.[4] In reality, Nebraska is both a Midwest state and a Great Plains state. For that reason alone, Nebraska claims a legitimate

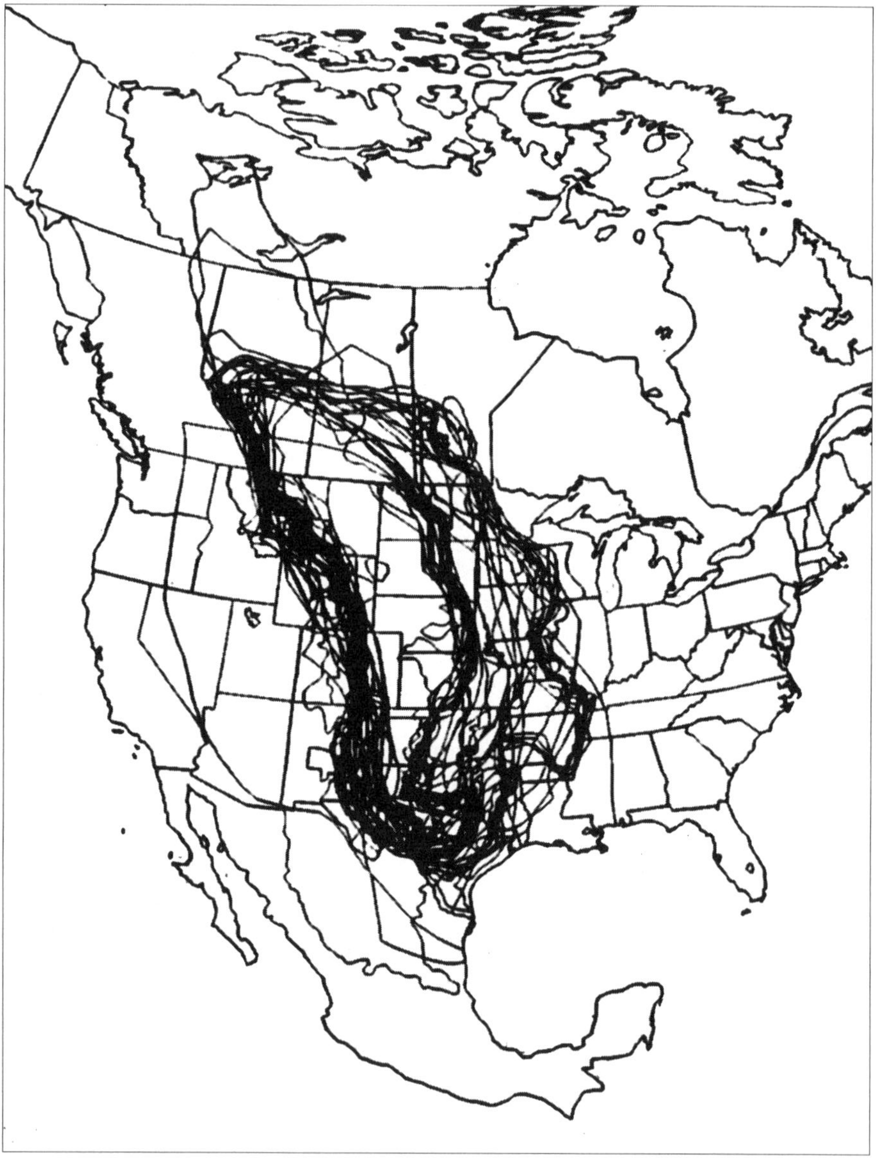

Map 0.1. Fifty published versions of the Great Plains regional boundary. *Reprinted by permission of the University of Nebraska–Lincoln Center for Great Plains Studies*

place in a series studying the legal history and the culture and politics of law in the Midwest, but we have additional reasons.

Nebraska's roots lie deep in the Midwest. More than three-fourths of the population of the Nebraska Territory at the time of the 1860 census claimed to be native-born Americans. They represented a stream of migration that had moved across the Old Northwest from New England and the Middle Atlantic states. The leading states of origin for the 1860 Nebraska population were, in order, Ohio, New York, Pennsylvania, Illinois, Iowa, Indiana, and Missouri.[5] Professor Ronald C. Naugle observed that the same patterns of settlement established in 1860 continued to hold for at least fifty years—significant numbers of native-born migrants to Nebraska continued to come along the same path from western Pennsylvania and from Ohio, Indiana, Illinois, and Iowa.[6]

Even more noteworthy for our present purpose, 31.92 percent of Nebraska's 1860 residents claimed states of the Old Northwest as their native states. Specifically, 10.81 percent of Nebraska's 1860 residents claimed Ohio as their native state; 6.91 percent, Indiana; 5.74 percent, Illinois; 5.51 percent, Iowa; 1.72 percent, Wisconsin; and 1.23 percent, Michigan. None claimed Minnesota.[7] By the next census, 32.33 percent of Nebraska's residents listed Old Northwest states as their native homes.[8] Of Nebraska's 1880 residents, 35.15 percent made that claim.[9] Over the next decade, the percentage dropped to 33.05.[10] In 1900, it declined further to 25.91 percent.[11] By 1910, the last year for which the census statistics measured the native state claims of responding parties, only 21.924 percent of Nebraska residents claimed states of the Old Northwest.[12] The importance of these demographic statistics lies in the recollections and preferences that many of these folks brought with them from their native states.

In fact, Nebraska modeled its first territorial laws and some of its first state laws on those enacted by states created out of the Northwest Territory. Nebraska's first state constitution was based on the U.S. Constitution and the Nebraska Enabling Act, but its second state constitution, largely still in effect in 2006, found its origins in the Illinois constitution of 1871. Whether the English common law and statutes applied in Nebraska did not become an issue as it did in parts of the Old Northwest.

Taken at face value, the Nebraska adoption statute stated that the common law applied; the English statutes did not. Roscoe Pound, dean of the Nebraska College of Law (1903–7) and future dean of the Harvard Law School (1916–36), also served as a Nebraska Supreme Court commissioner for a time. Pound's discussion of the meaning of "common law of England," as used in Nebraska's common law adoption statute, is worth reading for its uniqueness among American understandings of that phrase.[13] Pound's interpretation remains controlling in Nebraska today. Applying the common law inflexibly was not one of Pound's preferences.

In *Williams v. Miles,* Commissioner Pound wrote:

> We can not think, and we do not believe this court has ever understood, that the legislature intended to petrify the common law, as embodied in judicial decisions at any one time, and set it up in such inflexible form as a rule of decision. . . . The term "common law of England," as used in the statute, refers to that general system of law which prevails in England, and in most of the United States by derivation from England, as distinguished from the Roman or Civil Law system, which was in force in this territory prior to the Louisiana purchase. Hence the statute does not require adherence to the decisions of the English common-law courts prior to the Revolution, in case this court considers subsequent decisions, either in England or America, better expositions of the general principles of that system.[14]

As in the other volumes in this series, the essays presented here offer both basic information and bases for future in-depth research into the areas covered, which range from the narrowly legal to the more general. Our chapter authors include history professors, political science professors, law professors, and psychology professors as well as a psychology graduate student, practicing lawyers, and sitting judges. Some of the essays deal solely with nineteenth-century activity. Some bring the reader nearly up to the present. History deals with the past, yet, to be included in the past, events need only have happened a millisecond ago—or less—by passing through the lens of the present, which passage renders a subject fit for historical inquiry.[15] The essays in this volume briefly examine areas of Nebraska legal history showing both Nebraska's membership in the legal mainstream and its development of unique legal institutions and approaches to problem solving and interdisciplinary legal education. While each of the essays could stand alone, the reader will notice several places where the essays dovetail into each other.

Professor Thomas H. Cox explores the adoption of the Kansas-Nebraska Act, Nebraska's first state constitution, statehood, and the adoption of Nebraska's second state constitution. Cox demonstrates that Nebraska's quest for self-government represents a noteworthy glimpse into the larger issues of reconstructing the Union, civil rights, and federal-state relations with which many Americans were grappling in the aftermath of the Civil War.

Judge Alan G. Gless discusses various aspects of Nebraska's criminal codes from 1855 through 2007. Ohio, Illinois, Iowa,[16] and Michigan were the greatest contributors to the development of Nebraska's nineteenth-century criminal law. In the twentieth century, the National Conference of Commissioners on Uniform State Laws and the American Law Institute became the primary contributors to Nebraska's criminal law. Gless posits that the legislature's alterations of and additions to Nebraska's criminal law reflected changes in the perceived needs of society, both local and national, lending direct support to the proposition that society and culture shape law and only tangential support to the idea that law shapes society.

Professor Mark R. Ellis presents the professional career of Nebraska Supreme Court Justice Francis Hamer, a pioneer lawyer and jurist instrumental in the development of Nebraska's early water law. Hamer came to Nebraska by way of Ohio, Indiana, Illinois, and Iowa. In Ellis's hands, Hamer's forty-eight-year career as a pioneer lawyer, district court judge for western Nebraska, and state supreme court justice becomes a window from which to view the legal and judicial development of the state. Among the highlights of his career as a trial judge during the agricultural crash of the 1890s, Hamer single-handedly held off the clamoring creditors in his district, saving the homes of many farmers, without the support of moratory statutes. Hamer's varied legal and judicial career is, in many ways, the story of hundreds of other young attorneys who migrated to Nebraska and made it their home.

Professor Anthony B. Schutz contributes a chapter detailing the history of Nebraska livestock production land use regulation. Nuisance law was the initial means of dealing with the various conflicting interests, and it still plays a large role in this area. History shows that nuisance law is flexible enough to accommodate changing facts in changing times, even though the legal doctrine itself has remained amorphous. But an impatience with nuisance law or the uncertainty associated with nuisance lawsuits, or perhaps both, led the Nebraska Legislature to take actions that limit producers' liability. The emergence of concentrated animal feeding operations, or CAFOs, as the dominant model of livestock production has resulted in land use regulation at a more local level, leading to increased use of zoning power and, in some instances, municipal rule making. The initial push against such livestock operations, however, may be waning. Specifically, the state has begun to encourage economic development through livestock-friendly legislation, while at the same time maintaining state-level environmental regulations. State-level efforts, however, have not resulted in any legislative rollback of local zoning and regulatory authority. Local control remains a staple of Nebraska's land use law as it applies to livestock production. Given the regulatory regime that has resulted from environmental concerns, Schutz argues that CAFOs face a complex body of law.

Professor Peter J. Longo and Judge Alan G. Gless depict the history of Nebraska water law in chapter 5. Nebraska initially applied water law derived from English common law and the laws of the states in the East. However, climate differences between the other Midwest states and eastern Nebraska on one hand and between eastern and western Nebraska on the other[17] necessitated looking to the West for more useful water law concepts.[18] After only nine years of statehood, Nebraskans discovered the English and eastern water laws would not work in Nebraska's climate. Nebraska then turned to water laws from western states and territories. As Mark R. Ellis explains in chapter 3, Justice Francis Hamer was one of the leaders among Nebraska's legal profession in turning the face of Nebraska water law toward the West. This chapter also explains the dual system of control through which Nebraska surface water administration operates at the state level, whereas groundwater control comes from local government entities.

Professor J. David Aiken presents the story of Nebraska's legislative responses to the agricultural crisis of the 1920s and 1930s and the agricultural financial crisis of the 1970s and 1980s as well as the judiciary's reception of those laws. In both instances, efforts were made to hold off creditors by way of mortgage foreclosure moratoria. Aiken also examines the differing state and federal legislative responses to the two crises and compares the results of each. A changed judicial perspective as well as the farm credit mediation and farm-specific bankruptcy legislation of the late twentieth century made the crisis of the 1970s and 1980s far less devastating than that of the 1920s and 1930s.

Professor James W. Hewitt explores the history of Nebraska's unique unicameral legislature. Nebraska remains the only state to have removed the antidemocratic institution of the conference committee from its legislature. Hewitt discusses the movement that led to creation of the unicameral legislature and explains the advantages and disadvantages of unicameralism, the changes to the system over the years, the effects of nonpartisanship on lobbyists, and the consequences of the legislature's lobbyist gift-giving rules.

Professor John M. Gradwohl, a former judge of the Court of Industrial Relations, now the Commission of Industrial Relations (CIR), describes the history of this unique Nebraska institution. The Nebraska Commission of Industrial Relations deals with public employment collective bargaining and impasse resolution. The CIR has authority to decide representation and negotiation issues and to establish rates of pay and conditions of employment for public employees. The CIR judges exercise a healthy mix of traditional judicial jurisdiction and other decision-making authority made possible by a relaxation of the strict separation of powers doctrine.

Professors Brian H. Bornstein, Richard L. Wiener, and Evelyn M. Maeder explain the history of the University of Nebraska–Lincoln's pioneering Law and Psychology Program (LPP), the nation's first interdisciplinary education program in law and psychology. The program offers dual degrees at the graduate and professional level, as well as at the undergraduate level. As its history demonstrates, UNL's LPP has evolved into one of the nation's most respected programs for psycholegal research.

Professor Mark R. Scherer provides an overview of the legal history of the eastern Nebraska Native American tribes: the Omaha, the Otoe-Missouria, the Pawnee, the Ponca, the Santee Sioux, and the Winnebago. He demonstrates Nebraska's prominent position in the field of Native American legal history, describing how the state's native inhabitants have been at the center of many sweeping developments in federal Indian policy. Scherer also relates stories of failure and success, triumph and heartache, hope and misery and explains how Nebraska's aboriginal inhabitants have endured more than their fair share of suffering and hardship yet remain today a vibrant and significant force in the state's social, cultural, and political milieu. The histories of western Nebraska tribes (Lakota, Cheyenne) are omitted because the presence of these peoples in what is today Nebraska has always been more transitory than that of the eastern tribes. Despite their traditional use of much of the state for roaming, hunting, and raiding, there have been no Lakota or Cheyenne reservations established in the state (other than the Santee), and their land claims and Indian Claim Commission litigation have not addressed Nebraska lands per se.

Charles E. Wright depicts one of the rare bright spots in our nation's nineteenth-century treatment of Native Americans. Wright describes the conditions leading up to the 1879 decision in what could have but did not become an obscure habeas corpus hearing in the U.S. District Court for the District of Nebraska. Wright also reexamines the meaning of U.S. district court judge Elmer Dundy's decision in Standing Bear's case as it relates to the legality of the activities of the U.S. Army that led to Custer's demise at Little Big Horn. His conclusion applies to other hostile actions undertaken by the United States against other Native American tribes, as well.

Nearly a century after the Standing Bear trial, U.S. district court judge Warren K. Urbom presided over the bulk of the criminal trials that collectively came to be known as the Wounded Knee trials. Professor Tim A.

Garrison introduces Urbom's chapter, providing background information relating to the events at Wounded Knee that readers may need to understand the significance of the trials that Urbom describes from his vantage point as a participant. His address to the International Society of Barristers—a primary source, as historians view sources—included in this volume with the permission of the association, makes up the substance of chapter 12.

Judge Susan I. Strong describes the treatment of women in Nebraska's legal system. Strong concludes that the courage and determination of the first women of Nebraska law blazed the way for others who later entered the legal profession as a matter of right, without even realizing the sacrifices that had gone before. The first women of Nebraska law were not content with merely being the first. As Strong shows, they went beyond their first achievements and strove to be the best in their profession, not merely the best woman in their profession. Without question, these women were role models not only for other women but for all in the legal profession. Strong predicts that, while Nebraska women have already accomplished many firsts, there are many more yet to come.

Professor William G. Ross examines *Meyer v. Nebraska* (1923),[19] a case involving a teacher in a one-room schoolhouse in rural Hamilton County, Nebraska, which changed the course of American constitutional doctrine and has become one of the cornerstones of civil liberties law. Ross posits that, although the specific ethnic and cultural conflicts that inspired the case have long since disappeared and are nearly forgotten, the U.S. Supreme Court's decision remains at the heart of modern controversies involving parental rights, privacy law, abortion, and regulation of sexual conduct. Although the scope of the liberties recognized by *Meyer* is likely to continue to cause controversy, Ross predicts that the *Meyer* ruling that "the individual has certain fundamental rights which must be respected" is likely to endure for as long as the nation has citizens who are as willing to fight for their rights as courageously as did a Nebraska schoolmaster nearly a century ago.

Finally, Professor Richard E. Shugrue, in part 1 of chapter 15, briefly describes Roscoe Pound's life in Lincoln and discusses the extent to which Pound's service as a Nebraska Supreme Court commissioner may have contributed to the legal philosophy that he eventually developed. In part 2, Judge Alan G. Gless examines what Pound accomplished that made him arguably Nebraska's single greatest contribution to American legal history.

This volume provides one more brick in a foundation upon which future writers may develop regional histories for the nation. Writing true regional histories requires multiple perspectives from historians of many different specialty areas within the field. State legal histories like this one bring together in a single volume more disciplinary viewpoints and professional emphases than any single historian is able to provide. And state legal histories like this one bring us closer to laying the basic groundwork for a history of American law based upon the experiences of all the states, not just the most populous or the oldest. Regional historians can use state legal histories like this one to identify within the represented regions that which is merely local and control for its effects in their work.[20]

Notes

1. See, e.g., University of Nebraska Center for Great Plains Studies, *Map of the Great Plains,* http://www.unl.edu/plains/about/map.html. Geographers have developed at least fifty different descriptions of the Great Plains region's boundaries. Some extend the eastern boundary as far to the east as the middle of Wisconsin and Illinois. The western, southern, and northern boundaries seem agreed. David J. Wishart, ed., *Encyclopedia of the Great Plains* (Lincoln: University of Nebraska Press, 2004): xvi–xvii.

2. "The regions of the United States are geographic areas which include multiple states. The regional groupings presented here and their definitions are from standard language used by libraries and reflect the groupings used in the classification system for maps." Library of Congress, *American Memory,* "Railroad Maps Collection," http://memory.loc.gov/ammem/gmdhtml/rrhtml/regdef.html.

"The 'Middle West' region[, in standard library language and groupings, includes]: [the] Rocky Mountains to Allegheny Mountains, North of Ohio River and southern border of Missouri and Kansas: Illinois, Iowa, Indiana, Kansas, Michigan, Minnesota, Missouri, Nebraska, North Dakota, Ohio, South Dakota, Wisconsin." Ibid., http://memory.loc.gov/ammem/gmdhtml/rrhtml/regions3.html.

3. Warren R. Hofstra, "Reconsidering Regional History," *OAH Newsletter* 34, no. 1 (2006): 22.

4. The geographic center of the coterminous United States lies fourteen miles south of the southern border of Nebraska near Lebanon, Kansas. Roadside America, *Lebanon, Kansas—Geographical Center of the 48 States,* http://www.roadsideamerica.com/tips/getAttraction.php3?tip_AttractionNo==7032.

5. James C. Olson and Ronald C. Naugle, *History of Nebraska,* 3d ed. (Lincoln: University of Nebraska Press, 1997), 156.

6. E-mail from Ronald C. Naugle to author, March 6, 2006 (copy on file with author).

7. Compiled by Ronald C. Naugle from U.S. Department of the Interior, Bureau of the Census, *Population of the United States in 1860* (Washington, D.C.: Government Printing Office, 1864), 560 (copy on file with author).

8. Compiled by Ronald C. Naugle from U.S. Department of the Interior, Bureau of the Census, Ninth Census, vol. 1: *The Statistics of the Population of the United States in 1870* (Washington, D.C.: Government Printing Office, 1872), 328 (copy on file with author).

9. Compiled by Ronald C. Naugle from U.S. Department of the Interior, Census Office, *Statistics of the Population of the United States at the Tenth Census: 1880* (Washington, D.C.: Government Printing Office, 1883), 484–47 (copy on file with author).

10. Compiled by Ronald C. Naugle from U.S. Department of the Interior, Census Office, *Report on the Population of the United States at the Eleventh Census: 1890* (Washington, D.C.: Government Printing Office, 1895), 560–63 (copy on file with author).

11. Compiled by Ronald C. Naugle from U.S. Census Office, *Twelfth Census of the United States Taken in the Year 1900*, vol. 1, *Population*, Part 1 (Washington, D.C.: Government Printing Office, 1901), 686 (copy on file with author).

12. Compiled by Ronald C. Naugle from U.S. Department of Commerce, Bureau of the Census, *Thirteenth Census of the United States Taken in the Year 1910, Population* (Washington, D.C.: Government Printing Office, 1913), 3:45 (copy on file with author). Consistently less than 1 percent of Nebraskans claimed Minnesota as their native state over the entire period.

13. See, e.g., Joseph Fred Benson, "Reception of the Common Law in Missouri: Section 1.010 as Interpreted by the Supreme Court of Missouri," *Missouri Law Review* 67, no. 2 (2002): 595–617.

14. 68 Neb. 463, 469–71, 94 N.W. 705, 708 (1903) (citations in original omitted).

15. The metaphor of the present as a lens was inspired by the discussion of time, the future, the past, and the present appearing in John Lewis Gaddis, *The Landscape of History: How Historians Map the Past* (Oxford: Oxford University Press, 2002), 29–31.

16. Nebraska's eastern neighbor, Iowa, was part of the area acquired in the Louisiana Purchase and was not part of the Old Northwest; nevertheless, it was heavily influenced by Old Northwest legal traditions.

17. On the east side of Ohio, annual rainfall averages thirty-nine to forty inches. Heading west from there, by Omaha, annual rainfall averages drop to twenty-nine to thirty inches, and, by Scottsbluff annual rainfall averages only fifteen inches. About.com, *Geography*, "The 100th Meridian," http://geography.about.com/od/learnabouttheearth/a/100thmeridian.htm.

18. Ironically, now, more than a century later, the East is looking to the West for solutions to its new water problems. See, e.g., Steven T. Miano and Michael E. Crane, "Eastern Water Law: Historical Perspectives and Emerging Trends," *Natural Resources and Environment* 18, no. 2 (2003): 129–33.

19. 262 U.S. 390 (1923).

20. Kermit L. Hall, "The Legal Culture of the Great Plains," in *Law and the Great Plains: Essays on the Legal History of the Heartland*, ed. John R. Wunder (Westport, Conn.: Greenwood, 1996), 12.

ONE

Thomas H. Cox

FRONTIER FRAMERS

Constitution Making in Nineteenth-Century Nebraska

Throughout the 1860s and 1870s, Nebraskans participated in a complex process of political give-and-take to create a workable state constitution in a frontier environment. Their attempts resulted in no fewer than three separate constitutions created in 1866, 1871, and 1875. The controversies surrounding the creation of these documents shed light on the inner workings of Nebraska politics in the late nineteenth century. Equally important, these struggles reveal the ways in which local Nebraskans participated in national trends, such as the development of the transcontinental railroad, the legacy of slavery, Reconstruction, and woman suffrage.[1]

Nebraska's geographic and constitutional development sprung from the American frontier experience of the mid- to late nineteenth century. The United States initially acquired the land that eventually became Nebraska as part of the Louisiana Purchase in 1803. For much of the early nineteenth century, roughly fourteen thousand Native Americans, including the Omaha, Otoe-Missouria, Pawnee, and Ponca tribes dominated Nebraska. In 1834, Congress designated this territory "Indian Country" and attempted to regulate trade and travel among the tribes. Yet waves of white settlers, inspired by John C. Fremont's romantic depictions of western life, continued to pour into Nebraska in the 1840s. The federal government accommodated these newcomers by pressuring local tribes to cede territory south of the Platte River.[2]

Northern desires to establish a transcontinental railroad also influenced the settlement of the Nebraska Territory. Eager to establish a northern route with a terminus in Chicago, Representative Stephen A. Douglas, of Illinois, promoted the rapid institution of territorial governments that could provide an infrastructure for railroad development. Southern political leaders, however, worried about the implications of the addition of more free-labor states to the Union and so quietly tabled Douglas's motions in 1844.[3]

Despite this setback, railroad speculation continued to influence the settlement and territorial politics of Nebraska. In 1853, a group of businessmen in Kanesville (later Council Bluffs), Iowa, sponsored a town named Omaha on the western bank of the Missouri River. The following year, local merchant and businessman Peter A. Sarpy and his business associates organized the town of Bellevue, Nebraska, near the intersection of the Platte and Missouri rivers. After the passage of the Kansas-Nebraska Act on May 30, 1854, both communities vied to become the territorial capital and major railhead in the region.[4]

After the arrival of nearly three thousand inhabitants, Nebraskans eagerly awaited the establishment of a territorial government. In spring 1854, President Franklin Pierce, a Democrat, appointed Francis Burt, a proslavery South Carolinian, as the first governor of the Nebraska Territory. Following Burt's unexpected death from a stomach ailment on October 16, Nebraska's territorial secretary, Thomas Cuming, became its acting governor. Whereas Burt had been a political outsider, his successor held financial and political ties to the Council Bluffs community. In November, Cuming ordered a territorial census to determine proportional representation for the territory's first legislative session, scheduled for January 1855. Perhaps not surprisingly, Cuming allotted more representatives to the counties centered around Omaha than to counties south of the Platte, where the bulk of Nebraska's population lay. Southern Platte residents and Bellevue townsfolk consequently joined forces to protest what they considered an abuse of political power.[5]

Despite these protests, the first Nebraska Territorial Assembly convened on January 16, 1855. The delegates represented a cross section of frontier society. J. W. Pattison, a young reporter for the *New York Times,* noted somewhat caustically,

> It is a decidedly rich treat to visit the general assembly of Nebraska. You see a motley group inside of a railing in a small room crowded

> to overflowing, some behind their little school-boy desks, some seated on the tops of desks, some with their feet perch on top of their neighbor's chair or desk, some whittling—half a dozen walking about in what little space there is left . . . . It is one continued personal and local fight—a constant attempt at bargain, sale and argument.[6]

The arrival of Mark W. Izard, another staunch Democrat, as territorial governor in February 1855 helped provide focus for the fledgling legislature. At his urging, Nebraska adopted Iowa state laws as the basis for a new legal code and formulated plans for a public school system. Izard also ensured that posts in the Nebraska territorial government remained filled by loyal Democratic secretaries, judges, and military officers.[7]

Throughout the 1850s, Nebraska continued to grow. Railroad speculation increased property values throughout the Platte River valley. Prospectors headed for the gold fields of Colorado and California also contributed to the local economy. By 1859, Nebraska had a population of 28,841 inhabitants. Despite such growth, however, Nebraska remained bitterly politically divided. In 1854, the Kansas-Nebraska Act had prompted the rise of the Republican Party. Four years later, a coalition of eastern Nebraska attorneys and businessmen formed the Union Party. On November 1, 1858, Unionist representative Samuel G. Daily boldly offered a motion in the territorial legislature to abolish slavery within the borders of Nebraska. On December 8, 1859, Representatives William H. Broadhead and Mills S. Reeves, of Otoe County, proposed bills to frame a state government and to petition Congress for statehood. Harping upon the popular issue of railroad development, Reeves pointed out that "[t]he question of the location of the Pacific railroad, which, since the discovery of the untold millions of gold on our western border [the Pikes Peak gold fields], all conceded must and will be built, may be decided in our favor by the votes of our own representatives. If we are, as we should be, admitted into the Union at the same time with Kansas."[8]

In 1860, Union Party leaders felt secure enough to formally join the national Republican Party. At a convention in Plattsmouth, they endorsed Abraham Lincoln for president and Samuel Daily for territorial delegate to Washington, D.C. Nebraska Democrats met in Omaha and nominated J. Sterling Morton—who, at age twenty-seven, already had served as territorial secretary—as their candidate for territorial delegate. After a bitter campaign, Morton defeated Daily by a margin of 2,957 to 2,943. While the

Nebraska public remained occupied with the outcome of the election, the territorial legislature continued to debate the issue of statehood. In early January 1860, Representative Robert W. Furnas proposed a special election to determine whether a convention should be held to frame a state constitution and to elect delegates to attend such a gathering. The territorial assembly passed the motion and scheduled a special election to be held on March 5, 1860. Despite initial enthusiasm from Southern Platte delegates, northern representatives feared the relocation of the state capital away from Omaha and joined forces with Democrats to defeat the proposed convention. Critics of statehood effectively argued that a state government would increase taxes and governmental control over local affairs. As a result, Republicans won forty of the fifty-two races for delegates, but Nebraska voters decided against holding the convention at all.[9]

The outbreak of the Civil War in 1861 decisively influenced Nebraska territorial politics. In a show of support for the Union, the territorial legislature on January 5, 1861, outlawed slavery in the Nebraska Territory over the veto of Governor Samuel Black, a pro-Southern Democrat. In 1862, President Lincoln replaced Black with Alvin Saunders, a merchant, attorney, and former Republican state senator from Mount Pleasant, Iowa. Later that year, Lincoln appointed Algernon S. Paddock, a native New Yorker and cofounder of the Nebraska Republican Party, as territorial secretary. Furthermore, Republican Samuel Daily won reelection as territorial delegate in a hotly disputed race. Despite these Republican gains, the Nebraska Democratic Party retained considerable strength throughout the Civil War.[10]

While the Lincoln administration campaigned to restore federal authority over the South, it also sought to expand control over the western frontier. In 1862, Congress passed several pieces of legislation crucial to the development of Nebraska. The Homestead Act offered millions of acres of free western land to settlers. The Pacific Railroad Act guaranteed that the long-anticipated transcontinental railroad would take a northern route. Two branches of the Union Pacific Railroad were to run through Nebraska, terminating in Omaha and Sioux City, Iowa, respectively. Saunders participated in an official groundbreaking ceremony for the Union Pacific Railroad on December 2, 1863.[11]

Republican leaders envisioned a series of loyal state governments that would collaborate with Washington, D.C., to develop the frontier. For instance, in a speech delivered on January 8, 1864, Saunders touted the advantages that Nebraska statehood would bring, such as grants of federal land and increased revenue for internal improvements. To delay was to risk losing business and immigrants to other territories, such as Nevada and Colorado. In response to Saunders's urging, Nebraska congressional delegate Alfred H. Jackson, of Dakota County, presented a memorial to Congress to ask for enabling legislation to join the Union. Throughout the spring of 1864, Benjamin F. Wade, senator from Ohio and chair of the congressional Committee on Territories, promoted the cause of Nebraska statehood in the Senate. National Republican leaders like Wade were eager to bring the Nevada, Colorado, and Nebraska territories into the Union as quickly as possible, to enfranchise fresh Republican voters for the November 1864 presidential election. On April 19, Congress authorized Nebraska to create a state government as a prerequisite for eventual statehood.[12]

Five weeks later, Saunders called for a territorywide election to choose delegates for a constitutional convention that would meet in Omaha on July 4. In late June, Nebraska Democrats met at Plattsmouth to choose delegates for their national convention in Chicago. Although many Democrats eagerly supported statehood, they hoped to postpone the process until their party secured both the White House and the territorial legislature. Led by George L. Miller, editor of the *Omaha Herald,* and J. Sterling Morton, former territorial secretary and congressional delegate, the Democratic Party denounced the upcoming Omaha convention. They once again warned that a state government would only increase taxes and add another layer of bureaucracy to daily life. When Nebraska's first constitutional convention convened on July 4, 1864, the delegates elected Sterling P. Majors as president of the convention on the first ballot. Delegate Alfred Jackson, who had pushed so hard for statehood six months earlier, moved that the meeting adjourn. Jackson's resolution passed by a vote of 35 to 7, and Nebraska's first attempt at creating a state government ended before it had even begun.[13]

Despite these delaying tactics, public interest in statehood continued to grow. Many Nebraskans expressed concern in October 1864, when Nevada became the thirty-sixth state. Furthermore, Omaha residents contemplated the need to defend their railroad interests at the national level. Perhaps most decisively, homesteaders continued to patent federal land that might otherwise have gone to the state of Nebraska. Ironically, many new settlers were Union army veterans who supported statehood for Nebraska as soon as possible.[14]

Frustrated by the obstructionists, Saunders took a strong stance on the issue of statehood in his January 1865 address to the territorial legislature. In particular, he implied that constitutions need not come directly from the public. Saunders's speech provoked an angry response on January 26 from Charles H. Brown, a Democratic representative from Douglas County. Brown railed against a "certain politician" who had, through "fraud and chicanery," forced the issue of a constitution on the public and warned the territorial legislature against "any steps, which would throw this question upon the people without their first having asked for its submission to them."[15]

Throughout the summer and fall of 1865, local Republican newspapers like the *Nebraska Daily Republican* promoted the idea of statehood. One article asked, "So we need a good strong representation in Congress, to defend and protect our rights while the Railroad lines are being established through our territory—more might be gained or lost for our territory by one act than all the additional tax would amount to for the next twenty years to come." Saunders restated the issue in his 1866 address to the legislature. He announced that in his "candid opinion . . . the resources of Nebraska would be sooner developed, and her wealth and population increased by becoming a State, than if she remains a Territory." Saunders elaborated on his comments made the previous year by remarking that a territorial legislature could bypass a constitutional convention, create its own blueprint for a state government, and submit it to the public directly.[16]

Saunders's plan represented a bold departure from established American constitutional traditions. Throughout the spring of 1866, a secret committee made up of Saunders, Paddock, territorial chief justice William Pitt Kellogg, and representatives Experience Estabrook, Hadley D. Johnson, and Oliver P. Mason met in the Omaha law office of William A. Little to devise a state constitution. To counter Democratic scare tactics regarding spending, the committee designed as spare and economical a state government as possible. For example, state officers consisted of only a governor, a state auditor, a secretary of state, and three judges who served on both the state supreme and district courts. The proposed constitution also featured a bicameral legislature that met every other year and that could not run up a public debt greater than $50,000, except during times of war. The state was to finance public education from a perpetual fund based on the sale of state land. Although the constitution banned slavery, only white males received the right to vote.[17]

On February 5, 1866, J. R. Porter, one of the few Democrats who favored statehood without delay, submitted the proposed constitution to the territorial legislature. Saunders and his Republican allies used pamphlets, promises of patronage, and demands of party loyalty to push the constitution through the legislature as quickly as possible. James M. Woolworth, an Omaha attorney and Democratic representative, later stated, "Meeting after meeting was held and the matter urged by all the eloquence and sophistry possible, while private conversations were converted into private appeals and private bargains. One by one was won over—promises of offices and contracts and yet more tangible influences doing the work." Despite Democratic protests, the Nebraska Council approved the constitution within hours of its submission by a narrow 7-to-6 vote along straight party lines. On February 9, the House likewise approved the constitution by a vote of 22 to 16. The same day, Saunders called for a special election to be held on June 9 to ratify the constitution and to elect officers to the new state government, provided that the public accepted the document.[18]

Although Saunders and his supporters could boast of two quick victories in the territorial legislature, they still had to convince a majority of Nebraskans that a constitution proposed by extraordinary means represented their best interests. On April 12, Nebraska Republicans convened at Plattsmouth and nominated David Butler for governor on a platform that supported the newly drafted constitution. Two weeks later, a badly divided Democratic Party met in Nebraska City. The faction led by J. Sterling Morton wanted no part of the proposed state government. A more moderate faction led by George L. Miller hoped to put forth candidates and possibly to take over the new administration. After several days of negotiation, the delegates closed ranks to nominate Morton for governor on a platform that declared support for Andrew Johnson, opposed the radical Republicans in Congress, and remained silent on the issue of statehood."[19]

Both Republicans and Democrats avidly discussed the issue of statehood in the election of 1866. Republicans charged the Democrats in general—and Morton in particular—with wartime disloyalty. The pro-Democrat *Omaha Weekly Herald* countered that Republicans sought to turn Nebraska into "a negro colony to which plantation negroes may be imported to vote down white men." The *Nebraska City News* also stated, "[A] vote against the Democratic ticket is a vote in favor of negro-suffrage and for negro equality."[20]

At the polls, Nebraska voters approved the proposed constitution by a slim majority of 3,938 to 3,838 and elected David Butler as the state's first governor by a vote of 4,093 to 3,984. Although the Democrats had mounted a formidable campaign, Republican officials controlled many of the local canvassing boards that oversaw the election. After the election, Democrats charged Republican officials with fraud for throwing out votes from pro-Democratic Cass County on the grounds that election officials had left ballot boxes unattended, while ignoring similar technical breaches in Republican-controlled districts. Democrats also condemned Republicans for accepting votes from soldiers native to Iowa stationed at Fort Kearny and from Native Americans on a local reservation. Because the Republicans now controlled the state government, however, these charges of corruption went largely unaddressed. George Miller bitterly reported to J. Sterling Morton, "The damned scoundrels are swindling us out of a victory fairly won against great odds."[21]

Between the summer of 1866 and March 1867, Nebraska politics became even more complicated as the existing territorial government and the emerging state government contended for power. In July 1866, the first session of state legislature elected two U.S. senators, John Thayer and Thomas W. Tipton. The legislature, however, also called another public election to be held on October 9 for either a U.S. representative and a new state legislature or a congressional delegate and a new territorial legislature, depending upon whether the federal government accepted Nebraska as a state.[22]

In mid-July, the state legislature officially petitioned Congress for admission to the United States, and for a brief period local politics became directly connected to the national turbulence of the Reconstruction era. After the assassination of Abraham Lincoln in April 1865, vice president and former Tennessee Democrat Andrew Johnson had become the seventeenth president of the United States. Johnson attempted to continue Lincoln's policy of reconciliation toward the defeated South. Radical Republicans in Congress, however, had devised their own Reconstruction plans, plans that included the Civil Rights Act of 1866 and the Fourteenth Amendment to the U.S. Constitution, which declared all persons born or naturalized in the United States to be both federal and state citizens, entitled to equal protection and due process under law. Congress passed the Fourteenth Amendment on June 13 and submitted it to the states for ratification. Nearly six weeks later, on July 23, Senator Wade introduced a bill for the admission of Nebraska to the Union.[23]

Recent relations between the territorial government and the Johnson administration gave Nebraska Republicans cause for concern about their chances for statehood. Territorial Democrats had supported Johnson throughout the political battles of 1865 and 1866 and had frequently chided local Republicans for their unwillingness to back their own party's president. Aware that the president still wielded formidable patronage powers,

Nebraska Republicans divided between those who loosely allied with Nebraska Democrats in their mutual support of Johnson and those who backed the Congress dominated by the radicals. At the urging of local Democrats, Johnson attempted to replace Saunders and several high-ranking Republicans in the Nebraska territorial government. However, Johnson lacked congressional support to replace more than a few appointees, and his actions pushed Nebraska Republicans to side with Congress.[24]

The introduction of Wade's Nebraska bill in late July caused an immediate controversy. The state constitution disfranchised African Americans. Senator Charles Sumner argued that such a constitution could not be called republican in form, and he moved to strike the word "white" from the document. Wade and other Republican leaders, however, wished to admit Nebraska to the Union as quickly as possible, so as to gain for the radicals two more senators and a representative in their battles against the Johnson administration. On July 27, both houses of Congress passed the Nebraska Statehood Act. Johnson realized the motives of his rivals and defeated the measure with a pocket veto.[25]

The future of Nebraska was still in doubt, and local Democrats once again nominated J. Sterling Morton for both congressional delegate and territorial secretary and Algernon S. Paddock for representative. Nebraska Republicans chose John Taffe and Turner M. Marquette as their candidates for territorial delegate and representative, respectively. To further complicate matters, eccentric shipping magnate George Francis Train ran for the open House seat as an independent with the backing of the Union Pacific Railroad. Through strong appeals to patriotic sentiment, Republicans won handily and dispatched Taffe and Marquette to Washington.[26]

Once Republicans were firmly in control of the embryonic Nebraska state government, Wade reintroduced the issue of Nebraska statehood to the Senate on December 5, 1866. Democrats and conservative Republicans argued that Nebraska still lacked sufficient population to qualify for statehood and that the creation of the 1866 state constitution by the territorial legislature circumvented the requirements of the Nebraska Enabling Act of 1864. Charles Sumner, B. Gratz Brown, and other radical Republicans once again objected to the Nebraska constitution's suffrage restrictions against African Americans. Sumner and other Republicans also worried that if Nebraska entered the Union as a state in which only whites could vote, there was nothing to prevent Southern states from rejoining the Union under similar conditions. To overcome this problem, Senator George F. Edmunds, of Vermont, proposed an amendment to the Nebraska statehood bill. The amendment stipulated that Nebraska would become a state, provided that its state constitution did not withhold "the elective franchise, or any other right, to any person by reason of race or color, excepting Indians not taxed." With the addition of the Edmunds amendment, the Senate passed the Nebraska bill on January 9 by a vote of 28 to 14, and six days later the House followed suit by a vote of 103 to 55.[27]

Not surprisingly, President Johnson promptly vetoed the Nebraska Statehood Act on January 29. His veto message attacked the Edmunds amendment as a "clear violation of the Federal Constitution, under the provisions of which, from the very foundation of the Government, each State has been left free to determine for itself the qualifications necessary for the exercise of suffrage within its limits." Despite this setback, Senator Wade reintroduced the Nebraska statehood for a third time to Congress. On February 8, the Senate approved the measure with a veto-proof vote of 31 to 9, and the next day the House concurred, 120 to 43 (with 28 absences and abstentions). At a special meeting of the state legislature on February 20, Governor Saunders read the admissions bill. Despite scattered protests, the legislature agreed to amend Nebraska's constitution to allow universal male suffrage. After the removal of this last barrier, President Johnson reluctantly signed the act into law on March 1, 1867, and Nebraska officially became the thirty-seventh state.[28]

The admission of Nebraska, however, did little to stabilize the volatility of frontier politics. The newly empowered Governor Butler opened another special session of the state legislature on May 16 to debate a variety of topics, such as the creation of general laws, new counties, public buildings, internal improvements, and public schools. Butler also led a commission of delegates to scout land suitable for a new state capital. In June, Butler announced that the new capital would be located near the hamlet of Lancaster, near several large salt flats in Seward County. In the meantime, Omaha representatives hoped to block the decision to move the state capital by suggesting that Lancaster be renamed Lincoln, a name despised by many Democrats. This ploy backfired when the Nebraska Democrats swallowed their pride and accepted the name change as a necessary measure to guarantee a state capital south of the Platte River.

In the fall of 1867, the first public lots went on sale in Lincoln. The creation of the new state capital was a complicated and, at times, corrupt process. Butler and his fellow commissioners planned to locate the capital on local land donated by the town of Lancaster rather than on state lands set aside for specifically that purpose. Butler and his allies then sold the earmarked state land to speculators and pocketed the proceeds. The governor also negotiated contracts for construction of a public university and state asylum that greatly exceeded funds set aside for both projects and lent public money to friends as political favors. On March 6, 1871, the Nebraska Senate began impeachment proceedings against Butler. The embattled governor defended his actions publicly, but on June 1, by a vote of 9 to 3, the Senate found Butler guilty of misappropriating public funds, and the Supreme Court removed him from office.[29]

Nebraska's statehood led to an influx of settlers in the late 1860s. By 1870, the state had a population of 122,993 residents. This rise in population, coupled with public anger over the Butler controversy, concerns about the power of large businesses, and progressive desires for political and educational reform, led to calls for a new state constitution. On June 13, 1871, fifty-two delegates gathered in Lincoln to create a new framework for government. Democrat Nathan K. Griggs, a former territorial representative and Nebraska political veteran, served as a delegate and revealed the inner workings of the convention to his wife and colleagues in a series of letters. In mid-June, the convention agreed on procedural rules and created committees on a variety of issues ranging from banking to federal relations. Perhaps the most controversial issue faced by the delegates was that of woman suffrage. Nebraska progressives flooded the convention with petitions and letters urging delegates to extend the vote to women under the new constitution. Two days after the convention began, Elizabeth Cady Stanton delivered a speech in Lincoln on the necessity of women's rights. On July 16, Delegate John Nelson Cassell proposed that women should receive the right to vote under the new constitution, but opponents of the motion tabled it indefinitely.[30]

A bitter controversy emerged on July 20, when Seth Robinson, of Lancaster County, demanded that a clause giving thanks to God be removed from the preamble of the proposed constitution. Griggs quipped in response, "When the people of Nebraska cannot be thankful to Almighty God for his blessings, I think they are pretty hard up." Not surprisingly, Robinson's motion fell by a vote of 42 to 2 (with 8 absences and abstentions). The next day, delegates debated the salaries of public officials only to receive the cleverly timed motion of Victor Vifquain, of Saline County, that delegates should not be paid for convention meetings that they failed to attend. After considerable disagreement, the convention postponed Vifquain's proposal.[31]

On May 25, the constitutional convention voted to reduce debate time and to begin evening sessions in order to conclude matters as quickly as possible. One particularly grueling debate centered on mandatory public education. Some delegates, such as R. F. Stephenson, argued, "Let us erect school houses: give the children a chance to attend, and if they do not embrace the opportunity, the state is not to blame." A. J. Weaver responded, "Under a Republican form of government there is safety and prosperity only to the extent of the enlightenment of the people. . . . I ask the question whether education is not the strong armor with which to fight the battle of life?"

In early August, the convention discussed issues such as impeachments of public officials, the methods by which companies could become incorporated under Nebraska state law, state contracts, and appointments. On August 3, Delegate Oliver P. Mason launched a diatribe against state legislators who used public funds for their own purposes, bellowing, "I want to cut this evil up by the roots, and to make it a penitentiary offense to do this thing." This angered convention president and Civil War veteran Silas A. Strickland, who sharply responded, "Standing the entire legislature of the state of Nebraska as unworthy of any trust of honor! . . . It is a standing insult to every man who aspires to the position of serving his constituency in the legislature." Following Strickland's emotional appeal, Mason offered no further such attacks. The next day, delegates again argued hotly over the permanent location of the state capital. Rhetoric had reached a fever pitch when Delegate D. T. Moore wryly reminded his fellow delegates that reporters present at the convention would preserve such arguments for all posterity.[32]

In an attempt to defuse tensions, delegates turned to a debate on county government and taxation issues. On August 8, Barzillai Price, of Jefferson County, gave another speech in favor of woman suffrage. Again, delegates postponed the matter. Griggs informed his wife, "We are having hot times here. We have just voiced down the woman suffrage question by a vote of 23 to 10 and the other side is trying to again resurrect the question." Griggs concluded, "The Woman Suffrage question has entirely turned the convention wrong side up." On August 18, delegates agreed to present woman suffrage as a separate proposal to be submitted to the Nebraska public alongside the constitution. Having disposed of the matter temporarily, the convention adjourned at 3:00 on the morning of August 19.

Based primarily on the Illinois state constitution of 1871, the new Nebraska constitution was a moderate document with some liberal concessions. For instance, the new constitution retained the basic governmental structure of its 1866 predecessor—three separate branches of government and a system of checks and balances. Under this new framework, however, the state legislature could regulate railroad rates and fees, restrict local attempts to entice railroad companies, increase the salaries of public officials, designate Lincoln as the permanent capital of the state, and allow for the taxation of church property valued at more than $5,000. In addition, five proposals were submitted to voters separately, to become part of the constitution only if agreed upon by a majority of the public. In addition to woman suffrage, these measures included limited liability for corporations, restrictions on local financial aid to corporations, compulsory public education, and the prohibition of alcohol.[33]

In late August, the state legislature submitted the proposed constitution to the public for ratification. A variety of groups opposed the document. Railroad magnates aggressively criticized the constitution as a threat to free trade. Roman Catholics in Omaha opposed the tax on religious property because it singled out their large, urban cathedrals still under construction and exempted smaller, well-established Protestant churches. Many Nebraskans also worried about the expense and added bureaucracy that the new government might bring. In October 1871, the Nebraska public rejected the new constitution by a vote of 8,627 to 7,986. Voters likewise rejected each of the separate proposals by wide margins.[34]

The rejection of the 1871 state constitution did not end Nebraska's ongoing political problems. In 1872, Republican Robert W. Furnas was elected governor, and soon thereafter the *Omaha Herald* accused him of accepting a bribe of $3,000 in the early fight over removal of the state capital from Omaha. Furnas sued the *Herald* for libel. The jury, however, disagreed. The case was dismissed.[35] Rural Nebraskans refused to pay land taxes, and local governments continued to attract railroads through risky bond schemes. Already in financial trouble, the state government almost went bankrupt when the nation suffered through a crippling recession known as the panic of 1873. State leaders also continued to organize a steady stream of western counties whose residents received little or no representation in the state legislature. Nebraska newspapers such as the *Lincoln Blade, Omaha Bee, Omaha Daily Herald,* and *Seward County Reporter* repeatedly called for another constitutional convention to address these problems.[36]

The legislature bowed to public pressure, and on February 20 it called for a statewide election of sixty-nine delegates to meet at a constitutional convention in Lincoln on May 11. After the ballots were counted, Republicans controlled fifty delegates; the sixteen Democrats and three independents could provide only the semblance of political diversity. In May, the delegates gathered in the already dilapidated state capitol building in Lincoln. Public attention centered more on a plague of grasshoppers that had infested the Great Plains than on the deliberations of the delegates. One reporter for the *Omaha Daily Herald* sarcastically noted, "[T]here are some good men in the convention but if Abraham was to interview the Almighty with a view to their salvation on basis of numbers he would have to be modest in his arithmetic."[37]

Perhaps in response to such comments, the delegates quickly sought to project an image of humility and frugality to the public by voting against salaries for a chaplain or convention secretary and against free postage stamps for delegates. Instead, delegates agreed to share ministerial duties and hired several newspaper reporters covering the convention to double as temporary recorders. On May 12, representatives organized committees and adopted rules for the convention. One faction among the delegates wanted to reconsider the 1871 constitution in its entirety. Convention leaders, however, opted to create thirty-two special committees, each charged with drafting portions of an entirely new document. Debate began when Delegate James E. Doom, of Gage County, successfully campaigned to have the state auditor deliver a report on all state expenses for the past two years. Other controversies soon broke out over such issues as the direct election of Nebraska's U.S. senators, the size of the state militia, the ability of county and city governments to sell bonds, the organization of the state court system, funding for public education, and whether the state capital could be moved by an act of the legislature. To deal with this onslaught, Delegate Charles Van Wyck, of Otoe County, proposed that sessions begin at 8:00 AM each day. This measure failed, but the delegates agreed to evening sessions as a time-saving measure.[38]

After a remarkably short session, the convention adjourned on June 12, 1875. The delegates presented to the Nebraska public a document that bore striking similarities to the proposed constitution of 1871, but with several differences. For instance, the constitution's bill of rights listed property as a natural right and gave considerable emphasis to religious freedom. In addition, grand juries became optional in the state court system at the discretion of local judges. The new constitution imposed a limitation on the state's power to take private land for railroad use. If the railroads failed to use private land taken under the state's eminent domain power for railroad purposes, then the lands so taken reverted to private ownership. The new constitution also increased the size of the state legislature and added state offices such as lieutenant governor, state superintendent of public instruction, attorney general, and commissioner of public lands. Ironically, however, neither the state superintendent nor the attorney general could hire a clerk at state expense. To give the legislature more power, the constitution required only a three-fifths vote to overcome a veto from the governor. The new state government also established distinct district and state supreme courts and provided for the creation of six judicial districts throughout Nebraska. Unlike previous documents, the 1875 constitution called for a system of publicly funded secondary education as well as a state university. The proposed constitution also dropped any taxation of church property. The state government maintained restricted powers to tax and could not raise the state debt above $100,000 except during wartime. Despite the strident campaigning of social reformers, the 1875 constitution did not extend the vote to women.

The state legislature submitted the constitution to Nebraska voters along with two separate provisions. The first gave voters the option to express their preference for U.S. senator before the legislature voted on the matter. The second provided that the state capital could not be moved unless voters agreed to it in a public referendum. In the fall of 1875, the Nebraska public, by popular vote of 30,332 to 5,474, approved of the new state constitution. The two separate provisions likewise passed. After nearly a decade of conflict, Nebraskans had finally created a stable constitutional order.[39]

Although many states joined the Union in the mid-nineteenth century, Nebraska's journey was nevertheless a singular one. For instance, the national attention focused on Nebraska's sporadic attempts at constitution building reflected the growing sectional importance of the West in national political and economic affairs. Furthermore, Nebraska's entry into the Union at the height of Reconstruction as a free-labor state helped ensure that other states would enter the Union under similar conditions. Finally, the controversies surrounding Nebraska's three constitutional conventions provide unique insight into the ways in which Nebraskans dealt with complex social issues like emancipation, religious toleration, public education, governmental regulation of the economy, and women's rights. Nebraska voters debated these important topics at the grassroots level in ways that foreshadowed the progressive movement of the early twentieth century. As such, Nebraska's early attempts to create a local framework for government represent a noteworthy chapter in the development of a distinctively American constitutional tradition.

Notes

1. James B. Potts, "Nebraska Statehood and Reconstruction," *Nebraska History* 69, no. 2 (1988): 73–83.

2. Addison Sheldon, *Land Systems and Land Policies in Nebraska* (Lincoln: Nebraska State Historical Society, 1936), 5–24; James C. Olson and Ronald C. Naugle, *History of Nebraska,* 3d ed. (Lincoln: University of Nebraska Press, 1997), 49–72.

3. Olson and Naugle, *History of Nebraska,* 67–77; Roy F. Nicholas, "The Kansas-Nebraska Act: A Century of Historiography," *Mississippi Valley Historical Review* 43 (September 1956): 187–212.

4. 10 Stat. 277 (1854).

5. Mark R. Ellis, "The State of Nebraska," in *The United States: The Story of Statehood for the Fifty United States,* vol. 2, *Louisiana to Ohio,* ed. Benjamin F. Shearer (Westport, Conn.: Greenwood, 2005), 731–35.

6. Cited in J. Sterling Morton and Albert Watkins, *History of Nebraska: From the Earliest Explorations of the Trans-Mississippi Region* (Lincoln, Neb.: Western Publishing and Engraving, 1918), 218–19.

7. Olson and Naugle, *History of Nebraska,* 133–34.

8. Albert Watkins, "How Nebraska Was Brought into the Union," *Nebraska State Historical Society Publications* 18 (1917): 377–78.

9. Olson and Naugle, *History of Nebraska,* 135–36.

10. A. T. Andreas, *History of the State of Nebraska* (Chicago: Western Historical, 1882), also available at the Kansas Collection, *History of the State of Nebraska,* http://www.kancoll.org/books/andreas_ne/hon_cnty.html; Olson and Naugle, *History of Nebraska,* 136–37.

11. James B. Potts, "Nebraska Territory, 1854–1867: A Study of Frontier Politics" (Ph.D. diss., University of Nebraska–Lincoln, 1973), 271–73.

12. Douglas Bakken, "Chronology of Nebraska Statehood," *Nebraska History* 48 (Spring 1967): 81–89; Ellis, "State of Nebraska," 738–39; Watkins, "How Nebraska Was Brought into the Union," 388–89.

13. Watkins, "How Nebraska Was Brought into the Union," 389–96.

14. Larry D. Duke, "Nebraska Territory," *Journal of the West* 16, no. 2 (1977): 81–83.

15. Alvin Saunders, "Opening Message to the Eleventh Session of the Legislative Assembly, January 9, 1865," in *Messages and Proclamations of the Governors of Nebraska, 1854–1941* (Lincoln: Works Progress Administration, 1941), 1:188–189.

16. Saunders, "Opening Message," 198–200.

17. Addison E. Sheldon, "Nebraska Constitutions of 1866, 1871, and 1875," *Nebraska State Historical Society Bulletin* 13 (September 1920).

18. James W. Woolworth, "Admission of Nebraska as a State," *Nebraska State Historical Society Publications* 5 (1893): 84; Bakken, "Chronology of Nebraska Statehood," 85–87.

19. Potts, "Nebraska Territory, 1854–1867," 288–89.

20. *Nebraska Daily Republican,* June 1, 1866; *Omaha Weekly Herald,* June 1, 1866; *Nebraska City News,* May 26, 1866; all cited in Potts, "Nebraska Territory, 1854–1867," 290–91.

21. Olson and Naugle, *History of Nebraska,* 140–42; George L. Miller to J. Sterling Morton, June 12, 1866, quoted in Wallace Brown, "George L. Miller and the Struggle over Nebraska Statehood," *Nebraska History* 41 (December 1960): 312.

22. Potts, "Nebraska Statehood and Reconstruction," 76–77.

23. Eric Foner, *Reconstruction: America's Unfinished Revolution, 1863–1877* (New York: Harper Perennial Illustrated Classics, 2002), 239–60.

24. Potts, "Nebraska Territory, 1854–1867," 291–95.

25. *Congressional Globe,* 39th Cong., 2d sess., 4206–13 (July 27, 1866); Ellis, "State of Nebraska," 744–45.

26. Potts, "Nebraska Statehood and Reconstruction," 78–79.

27. *Congressional Globe,* 39th Cong., 2d sess., 121–29, 162–70, 216–39, 354–58, 448–81 (December 5, 1866–January 9, 1867); Potts, "Nebraska Statehood and Reconstruction," 79–81.

28. Andrew Johnson, "Veto Messages," in *A Compilation of the Messages and Papers of the Presidents, 1789–1897,* ed. James D. Richardson (Washington, D.C.: Government Printing Office, 1897), 8:3688–89.

29. Olson and Naugle, *History of Nebraska,* 150–53.

30. Andreas, *History of the State of Nebraska;* Ruth Moore Stanley, "N. K. Griggs and the Nebraska Constitutional Convention of 1871," *Nebraska History* 46 (March 1965): 39–41.

31. Stanley, "N. K. Griggs and the Nebraska Constitutional Convention of 1871," 41–51.

32. Ibid., 51–56.

33. Sheldon, "Nebraska Constitutions"; Olson and Naugle, *History of Nebraska,* 180–82.

34. Addison Sheldon, *Nebraska: The Land and the People* (Chicago: Lewis, 1931), 1:422–57.

35. Addison Sheldon, *The True History of Nebraska* (Lincoln: Nebraska Press Association, 1940), xvi, and accessible online at http://www.rootsweb.com/~neresour/OLLibrary/wh01940/hist/wwnhista.html.

36. Sheldon, "Land and the People," 1:457–59.

37. *Omaha Daily Herald,* May 18, 1875.

38. Olson and Naugle, *History of Nebraska,* 516–19.

39. Ibid., 516–22.

TWO

Alan G. Gless

NEBRASKA'S CRIMINAL CODES

Sometimes criminal justice eludes those who seek it. This slippery quality became evident early in the history of Nebraska's criminal codes, in the territory's second year of existence.[1] On April 23, 1856, Simpson Hargus, insisting that James Lacy had jumped Hargus's claim to the west eighty acres of a quarter section of land near the courthouse in Nebraska City, shot and killed the alleged trespasser. Hargus was indicted for manslaughter, tried, convicted, and sentenced to prison. For an unsettling reason, as explained below, the territorial supreme court reversed the conviction and ordered Hargus released with no possibility of his ever being reprosecuted for killing Lacy. This chapter examines the development of Nebraska's statutory criminal law, beginning in 1855.[2] Some second-degree murder cases will illustrate the mischief that statutory change can unleash. The *Hargus* case, some chicken-stealing cases, a flag misuse case, and the unfortunate case of a financially stressed yet patriotic soul will serve as vehicles to illustrate other developments.

Like every other nonoriginal American territory and state, Nebraska faced the project of settling its law for itself.[3] Also, like most nonoriginal states, Nebraska achieved the initial settlement—and subsequent resettlements—of its criminal law in the nineteenth century by borrowing from other jurisdictions, of which Ohio, Illinois, Iowa, and Michigan were the greatest contributors.[4] In the twentieth century, the National Conference of Commissioners on Uniform State Laws and the American Law Institute became the primary contributors to the development of Nebraska's criminal law. The Nebraska Territory initially settled its criminal law very quickly, only to witness its complete demise within two years. The first resettlement of Nebraska criminal law survived for the remainder of the territorial period and the first six years of statehood, only to be entirely replaced again. The state's criminal law remained fairly stable for more than a century, with the usual systemic alterations, additions, and amendments. The legislature's alterations of and additions to Nebraska's criminal law reflected changes in the perceived needs of society, both local and national, lending direct support to the proposition that society and culture shape law and only inferential support to the idea that law shapes society. This chapter will establish the basic chronology of the adoption of Nebraska's first criminal code, examine the unforeseen effects of a statutory amendment, and turn to selected[5] reflections of the felt needs of the times as they appeared in the state's criminal codes.[6]

The 1855 Legislative Assembly of the Territory of Nebraska adopted the Iowa criminal code in toto as Nebraska's territorial criminal code.[7] Identifying the jurisdictional source of the 1855 Nebraska territorial criminal code is easy—the territorial assembly named the Iowa code, undated, in its adoption statute. But Nebraskans have been led to believe, incorrectly, that it was the 1838 Iowa territorial criminal code that became the 1855 Nebraska territorial criminal code.[8] The Nebraska assembly did not adopt the 1838 Iowa territorial criminal code; it adopted the Iowa state criminal code of 1851. This code should have more than sufficed in a territory with fewer than five thousand inhabitants at the time of its enactment.[9] But the 1855 criminal code was not destined to last.

In an unusual move, the 1857 territorial legislature repealed the 1855 criminal code over a gubernatorial veto and eventually adjourned without adopting a replacement.[10] The territorial code of criminal procedure, because it was part of the criminal code, also was repealed. The legislature failed to include either a savings clause preserving prosecutions for crimes committed before the repeal of the code[11] or a clause readopting the common law of crimes. As a result, Nebraska was left without any criminal law, code based or common law based.[12]

In the *Hargus* case, the crime was committed before the repeal, but the trial did not begin until after the repeal. Territorial judge Samuel W. Black reasoned that the common law recognized the crime of manslaughter. The territory had adopted the common law by statute and the legislature had not repealed that statute. He concluded that because the 1855 code had not defined the crime of manslaughter, but simply had made it an offense with a prescribed penalty range, the court's jurisdiction continued under the common law definition. The territorial supreme court disagreed, vacated the conviction and sentence, and discharged the prisoner.[13] The supreme court's position meant that territorial crimes committed but not prosecuted to final judgment before the repeal took effect could never be prosecuted at all.

Governor William A. Richardson called a special session of the territorial legislature in September 1858, in part to urge the adoption of a criminal code.[14] The legislature obliged and adopted a new criminal code copied from the Illinois criminal code of 1845.[15] The 1858 criminal code was readopted nearly in its entirety as part of the territorial revised statutes of 1866. Admitted to statehood in 1867,[16] Nebraska adopted the territorial revised statutes of 1866, in their entirety, as its first state statutes.[17] The 1858 Illinois-based code, with annual amendments, remained Nebraska's criminal code until 1873.

In that year, the legislature adopted the 1869 Ohio code of criminal procedure[18] and the 1835 Ohio criminal code,[19] supplemented through 1868,[20] as the Nebraska criminal code of 1873.[21] The criminal procedure code, as modified and supplemented over time, remained largely in effect in 2005.[22] The criminal code remained in effect until 1979,[23] with amendments—some major, most minor—and many additions, only a few of which were repealed before the adoption of the new code.

The 1858 criminal code had expressly recognized several affirmative defenses and justification defenses, including defense of self, others, and property; unavoidable necessity; and duress.[24] The 1873 code recognized none of these affirmative defenses, but the case law did. By recognizing insanity, self-defense, and entrapment as affirmative defenses, Nebraska decisional law also recognized the potential existence of other overt affirmative defenses and some justification defenses. The 1873 criminal code did not expressly recognize any major overt affirmative defenses[25] or justification defenses until 1972, when the legislature adopted several of the justification defense provisions of the American Law Institute's Model Penal Code: self-defense, defense of another, defense of property, and choice of lesser harms. It chose not to adopt the defense of duress.[26]

The Nebraska Legislature modeled elements of the present Nebraska Criminal Code,[27] adopted in 1977[28] and effective in 1979,[29] on the Model

Penal Code (MPC).[30] Several parts of the MPC—especially its property crime definitions, its consolidation of theft offenses, and its assault, general attempt, general conspiracy, and escape provisions, for example—became parts of the Nebraska Criminal Code. Most other parts of the present Nebraska Criminal Code retained the operative language, with some cosmetic modernizing, of earlier Nebraska criminal statutes in order to preserve the state's body of precedent and adopted only the penalty classification approach of the MPC.[31] One notable exception lay in the second-degree murder statute. The legislature's inexplicable tinkering with the definition of second-degree murder unleashed a major legal and political controversy and an ensuing high judicial drama.[32]

The legislature had intended to avoid an avalanche of appeals by retaining the operative definitions of most crimes. It earned at least a minor cascade of them, though, all arising out of convictions for second-degree murder. The 1873 criminal code declared that "[i]f any person shall purposely and maliciously, but without deliberation and premeditation, kill another, every such person shall be deemed guilty of murder in the second degree." That statute remained in force until 1979, when the present criminal code took effect. The legislature, without explaining why a change was necessary—but clearly cognizant that it was making the change—altered the statute to declare: "A person commits murder in the second degree if he causes the death of a person intentionally, but without premeditation." In Nebraska criminal law, the word "purposely" always has been used interchangeably with the word "intentionally"; the statutory change from "purposely" to "intentionally," therefore, caused no difficulty. Removing the word "maliciously" from the second-degree murder definition, however, caused major difficulty. "Malice" had always been given its older common-law meaning throughout the history of Nebraska criminal law until 1994, when it suddenly became a problem word.

In *State v. Myers,*[33] seventeen years after the criminal code revision, the Nebraska Supreme Court suddenly, and without anyone's asking it to do so, ruled that the new second-degree murder statute still required proof of malice, even though the legislature had dropped it from the definition. In the trial court, the judge, prosecuting attorney, and defense counsel all believed malice had been eliminated as an element of second-degree murder. Before the supreme court, neither the state nor the convict raised any question about malice and second-degree murder. The supreme court acted on the question without briefing and without any indication that it intended to go off on its own. The court also covertly, or perhaps inadvertently, adopted a newer common-law meaning of malice in *Myers,* overturning 134 years of Nebraska legal usage and never openly acknowledging what it had done.

The supreme court continued down this path through numerous decisions, almost always on its own initiative, eventually creating a situation in which as many as 130 second-degree murder convictions were open to attack and likely needed new trials. The state released thirteen second-degree murder convicts because prosecutors could not retry them with the judicially revitalized malice requirement. The public eventually manifested its outrage through the removal of the first supreme court justice to stand for retention election after the *Myers* decision— the only supreme court justice Nebraska voters ever have removed.

The removal of that justice, coupled with the departure of another for the federal bench and the retirements of four other *Myers* court members between 1993 and 1998, resulted in an entirely new supreme court membership. Each of the new appointees disagreed with the old supreme court members on the continuing vitality of malice as an element of second-degree murder. By August 1998, the controversy had reached its end. The new supreme court majority overruled all of the recent second-degree murder cases requiring that malice be shown as an element, recognized that the legislature could remove malice as an element of the crime of second-degree murder,[34] and reinstated Nebraska's historical definition of malice.[35] Despite this attempt to return to the status quo ante, more legal questions than ever in second-degree murder cases await appellate resolution as a result of the legislature's definitional tinkering, but none as controversial as the removal of the malice requirement.

Nebraska's criminal codes reflected the felt needs of the times.[36] In a very real sense, everything is related to everything else. The image of the law as a seamless web readily transposes to the greater society in which law plays a part. Natural and social conditions determine what law may become necessary or useful. Context matters.

The 1873 criminal code included a standard larceny statute prohibiting thefts of personal property. The code also included a procedural provision requiring juries in larceny cases to determine the value of the property stolen. The value the jury determined then automatically classified the offense. Grand larceny, $35.00 or more, was a felony carrying a penitentiary sentence—neither probation nor lesser forms of imprisonment were possible. Petit larceny, less than $35.00, was a misdemeanor carrying only a very short county jail sentence or a small fine. The penalty was based on the value, not on the specific nature or identity of the property involved.

During the late nineteenth century, the Nebraska Supreme Court worked toward more clearly defined and more stringent rules relating to evidence of value and toward more reliable jury verdicts. These supreme court activities resulted in reversals of a large a number of grand larceny convictions because of insufficient evidence of value and verdicts in which juries openly estimated, as opposed to determined, fair market values for the stolen property. Nebraska's legislature responded by adopting statutes prohibiting the theft of specific types of property "of any value," for which penitentiary sentences were the only allowable dispositions.

Except for some tinkering with sentencing options, most of these statutes remained in effect until 1979. The legislature apparently compared the penalty provisions of the 1873 criminal code, as amended through the years, with one another only occasionally. The legislature's neglect of the penalty provisions resulted in differences in possible penalties for conduct seemingly of the same nature, differences inexplicable to some later twentieth-century legislators. To those legislators, theft remained theft, regardless of the nature of the property stolen. It was the value of the property stolen that should define the crime of theft and that should determine the penalty, or so went the argument. By the 1970s, conditions differed sufficiently from those of earlier days that the argument made sense to the legislative presentists then in office, folks lacking an appreciation of the historical context.

However, these late twentieth-century legislators failed to appreciate the problems faced by a nineteenth-century rural state criminal justice system, one that lacked the support of low-cost, high-speed communications, a reliable, hard-surfaced road system,[37] and even electricity and telephones outside the major towns until well into the twentieth century. If a prosecutor must charge theft, with the applicable penalty gradations based on fair market value of the stolen property, that prosecutor must have adequate resources and evidence to prove value. That was easily done in the Nebraska of the 1970s. It was not easily done in the Nebraska of the 1870s through the 1940s. The legislative choice of proscribing theft and basing the possible penalties on the nature of the property stolen had made good sense at the time.

If a prosecutor could charge the theft of poultry, horses, cattle, or hogs, without regard to their value, the job was fairly clear-cut. Everyone knew what poultry, horses, cattle, and hogs were. Very few people, if any, had access to reliable information on current market value in forms admissible in evidence. Furthermore, poultry, horses, cattle, and hogs formed a vital part of Nebraska's economy as well as the livelihoods and even subsistence of their owners at the time. Thus it was that under the 1873 criminal code, as amended, stealing a chicken carried a possible penalty range of not less than one year's nor more than five years' imprisonment.[38] Stealing a horse carried a possible penalty range of not less than three years' nor more than fifteen years' imprisonment.[39] Stealing a cow carried a possible penalty range of not less than one year's nor more than ten years' imprisonment.[40] And stealing a pig carried a possible penalty range of not less than one year's nor more than five years' imprisonment.[41] All of those penitentiary sentences applied without regard to the value of the stolen chicken, horse, cow, or pig,[42] a legislative approach that reflected both the felt needs and the practicalities of the times.

The state supreme court understood and appreciated the situation. For example, after the legislature freed chicken-stealing from proof of value, a father and son convicted of receiving stolen chickens argued to the Nebraska Supreme Court that their convictions were invalid because the prosecutor had not alleged any value for the chickens, nor had the jury declared one. The statute prohibited stealing or receiving stolen chickens "of any value." The chief justice, writing for the unanimous court, explained: "Judges, as well as other people, in this jurisdiction, know . . . that chickens, alive and well enough to run around, are at least a basis upon which juries in this jurisdiction may ground a finding of some inferential value."[43]

Other felt needs of the times become readily apparent when one examines the dates of initial enactment of various Nebraska criminal laws in connection with roughly contemporaneous natural and social conditions, events, and movements, both local and national. Extreme nationalism swept the country in the 1890s and early 1900s and manifested itself in Nebraska's flag desecration laws and prohibitions on various uses of the American flag.[44] Nebraska's lone reported flag misuse case, *Halter v. State,* went on to the U.S. Supreme Court. Nicholas Halter and Harry Hayward were beer retailers. One of the brands they sold came in bottles that carried an image of the U.S. flag as part of the brewery's registered trademark. Nebraska's flag desecration statute prohibited the use of any representation of the American flag as a marking on any merchandise or receptacle of merchandise as a means of distinguishing the merchandise. Halter and Hayward were convicted and fined for their misuse of the national flag, and they challenged the constitutionality of the statute as exceeding the power of the state. The Nebraska Supreme Court ruled that the state constitutionally could regulate the use of the national flag. The U.S. Supreme Court agreed.[45]

The 1901 assassination of President William McKinley by an anarchist, World War I, the Bolshevik revolution in Russia, the activities of the Industrial Workers of the World, and the growth of socialist, communist, and anarchist movements in the United States combined to produce a virulent strain of American xenophobia in the early twentieth century. This xenophobia appeared in Nebraska's criminal code in several forms, including a prohibition of the teaching of the German language;[46] a requirement that public meetings be conducted in English only;[47] prohibitions relating to red (communist) and black (anarchist) flags and to symbols of any organization advocating the violent overthrow of the U.S. government;[48] and a sedition law, enacted in 1918 and repealed only in 1933.[49]

The 1918 sedition law ensnared one soul deemed less than acceptably patriotic by other members of his community.[50] The Beatrice, Nebraska, committee formed to raise money for war bonds had determined for itself how much and when various community members should contribute. When two committee members visited a certain Mr. Gerdes for the purpose of securing those funds, he could not immediately raise the sum demanded of him. He was in difficult financial straits just then but was agreeable to contributing that amount at a later time, after he had sold some of his corn. That did not satisfy the committee members. An altercation ensued. Gerdes, who was the father of two American soldiers and who was encouraging a third son to enlist, eventually found himself convicted and sentenced for sedition. The Nebraska Supreme Court held in a 4-to-3 decision that intent "to obstruct the government in prosecuting the war" was an essential element of the offense of sedition and ruled that the evidence adduced at trial failed to prove that Gerdes had argued with the committee members with the required intent.

The national labor unrest of the second half of the nineteenth century has been credited with contributing to the felt need for firearms regulation.[51] Nebraska lagged behind its eastern neighbors in experiences with labor strife, but the experiences eventually came. Nebraska's first major experience with labor strife, Omaha's Camp Dump Strike of 1882, started at the Burlington and Missouri Railroad site, spread to other industries, and developed into a riot. The governor, as had governors in other states, called on the National Guard to put down the riot.[52] In some states, struck businesses hired private police or paid the salaries of local police, who served as strikebreakers.[53] The Nebraska Legislature responded to the threat of these practices by prohibiting the importation of nonresidents into Nebraska for service as private police, prohibiting police service by persons who were not Nebraska residents, and prohibiting appointment of nonresidents as undersheriffs and deputy sheriffs.[54]

Nebraska moved to regulate firearms only slowly, beginning with an 1858 prohibition of assault with a deadly weapon.[55] In 1873, the legislature added the offenses of shooting or shooting at another with intent to kill, wound, or maim;[56] carrying concealed dangerous weapons (specifying pistols as a type of dangerous weapon);[57] and dueling.[58] Memories of the battle at Little Big Horn (1876) and the massacre at Wounded Knee (1890) were still fresh, and fears of a continued struggle between whites and Indians manifested themselves in the 1891 creation of the felony offense of sales of firearms and ammunition to noncitizen Indians.[59] In the early decades of the twentieth century, fear of foreigners and immigrants supplanted fear of Indians; in 1921, the Nebraska Legislature adopted a provision prohibiting aliens from owning, possessing, or keeping any form of firearms for any purpose.[60]

The combination of the strong nativist movement and the violent gangsterism of the 1920s led the National Conference of Commissioners on Uniform State Laws (NCCUSL) to develop the Uniform Machine Gun Act.[61] Nebraska was among the states that adopted this law, which forbade sales of machine guns to and possession of machine guns by anyone except law enforcement officers and soldiers. The act also contained a specific provision prohibiting ownership or possession of machine guns by aliens. Nebraska did not adopt any more noteworthy firearm regulations until 1961. In that year, the legislature proscribed possession of firearms by felons[62] and possession of pistols and revolvers with serial numbers removed.[63] In 1969, use of a firearm in the commission of a felony was made a separate offense.[64]

Labor unrest, World War I, and aggressive attempts by communist organizers to spread their program in the United States combined to provoke adoption of statutes prohibiting criminal syndicalism and regulating picketing. The legislature first defined "criminal syndicalism" as "the doctrine which advocates crime, physical violence, arson, destruction of property, or sabotage, as a means of accomplishing or effecting industrial or political ends, or for profit."[65] Then, the legislature made it a felony to advocate, teach, or affirmatively suggest crime, physical violence, or sabotage to accomplish industrial or political ends, or for profit, and prohibited assemblages for the purpose of such advocacy, teachings, or suggestions.

Furthermore, the legislature proscribed, as a misdemeanor, permitting the use of any place, building, rooms, or premises for such assemblages. Sabotage was a separate and substantive felony offense.[66] The legislature regulated picketing in 1921 and prohibited mass picketing in 1949.[67] A new wave of fear, inspired by the Soviet pledge to overthrow the United States from within and by Cold War domestic propaganda, manifested itself in the forms of a new sedition law and an act outlawing the Communist Party and declaring membership in that organization a form of felony sedition prosecutable by the state's attorney general.[68]

The development of Nebraska's criminal code also reflects technological advancements and the new actions that they made possible. The need to control the spread of animal diseases through the normal course of local commerce[69] and through transportation by rail appeared in 1877.[70] The proliferation of motor vehicles in the state led inevitably to a need to deal with various forms of criminality that they made possible.[71] The first joyriding statute came in 1915.[72] The offenses of stealing motor vehicles,[73] receiving automobiles with altered or defaced vehicle identification numbers, altering or defacing vehicle identification numbers first appeared in 1917, as did statutes creating strict record keeping regulations for motor vehicle repair garages with criminal penalties for violations.[74] The legislature enacted a similar protection of manufacturers' serial numbers affixed to general merchandise in 1929[75] and to farm machinery in 1953.[76] The offense of breaking and entering an automobile with intent to steal made its first appearance in 1935.[77] Failure to return a rented motor vehicle first became a crime in 1961.[78]

Nebraska first criminalized the unlicensed distribution of old drugs, such as cocaine, morphine, and opium as well as various forms of their abuse in 1915.[79] In 1935, Nebraska adopted the Uniform Narcotic Act[80] and the Hypnotic Drug Law[81] to combat the spread of newly developed drugs; this was followed at intervals by adoption of revised versions of the Uniform Narcotic Act and its successor, the Uniform Controlled Substances Act, which the legislature regularly updates to match federal drug schedule changes.[82] Special statutes aimed at controlling the manufacture of methamphetamine by criminalizing possession of anhydrous ammonia and ephedrine for that purpose became part of the criminal code in 2001.[83]

The development and proliferation of personal computers and broad Internet access prompted an attempt to control the forms of criminality that the emerging computer technology enabled. Nebraska's first laws aimed at deterring the criminal use of computer technology included a financial transaction device act of 1989[84] and the Computer Crimes Act of 1991.[85] The legislature bolstered these laws by adopting a personal information act in 2002,[86] which included additions to the financial transaction device laws and an act prohibiting the use of computers in enticing children into sexual offense situations.[87]

Nebraska's criminal codes have always included general laws to combat various forms of interpersonal violence, such as various forms of assault or sexual assault, as well as other social ills, such as pornography. Since the 1980s, legislators have focused some of their efforts on extra protection for special identity victims, such as children, victims of domestic assault, vulnerable adults, and other identifiable groups. These efforts have manifested themselves in laws aimed at combating child abuse, domestic abuse, and hate crimes and carrying special penalty provisions not available under the generally applicable proscriptions. Examples, among others, include the visual depiction of sex acts with minors in films,[88] gun transfers to minors and gun possession on school property,[89] sexual abuse of inmates and parolees,[90] criminal child enticement,[91] domestic assault,[92] and enhanced penalties for discrimination-based crimes.[93]

Nebraska accomplished its initial criminal law settlement and resettlements in the nineteenth century by borrowing from other jurisdictions, with Ohio, Illinois, Iowa, and Michigan serving as the greatest contributors to Nebraska's criminal law. In the twentieth century, the National Conference of Commissioners on Uniform State Laws and the American Law Institute became the primary contributors to Nebraska's criminal law. Its criminal law remained fairly stable for more than a century. The legislature's alterations and additions to Nebraska's criminal law reflected the changing locally, regionally, and nationally felt needs of the times; in other words, society and culture shaped Nebraska's criminal law.

Notes

1. Congress created the Nebraska Territory in 1854 under the Kansas-Nebraska Act, discussed in chapter 1. The Nebraska Territory put its government into operation in 1855.

2. The criminal laws that applied to the region that would become Nebraska while it was encompassed within the Province of Louisiana (1803–4), the District of Louisiana (1804–5), the Territory of Louisiana (1805–12), the Territory of Missouri (1812–20), and the Indian Country (1834–54) lie outside the scope of this chapter, as does almost all of Nebraska's criminal procedure. A large number of criminal laws dealing with special situations have always appeared outside the criminal code in

scattered areas of Nebraska's statutes (e.g., election laws, livestock health regulations, and so on); those laws generally lie outside the scope of this chapter as well.

3. "Settling the law" is a conceptual approach to American legal history formulated by Eben Moglen. For Moglen's basic explanation of his approach, see Eben Moglen, "Settling the Law: Legal Development in New York, 1664–1776" (Ph.D. diss., Yale University, 1993), 12–16. Settling the law does not end: the law, as a dynamic system, periodically becomes unsettled again and must be resettled.

4. Adopting laws and even entire codes from existing states and territories was a common practice in the formative years. See Lawrence M. Friedman, *A History of American Law,* 2d ed. (New York: Simon and Schuster, 1985), 166–67, 410; and William Wirt Blume and Elizabeth Gaspar Brown, "Territorial Courts and Law: Unifying Factors in the Development of American Legal Institutions; Part II: Influences Tending to Unify Territorial Law," *Michigan Law Review* 61, no. 3 (1963): 467–538.

5. "Selected" because Nebraska statutes define no fewer than 530 substantive offenses for which jury trials constitutionally are required, of which no fewer than 373 are felonies and another 157 are Class I misdemeanors. No fewer than 880 other offenses are misdemeanors for which jury trials statutorily are required on defense demand.

6. Justice Holmes applied his "felt necessities of the times" in discussing common law development. Oliver Wendell Holmes Jr., *The Common Law* (Boston: Little, Brown, 1923), 1. The concept also applies to statutory development as well, perhaps even more aptly.

7. 1855 Laws of Nebraska Territory 212, adopted just two months after the first territorial legislature assembled on January 16, 1855. James C. Olson and Ronald C. Naugle, *History of Nebraska,* 3d ed. (Lincoln: University of Nebraska Press, 1997), 84, 86. The 1855 code included both the substantive law of crimes and the code of criminal procedure.

8. Roland A. Luedtke, "Nebraska Criminal Code Revision—A Decade of Legislative Perseverance," *Creighton Law Review* 11, no. 1 (1977): 79–80. The late Lt. Gov. Luedtke chaired the Nebraska Legislature's Judiciary Committee from 1971 through 1976 and led the Nebraska criminal law revision efforts of the 1960s and 1970s. His article has been Nebraska's only published authority on the history of the state's criminal code. Luedtke did not even mention Nebraska's 1857 repeal of the 1855 criminal code or the adoption of the 1858 criminal code or the adoption of the 1873 criminal code. By omitting those events, Luedtke misled readers into believing that the 1855 code persisted with piecemeal revisions from its adoption until 1979. In addition, Luedtke said of the alleged 1838 Iowa code: "The Legislature merely adopted the Iowa Criminal Code passed in 1838 by the Iowa Territorial Legislature. Although the source relied upon by the Iowa legislature is uncertain, it may be assumed that the English statutes and common law had a profound influence." Ibid., 79–80.

Iowa Territory had no 1838 criminal code adopted by its territorial legislature. The immediate source of Iowa Territory's first criminal code lay in the congressional enactment, Iowa Organic Act, ch. 96, § 12, 5 Stat. 239 (1838), that the existing laws of Wisconsin Territory would govern in Iowa until altered, amended, or repealed by the territorial government. In like manner, the laws of the Territory of Michigan formed Wisconsin Territory's first laws. Wisconsin Organic Act, ch. 54, § 12, 5 Stat. 15 (1836). Congress created Iowa Territory out of Wisconsin Territory in 1838, including in the Iowa Organic Act a provision that all laws then in force in Wisconsin would be in force in Iowa. Iowa Organic Act, ch. 96, § 12, 5 Stat. 239 (1838). Iowa Territory comprised the present states of Iowa, Minnesota west of the Mississippi River, and the Dakotas east of the White Earth and the Missouri rivers. The act of Congress approving the new division went into effect July 4, 1838.

The first Iowa territorial legislature promptly repealed all laws of Michigan and Wisconsin then in force in Iowa. 1840 Laws of the Territory of Iowa 20. The Iowa Territorial Assembly enacted Iowa's first criminal code on January 4, 1839, to take effect on January 1, 1840. 1838–39 Laws of the Territory of Iowa 109. Within five years after statehood, the Iowa state legislature adopted the Iowa Code of 1851. Iowa General Assembly, *The Code of Iowa: Passed at the Session of the General Assembly of 1850–1 and Approved 5th February, 1851* (Des Moines: Palmer and Paul, 1851; repr. Emory H. English, 1912).

9. The census used to create the territory's first election districts showed only 2,732 inhabitants in November of 1854. An 1855 territorial census showed the territory's population had increased to 4,494 by October of 1855. An 1856 estimated census showed the territory's population had increased to 10,716. The official 1860 census showed the population had swollen to 28,841. Olson and Naugle, *History of Nebraska*, 87.

10. 1857 Laws of Nebraska Territory 137. See also Western Historical Company, *History of the State of Nebraska* (Chicago: Western Historical, 1882), 1:115. That session of the territorial legislature was riddled with heated conflict over locating the site of the territorial capital and continuing unhappiness with acting governor Thomas B. Cuming's 1855 legislative apportionment to the extent that a majority of the members of the legislature even seceded and attempted to conduct business in a place other than the place the governor had designated for holding the session. Both legislative camps adjourned sine die leaving a number of pressing problems unresolved. The repeal of both the criminal and civil codes could have been part of a larger effort to inflict heavy political embarrassment on the federally appointed executive. Cuming created the legislative unrest, which the unpopular Governor Mark W. Izard was unable to calm.

11. An omission that neither the territorial nor state legislature would ever repeat.

12. Although the relatively few federal criminal statutes still applied in the Nebraska Territory and the territorial courts had federal jurisdiction, because there was no federal common law of crimes, the territory had essentially no criminal law at all. See, e.g., Dwight F. Henderson, *Congress, Courts, and Criminals: The Development of Federal Criminal Law, 1801–1829* (Westport, Conn.: Greenwood, 1985).

13. Judge Black's multipage trial court opinion was printed in full in the local newspaper. *Nebraska City News*, January 9, 1858. The supreme court opinion consisted of a six-line journal entry. Nebraska Territorial Supreme Court Journal, Criminal Case No. 3-502, December 21, 1858, page 45, Nebraska State Historical Society, RG 58, series 3, box 4.

Earlier historians who have investigated the case concluded the discharge of the prisoner was precisely the goal of the territorial legislator, Alan A. Bradford, who introduced and promoted the repeal of the criminal code. Bradford was one of Hargus's lawyers. Michael W. Homer, "The Territorial Judiciary: An Overview of the Nebraska Experience, 1854–1867," *Nebraska History* 63 (Fall 1986): 348, 366–67; J. Sterling Morton and Albert Watkins, *History of Nebraska,* rev. ed. (Lincoln: Nebraska Historical Society, 1918), 228–30; and A. T. Andreas, *History of the State of Nebraska* (Chicago: Western Historical, 1882), 1:115–16.

14. Message of the governor, *Council Journal of the Legislative Assembly of the Territory of Nebraska,* 5th sess., 12 (September 21, 1858).

15. 1858 Laws of Nebraska Territory 6.

16. Nebraska Admission Act, 14 Stat. 391 (1867); Nebraska Enabling Act, 13 Stat. 47 (1864).

17. Neb. const. of 1866, schedule, § 1.

18. 66 Laws of Ohio 287.

19. Republished in the 1854 Statutes of Ohio, as Ohio Stat., ch. 33 (1854), and in Joseph R. Swan and Leander J. Critchfield, eds., *The Revised Statutes of the State of Ohio, of a General Nature, in Force August 1, 1860* (Cincinnati, Ohio: R. Clarke, 1860).

20. Joseph R. Swan and Milton Sayler, eds., *Supplement to the Revised Statutes of the State of Ohio, Embracing All Laws of a General Nature, Passed since the Publication of Swan and Critchfield's Revised Statutes, 1860: In Force August 1, 1860* (Cincinnati, Ohio: R. Clarke, 1868).

21. Neb. Gen. Stat., ch. 58 (1873). The state librarian and legislative historian could find no record of a separately published compilation of the public general session laws for 1873. The legislature ordered the session laws for that year to be integrated into the Nebraska General Statutes of 1873, a work in progress during the 1873 regular legislative session. Neb. Gen. Stat. 1083 (1873). The legislature took the same approach to the laws passed during the special session of 1873. Ibid.

"The criminal law of the state of Ohio was adopted by the legislature of this state in 1873, almost bodily, and by the one act entitled 'An act to establish a Criminal Code,' passed March 4th of that year. By it the entire criminal law of that state was substantially transferred to the statute books of Nebraska." Bohanan v. State, 18 Neb. 57, 73, 24 N.W. 390, 398 (1885). See also Larson v. State, 161 Neb. 339, 73 N.W.2d 388 (1955); Schultz v. State, 88 Neb. 613, 130 N.W. 105 (1911); Wheeler v. State, 79 Neb. 491, 113 N.W. 253 (1907); Morgan v. State, 51 Neb. 672, 71 N.W. 788 (1897); and Walrath v. State, 8 Neb. 80, 1878 WL 3183 (1878). Contra, Stevens v. State, 19 Neb. 647, 648–49, 28 N.W. 304, 304–5 (1886) (Maxwell, C.J.: "Many of the provisions of our Criminal Code are copied, substantially, from the statutes of Illinois,—some sections verbatim"). However, in *Stevens,* Chief Justice Maxwell was referring to procedural statutes first adopted in 1885, not to the 1873 code.

22. From 1855 through 1872, Nebraska prosecutors could not compel the accused to submit to cross-examination because the accused were not permitted to testify even voluntarily as witnesses in their own favor; that is, the criminally accused were neither compellable nor competent. Joining a movement that would become national in scope and as part of the 1873 criminal procedure code, the legislature removed

the testimonial incompetency of the criminally accused in 1873. Neb. Gen. Stat., ch. 45, § 473 (1873). The constitutional immunity from testimonial compulsion remained. Neb. const. of 1866, art. I, § 8 ("[N]or shall [any person] be compelled in any criminal case to be a witness against himself"); and Neb. const. of 1875, art. I, § 12 ("No person shall be compelled in any criminal case to give evidence against himself").

The 1885 legislature replaced the grand jury system with the preliminary examination by magistrate system as Nebraska's routine felony charge screening mechanism. The Nebraska constitution of 1866 mandated grand jury proceedings in the prosecution of serious offenses. Neb. const. of 1866, art. I, § 8. The Nebraska constitution of 1875 continued the grand jury system as it had been, but it also contained the following permissive language: "Provided, That the Legislature may by law provide for holding persons to answer for criminal offenses on information of a public prosecutor; and may by law, abolish, limit, change, amend, or otherwise regulate the grand jury system." Neb. const. of 1875, art. I, § 10. The legislature eventually did so in 1885 (1885 Laws of Nebraska 397 [conferring on the state's courts jurisdiction to hear prosecutions initiated by information]), adopting nearly verbatim Michigan's 1859 prosecution by information statutes (1859 Laws of Michigan 391). Michigan had been the first state to replace its grand jury system with prosecution by information. For a full account of the Nebraska grand jury story, see Richard E. Shugrue, "The Grand Jury in Nebraska," *Creighton Law Review* 33, no. 1 (1999): 39–64. Grand juries still could be called by special order of a district judge or by petition of the people to the district court, but no longer were they to be called routinely to sit for every term of the district court. See 1885 Laws of Nebraska 397 and 1988 Laws of Nebraska 573 (providing that a grand jury shall be called whenever a person dies in the custody of Nebraska law enforcement officers).

23. Luedtke claimed that the 1855 criminal code, with the major revisions adopted in 1875 (citing 1875 Laws of Nebraska 2 and 1875 Laws of Nebraska 18), remained largely in effect in 1977, when the present criminal code passed the legislature. Luedtke, "Nebraska Criminal Code Revision," 80–81. Both 1875 Laws of Nebraska 2 and 1875 Laws of Nebraska 18 contain numerous internal references to amending various sections in "Gen. Stat." The only set of Nebraska statutes ever identified as "Gen. Stat." was the Nebraska General Statutes of 1873, in which, as we have seen, the legislature adopted the 1873 criminal code.

24. 1858 Laws of Nebraska Territory 459–61.

25. The 1873 code did recognize an affirmative defense to a charge of carrying a concealed weapon. Neb. Gen. Stat., ch. 58, § 25 (1873).

26. 1972 Laws of Nebraska 276. Nebraska has produced no case law on duress either. Nebraska Supreme Court, *Nebraska Jury Instructions, Criminal,* 2d ed. (Minneapolis, Minn.: Thomson-West, 2004), 87.

27. "Nebraska Revised Statutes §§ 28-101 to 28-1350 shall be known and may be cited as the Nebraska Criminal Code." Neb. Rev. Stat. § 28-101 (Cum. Supp. 2004).

28. 1977 Laws of Nebraska 88 (LB 38). Three companion bills, also adopted in 1977, completed the criminal code package: 1977 Laws of Nebraska 230 (LB 39), 1977 Laws of Nebraska 363 (LB 40), and 1977 Laws of Nebraska 503 (LB 41). The Nebraska justification defense provisions, also based on the MPC (see Judiciary Com-

mittee Statement on LB 895 [1971]) and now appearing as Neb. Rev. Stat. §§ 28-1406 to 28-1416, denominated as noncode provisions, were retained in 1977.

29. Initially, the effective date for the Nebraska Criminal Code was established as July 1, 1978 (1977 Laws of Nebraska 141 [LB 38, § 325]), but was delayed until January 1, 1979, as part of a later harmonizing act. 1978 Laws of Nebraska 725 (LB 748, § 54).

30. American Law Institute, Model Penal Code (Proposed Official Draft 1962).

31. Luedtke, "Nebraska Criminal Code Revision," 78, 91. The 1962 Proposed Official Draft of the MPC and the supportive commentary accompanying the various earlier tentative drafts formed the direct source materials for interpreting the parts of the Nebraska Criminal Code based on the MPC.

32. See Richard E. Shugrue and John R. Snowden, "*State v. Burlison* Redefines the Malice Requirement: Now What? A Dialogue on Nebraska's Evolving Homicide Law," *Creighton Law Review* 32, no. 2 (1998): 645–67; John R. Snowden, "Second Degree Murder, Malice, and Manslaughter in Nebraska: New Juice for an Old Cup," *Nebraska Law Review* 76, no. 3 (1997): 399–451; Don Stenberg, "Malice in Wonderland," *Creighton Law Review* 30, no. 1 (1996): 15–27; and Richard E. Shugrue, "The Second Degree Murder Doctrine in Nebraska," *Creighton Law Review* 30, no. 1 (1996): 29–66.

33. 244 Neb. 905, 510 N.W.2d 58 (1994).

34. State v. Burlison, 255 Neb. 190, 583 N.W.2d 31 (1998).

35. Snowden, "Second Degree Murder, Malice, and Manslaughter in Nebraska," 399–451.

36. The national criminal code revision movement may have been the trend that most influenced Nebraska criminal law during the 1960s and 1970s. This chapter, however, will not discuss that movement. By 1997, thirty-six states had adopted revised criminal codes influenced by or modeled on the MPC. See, e.g., Dannye Holley, "The Influence of the Model Penal Code's Culpability Provisions on State Legislatures: A Study of Lost Opportunities, Including Abolishing the Mistake of Fact Doctrine," *Southwestern University Law Review* 27, no. 2 (1997): 229–63; and Herbert Wechsler, "The Model Penal Code and the Codification of American Criminal Law," in *Crime, Criminology and Public Policy: Essays in Honour of Sir Leon Radzinowicz*, ed. Roger Hood (London: Heinemann Educational, 1974), 419.

37. In 1905, no paved roads existed anywhere in the United States. Although the 1904 Nebraska road inventory in the first federal census of roads showed more than 79,000 miles of roads in the state, they were mostly county section line roads, which were dirt-surfaced at best. Most of these county section line roads, in reality, were only trails. In 1908, only sixteen of the state's ninety-three counties had any improved roads at all. Olson and Naugle, *History of Nebraska*, 298. By 1914, only 1.5 percent of all of Nebraska's roads, state highways included, had been improved ("improved" meant only graded with a dirt surface). State Board of Irrigation, Highways and Drainage, *Tenth Biennial Report of the State Board of Irrigation, Highways and Drainage, 1912–1914* (Lincoln: Nebraska State Board of Irrigation, Highways and Drainage, 1914), 221. By 1930, the state highway system included 9,752 miles of roads, 4,760 miles of which were graveled, 1,725 miles dirt-surfaced, 368 miles hard-surfaced, 29 miles oiled, and only 6,882 miles maintained. U.S. Highway 30 became Nebraska's first border-to-border hard-surfaced highway spanning 442 miles

only in 1935. By 1940, the state highway system included 11,220 miles of roads, of which 4,784 miles were graveled, 412 miles dirt-surfaced, 3,804 miles hard-surfaced, and only 9,000 miles maintained. George E. Koster, *A Story of Highway Development in Nebraska* (Lincoln: Nebraska Department of Roads, 1997), 8, 13, 36, 51; and Mead and Hunt, Inc., and Heritage Research Ltd., *Nebraska Historical Roads Survey* (Lincoln: Nebraska Historical Society and Nebraska Department of Roads, 2002), 21, 54–55.

38. 1907 Laws of Nebraska 500.

39. Neb. Gen. Stat., ch. 58, part 1, § 117 (1873).

40. 1899 Laws of Nebraska 358.

41. 1907 Laws of Nebraska 499.

42. Wells v. State, 11 Neb. 409, 9 N.W. 552 (1881) (the character of the crime is the same whether the value of the animal, a horse, is $500 or only $20).

43. Halbert v. State, 116 Neb. 1, 215 N.W. 459, 461 (1927).

44. 1905 Laws of Nebraska 694. Twenty-eight of the nation's forty-five states adopted similar laws between 1891 and 1906.

45. Halter v. Nebraska, 205 U.S. 34 (1907), *aff'g* Halter v. State, 74 Neb. 757, 105 N.W. 298 (1905).

46. Meyer v. Nebraska, 262 U.S. 390 (1923), discussed in chapter 14.

47. 1919 Laws of Nebraska 991.

48. 1919 Laws of Nebraska 916.

49. 1918 Laws of Nebraska 36, repealed by 1933 Laws of Nebraska 459. On the restrictions imposed on speech and political activity generally from 1900 through 1960, see Thomas I. Emerson, David Haber, and Norman Dorsen, *Political and Civil Rights in the United States*, 3d ed., 2 vols. plus supp. (Boston, Mass.: Little, Brown, 1967); and Zechariah Chaffee Jr., *Free Speech in the United States* (Cambridge, Mass.: Harvard University Press, 1948).

50. Gerdes v. State, 104 Neb. 35, 175 N.W. 606 (1919).

51. On labor unrest in other places vis-à-vis firearm regulation, see Clayton E. Cramer, *For the Defense of Themselves and the State: The Original Intent and Judicial Interpretation of the Right to Keep and Bear Arms* (Westport, Conn.: Praeger, 1994), 132–34, 168–69.

52. Olson and Naugle, *History of Nebraska,* 220.

53. See Cramer, *For the Defense of Themselves and the State,* 168.

54. 1893 Laws of Nebraska 403. Violations were classified as felonies. Ibid., § 3.

55. 1858 Laws of Nebraska Territory 462.

56. Neb. Gen. Stat., ch. 58, § 16 (1873).

57. Neb. Gen. Stat., ch. 58, § 25 (1873).

58. Neb. Gen. Stat., ch. 58, § 9 (1873).

59. 1891 Laws of Nebraska 267. The legislature finally repealed the restriction on sales of firearms and ammunition to Indians in 1955. 1955 Laws of Nebraska 286.

60. 1921 Laws of Nebraska 606. The idea probably originated with New York's 1905 prohibition of possession of firearms by aliens "in any public place at any time," 1905 Laws of New York 1:130, which was carried over into New York's Sullivan Law of 1911. Don B. Kates Jr., "Toward a History of Handgun Prohibition in the United States," in *Restricting Handguns: The Liberal Skeptics Speak Out,* ed. Don B. Kates Jr.,

(Croton-on-Hudson, N.Y.: North River, 1979), 17. The legislature finally repealed the alien gun restriction in 1957. 1957 Laws of Nebraska 358.

In 1922–23, the United States Revolver Association created a proposed Uniform Revolver Act, sent copies with supporting materials to the state legislatures and to the NCCUSL, and worked with the NCCUSL on the development of a proposed uniform state law. See National Conference of Commissioners on Uniform State Laws, *Handbook* (Chicago: NCCUSL, 1926), 571–84; and National Conference of Commissioners on Uniform State Laws, *Handbook* (Chicago: NCCUSL, 1924), 172–73, 711–48. Nebraska did not adopt any of the NCCUSL's Uniform Firearms Act sales regulation scheme.

Creation and adoption of a system of uniform state laws became another of the national movements of the times to which Nebraska responded favorably. On the uniform state laws movement generally, see Walter P. Armstrong Jr., *A Century of Change: A Centennial History of the National Conference of Commissioners on Uniform State Laws* (St. Paul, Minn.: West, 1991).

61. 1929 Laws of Nebraska 674. See also Cramer, *For the Defense of Themselves and the State,* 179–82, 184–90.

62. 1961 Laws of Nebraska 376.

63. Ibid.

64. 1969 Laws of Nebraska 808.

65. 1919 Laws of Nebraska 1058.

66. 1918 Laws of Nebraska, spec. sess., 50.

67. 1921 Laws of Nebraska 836 (picketing); 1949 Laws of Nebraska 181 (mass picketing). In 1946, Nebraska also adopted so-called right to work amendments to its state constitution. Neb. const. of 1875, art. XV, §§ 13, 14, and 15.

68. 1961 Laws of Nebraska 367. Nebraska's enactments in this area resembled parts of the earlier federal laws on the same topics. See Subversive Activities Control Act, Title I of the Internal Security Act of 1950, ch. 1024, 64 Stat. 987 (1950); and Communist Control Act, ch. 886, 68 Stat. 775 (1954).

69. See Johnson v. Chilson, 29 Neb. 301, 45 N.W. 462 (1890) (two separate provisions made it unlawful to sell diseased animals); Neb. Comp. Stat. Ann., ch. 4, § 13, and Criminal Code, ch. 10, § 76 (1887).

70. 1877 Laws of Nebraska 149.

71. From 1,087 registered vehicles in 1906 to 211,750 in 1919. Mead and Hunt, Inc., and Heritage Research, Ltd., *Nebraska Historical Roads Survey* (Lincoln: Nebraska Historical Society and Nebraska Department of Roads, 2002), 12.

72. 1915 Laws of Nebraska 582.

73. 1917 Laws of Nebraska 479.

74. 1917 Laws of Nebraska 480.

75. 1929 Laws of Nebraska 498.

76. 1953 Laws of Nebraska 258.

77. 1935 Laws of Nebraska 217.

78. 1961 Laws of Nebraska 363.

79. 1915 Laws of Nebraska 110.

80. 1935 Laws of Nebraska 232.

81. 1935 Laws of Nebraska 221.

82. 1967 Laws of Nebraska 460; 1969 Laws of Nebraska 793; 1969 Laws of Nebraska 800; 1971 Laws of Nebraska LB 326 (Uniform Controlled Substances Act).

83. 2001 Laws of Nebraska 254.

84. 1989 Laws of Nebraska 1441.

85. 1991 Laws of Nebraska 256.

86. 2002 Laws of Nebraska 75.

87. 2004 Laws of Nebraska 308.

88. 1988 Laws of Nebraska 76.

89. 1994 Laws of Nebraska 747.

90. 1999 Laws of Nebraska 764.

91. 1999 Laws of Nebraska 66.

92. 2004 Laws of Nebraska 154.

93. 1997 Laws of Nebraska 143.

THREE

Mark R. Ellis

THE LEGAL AND JUDICIAL CAREER OF FRANCIS "FRANK" HAMER

Pioneer Lawyer, District Court Judge, and Nebraska Supreme Court Justice

On August 10, 1918, Francis "Frank" Hamer died of stomach cancer at his home in Kearney, Nebraska. Hamer was seventy-five years old, and he had been a resident of Nebraska for nearly fifty years. He arrived in 1869 as a young lawyer in search of a suitable location to hang out his shingle, and he died while serving as an associate justice on the Nebraska Supreme Court. Hamer's forty-eight-year career as a pioneer lawyer, district court judge for western Nebraska, and state supreme court justice serves as a window from which to view Nebraska's evolution from a sparsely settled frontier territory into a modern Great Plains state.[1]

Frank Hamer was born on February 20, 1843, in a log cabin near Fostoria, Seneca County, Ohio. Shortly after Hamer's mother died in 1852, the family pushed westward to Carroll County, Indiana, where the extended Hamer clan farmed and participated in the public affairs of the community. The Hamer family knew hard work, and Frank spent his childhood on the family farm, clearing land and chopping wood. Like his father, young Hamer was a voracious reader who reportedly pored over books and newspapers whenever they were available.

At the age of sixteen, Hamer left the neighborhood to acquire a teacher's certificate at a school near Springfield, Illinois. After eighteen months, he returned to the family farm and began teaching in the rural schools around the county seat, Delphi. Hamer joined a literary and debating society, where he listened and learned how to debate from lawyers, newspaper editors, and politicians. From an early age, Hamer had an interest in the law, and the lawyers in his debating society encouraged him to follow this bent. Thus, at the age of eighteen, he borrowed a copy of Blackstone's *Commentaries* and in his spare time began learning the law. In 1861, Hamer moved to Indianapolis, where he read law with a prominent legal firm and began taking classes at a law school operated by Samuel E. Perkins, a justice of the Indiana Supreme Court. Hamer graduated at the top of his class and was admitted to the bar in 1864.

In 1869, Hamer made several decisions that would change his life. On December 6 of that year, he married Rebecca Almira McCord at her brother's farm near Eddyville, Iowa. Both Frank and Rebecca had taught in the rural schools around Delphi, and their relationship was more than likely fostered by their mutual interest and participation in the local debating societies that were popular in Indiana. Now having a wife to support, Hamer also decided in 1869 to give up farming and teaching, and to make the legal profession a full-time career. He began searching throughout Iowa and Wisconsin for a suitable location to open a law office but finding these states teeming with established attorneys, the twenty-six-year-old lawyer decided to test out the young state of Nebraska.

Hamer was one of hundreds of young midwestern lawyers who recognized the career opportunities that the newly settled Great Plains states offered. The extension of railroads across the plains and the emergence of hundreds of new communities provided lawyers with opportunities that would have taken them decades to attain in their native states. Remaining in Ohio, Illinois, or Indiana meant a slow climb up the legal ladder to economic, social, and political success. In the recently settled states of the Great Plains—Kansas, Nebraska, and the Dakotas—the bar was not yet established, and a young and ambitious lawyer could advance quickly on his merits and initiative.[2]

Like most migrant lawyers, Hamer did not venture onto the Great Plains without first doing some investigation. Hamer scouted neighboring states and must have gathered information about Nebraska before setting off for the Cornhusker State. Those seeking suitable communities usually appeared with letters of introduction from their hometown mayors, teachers, judges, or others of high community standing. The *North Platte Republican* regularly reported on young professionals like Hamer who passed through town while "looking up western locations" to begin their careers. Harrison Babb, for example, a young lawyer from Illinois and recent graduate of the University of Iowa's law school, scouted out dozens of communities in several states during the summer of 1876 before settling in North Platte. The *North Platte Republican* was quite impressed with Babb, reporting that he was a young man with "regular western push and enterprise."[3]

Other migrant lawyers did not necessarily need to do as much scouting because they were part of migration networks centered on a particular law school. The law schools at the universities of Iowa and Michigan, for example, sent hundreds of graduates into Nebraska and Kansas during the 1870s and 1880s. Once a graduate or two had settled in a particular community, others from the same university tended to follow shortly thereafter. North Platte and Grand Island drew lawyers from the University of Iowa, while graduates of the University of Michigan migrated to Hastings and Seward.[4]

It is unclear what connections, if any, Hamer might have had when he arrived in Omaha in December 1869. He certainly would have carried papers from his law school and letters from the lawyers under whom he had studied, particularly Samuel Elliott Perkins. Hamer briefly considered opening a law office in Omaha. The bustling commercial city, however, was overstocked with experienced lawyers, and it apparently intimidated the inexperienced Hamer. Later in life, Hamer admitted that he had been "timid about practicing law in Omaha." In January 1870, therefore, he pushed on to the new but growing capital city of Lincoln. Lincoln had been founded only a few years before and had a population of around seventeen hundred. The town was not yet accessible by railroad, although the Burlington line would soon arrive from Plattsmouth. Still, Lincoln appeared promising—after all, it was home to the state capital, penitentiary, and university.

Arriving in Lincoln on January 7, 1870, Hamer was the thirty-ninth lawyer to hang out his shingle in that city. Although a number of Lincoln attorneys were already well established and had many years of legal experience, the majority were young and inexperienced recent migrants. Hamer opened his first office among a string of shanties on Tenth Street that were rented by what he called a group of "young fellows" of similar standing. Because there were so many lawyers in the capital city, work was hard to come by during the first few months. Work for new arrivals like Hamer usually consisted of trying cases before the local justice of the peace. His first case involved a tort suit that netted the plaintiff ten cents for damaged crops. Hamer earned $2.50 for his effort. Hamer later recalled that such cases were often hotly contested between the young lawyers who worked out of the Tenth Street offices. On one occasion, violence nearly broke out in the court when an opposing lawyer "offered to lick" Hamer. The justice of the peace temporarily halted court and offered to adjourn if Hamer and his challenger wanted to go outside and fight. Both parties declined, and the case proceeded. Although Hamer advertised his services in the local press and continued to pick up petty cases in the local justice of the peace court, he still had a difficult time paying the bills. During his second month in Lincoln, Hamer paid his office rent by defending his ill-tempered landlord, who frequently found himself involved in minor legal disputes.[5]

Hamer's fortune changed in 1871, when he entered into a partnership with Alexander Connor, a lawyer and newspaper editor from Indianapolis whom Hamer apparently had met while attending law school. Connor was a renowned public speaker and may have been one of Hamer's law school instructors. Connor's experience, name recognition, and financial resources, combined with Hamer's energy and work ethic were the perfect mix for a successful law partnership. The senior partner immediately moved Hamer into a larger law office among the more established Lincoln attorneys on O Street, purchased law books for the firm, and began picking up more lucrative legal work in the district court.[6]

Little is known about the Hamer and Connor law firm's operations in Lincoln. Their names do not appear as counsel in any of the early Nebraska Supreme Court reports, so the firm must not have been considered one of the high-caliber practices. Lincoln had an established bar that Hamer and Connor may not have been able to break into. Many of the prominent law firms had been in operation since the territorial period, and corporations like the Burlington and Union Pacific railroads employed others. The firm, therefore, made a bold move in 1872 by migrating westward to find better opportunities. The young Hamer did the investigative work for the move, traveling 125 miles west to the so-called paper town of Kearney Junction, where he searched for available land and ascertained the possibilities of opening a law practice. Kearney Junction was where the Burlington Railroad planned a junction with the Union Pacific Railroad. The town did not yet exist when Hamer arrived, but he realized that once the Burlington Railroad reached this point, the area would quickly become a boomtown. Hamer filed a claim on a section of government land, located another for his partner, and hurried back to Lincoln to prepare for the move.

Nascent railroad towns like Kearney Junction—without established lawyers, doctors, or businessmen—provided young, enterprising professionals the chance of a lifetime. In Kearney Junction, Frank Hamer became the first lawyer in a budding Great Plains commercial town. Although other lawyers appeared shortly after Hamer's move to Kearney, he already had made clients of the primary businessmen in town and had handled the legal work of the county commissioners. Hamer's career grew with the town.[7]

Hamer did not find immediate financial success, though, in Kearney. Although the firm had a growing clientele that included bankers, land seekers, and the county commissioners, remuneration often was paid in kind. Clients paid Hamer in labor, cattle, crops, and, on occasion, with town lots. During his campaign for the Nebraska Supreme Court, Hamer recalled that he had a sizable "clientage of poor people who got in trouble perhaps oftener than they should." Hamer added that he never had hesitated to spend his "time and often a little [of his own] money" to properly defend such clients.[8]

For the first nineteen months in Kearney, the Hamers lived several miles northwest of town in a one-room, twelve-by-sixteen-foot cabin on their government claim. Shortly after arriving, Frank's wife Rebecca expressed her concern about the move in a letter to her sister. "We are poor to be sure," Rebecca explained, "but we expect to get through the worst this summer. Leaving a living law practice [in Lincoln] and coming here where there is nothing does not fill ones pockets very fast."[9] Within a few years, the law practice began to prosper, and in early 1874, the Hamers built what they remembered as "the best house in town" for $825 and moved off the homestead.[10]

As the first lawyers in a new town, Hamer and Connor took on all types of cases. Unlike their counterparts in Omaha and Lincoln, who could specialize in railroad law, torts, or criminal law, frontier lawyers offered a multitude of legal services. Hamer later commented that during his career, he had done the "legal business of a country community." Their early legal work reflects the issues faced by a community in its pioneer stage. The partnership regularly represented the interests of the county government in suits against the railroads as well as in property disputes, taxation issues, and internal improvement projects, such as road and bridge building. Through their legal work, the firm assisted in the economic development of this nascent Great Plains community. The firm, for example, successfully defended Kearney's claim to status as the county seat. Their legal work also led to the bridging of the Platte River, which opened Kearney businesses to the people of Phelps and Kearney counties to the south.[11]

In preparing a case for trial, Hamer did most of the legwork. He familiarized himself with the evidence, interviewed witnesses on both sides, and reviewed related case law. As the trial date neared, Hamer presented his findings and defense strategy to Connor, who usually argued the case before the court. Connor was charismatic and could be both "eloquent and forceful" in the courtroom. At times, however, his fiery, emotional style evoked criticism. In the July 1883 murder trial of Maria Brown, the *Kearney New Era* declared that Connor's "western style of bully-ragging, pounding on tables, and questioning the truthfulness of the prosecution was decidedly unprofessional." The newspaper was obviously unhappy that Connor and Hamer got a manslaughter conviction for their client in what most people thought was an obvious case of first-degree murder.[12]

The pair found themselves involved in almost every criminal case in Buffalo County and gained statewide notoriety as proficient defense lawyers in several high-profile murder cases during the 1870s. The first grew out of a conflict between cowboys and the citizens of Kearney. The area around Fort Kearny served as a stopover point for cattle being driven to Indian reservations and Wyoming ranches. Young cowboys frequented the saloons in Kearney and on occasion rode wildly through the streets, shooting their revolvers indiscriminately. Such behavior naturally stirred the emotions of the middle-class families who by then called Kearney home. To protect themselves, the citizenry founded the Kearney Guards, a quasi-militia unit that could organize quickly if called upon. According to one source, Hamer had "acquired something of a reputation as a scrapper," and on one occasion he challenged a sizable group of drunken cowboys to fight him or get out of town. None took up Hamer's offer, and the group reportedly heeded the lawyer's advice and left. Such tension between cowboys and townsfolk eventually led to tragedy. On September 17, 1875, Milton Collins, a farmer and son of one of Kearney's founders, was shot and killed by a drunken cowboy.

The Kearney Guards quickly turned out and arrested more than a dozen herders. Three men were charged with murder: Jordan Smith, as the shooter, and Frederick Copeland and Bernardino Roach, as accomplices. Judge William Gaslin appointed Hamer to defend Copeland and Roach. In order to minimize Copeland and Roach's connection to Smith, who reportedly had shot Collins without provocation, Hamer requested that his clients be tried separately from the alleged triggerman. Hamer argued that although his clients had been present at the murder, they had not participated in the shooting. They were simply at the wrong place at the wrong time. A Buffalo County jury accepted the argument and acquitted both men.[13]

After the acquittal of Copeland and Roach, Jordan Smith's family hired Hamer and Connor to assist in their son's defense. Defending Smith was more difficult. Dozens of people, including the deceased's wife and father, had seen Smith pull the trigger. Moreover, public sentiment weighed heavily against the accused, and talk of extralegal violence could be heard in and around Kearney. The defense, therefore, requested and was granted a change of venue. There was little doubt that a jury, whether in Buffalo County or elsewhere, would convict Smith. To save their client from the gallows, Hamer argued that Smith had been intoxicated and that the murder had not been premeditated. In the end, after two changes of venue and three trials, a jury convicted Smith of the lesser offense of manslaughter, and Judge Gaslin gave him the maximum sentence of ten years.[14] Defending the three cowboys put the Hamer and Connor firm in the headlines. In what appeared to be open-and-shut cases, the lawyers had gained two acquittals and a conviction on a lesser charge for their clients. The firm's legal work marked them as proficient defense lawyers, and they were soon representing defendants in criminal cases throughout western Nebraska.

Hamer and Connor's most publicized criminal trial came several years after the cowboy trials, when cattlemen led by Isom Prentice "Print" Olive killed two homesteaders in Custer County. The murders of Luther Mitchell and Ami Ketchum grabbed national attention because of the gruesome nature of the killings: the perpetrators, after murdering their victims, burned the bodies. Photographs were taken of the remains, and the killers became known across the nation as the "Man Burners." Print Olive, who was tried with several accomplices for the murders, was a wealthy cattleman, and he hired a team of ten lawyers, including Hamer and Connor. "It was a legal staff," according to one source, "that only a cattle king could afford."[15] Although the legal team included experienced trial lawyers, such as Connor and Beach Hinman, of North Platte, the younger and less experienced Hamer led the defense. Hamer examined and cross-examined the witnesses and delivered the closing argument. A jury convicted Olive and Fred Fisher, and Judge Gaslin sentenced them to life in prison. The supreme court, however, reversed the convictions, and the pair walked out of the state prison in 1881 after serving only two years.[16]

People throughout the state and beyond followed the Olive trial, which pitted wealthy cattlemen against poor homesteaders, and Hamer's name was splashed across newspaper headlines. However, this was not the type of recognition Hamer desired. Had Olive's conviction been affirmed by the high court, and had he served out his life sentence, Hamer would have been viewed as a lawyer who had done his best to defend his client. Olive, however, walked out of prison and was never reprosecuted. To many people, Hamer had helped free a cold-blooded murderer. Hamer avoided connecting himself to the case in later years. In the many autobiographical sketches that he penned, he made no mention of his role in the trial.

By 1883, Hamer had made a name for himself as an accomplished lawyer, particularly in the territory west of Lincoln. When agitation arose in 1883 to elect a Nebraska Supreme Court justice from the western part of the state, Hamer, along with other leading western attorneys, threw their hats into the ring. Although Hamer did not gain the nomination, he garnered enough attention at the state level to be appointed district court judge after Judge Samuel Savidge died unexpectedly in December 1883. Governor James W. Dawes made Hamer the judge of the Tenth Judicial District, the largest in the state. Hamer served out the remainder of Savidge's term and subsequently was reelected by large majorities in 1884 and 1887.[17]

While riding the circuit, district court judges traveled by a variety of conveyances, experienced rustic living accommodations, and held court in a host of different buildings. Simply getting to distant courthouses could be an adventure. Many counties, particularly those in western Nebraska, lacked improved roads or rail service. According to one source, many isolated county seats were reached only by "long and dreary stage rides over sparsely settled prairies."[18] As late as 1900, traveling to court in some Sandhills counties required hardiness. In December 1902, for example, Judge Hanson Grimes and a contingent of lawyers from North Platte traveled more than forty miles across snow-covered prairies to hold district court in McPherson County. The county seat, Tryon, was not accessible by train via North Platte, so the weary group had to travel by horse and buggy. "Holding court in McPherson County," reported the *North Platte Independent Era,* "is no joke of a winter's job."[19]

Accommodations at county seats during the first decades of statehood were often spartan at best. While riding the circuit during the early 1870s, Judge George Lake claimed that he always carried his own bedding and slept wherever he could find a place, including on floors and tables. "There was no such thing," remembered Lake, "as the Judge having a room to himself."[20]

When a full corps of lawyers attended district court in McPherson County, visitors reportedly pitched tents on the courthouse grounds.[21] Fortunately, the citizens and resident lawyers of most county seats offered room and board to visiting court personnel and out-of-town lawyers. At Hayes Center, for example, Dad Hatch provided accommodations for Judge George Norris (later a U.S. senator) whenever he held court in town.[22]

The courthouses were not what would be expected of a temple of justice. Elaborate and ornate courthouses took time and money to construct; most newly organized counties used whatever building was available. Lincoln County, for example, used a one-room log building for the first six or seven years of its existence. Hall County rented space in the Union Pacific depot. Several counties took over the local opera house or hotel lobby during district court sessions. Many Sandhills counties, because they were thinly populated and had sparse resources, built sod courthouses.[23] In 1890, for example, the *North Platte Telegraph* reported that McPherson County had constructed a twenty-four-foot-square sod courthouse and was installing a brick vault to protect court documents from fire.[24]

Hamer would have experienced many of these conditions while riding the circuit. In 1883, his district stretched from Buffalo County to the Wyoming border, an area approximately 300 miles in length and an average of 150 miles wide—almost two-thirds of the entire state. By 1887, the Tenth Judicial District encompassed ten counties within its borders and had a population of around a hundred thousand people. The state legislature made Hamer's job easier by assigning a second judge to the district in 1889. Thereafter, Alonzo Church, of North Platte, took over the western half of the district, while Hamer held court in the eastern counties of Buffalo, Custer, Phelps, and Sherman.[25] Hamer's tenure on the district court bench coincided with a period of judicial expansion in Nebraska. When Nebraska's population exploded during the 1880s and the work of the trial courts increased, the legislature subdivided judicial districts. From 1875 to 1891, the legislature liberally added new judicial districts, so that within the span of sixteen years, the number increased from three to fifteen.[26]

On the first day of January each year, district court judges set their court calendars. In Hamer's expansive district, this meant spending a good part of his time traveling across the western two-thirds of the state. Hamer reported that on average, he held court forty-two weeks per year. In most counties, he set a spring and fall term of court. If needed, the judge held adjourned sessions to clear up the dockets. In some smaller counties, the judge visited only once a year, and in thinly populated Sandhills counties, such as Logan and McPherson, district court sessions were held only when the county commissioners made a written request.[27] Hamer kept court open day and night to keep the dockets clear in more densely populated Platte Valley counties, such as Lincoln (North Platte) and Buffalo (Kearney). The judge opened court at nine o'clock in the morning and, other than breaks for meals, did not adjourn until ten o'clock at night. If the docket was especially heavy, he sometimes kept court open until four o'clock in the morning. The *Broken Bow Republican* praised Hamer for keeping his court open, writing that his work ethic was "highly appreciated and is quite a savings in expenses to the county."[28]

Evaluating Hamer's competence as a trial court judge is difficult. He heard more than five thousand cases during his seven years on the bench, but the vast majority of the related court documents have not survived the ravages of time. If press reports are a reliable indicator, Hamer's judicial district praised his work. The *North Platte Tribune* claimed that Hamer had "proved himself preeminently qualified for the bench" and that "the people are proud of his record."[29] The *Loup City Northwestern* boasted that "Judge Hamer has made the best judge this district has ever had," while the *Plum Creek Pioneer* claimed that Hamer "has made a most excellent judge, presiding with dignity and strict impartiality."[30]

Hundreds of other newspaper clippings testified to Hamer's skill on the bench, but perhaps a better indicator of his competence are appeals to the state supreme court. Parties appealed only eighty-six cases of the more than five thousand that Hamer tried in the Tenth Judicial District. The high court affirmed thirty-eight, or 44 percent, and reversed forty-eight, or 56 percent of the total.[31] During the same period, the high court reversed only about 27 percent of Judge T. L. Norval's cases and 35 percent of Judge William Gaslin's cases. Although Hamer had a reversal rate higher than those of his contemporaries, far fewer of his cases were appealed to the high court. Over the same period (1884–91), 226 of Gaslin's decisions were appealed from a district much smaller than Hamer's.[32]

The district court judges of western Nebraska often tried cases involving dangerous criminals. Gaslin, for example, who sat on the bench in western Nebraska during the 1870s, regularly sentenced horse thieves, highwaymen, and murderers to long terms in the state penitentiary. The abrasive judge reportedly held court with two revolvers on the bench in some western counties and, because of his harsh sentences, gained a reputation as "a terror to evil-doers." Judicial realignment eventually relegated Gaslin to the less turbulent counties of the Republican River valley during the early

1880s.[33] Soon after, Hamer found himself sitting on the bench of Gaslin's former district. Hamer sent hundreds of criminals to the state prison and sentenced more than a dozen murderers to death. Recalling his days as a judge in western Nebraska, Hamer told members of the Western Nebraska Bar Association, "[W]e were on the frontier but we had important responsibilities upon us and the lawyers of this immense district always acquitted themselves creditably."[34]

Perhaps Hamer's most harrowing experience as a judge came on April 17, 1891, when he faced a lynch mob in Broken Bow, Custer County. The incident erupted when Governor James E. Boyd granted convicted murderer Albert Haunstine a thirty-day reprieve from his death sentence. Upon hearing that the execution would not take place, friends and relatives of the two men killed by Haunstine began milling about the courthouse, threatening to take justice into their own hands. As the crowd grew more restless, Hamer climbed the steps of the courthouse and addressed the assembled masses, explaining that the governor had only done his duty and that the respite would in no way interfere with the law. Although the crowd appeared satisfied with Hamer's explanation and dispersed, it was not long after that two columns of men armed with crowbars and sledgehammers marched into the courthouse, intent on gaining entrance into the basement jail cell where Haunstine lingered. Hearing the commotion, Hamer rushed into the crowd, grabbed one of the ringleaders, and pleaded with him to stop. The crowd shoved the judge aside, but Hamer did not give in so easily. Just as he had done almost twenty years earlier when facing drunken cowboys on the streets of Kearney, Hamer charged back into the crowd and in a booming voice shouted, "[I]n the name of the law, I command you to keep the peace." The emotion and determination of Hamer must have caught the mob off guard; they stopped in their tracks and allowed the judge to speak. Hamer pleaded with the crowd to show "moderation, reason, and patience" and again reiterated that the law would be properly executed. In the middle of his thirty-minute speech, somebody brought the judge a chair and allowed him to sit while he finished speaking. Hamer's well-reasoned address finally convinced the crowd to disperse. Hamer gained statewide notoriety for his bravery in Broken Bow. "His calm and judicious action," claimed one newspaper, saved our county "the unfortunate name of having resorted to lynch mob law."[35]

Later in 1891, Hamer once again garnered statewide news coverage when he refused to confirm dozens of Custer County real estate foreclosures.

Drought and an economic downturn caused severe hardship in Nebraska during the early 1890s. Farmers could not pay their loans, and creditors were foreclosing on one farm after another in places like Custer County. When creditors sold the foreclosed properties, however, that sale had to be confirmed by the district court judge, and Judge Hamer was determined to protect the farmers.[36]

When the first confirmation case came up, Hamer asked: "Does this man live on the land?" The lawyer representing the creditors confirmed that the farmer was still on the land. Hamer replied, "[T]hen he shall have a chance to raise a crop." To keep the farmers from losing their land, he continued all the confirmation cases to the next session. Those in attendance "appeared dumbfounded, as if struck by a thunder-bolt."[37] Hamer then explained his reasoning with an address directed at the attorneys. "The act of God, for which the people are not responsible, has reduced one-half of them almost to beggary, and this calamity shall not be made worse by any act of mine. We are asked to turn over 100 farms over to money lenders, and 500 women and children over to pauperism. It shall never be done in this district while I am judge."[38] Hamer continued by suggesting that farmers would be better able to pay their creditors if allowed to stay on their land and raise a crop. When questioned about the legality of his decision, Hamer fired back, informing the lawyers that he had the right to refuse a sale if it failed to bring two-thirds of the property's value, a debatable legal position.

The country press of western Nebraska praised Hamer for his bold decision. "Judge Hamer," wrote the *Custer County Beacon,* "will be honored in hundreds of homes as a judge from whose heart considerations of humanity have not fled."[39] The paper encouraged other judges to follow Hamer's example and chastised those who confirmed foreclosure sales. To Hamer's opponents, however, his ruling must have seemed nothing more than campaigning. Hamer was in the middle of a campaign for his third term on the district court, and he was running against Silas Holcomb, a candidate from Custer County supported by the Alliance-Independent Party (the predecessor of the Populist Party).

The 1890s were difficult for Republican politicians in Nebraska. The Alliance-Independent Party and later the People's, or Populist, Party drove many of them out of office. Drought, high interest rates, railroad monopolies, and economic malaise in general gave the independent and populist candidates plenty of ammunition against candidates from the traditional parties. In elections during the early 1890s, the independents attacked the judiciary, which was stocked with mostly Republican judges and was believed by Nebraska farmers to be the protector of banks, railroads, and corporations. Despite being viewed as a friend of the farmer, Hamer's tenure on the district court bench was terminated by this political revolution against the established parties. At the local level, Republicans were swept from office in the elections of 1890 and 1891. Whereas most Republicans lost by huge majorities, some by as many as three thousand votes, Hamer lost his seat on the bench by only thirteen votes, indicating that he still had strong support among rural voters.[40]

On January 6, 1892, Hamer served his last day on the district court bench. It must have been a sad day for Hamer, who thoroughly enjoyed the job. "During the time I was judge of the district court," he remembered, "I was never happier. It is a pleasant job to be judge . . . even though the responsibilities are great."[41] Hamer was forty-eight years old when he left the bench. Real estate investments and various business ventures provided a comfortable living for Hamer, his wife, and their two children, but he was not ready to retire. Never one to sit idle, Hamer went back into private practice, forming a high-caliber partnership with Norris Brown (future Nebraska attorney general and U.S. senator) and Hector Sinclair (future district court judge). This firm, in one form or another, conducted legal business across the state until Hamer was elected to the state supreme court in 1911. As the senior partner of Hamer, Sinclair, and Brown, the former district court judge built the firm into one of the most powerful law partnerships outside of Lincoln and Omaha.[42]

Although it is impossible to estimate the number of cases he handled during the next twenty years of private practice, Hamer's appeals to the high court provide a glimpse into the type of legal work he conducted. The Hamer firm argued 101 appeals before the Nebraska Supreme Court and successfully appealed one case to the U.S. Supreme Court. Because of his experience as a district court judge, Hamer was highly sought after in criminal cases, particularly murder cases. Between 1895 and 1911, Hamer argued thirty-six criminal appeals (36 percent of his total appeals) before the state high court. Although most of these cases originated from counties in his old judicial district—Buffalo, Phelps, Dawson, and Kearney—he also took on cases from Box Butte, Cherry, Douglas, Harlan, Lancaster, Sarpy, Sioux, and Webster counties.[43]

Hamer also specialized in the emerging field of water law. As a lawyer and judge in western Nebraska, a region that averages less than twenty inches of rainfall per year, Hamer understood that irrigation was a necessity for farming the western plains. He had been a strong supporter of irrigation in and around Buffalo County and played a part in the construction of the Kearney Canal during the 1880s. Before 1900, one of the problems for irrigators was a judiciary unfamiliar with water law and with the need for irrigation in an arid climate. The courts regularly upheld the common-law doctrine of riparian water rights, which restricted the amount of water that could be taken from waterways. In a speech delivered to the Western Nebraska Bar Association in 1915, Hamer pointed to the problem. "I question whether you can raise a first class irrigation judge on a sand hill," he suggested, "unless he gets where he can put his feet in the water of a ditch."[44] After several failed appeals before the court, Hamer invited the justices out west to see for themselves the importance of irrigation and the necessity of revising Nebraska water law for the west's arid climate. According to Hamer, "not a single judge would budge." By 1900, however, the attitude of the supreme court had changed with the election of Silas Holcomb. As a former district court judge from western Nebraska and a former governor elected as a Populist, Holcomb understood that Nebraska, with its varied climate and rainfall, needed a broader and more flexible water law.

Hamer counted as his most important legal battle an irrigation case that effectively changed Nebraska's water law. The case grew out of a legal struggle in Dawes County in northwest Nebraska, where the Crawford Company was diverting water from the White River for irrigation and for municipal uses in the town of Crawford. Downstream riparian proprietors challenged the company for diminishing the flow of the river and violating their riparian rights to the water. The lower court sided with the riparian proprietors, and the Crawford Company appealed to the state supreme court. As an expert on water law, Hamer was brought in to assist the Crawford Company's attorneys. *Crawford Company v. Hathaway* first came before the high court in 1900. Basing their opinion on Nebraska's statutory protection of riparian users, the justices affirmed the lower court's decision. By 1903, however, Nebraska newspapers were involved in a lively debate over the necessity of irrigation and the revision of state water law. Moreover, the court by then had two justices who understood the need for irrigation. Justices Silas Holcomb and John J. Sullivan, both elected to the court during the Populist upheaval that swept the state in the 1890s, played an important role in changing the views of the high court. In early 1903, therefore, Hamer requested a rehearing, and the court obliged. In a twenty-six-page opinion by Justice Holcomb that thoroughly reviewed case law involving water, the supreme court reversed the lower court's decision. The decision altered the course of the state's water law by establishing that riparian water rights and prior appropriation rights coexisted in Nebraska. Thereafter, irrigators like the Crawford Company could appropriate water for "beneficial uses" and the public good.[45]

Hamer's law practice continued to grow during the first decade of the 1900s. He trained a host of young Kearney lawyers, argued cases throughout the state, and made yearly appearances before the state supreme court. The law firm changed names as the partners moved on to high elective and appointed offices. Sinclair left the firm when he was elected to the district court bench, and Brown moved on to become Nebraska's attorney general. Willis Oldham, another Kearney attorney of high standing and a former Nebraska Supreme Court commissioner, joined the firm after 1907. Hamer also brought in his son, Thomas, as the junior member of the firm.

As a former district court judge and senior member of the Nebraska bar, Hamer was often asked why he had not made a bid for the state supreme court. Hamer had sought but failed to gain the Republican nomination for the high court in 1883, but he had not given another bid much thought until 1908, when the state legislature expanded the court from three members to seven. To sit on the state's highest court, a justice had to be thirty years of age, a citizen of the United States, a three-year resident of Nebraska, and a practicing attorney in the state. Hamer far exceeded the qualifications for the high court. In 1908, Hamer was sixty-five years old and had been a resident of Nebraska for almost forty years.[46] In explaining his reasoning for seeking a post on the supreme court, Hamer concluded that "old Father Time . . . sort of suggested that I was not going to live always and if I wanted to be a judge of the supreme court I had better get at it."[47]

Hamer failed to obtain one of the initial four governor-appointed justiceships in 1908, but when three seats were up for election in 1911, he threw his hat into the ring. Hamer's bid for the supreme court was aided by Nebraska's new direct primary law, which ended the old system of backroom party politics under which the best candidate was not always given the opportunity to run for election. In his campaign speeches and literature, Hamer always stressed the point that western Nebraska had never been represented on the supreme court: "Is just one judge in seven too many for our share, considering we have two-thirds of the territory of the state?" Hamer was not being entirely honest. T. O. C. Harrison, of Grand Island, had served one term on the court, and Silas Holcomb, although living in Lincoln when elected, hailed from Custer County. Somebody must have pointed this out to Hamer as the campaign progressed because in later campaign literature he qualified Holcomb's election (elected from Lincoln) and explained that western Nebraska, by his reckoning, began west of Grand Island.[48]

Hamer faced a heated battle in the primaries. Prohibition was a divisive topic in Nebraska during the 1910s. Because Hamer had received more primary votes in Omaha (a wet city) than any of the other six Republican candidates, the Anti-Saloon League accused him of being the "Brewery Candidate." Hamer denied the charges and at first refused to pay attention to the attacks. Because these enemies "have not branded me as a criminal, a wife beater, or any of the other higher forms of law breaking," Hamer responded, "I do not deem it advisable to attack them."[49] He eventually refuted charges that his campaign was financed by the liquor interests by pointing out that in addition to his strong showing in Omaha, he had received more votes than any other candidate in six dry counties.[50]

Hamer's friends and supporters flocked to his side. Wesley Wilcox, a lawyer from North Platte who had known Hamer for more than twenty-five years, wrote a letter that appeared in newspapers throughout the state. Titled "Stand Up for Western Nebraska," it called on the citizens of western Nebraska to "look after Judge Hamer's interests on election day." Wilcox was aghast at the accusations that Hamer was in cahoots with the liquor interests. "I have never seen him enter a saloon or drug store, either through front or back door," Wilcox wrote. "There is not a man, woman, or child in this whole territory . . . who ever saw him take a drink of liquor . . . . [H]e has always been a total abstainer." The only reason for such an attack, Wilcox concluded, was to prevent the western part of the state from being represented on the high court.[51]

Although the unfounded attacks turned many voters away, Hamer still managed to squeak out a victory in the general election, finishing third among the six candidates.[52] Hamer was the twentieth man to sit on the Nebraska Supreme Court, and it put him in company with some of Nebraska's best legal minds. Previous members of the court included former governors Lorenzo Crounse and Silas Holcomb. Four of the first five justices had helped write the state constitution. The longest-serving member of the court, Samuel Maxwell, was a noted writer of legal treatises. Nebraska's justices were all cut from the same cloth. All but one had been born in northeastern states, such as New York and Pennsylvania, or midwestern states, such as Ohio, Indiana, and Illinois. Nineteen of the first twenty-four justices were affiliated with the Republican Party. Finally, each member of the court, like Hamer, had come to the state as a young man and was "essentially Nebraskan" in his legal career.[53]

In 1912, when Hamer first sat on the court, the duties of supreme court justices were dramatically different from what they had been during the early days of statehood. Under Nebraska's original constitution, justices had ridden the circuit as trial judges when not sitting as an appellate body. Several of the early justices reportedly had traveled more than ten thousand miles per year while riding the circuit.[54] The constitution of 1875 finally relieved the justices of their trial court duties by dividing the state into six judicial districts presided over by elected district court judges. Although the court now sat continuously at the state capital, the increased case load during the late 1880s and 1890s overburdened the three justices.

The expansion of the state supreme court in 1908 occurred only after a long, drawn-out battle. Although the legislature regularly increased the number of judicial districts as the state's population increased, the number of justices had remained unchanged until 1909. As early as 1874, North Platte's *Western Nebraskian* had called for an increase in the number of justices, claiming that "the work done by our three judges could hardly be properly done by five."[55] The newspaper foresaw an important issue. The state's population had more than doubled between 1875 and 1891, and although the number of district court judges had increased from three to twenty-eight between these years, the number of justices remained unchanged. The result was an overworked supreme court with a heavy backlog of cases that, by 1893, had reached 1,285.

There had been several attempts to increase the number of justices, but such an expansion could be accomplished only by a constitutional amendment approved by the public. In 1890 and 1896, the legislature approved an amendment to expand the court only to see each defeated by the public in the general elections. Uneasy with prevailing economic conditions and distrustful of public officials in the 1890s, Nebraskans refused to expand the court.[56]

To provide some relief for the overburdened supreme court, in 1893 the legislature authorized the creation of a supreme court commission consisting of three appointed commissioners who possessed the same qualifications as supreme court justices. In essence, the commission sat as a second supreme court, reviewing appeals and writing opinions. Officially, opinions written by the commissioners were only recommendations that the justices had to approve. Burdened by their own heavy workload, the justices rubber-stamped the commission's written opinions with the following phrase: "For the reasons stated in the foregoing opinion, it is ordered that the judgment of the district court be affirmed / reversed." The commission operated until 1899, when Governor William Poynter refused to sign a bill that would have extended its work for another three years. In vetoing the bill, Poynter stated that the commission had been created only as a temporary relief until the number of justices on the court could be expanded.[57]

Just two years later, the supreme court faced a backlog of more than seventeen hundred appeals, and it was estimated that any new case brought before the court would take eight years to reach final judgment. In his inaugural speech that year, Governor Charles Dietrich recommended that an amendment to expand the court be submitted again to the voters. Although Dietrich's request was not granted, a second supreme court commission, composed of nine commissioners, began operation in 1901 and lasted until 1909. This new commission sat in three panels of three and included legal theorist and future Nebraska and Harvard law dean Roscoe Pound.[58]

Difficulties marked Hamer's tenure on the Nebraska Supreme Court. Although he was older than most of the justices and had more experience in trying cases than all but Justice John Barnes, Hamer did not seem to get the respect that he thought he deserved. In a 1915 essay about the workings of the court, Hamer tactfully criticized several unnamed justices for their behavior. "At least two of the judges," he claimed, "are ready to assume that if the matter is difficult, they can do it better than anyone else." Hamer added, "I have met a few headstrong politicians [and] listened to some turbulent preachers but if you want to [see] a man who has confidence in himself then meet a supreme court judge who is growing old in service." Hamer was particularly upset about how he was treated during his first few months on the court. After spending several weeks writing an important opinion, Hamer attempted to present his reasoning to the other six members of the court. Thirty seconds into his speech, one justice asked a question, which was then answered by another justice. The two justices, who had opposing views about the case, then began arguing with one another and never allowed Hamer to finish his presentation. Hamer captured his frustration in the following phrase: "I found that those fellows could thrash my buckwheat without my consent and that I was utterly helpless in their presence."[59]

Hamer also had a difficult time writing clear, cohesive, and succinct opinions. A review of Hamer's personal writings and legal briefs indicates that he was a voluminous but cumbersome and sometimes meandering writer. Hamer claimed that in composing his opinions, he often wrote more than a hundred pages before painfully whittling them down to the essential ten to twelve. Justice Barnes noted that "in the work of writing opinions he [Hamer] was not always felicitous." According to Barnes, Hamer's biggest problem was his inability to condense his views "so as to meet the approval of his associates."[60] As a consequence, Hamer was the least productive member on the court. During his six-and-a-half-year tenure, Hamer wrote 174 opinions, an average of about 25 per year. Justice Barnes wrote 268 opinions during this same period, and Justice Charles Letton produced 322. Justice Samuel Sedgwick was the most productive writer, with 369 opinions—almost 200 more than Hamer wrote.[61]

Poor health plagued Hamer during his service on the court and contributed to his writing fewer opinions than his fellow justices. In 1917, for example, ill health forced him to be absent for much of the term. Hamer apparently suffered from a stomach ailment throughout his tenure on the high court, and although he did not know it until 1918, he was suffering from cancer. Facing reelection in 1918, Hamer formed a campaign committee, but his failing health eventually caught up with him. During the summer of 1918, Hamer withdrew his name from the election, took another leave of absence from the court, and returned to convalesce at his home in Kearney. Frank Hamer finally succumbed to cancer, dying at his home on August 10.[62]

What makes Frank Hamer's legal and judicial career worth telling? After all, he was not the most noted Nebraska lawyer or district judge, and legal historians would have to rank him quite low as a supreme court justice. Dozens of other Nebraska lawyers and judges gained greater notoriety or went on to higher elected offices. Hamer's former law partners, for example, served in the state legislature, as state attorney general, and in the U.S. Senate. Hamer's career is special and worth highlighting for its length and its uniqueness as well as for what it reveals about the early legal and judicial history of the Cornhusker State. Few Nebraskan attorneys had a career as lengthy as Hamer's. For forty-eight years, he served the people of Nebraska as a lawyer and judge. He arrived in Nebraska less than two years after statehood, practiced law in Lincoln during its infant years, and became the first attorney in the frontier community of Kearney Junction. These feats alone are noteworthy, and they reveal much about how young and enterprising midwestern lawyers migrated to Nebraska and built successful law firms in pioneer communities. Likewise, Hamer's service on the district and supreme court benches reflects how a Great Plains state struggled as its population expanded and its economy was transformed from a frontier crop exchange into a modern agriculture state. It is important to remember that each and every frontier community in Nebraska had its own version of Frank Hamer. Of course, not all Nebraska communities could boast of having a district court judge in their midst, and even fewer could claim to have produced a justice of the Nebraska Supreme Court. Frank Hamer's varied legal and judicial career is, in many ways, the story of hundreds of other young attorneys who migrated to Nebraska and made it their home.

Notes

1. On Francis Hamer's life and career, see Francis G. Hamer, Papers, RG 4471, Nebraska State Historical Society, Lincoln (Hamer Papers); Mark R. Ellis, "Hanging Out the Shingle: Nineteenth-Century Lawyers in Nebraska's Platte Valley," *Nebraska History* 85 (Spring 2004): 38–52; A. T. Andreas, *History of the State of Nebraska* (Chicago: Western Historical, 1882), 433; Samuel Clay Bassett, *Biographical Souvenir of the Counties of Buffalo, Kearney, Phelps, Harlan, and Franklin, Nebraska* (Chicago: F. A. Batty, 1890), 158–63; Samuel Clay Bassett, *Buffalo County, Nebraska, and Its People* (Chicago: S. J. Clarke, 1916), 90–94.

2. On the migration of lawyers to Nebraska, see Ellis, "Hanging Out the Shingle," 39–45.

3. *North Platte Republican,* August 19, 1876.

4. Ellis, "Hanging Out the Shingle," 45.

5. On Hamer's arrival and early practice in Lincoln, see "Life Sketch," Hamer Papers; "Lincoln in the Early Seventies," Newspaper Clippings, Hamer Papers.

6. On Alexander Connor, see Bassett, *Biographical Souvenir,* 473–74.

7. Ellis, "Hanging Out the Shingle," 38–42; "Reminiscences of the Early History of Kearney, Nebraska," Hamer Papers; "To the Voters of Nebraska," *Omaha Daily Bee,* August 13, 1911.

8. "Miscellaneous Campaign Writings," Hamer Papers.

9. Rebecca Hamer to Elizabeth, February 23, 1873, Hamer Papers; Mark R. Ellis, "Dear Lib: A Letter from Kearney Junction," *Buffalo Tales* 26 (May–June 2003).

10. "Reminiscences of the Early History of Kearney."

11. On the firm's early work in Kearney, see "Campaign Committee," Hamer Papers; Bassett, *Buffalo County,* 115, 126, 191–92, 224–25, 314–23.

12. *Kearney New Era,* July 14, 1873; Bassett, *Buffalo County,* 191.

13. On the murder of Milton Collins and the ensuing trials, see State v. Copeland and Roach, Criminal Case Files, Buffalo County District Court, RG 221, Nebraska State Historical Society (BCDC); Bassett, *Buffalo County,* 314–25.

14. State v. Smith, Criminal Case Files, BCDC; Richard Crabb, *Empire on the Platte* (New York: World, 1967), 314.

15. Crabb, *Empire on the Platte,* 311.

16. On the Olive trial, see Olive v. State, 11 Neb. 1, 7 N.W. 444 (1881); Crabb, *Empire on the Platte.*

17. "Judge F. G. Hamer Is Dead," *Nebraska State Journal,* August 11, 1918; "Life Sketch," Hamer Papers; *Kearney New Era,* November 15, 1884, and November 19, 1887.

18. W. Morton Smith, "Supreme Judges of Nebraska," *Transactions and Reports of the Nebraska State Historical Society* 4 (1892): 116.

19. *North Platte Independent Era,* December 18, 1902.

20. Henry E. Maxwell, "George B. Lake," *Nebraska Law Bulletin* 5 (February 1927): 360.

21. *North Platte Independent Era,* December 18, 1902.

22. Richard Lowitt, "Blackledge on Norris: Reflections on Nebraska Justice in the 1890s," *Nebraska History* 46 (March 1965): 67–76.

23. Mark R. Ellis, "Legal Culture and Community on the Great Plains: *State of Nebraska v. John Burley,*" *Western Historical Quarterly* 34 (Summer 2005): 189–90.

24. *North Platte Telegraph,* July 18, 1890.

25. "A Bit of Early Legal History," Miscellaneous Newspaper Clippings, Hamer Papers.

26. On judicial expansion, see Mark R. Ellis, "Law and Order in Buffalo Bill's Country"(Ph.D. diss., University of Nebraska, 1999), 78–87; William Gaslin, "Judicial Grafts," *Proceedings and Collections of the Nebraska State Historical Society* 15 (1907): 108–11; Lorenzo Crounse, "Veto Messages to the House of Representatives," March 18, 1893, in *Messages and Proclamations of the Governors of Nebraska, 1854–1941* (Lincoln: Nebraska State Historical Society, 1942), 2:215–16.

27. On the general duties and the jurisdiction of the district courts, see Neb. Comp. Stat., ch. 19, §§ 23–57 (1881).

28. *North Platte Tribune,* September 17, 1887.

29. *Kearney New Era,* September 24, 1887.

30. *Kearney New Era,* October 25, 1884.

31. Nebraska Reports, vols. 15–31 (1883–92).

32. Frank E. Landis, "Life and Judicial Career of T. L. Norval" (master's thesis, University of Nebraska, 1937), 56–58.

33. On Gaslin, see Roscoe E. Wright, "Judge William Gaslin, Jr." (master's thesis, University of Nebraska, 1934).

34. "Bit of Early Legal History."

35. On Hamer's role in the Haunstine case, see "How Hauinstine Was Saved," Miscellaneous Newspaper Clippings, Hamer Papers.

36. J. E. Cobbey, ed., *Consolidated Statutes of Nebraska, 1891 . . . Annotated* (Lincoln, Neb.: State Journal Company, printers, 1891), § 5033.

37. "A Grand Stand," Miscellaneous Newspaper Clippings, Hamer Papers.

38. "Judge Hamer on Foreclosures," Miscellaneous Newspaper Clippings, Hamer Papers.

39. "Grand Stand."

40. *Kearney Hub,* November 9, 1891, and November 10, 1891.

41. "Bit of Early Legal History."

42. "Office of Francis G. Hamer Campaign Committee," Hamer Papers.

43. Whitaker v. McBride, 197 U.S. 510 (1905); Nebraska Reports, vols. 40–92 (1893–1912).

44. "Bit of Early Legal History."

45. Crawford Company v. Hathaway, 67 Neb. 325, 93 N.W. 781 (1903).

46. On the duties and jurisdiction of the Nebraska Supreme Court and the eligibility of its justices, see Neb. const., art. VI (1875); Neb. Comp. Stat., ch. 19, §§ 1–22; and Code of Civ. Pro., tit. XVI, §§ 580–601a (1881).

47. "About the Supreme Court," Hamer Writings, Hamer Papers.

48. "Office of Francis G. Hamer Campaign Committee."

49. *Kearney Hub,* September 11, 1911.

50. *Kearney Hub,* September 8, 1911.

51. "Stand Up for Western Nebraska," *North Platte Telegraph,* November 2, 1911.

52. "Republicans Win in Nebraska," *Kearney Hub,* November 8, 1911.

53. J. Sterling Morton and Albert Watkins, *History of Nebraska* (Lincoln: Western Publishing and Engraving, 1918), 694–702.

54. Ibid., 694.

55. *North Platte Western Nebraskian,* August 20, 1874.

56. John M. Thayer, "Messages and Proclamations to the Senate and House of Representatives," February 6, 1889, *Messages and Proclamations of the Governors of the State of Nebraska,* 2:82–83; Silas A. Holcomb, "Second Inaugural Message," January 7, 1897, ibid., 2:287–88.

57. William A. Poynter, "Veto Messages," March 14, 1899, ibid., 2:436.

58. Charles H. Dietrich, "Inaugural Message," January 3, 1901, ibid., 2:453.

59. "About the Supreme Court."

60. John B. Barnes, "In Memoriam: Francis G. Hamer," 103 Neb. ix–x (1918).

61. Nebraska Reports, vols. 91–103 (1912–18).

62. "Judge F. G. Hamer Is Dead."

FOUR

Anthony B. Schutz

LAND USE LAW AND LIVESTOCK PRODUCTION

Raising livestock, like agriculture in general, had its genesis in the production of food for the family or a local market. Society, of course, has long since departed from that notion of farming, having replaced self-sufficiency with profit making. And, as a business, agriculture continues to change. This chapter focuses on the legal responses in Nebraska to one of the more recent changes in livestock production: concentrated animal feeding operations.[1]

The business of raising cattle, hogs, and poultry has changed in the last three or four decades. Not too long ago, all were produced through a system that spread production over a large number of farms that generally were family owned and operated. Such farms also diversified their pursuits among a variety of commodities. For example, it was common to find a single farm producing grain, cattle, and hogs. Today, such a diversified farming operation is increasingly uncommon. Costs of production have increased exponentially, while commodity prices have not. In such circumstances, generating profits depends heavily on the producer's ability to decrease costs, an endeavor that often involves an increase in overall production: a larger operation. Economic pressures have borne heavily on small farms, and as a result, much of Nebraska's livestock is produced by large operations. These often produce livestock within a relatively small geographic area, under conditions of confinement. These facilities are generally referred to as concentrated animal feeding operations, or CAFOs.

Various problems have arisen with the onslaught of CAFOs in Nebraska and across the country. Animal waste becomes a primary concern when large numbers of livestock are grown in close quarters like confinement facilities or feedlots. Producers collect the waste, store it, and then apply it to farm ground as fertilizer. But both the storage and the application of waste pose problems. For example, storage of large amounts of waste in lagoons poses a threat to groundwater through seepage; overapplication of waste to farm ground poses a threat to surface and groundwater through runoff, as well as a threat to the land's fertility; and the odor associated with storing and applying large amounts of waste is troublesome for those downwind. CAFOs also often increase dust volume, fly and insect populations, noise, and traffic on rural roadways.

The law has responded to these problems, and its responses reflect the various interests that such operations implicate. For example, adjoining landowners have often called upon the legal system to alleviate nuisances; city, county, state, and federal governments have enacted laws and erected administrative mechanisms to protect natural resources, facilitate economic development, and decrease the impact that such operations may have on their neighbors; and the system in general has tried to accommodate larger policy interests like the continued vitality of the agricultural economy and the family farm.

Nuisance Law

A nuisance action is one means of controlling the way in which landowners use their land. The plaintiff in such a case generally complains that a landowner is doing something on his property that adversely affects either the use and enjoyment of the plaintiff's own property or the public's welfare.[2]

Nuisance suits involving livestock operations are not a recent phenomenon. In 1884, for example, John Farrell bought land in Red Cloud, using some of it for a feed stable and renting some of it to other individuals. A neighbor across the street filed suit to stop the operation because "the premises was being used as a place for putting jacks and stallions to mares, in full view of plaintiff's dwelling, and to the great inconvenience and discomfort of the plaintiff and his family." Apparently the plaintiff, his wife, his two daughters, and his son found the animals' conduct offensive. The trial court held for the neighbor and enjoined Farrell's business. The Nebraska Supreme Court affirmed, citing two cases. The first, from Missouri, found that the "standing of jacks and stallions within the immediate view of a private dwelling was a nuisance." And the second, from Maryland, found that "the keeping of a brothel near one's dwelling" was a nuisance. To the Nebraska Supreme Court, the sum of those decisions fully supported the enjoining of Farrell's business.

The *Farrell v. Cook* court's exposition of the legal standard for nuisances is fairly protective of neighboring landowners:

> A nuisance may be defined as whatever is injurious, offensive to the senses, indecent, or an obstruction to the free use of property so as materially to interfere with the comfortable enjoyment of life or property. It is anything that unlawfully worketh hurt, inconvenience, or damage. It is a term applied to that class of wrongs that arise from the unreasonable, unwarrantable, or unlawful use by a person of his own property, real or personal, or from his own improper, indecent, or unlawful personal conduct, working an obstruction of or injury to the right of another or of the public, and producing such material annoyance, inconvenience, discomfort, or hurt, that the law will presume a consequent damage. There must not only be a violation of a right, but an essential inconvenience, annoyance, or discomfort must result therefrom. A party is entitled to the free use and enjoyment of his own property, but he must so use it as not to interfere with the rights of others. Enjoy your property in such a manner as not to injure that of another person, is the maxim of the law.[3]

Some years later, the court held that equine mating was not a nuisance when it occurred behind closed doors. In *Thatcher v. Dueser,* the court concluded that

> [t]he keeping of stallions and jacks for breeding purposes is a legitimate, proper and necessary business. They are usually kept at livery barns in villages, as being the most convenient places for carrying on the business. That such business may be carried on in such a manner as not to constitute a nuisance is beyond question; and, if it is so conducted as not to offend or shock the sense of decency and not to annoy those in the immediate vicinity, it cannot be enjoined as a nuisance.[4]

These two cases exemplify the controversy that may arise when a business pursuit clashes with the interests of neighboring landowners. When that happens, a court will consider the utility of the business being conducted, the feasibility of conducting that business in less intrusive ways, and the significance of the intrusion on the neighbor. Generally speaking, if the land use is desirable but is conducted in a manner that does little to control a significant impact on neighboring landowners, then a court will afford the plaintiff relief in the form of damages or an injunction. This balancing act, one that is quite familiar to students of tort law in general, appears to be the analysis that the court implicitly used in *Farrell* and *Thatcher.*

In the late 1980s and early 1990s, the Nebraska Supreme Court expressly adopted an approach to nuisance law from the *Restatement (Second) of Torts* for cases that involve claims for money damages.[5] That approach balances the utility of the defendant's land use with the significance of the harm intentionally inflicted by that land use.[6] To be actionable, the intentional harm must unreasonably invade the plaintiff's interests. An invasion can be unreasonable if "the gravity of the harm outweighs the utility of the actor's conduct."[7] This balancing act takes into account a variety of factors. The gravity of the harm refers to both the extent and character of the harm: the social desirability of the plaintiff's land use, its suitability to the locale, and the extent to which the plaintiff can avoid the harm.[8] The utility of the defendant's conduct refers to the social value of the defendant's land use, its suitability to the locale, and "the impracticability of preventing or avoiding the invasion."[9] The results in both *Farrell* and *Thatcher* can be reconciled through this approach: in *Farrell,* the balance favored the plaintiff, and in *Thatcher,* the balance favored the defendant.

Suits for injunctive relief, however, are governed by a different standard, one that does not take into account the notion of reasonableness. In such cases, "the invasion of or interference with another's private use and enjoyment of land need only be substantial."[10] A substantial-interference inquiry *could* be construed broadly enough to take into account the same notions of utility and harm considered in the restatement's reasonableness inquiry. After all, cases like *Thatcher* seem to do just that. But recent Nebraska decisions have not taken that path. Instead, the inquiry, at least in the initial stages of these lawsuits, focuses on the degree of harm posed to the plaintiff.[11] And the rubric "need only be substantial" fuels the belief that a suit seeking an injunction is somehow easier to win, from a plaintiff's perspective, than a suit seeking damages.[12] Thus, it may seem a harsher standard from the perspective of livestock producers.

Furthermore, even in cases governed by the reasonableness inquiry of the restatement, what should the courts do when a CAFO, producing food for consumers and bolstering the agricultural economy, causes neighboring landowners harm in the form of odor, flies, dust, rats, and noise? That is a difficult question, one complicated on the livestock operators' side by the changing face of agriculture, evolving technologies associated with waste handling, and implicitly value-laden judgments concerning the utility of their allegedly harmful conduct.

Along those same lines, the significance of the harm to a plaintiff can also change, and not only in terms of the perceived significance of offensive odors or swarming flies. For example, assume that a feedlot or hog confinement facility has been situated in a predominantly rural agricultural area for ten years and has been operating without complaints from the adjoining landowners. Assume further that over those ten years, some of the adjoining land has become a residential area. If those residents later decide to sue the livestock operator, complaining of flies, dust, and odor, will they win? Could the residents use the mere threat of litigation to affect the livestock operator's conduct? Under nuisance standards, it would appear that they could. Under the restatement's approach, plaintiffs may have a nuisance claim even if they "come to the nuisance." That circumstance "is a factor to be considered in determining whether the nuisance is actionable," but it is not dispositive.[13] The prospect of litigation in such circumstances, however, led the Nebraska Legislature to action.

This legislative response, discussed in more detail below, also illustrates a level of impatience with the somewhat uncertain nature of nuisance law in damages actions and the apparent disparity in standards between suits seeking damages and those seeking injunctions. This response, however, deals primarily with limiting claims by those who come to the nuisance. Thus, nuisance law remains one of many tools available to control CAFOs or, at least, those operations that postdate neighboring landowners' land use. And nuisance law is relatively well-suited to the task. Tort law has always dealt with difficult questions under somewhat vague standards. It recognizes that each case will be a bit different and that even similar cases may come out differently as community standards change. As time moves on, one can expect nuisance law to accommodate the challenges presented by CAFOs, including the utility of such operations and the harm they may pose to their neighbors.

Legislative Responses to Nuisance Suits

Nebraska's legislative response to nuisance actions evolved over the course of three legislative sessions. In 1977, the legislature amended section 81-1506 of the Nebraska Revised Statutes in the wake of *Botsch v. Leigh Land Co.* In 1980, the legislature revisited its amendment, attempting to strengthen it. And in 1982, the legislature passed the Nebraska Right to Farm Act.

The liability shield of section 81-1506 originated in a 1977 addition to that section, promulgated in the wake of *Botsch v. Leigh Land Co. Botsch* was a nuisance suit instituted by Glenn and Eola Mae Botsch, of Colfax County, who sought an injunction against the operations of the Leigh Land Company. Leigh operated cattle feed yards directly south of the Botsches' farmstead. In conjunction with its feeding operations, Leigh had four waste lagoons that caught runoff water and manure from the lots, and "the manure accumulating in the feedlots was not ordinarily removed, but was piled up into large mounds."[14] The Botsches complained of "odors, dust, and insects originating on the defendants' premises."[15] Various witnesses testified to the offensive nature of the odors, one describing it as a '"dead sour smell' that 'almost kills you.'"[16] The Department of Environmental Control (today's Department of Environmental Quality) inspected the operation and found that it complied with existing regulations. The trial court concluded that the Botsches' claim had failed, but the Nebraska Supreme Court reversed, holding that the evidence submitted was sufficient to establish that "the lagoons and the manner of handling manure constituted a nuisance."[17] On remand, Leigh was afforded the opportunity to rebut that evidence.[18]

The legislature did not like the outcome of that case and took action.[19] Section 81-1506, as amended in 1977, provided that livestock operations have "prima facie evidence" that they are not nuisances if they fulfill three conditions: (1) they are using "reasonable techniques . . . to keep dust, noise, insects, and odor at a minimum"; (2) they are "in compliance with applicable [Environmental Quality Council] regulations . . . and zoning regulations of the local governing body having jurisdiction"; and (3) they are being sued by a person whose lawful possession of his property began after the livestock operation received its permit or, if the livestock operation requires no permit, after the livestock operation began.[20]

The phrase "prima facie evidence that a livestock operation is not a nuisance," is odd on a variety of levels.[21] But it appears from the Agriculture Committee hearing transcript that the language was an effort to give feedlots only a limited shield even if they met the three conditions included in the bill.[22] In other words, reasonable management practices, regulatory compliance, and priority in time would not necessarily shield the producer from liability but would put the onus on the plaintiff to overcome the defendant's statutory presumption. The legislature did not discuss what would overcome that presumption, nor was the question ever presented in a reported judicial decision.

In 1980, the legislature repealed the "prima facie evidence" language of the section, replacing it with the current language: "An animal feeding operation is not a nuisance if" the three conditions are met.[23] In debate, one senator noted the difficulty that this change would cause for potential plaintiffs: "[I]f this change is made it is going to make it significantly harder for residents who have in some cases legitimate complaints . . . [to] prevail. Now I am sure that that is the purpose of the bill but I think people ought to recognize that if this thing is passed it is going to make a lawsuit against a feedlot . . . much more difficult than it is currently."[24] To increase the difficulty of bringing a successful action was, of course, one of the reasons behind the passage of the 1977 bill. But, as explained in the committee hearings in 1977, the bill was not meant to protect livestock operators from all regulatory control—it was meant to push control away from the courts and toward local zoning and state regulatory agencies.[25] Thus, the 1980 amendment can be seen as a further push in that direction.

The statute has not appeared in any reported judicial decision, leaving one to wonder whether the legislation is so effective that no party has sought to put the statute in issue. The statute invokes the term "reasonable" in its first prong, possibly as a legislative response to the common-law standard for injunctive relief, discussed above, which apparently disregards the reasonableness of the defendant's land use. In any event, such a modifier typically becomes a source of contention in lawsuits. Thus, given the lack of reported appellate case law on this point in the past twenty-five years, it seems likely that few factual scenarios have fit the pattern envisioned by the legislature. For example, it may be that most nuisance suits are initiated by landowners who complain of newly created land uses. Thus, many producers may not be able to fulfill the third prong of the statute. And other producers may not be able to fulfill the second prong because they are not in compliance with the wealth of regulatory controls now in place, including county zoning regulations, which are discussed below. One might also deduce from the lack of case law that those producers who comply with local zoning and state regulations are not inflicting objectionable harm on neighboring landowners. So it may be that the lack of litigation over this statute reveals the effectiveness of local regulatory controls. Indeed, the statute may be serving its purpose.

The other legislative response to nuisance suits concerning agricultural land uses is the Nebraska Right to Farm Act.[26] The act, which cleared the Nebraska Legislature with a passing reference to what the legislature did in 1977 and 1980, shields a farm operation[27] from nuisance liability if (1) its operations preceded the existing use or occupation of the plaintiff's land and (2) before the change in use or occupancy of the plaintiff's land, the defendant's farm would not have been a nuisance. Thus, if someone comes to the nuisance by establishing a residence near a CAFO, that person will not be able to sue the CAFO under nuisance law. To put it another way, a CAFO cannot become a nuisance simply because the neighborhood has changed. Neither a new neighbor nor the arrival of residential development is enough to transform prior nonnuisance land uses into nuisances.

The Nebraska Right to Farm Act has appeared in reported decisions. In *Flansburgh v. Coffey*, the court was faced with a hog operation that caused fly, starling, and rat infestations on the plaintiffs' property and produced such strong odors that the plaintiffs could not use their yard. The court held that there was sufficient evidence to substantiate the nuisance claim and that the Nebraska Right to Farm Act did not shield the defendant from liability. The act did not apply because the change in use had occurred on the defendant's property; the plaintiffs had maintained their property as a residence since well before the hog operation started.[28]

Although there are no reported appellate court opinions that include a successful use of the Nebraska Right to Farm Act, it has been invoked effectively at the district court level. In *Bolton v. M Farm, Inc.*, the district court ruled that a neighboring landowner could not sue a feedlot operator because the feedlot predated that landowner's occupancy of the neighboring property.[29] The unsuccessful plaintiffs did not appeal.

The Nebraska Right to Farm Act, although it shields some agricultural producers against nuisance suits in some circumstances, has not immunized CAFOs from land use regulation. A myriad of other land use mechanisms has been used to deal with the conflicting interests that CAFOs implicate.

County Zoning

One of the more recent efforts at land use regulation is the use of zoning. The Nebraska Legislature gave zoning authority to counties in the 1960s.

As noted above, when the legislature was considering its amendment to section 81-1506 of the Nebraska Revised Statutes in 1977, one of the reasons cited for the legislation was the greater acceptability of county zoning laws as a solution to the problems feedlots were causing, at least when compared to nuisance actions. But zoning with CAFOs in mind did not emerge until around 1996. Until that time, only twenty-three of Nebraska's ninety-three counties had been zoned for a number of years. By 2003, all but four of Nebraska's counties had been zoned.[30]

The influx of large hog confinement operations caused the counties' rush to zone. Such livestock operations caused concern on a number of fronts. The experiences of other states, like Iowa and North Carolina, illuminate the concerns that arise from the environmental damage that large operators may cause,[31] and Nebraska is working to avoid a repetition of such problems. Carolyn Johnsen, a University of Nebraska journalism lecturer, has thoroughly chronicled the resistance that large hog confinement operations have encountered in Nebraska.[32] As Johnsen demonstrates, the resistance stems not only from environmental concerns but also from the increasing inability of the agricultural economy to provide sufficient income to the traditional farming family and from the perceived gradual extinction of agrarian families and communities. The onslaught of so-called factory farms has been and continues to be seen as exacerbating that problem.[33]

In Nebraska, the confluence of all these factors led, among other things,[34] to an increased effort at county zoning and an apparent preference for local control.[35] Other states, like Iowa, have left agricultural land uses to state control, exempting such uses from the counties' zoning authority.[36] Nebraska, however, allows counties to exercise land use control through zoning regulations.[37] Under Nebraska law, a county may "regulate and restrict . . . the uses of land for agriculture . . . after considering factors relating to soil conservation, water supply conservation, surface water drainage and removal, or other uses in the unincorporated area of the county."[38]

One exemption in the statutes' language has caused problems in this regard. Section 23-114.03 appears to exempt farm buildings from county zoning authority,[39] even though section 23-114 allows counties to regulate "the uses of land for agriculture."[40] The conflicting language came before the Nebraska Supreme Court when Premium Farms attacked the validity of Holt County's zoning regulations as applied to the hog operation that Premium Farms was building. The court ruled that "[l]and use does not stop at the walls of a building"[41] and, after perusing the legislative history of the county zoning statutes, concluded that the farm building exemption operated only to shield farm buildings from building permit requirements.[42] Thus, agricultural land uses, including hog confinement facilities or other land uses that occur within the confines of a farm building, remain within the scope of counties' zoning authority.

There is also statutory support for further regulation by county government.[43] Under section 23-174.10, counties that have adopted zoning regulations may

> make regulations as may be necessary or expedient to promote the public health, safety, and welfare . . . ; to provide rules for the prevention, abatement, and removal of nuisances, including the pollution of air and water; and make and prescribe regulations for the construction, location, and keeping in order of all . . . stockyards, . . . stables, barns, commercial feedlots, dairies, . . . or other places where offensive matter is kept, or is likely to accumulate.[44]

The scope of this power has not yet been judicially tested.[45]

One issue that has come before the Nebraska Supreme Court is the extent to which an operation will be held to comply with local zoning restrictions if its construction started before the zoning regulations were in place. Zoning does not apply retroactively, so nonconforming land uses that exist when zoning regulations take effect are not governed by those zoning regulations. In fact, the nonconforming use does not have to be operational when the zoning regulation passes. A landowner who, "in good faith reliance on existing zoning, has substantially changed position either by causing substantial construction to be made or by incurring substantial expense related to construction, or both"[46] will have a vested right in his later completed nonconforming use. Thus, the landowner will be treated as if his nonconforming use had existed before the zoning ordinance took effect.

But a landowner cannot, with the prospect of adverse zoning regulations on the horizon, simply start building before the ordinance takes effect. In *Hanchera v. Board of Adjustment,* Furnas County Farms started building a large hog operation, knowing that Red Willow County was considering regulations that "would hinder, if not prohibit, its confined animal feeding operations."[47] The Nebraska Supreme Court concluded that the facts did not support the finding of good-faith reliance required to support the operator's claim of a vested right.

The legislative choice to let local governments deal with the types of problems that adjoining landowners are most likely to experience—e.g., odor, dust, and flies—is rational. Local control also can be justified on a geographic level, when one considers the wide variety of soil types and other geographic characteristics of Nebraska's land. From west to east and from north to south, topography, soil, rainfall amounts, and the volume and availability of groundwater and surface water vary considerably.[48]

One could just as easily fashion a contrary argument, however, by considering the statewide, nationwide, and even worldwide importance of the agricultural economy.[49] Although such economic concerns have not caused the Nebraska Legislature to roll back the county zoning regime, those issues have led to new efforts to promote livestock production in Nebraska. In 2003, the Nebraska Legislature passed a law geared toward promoting livestock production.[50] The legislative findings are telling:

> The Legislature finds that livestock production has traditionally served a significant role in the economic vitality of rural areas of the state and in the state's overall economy and that the growth and vitality of the state's livestock sector are critical to the continued prosperity of the state and its citizens. The Legislature further finds that trends in livestock production suggest a need to identify and address factors that affect the viability and expansion of livestock production. Those factors include the impact of livestock production on the state's economy and its communities, all applicable regulatory agencies, and the latest technology available to enhance the livestock industry. It is the intent of the Legislature to seek reasonable means to nurture and support the livestock sector of this state.[51]

Section 54-2802 instructs the director of agriculture to establish rules for designating a county as a "livestock friendly county" as a means of "recogniz[ing] and assist[ing] efforts of counties to maintain or expand their livestock sector." The statute goes on to direct the Department of Agriculture to "establish a resource data base to provide, upon written request of the county zoning authority or county board, information sources that may be useful to the county in evaluating and crafting livestock facility conditional use permits that meet the objectives of the county and livestock producer applicant."

The Department of Agriculture has promulgated regulations under the statute that touch on county zoning efforts.[52] A large part of the evaluation criteria and standards found in the regulations[53] speaks directly to types of requirements typically found in county zoning ordinances. One overarching regulatory theme is that the requirements counties place on animal feeding operations should be objective and science-based. Another is that the county restrictions should not exceed applicable state requirements under the Livestock Waste Management Act or the Wellhead Protection Area Act, unless the county's particular environmental circumstances justify a deviation. In sum, the regulations appear to encourage counties to insulate their zoning decisions from the more emotional responses that CAFOs engender. The state has not, however, repealed or changed the zoning statutes that have vested zoning authority in counties since the 1960s.

Once a county has been designated livestock friendly, it may use that designation in its promotional materials.[54] This designation is subject to a yearly review,[55] however, and the county is under a continuing duty to report any changes in its zoning requirements or its comprehensive development plan to the Department of Agriculture.[56]

The Department of Agriculture has designated Morrill, Hitchcock, and Webster counties as livestock friendly.[57] Hitchcock County applied for the designation for economic reasons. As one commissioner said, "Livestock is the biggest and best chance Hitchcock County has for (economic) expansion."[58] But the concerns about local control remain: "The loss of local control is a concern expressed by many in the zoning community."[59] Several other counties are considering whether to pursue the designation.[60]

Other Legislative and Administrative Land Use Controls

The environmental concerns associated with CAFOs' land uses have led to a huge and complex body of law. On the federal level, the Clean Water Act has a permit mechanism with which some livestock operations must comply. On the state level, the Nebraska Environmental Protection Act[61] places restrictions on such operations, as do the Livestock Waste Management Act[62] and the Wellhead Protection Area Act.[63] And a variety of state and federal administrative regulations have been promulgated under these statutes. Of particular relevance is Title 130 of the Nebraska Administrative Code, which regulates livestock waste and animal feeding operations. The particulars of these legislative and administrative controls are beyond the scope of this chapter, but it is worth noting that environmental concerns have been of primary importance in the evolution of regulatory approaches to agriculture and the relatively new phenomenon of

CAFOs. Such concerns will continue to affect the future of agriculture in Nebraska.

In sum, livestock production in general and CAFOs in particular have had an impact on Nebraska law. Nuisance law was the initial means of dealing with the various conflicting interests, and it still is flexible enough to accommodate changing facts in changing times. But the very effectiveness of nuisance law has also led the Nebraska Legislature to take actions to limit producers' liability. That legislative action may indicate that livestock production is politically popular, but it surely indicates that nuisance suits were seen as a poor means of dealing with the various ways in which some livestock producers affected some of their neighbors. As of now, legislative action and the rise of CAFOs (specifically, large hog operations) have pushed land use regulation to a more local level, resulting in increased uses of zoning power.The state has also begun to encourage economic development through livestock-friendly legislation. Notably, however, those state-level efforts have not resulted in any legislative rollback of county zoning authority. Thus, local control remains a staple of Nebraska's land use law as it applies to livestock production.

Notes

1. For a discussion of Nebraska's land use law as of 1977, see Craig Williams and Donald Shaneyfelt, *Land Use and the Law: A Nebraska Primer* (Lincoln, Neb.: C. Willams and D. Shaneyfelt, 1977).

2. There is a legal distinction between actions for public nuisances and actions for private nuisances. A private nuisance involves a complaint regarding a land use that has an impact on an individual's own use of land. A public nuisance involves a complaint regarding a land use that adversely impacts the public generally. In Nebraska, the ramifications of that distinction are not entirely clear. Thus, this chapter refers to nuisance actions in fairly general terms.

3. 16 Neb. 483, 484–85, 20 N.W. 720, 720–21 (1884).

4. 81 Neb. 349, 351, 116 N.W. 45, 46 (1908).

5. American Law Institute, *Restatement (Second) of the Law of Torts,* 2d ed., 4 vols. (St. Paul, Minn.: American Law Institute, 1965–79), §§ 825, 826, 827, and 840D.

6. Intentional invasions occur when a defendant "purposefully causes the invasion, knows that invasion is resulting from the [defendant's] conduct, or knows that the invasion is substantially certain to result from the [defendant's] conduct." Stephens v. Pillen, 12 Neb. App. 600, 606, 681 N.W.2d 59, 65 (2004) (relying on *Restatement [Second] of Torts* § 825, cmt. c, and Hall v. Phillips, 231 Neb. 269, 436 N.W.2d 139 [1989]); accord, Kopecky v. National Farms, Inc., 244 Neb. 846, 510 N.W.2d 41 (1994).

7. 244 Neb. at 852, 510 N.W.2d at 47–48 (quoting *Restatement [Second] of Torts* § 826). Unreasonable invasions can also occur when "the harm caused by the conduct is serious and the financial burden of compensating for this and similar harm to others would not make the continuation of the conduct not feasible." This middle ground recognizes that some suits for damages should take note of the financial burden the suit places on the defendant in light of the harm he is causing. See *Restatement (Second) of Torts* § 826, cmt. f. Although this language was quoted in *Kopecky,* no example of its proper role has arisen in a reported Nebraska case.

8. 244 Neb. at 853, 510 N.W.2d at 48 (quoting *Restatement [Second] of Torts* § 827).

9. Ibid., 510 N.W.2d at 48.

10. Goeke v. National Farms, Inc., 245 Neb. 262, 269, 512 N.W.2d 626, 632 (1994).

11. See ibid., 512 N.W.2d at 632 (explaining that the court has never "attempted to define substantial interference in the context of a suit to enjoin or abate a nuisance" but noting that "the annoyance must be such as to cause actual physical discomfort to one of ordinary sensibilities").

12. See also Hall v. Phillips, 231 Neb. 269, 278, 436 N.W.2d 139, 145 (1989).

13. *Restatement (Second) of Torts* § 840D.

14. Botsch v. Leigh Land Co., 195 Neb. 509, 511, 239 N.W.2d 481, 484 (1976).

15. Ibid., 510, 239 N.W.2d at 483.

16. Ibid., 511, 239 N.W.2d at 484.

17. Ibid., 517, 239 N.W.2d at 487. This is, of course, a truncated version of the court's analysis.

18. As a later appeal in the same case points out, Leigh offered no further evidence. Botsch v. Leigh Land Co., 205 Neb. 401, 405, 407, 288 N.W.2d 31, 33, 34 (1980).

19. In fact, Glenn Botsch testified at length before the Agriculture Committee when it was considering the legislative action. See Hearing Transcript on LB 132, Nebraska Legislature, Agriculture Committee, 24–34 (January 27, 1977).

20. Neb. Rev. Stat. § 81–1506(1)(b) (Supp. 1977) (superseded). The statutory language has been renumbered and much of it paraphrased.

21. For example, there was no presumption that livestock operations were nuisances, even though the statutory language seemed to assume that they were. A prima facie case of nuisance had been established by the plaintiff in *Botsch,* so it is possible that the drafters had the procedural posture of that case in mind. Another oddity of that choice of language was lack of any indication or discussion of what, if anything, a plaintiff could do to rebut the defendant's prima facie evidence. Finally, the statute seemed to conflate the relative burdens of proof by speaking in terms of prima facie evidence that a particular land use is *not* a nuisance, because the plaintiff generally has the burden of proving that a land use *is* a nuisance. Procedurally, it is difficult to imagine what should happen after both parties have presented a prima facie case on the same issue.

22. Hearing transcript on LB 132, Nebraska Legislature, Agriculture Committee (January 27, 1977).

23. Neb. Rev. Stat. §81-1506(1)(b) (Cum Supp. 2004).

24. *Nebraska Legislative Journal,* floor debate of LB 915, 7983–84 (March 7, 1980) (Senator Hoagland).

25. Hearing transcript on LB 132, Nebraska Legislature, Agriculture Committee (January 27, 1977).

26. The Nebraska Right to Farm Act is now codified at Nebraska Revised Statutes §§ 2-4401 through 2-4404 (Reissue 1997, Cum. Supp. 2004).

27. In this regard, the Nebraska Right to Farm Act is broader than section 81-1506. Section 81-1506 covers only "animal feeding operations." Neb. Rev. Stat. § 81-1506(b) (Cum. Supp. 2004). But a "farm operation" includes grain producers and many other types of farming operations. See Neb. Rev. Stat. § 2-4402 (Cum. Supp. 2004).

28. 220 Neb. 381, 370 N.W.2d 127 (1985). Similarly, in *Cline v. Franklin Pork, Inc.,* the plaintiff's ownership, use, and occupancy of his property predated the complained-of hog-raising use of the defendant's property, so the court held the act inapplicable. 219 Neb. 234, 361 N.W.2d 566 (1985). The Nebraska Right to Farm Act also made an appearance recently in *Soukop v. ConAgra, Inc.,* 264 Neb. 1015, 653 N.W.2d 655 (2002). There, the court held that a 1998 amendment to the act, which included grain elevators among the class of operations protected from nuisance actions, did not operate retrospectively. 264 Neb. at 1019, 653 N.W.2d at 658. Thus, the court held that the applicable version of the act was the one in effect at the time suit was filed.

29. Bolton v. M. Farm, Inc., No. CI01-135, judgment dated October 1, 2003 (5th Dist., York County).

30. Interview with Keith Marvin, planning department manager of JEO Consulting Group, Inc., in Wahoo, Nebraska, June 8, 2005.

Some examples of county zoning that are available online are

- Buffalo County: http://www.buffalogov.org/offices/Zoning/forms/Zoning Regulations.pdf
- Cass County: http://www.cassne.org/downloads/web%20page%20zoning%20regulations2.pdf
- Howard County: http://www.howardcounty.ne.gov/content/zoning_regs/zoning_regs.html
- Lancaster County: http://www.lincoln.ne.gov/city/plan/statreg/cozon.htm
- Madison County: http://www.co.madison.ne.us/mcjpc/faq_pdf/zon_regs.pdf (with additional conditional use permit information for livestock operations at http://www.co.madison.ne.us/mcjpc/faq_pdf/mclfo.pdf)
- Pierce County: http://www.co.madison.ne.us/mcjpc/faq_pdf/pie_zon.pdf (with additional conditional use permit information for livestock operations at http://www.co.madison.ne.us/mcjpc/faq_pdf/pclfo.pdf)
- Sarpy County: http://www.sarpy.com/pcommission/sarpy-zoning-ords.pdf

There is also a Web page with links to all Nebraska counties' Web pages at http://www.nebraska.gov/counties.phtml.

31. See Aaron McKown, "Hog Farms and Nuisance Law in *Parker v. Barefoot:* Has North Carolina Become a Hog Heaven and Waste Lagoon," *North Carolina Law Review* 77 (September 1999): 2355–76.

32. Carolyn Johnsen, *Raising a Stink: The Struggle over Factory Hog Farms in Nebraska* (Lincoln: University of Nebraska Press, 2003).

33. Ibid.

34. Professor Johnsen describes many of the state legislative efforts during this period, some of which failed. Notably, the influx of large hog operations was politically unpopular enough that the state legislature considered a temporary moratorium on the construction of hog confinement facilities. In fact, Senator M. L. Dierks went so far as to ask Attorney General Don Stenberg for his opinion regarding the constitutionality of such a moratorium. Adv. Op. 97044 (August 22, 1997). Although no moratorium was implemented, counties were allowed to adopt temporary zoning restrictions to apply to the incoming hog operations.

35. See generally Johnsen, *Raising a Stink.*

36. See Neil D. Hamilton, "Freedom to Farm! Understanding the Agricultural Exemption to County Zoning in Iowa," *Drake Law Review* 31, no. 3 (1981–82): 565–86.

37. For a more complete explanation of how rural zoning in Nebraska works, see Robert Coupland, "Rural Zoning in Nebraska," *Nebraska Law Review* 54, no. 3 (1975): 586–602. Zoning authority also exists at the city level, and in some circumstances the city's jurisdiction may extend beyond the city limits.

38. Neb. Rev. Stat. § 23-114(2)(g) (Cum. Supp. 2004).

39. Neb. Rev. Stat. § 23-114.03 (Cum. Supp. 2004).

40. Neb. Rev. Stat. § 23-114(2)(g) (Cum. Supp. 2004).

41. Premium Farms v. County of Holt, 263 Neb. 415, 422, 640 N.W.2d 633, 639 (2002).

42. Ibid., 438, 640 N.W.2d at 643.

43. This statutory provision was also cited by the *Premium Farms* court as support for the notion that farm buildings were within the county's zoning authority.

44. Neb. Rev. Stat. § 23-174.10 (Reissue 1997).

45. In *Enterprise Partners v. County of Perkins,* 260 Neb. 650, 619 N.W.2d 464 (2000), the court was presented with the validity of a county zoning regulation that required operators to cover "livestock waste storage containment structures" to reduce odor. After noting that "[t]he statutory language . . . grants extensive powers to counties to regulate their lands" (ibid., 656, 619 N.W.2d at 468), the court held the regulation invalid because the county had failed to satisfy one of the statutory requirements for enacting such a regulation—the adoption of a comprehensive development plan. Ibid., 659, 619 N.W.2d at 470.

46. Hanchera v. Bd. of Adjustment, 269 Neb. 623, 628, 694 N.W.2d 641, 646 (2005).

47. Ibid., 630, 694 N.W.2d at 647.

48. Interview with Keith Marvin, planning department manager of JEO Consulting Group, Inc., in Wahoo, Nebraska, June 8, 2005.

49. In the end, whether county zoning is a good or a bad idea is beyond the scope of this chapter. The point is that county zoning has been used as one tool to control CAFOs in Nebraska, and it gives the citizens of the state the opportunity to affect policy making through debate on a quite local level.

50. Neb. Rev. Stat. §§ 54-2801 and 54-2802 (Reissue 2004).

51. Neb. Rev. Stat. § 54-2801 (Reissue 2004).

52. Title 29 Neb. Admin. Code, ch. 2.

53. Ibid., § 008.05.

54. Ibid., § 009.

55. Ibid., §§ 011.02–011.04.

56. Ibid., § 010.

57. Phone Interview with Richard Sanne, administrator of agricultural promotion and development, Nebraska Department of Agriculture, March 30, 2006; "Morrill Is First Livestock Friendly County; Morrill County FB Is Partner," http://www.nebraska agconnection.com/story-state.cfm?Id=360&yr=2005 (June 16, 2005); "Gov. Heineman Designates Morrill County as Livestock Friendly County," http://www.gov.state.ne .us/news/2005_06/15_morrill_county.html (press release dated June 15, 2005).

58. "Hitchcock Could Be First 'Livestock Friendly' Nebraska County," *McCook Gazette,* April 25, 2005, available at http://nebraska.statepaper.com/vnews/display .v?TARGET=printable&article_id=426cc7ffafc1d (quoting Hitchcock County commissioner Dale Keeney).

59. Ibid. (quoting John Johnson, Pierce and Madison counties' zoning administrator).

60. Phone interview with Richard Sanne, administrator of agricultural promotion and development, Nebraska Department of Agriculture (March 30, 2006).

61. Neb. Rev. Stat. §§ 81-1501 through 81-1532 (Reissue 1999, Cum. Supp. 2004, Supp. 2005).

62. Neb. Rev. Stat. §§ 54-2416 through 54-2435 (Reissue 2004, Supp. 2005).

63. Neb. Rev. Stat. §§ 46-1501 through 46-1509 (Reissue 2004).

FIVE

Alan G. Gless and Peter J. Longo

AN OVERVIEW OF NEBRASKA WATER LAW

Nebraska is a place of transition. The westbound traveler witnesses the slow translation of the Midwest into the Great Plains, leaving behind the well-watered valleys of the east for the more severe regimes of the sandhill and the prairie. The hundredth meridian neatly bisects the state, separating the humid and subhumid regions to the east from the semiarid regions to the west. The hundredth meridian is, of course, an imaginary and static line projected onto a very real and dynamic landscape, one that is neither the Eden depicted by nineteenth-century boosters nor the wasteland once styled the Great American Desert.[1]

Lawyers and legislators, like geographers, have sought to draw lines and to establish boundaries, both in the law and on the land. Nature, however, dictates the where and when of water, and nature has no interest in cooperating with human-made laws. Out of this tension between the natural distribution of water resources and their political distribution have arisen many of the conflicts and compromises that have shaped the history of this state and its water law. Eastern Nebraska fronts the Missouri River, and surface water resources were central to the early development of territorial and state water law. Western Nebraska sits atop a large portion of the Ogallala Aquifer (or High Plains Aquifer), once considered a limitless

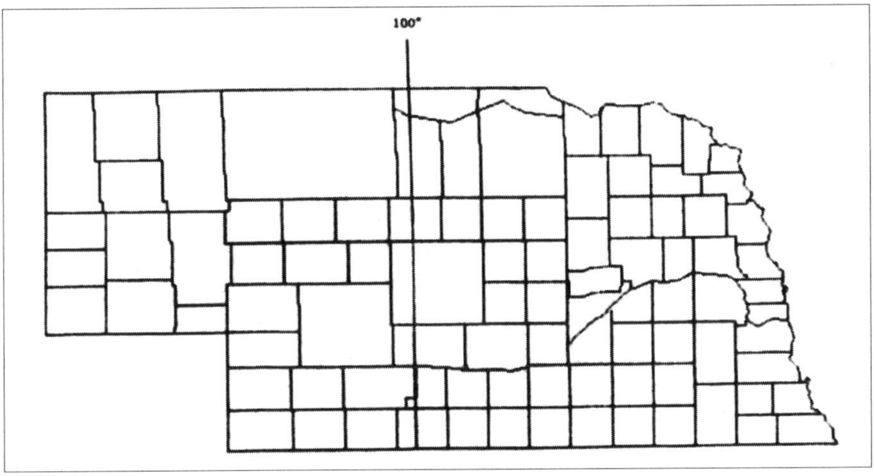

Map 5.1. Location of the 100th meridian through Nebraska

water supply; the scarcity of rain in that region and the necessity of groundwater for agriculture have brought about some of the thornier practical and legal problems in the state's history. Most recently, Nebraska's tributary groundwater resources have taken center stage. This chapter offers short descriptions of the highlights of Nebraska's historically significant water cases and legislative acts. It also illustrates competing views of the best manner in which to promote the common good and demonstrates how outcomes may be determined by whether citizens cooperate or fight over a finite resource.

Origins of Nebraska Water Law: Riparians and Appropriators

Nebraska's early water law derived from English common law, as modified by American courts in the East. This system of rights was known as riparianism, and it worked well enough in its rain-soaked country of origin and in the North American colonies to which it was first transplanted. However, differences of climate between Nebraska and the eastern states, on the one hand, and between eastern Nebraska and western Nebraska, on the other,[2] necessitated looking to the West for more useful water law concepts. In these lands of little rain, settlers developed an alternative system called prior appropriation; it sprang up first as a rule of necessity among mining camps on public lands and later was refined and regularized across the western territories and states. As historian Sam Kepfield wrote in 1994, "The best way to conceptualize water law on the Great Plains is to see a modified riparianism moving west colliding with a modified prior appropriation system moving east." He also concluded, however, that "[t]he true development of Great Plains water law, and Nebraska's in particular, comes not from the East, . . . but rather from the West."[3] Although Nebraska water law is considered a subset of the water law generally applied in seventeen western states, it also incorporates a number of unique approaches.[4]

English riparianism was a common-law doctrine and, as such, a creature of the courts. Courts can determine only those disputes that are brought before them, and these cases usually come one at a time—judges cannot go out and adopt integrated solutions to all the problems of the world outside the courtroom. As a result, development of the common law tends to be very slow, random, and context-based. For all their ability to narrowly tailor specific remedies for specific wrongs in specific cases, courts are not the instruments best suited to the crafting of broad public policy. In addition, courts are bound to decide cases on the evidence presented to them; they cannot venture forth and collect their own. So when a court makes a decision that doesn't entirely comport with scientific reality or with the state of the art, it may be because the litigants have presented low-quality evidence. When legislatures decide to enact comprehensive regulatory regimes, courts cannot escape the duty of figuring out how the legislation plays out in real-world disputes—or even what the legislation means—and they are almost always forced to interpret and implement these laws one case at a time. The history of Nebraska's water law presents no exception to these propositions.[5]

By 1867, Nebraska's first year of statehood, the line of settlement had begun to sweep beyond the hundredth meridian.[6] The settlers coming into the territory hailed primarily from eastern areas of the country, where few, if any, had experienced the drying up of rivers or significant shortages of water.[7] They had experienced conditions in which riparianism had tended to work well. Nearly every state and territory, by statute or by court decision, had adopted the common law.[8] Even in the East, however, the common law of water rights had been changing well before the settlement of Nebraska Territory.[9] It was no longer the preindependence common law of England, for American courts had been modifying it for years.

Riparianism in its purest English form (known as natural flow riparianism) declares that owners of land abutting a watercourse enjoy a usufructuary right in the flow of water past that land, subject only to the same right in other riparian landowners along the watercourse and to the requirement that one's use not diminish the flow.[10] The doctrine was predicated on a fiction—that all uses of water are nonconsumptive—but it was a fiction easily sustained in a land of hydrologic abundance, especially before the rise of industrialism. Courts in the new United States, recognizing that certain socially and economically desirable activities might consume some volume of water or partially restrict streamflow, began to read into the doctrine a principle of reasonable use:

> The true test . . . of the use is, whether it is to the injury of the other proprietors or not. There may be a diminution in quantity, or a retardation or acceleration of the natural current indispensable for the general and valuable use of the water, perfectly consistent with the existence of the common right. [It] is an implied element in the right of using the stream at all. The law here, as in many other cases, acts with a reasonable reference to public convenience and general good.[11]

This American variation became known as reasonable use riparianism, and it served well in the humid eastern regions. But as migrants moved westward, they encountered new climatic conditions and found new uses for limited water resources (hydraulic mining in the gold fields, for example, or irrigated agriculture on the plains) that required a rethinking of the law.

Their solution was the prior appropriation system. Under this approach, individuals (appropriators) were free to divert from the watercourse as much water as they could use, subject only to the equitable maxim of first in time, first in right.[12] Like their counterparts in the East, western courts soon found it necessary to read into their general rule an element of reasonable use—the requirement of a beneficial purpose, without waste.[13] The system was developed initially to adjudicate priority of appropriative rights as between mere occupants of public lands, the title to which was held by the federal government. But as more and more land passed into private ownership, there arose the question of whether adoption of the appropriative principle had supplanted the old doctrine of riparian rights as between owners in fee. Here the western jurisdictions split, largely along lines of scarcity. The truly arid, mountainous states hewed to a strict prior appropriations line, even enshrining the principle in their state constitutions. The coastal states and those straddling the semiarid-subhumid boundary of the hundredth meridian—Nebraska among them—struggled with the question of extinguishment of riparian rights and developed the hybrid system of water law that prevails in these jurisdictions today.[14]

Development of Nebraska Water Law: Surface Water Resources

Despite a severe drought that lasted from 1857 to 1877, the Nebraska Supreme Court heard no water rights cases, and no irrigation or water rights legislation came out of the state legislature.[15] Thus, the exact nature of riparian owners' water rights in Nebraska during this period remains forever an academic question.

The promoters of the Kearney Canal Company, which went bankrupt in 1890, left a legislative legacy of considerable value to irrigation developers. In 1877, they persuaded the legislature to pass a law recognizing irrigation ditches as works of internal improvement and conferring eminent domain powers on irrigation ditch companies for the purpose of obtaining rights of way to construct canals, dams, and reservoirs, and for related activities.[16]

Before that successful lobbying effort, irrigation had been a dirty word to Nebraska's leadership. Promoters of settlement had denied the necessity of irrigation out of fear that settlers would not come if they believed the climate too dry to support agriculture. The public good, in their view, required the attraction of as many immigrants as possible—and misleading potential settlers in pursuance of this greater good did not seem to prick their consciences overmuch. Furthermore, two prominent water scientists at the University of Nebraska, Samuel Aughey and Charles Dana Wilber, supported and promoted the idea that rainfall would be enhanced by tilling the land and that irrigation was, or shortly would become, unnecessary. The irrigationists, on the other hand, saw the public good in the proliferation of irrigation systems that would increase the state's economic activity.[17]

The 1877 act said nothing about water rights, although, some thirty-seven years later, the Nebraska Supreme Court detected within it an implication that a vested water right could be obtained by appropriating streamflow and applying it to a beneficial use.[18] No more legislation and no supreme court decisions dealing with water rights appeared until 1889.[19] In the interim, however, the position of the irrigationists was in the ascendancy.

In 1889, using a California law as its model, the legislature passed a (somewhat) comprehensive act by which the owners or claimants of land located on the banks of streams, or even in the vicinity of streams, had the right to use the streamflow for irrigating that land. Doing so entitled them to acquire a water right in the streamflow by its appropriation to "any useful or beneficial use."[20] The 1889 act, popularly known as the Rayner Law after its legislative sponsor, Representative Henry St. Rayner, was Nebraska's first statutory recognition of the doctrine of appropriation. To secure an appropriation right, one had only to post a notice on the stream bank at the planned point of diversion and to file a duplicate notice in the local county clerk's office. If an appropriator ceased using the water for some useful or beneficial purpose, the appropriative right terminated. The act also specifically forbade diverting or permitting water appropriated from a river or stream to run into the waters or channel of any river or stream other than that of its origin, effectively prohibiting transbasin diversion.[21]

The 1889 act also readopted the 1877 law relating to the eminent domain powers of irrigation companies, limited appropriators' water usage to that amount required by the exercise of good husbandry, and restricted the application of the act vis-à-vis the rights of riparian proprietors along streams less than fifty feet in width.[22] The legislature also provided for apportionment of streamflow in times of scarcity among all appropriators, with no consideration of what their initial allotments may have been. This apportionment provision represented a departure from the strict priority regimes that prevailed among the truly arid states. The 1889 act did not create any unified or centralized recording system for administration of the appropriations, neither did it expressly extinguish riparian rights nor establish any form of priority or preferences among uses. Although it did declare that first in time was first in right, the act provided no remedy for violations of priority. Once outside the county of filing, the appropriator was left to litigation or self-help to establish and defend the priority of the claim.[23]

The drought of 1890, one of the worst experienced after settlement began, gave the irrigation movement new energy. Political problems obstructed passage of a truly comprehensive surface water irrigation law, at least until the drought of 1894 arrived to persuade those whom the drought of 1890 had left unconvinced of the necessity of water law reform.[24] The following spring, the legislature adopted the 1895 Appropriation and Irrigation Law, which came to be called the Akers Law after the irrigator and legislator who guided the four bills making up the irrigation law package through the legislature (and who, by 1896 if not earlier, became the state engineer in charge of administering the act).[25] The 1895 irrigation law sought to codify the two underlying principles of a prior appropriation system: beneficial use as the basis of the right and priority in time as the basis of allocation in times of shortage. The act

> had five salient features: (1) it replaced inadequate judicial procedures for determining and enforcing water rights with state administrative control; (2) it declared the water of every natural stream, not heretofore appropriated, to be the property of the public, subject to appropriation for a beneficial use; (3) it provided statutory controls to prevent waste and an uneconomical distribution of water; (4) it established, subject to a preference for domestic use, a preference for agricultural uses over manufacturing uses; and (5) it protected existing rights to water appropriated and acquired prior to passage of the act. The legislation also incorporated additional provisions prohibiting transbasin diversion and change of location of use, limiting the application of the act to water from natural streams[,] encouraging investment in irrigation works, and providing a uniform method for measuring streamflow.[26]

The 1895 act removed initial adjudicatory duties from the district courts to a state agency with jurisdiction over surface water rights, the State Board of Irrigation.[27] The district courts continued to be involved in resolving disputes between water users, serving as the first level of appeal from the state agency and as the trial-level tribunal for the resolution of disputes between water users and the state. The supreme court was, and remains, the final arbiter of all such litigation upon further appeal.[28] Although the act succeeded in removing the district courts from the ensuing flood of trial-level surface water rights adjudications, it failed to stanch the flow of second- and third-level appeals from irrigation board decisions. The enactment of major legislation, and even of minor legislation, often leads to an increase in litigation as the courts are called upon to interpret the new laws.

Before the legislature's entry into the irrigation and surface water fray, remarkably few water rights cases had come before the state supreme court. Compared with the rest of the case load, the number of water rights cases seems a minor component of the courts' business.[29] However, in light of the importance of the questions decided, litigation in Nebraska has been and continues to be a major method of water policy making. It didn't take long for the 1895 act to appear in a supreme court opinion.

The legislature adopted the Akers Law in April 1895, and the Nebraska Supreme Court released its decision in *Clark v. Cambridge & Arapahoe Irrigation & Improvement Co.* in September of that same year.[30] This case involved a mill operator as the plaintiff, an irrigation company as the defendant, and several irrigation company customers as intervenors. Both the mill operator and the irrigation company were diverting water from the Republican River. Despite the priority of the mill operator's claim, the court ruled for the irrigation company and, as a consequence, for the farmers. The ruling in favor of the irrigators rested not on any argument relating to water law, but on the assertion of the equitable defense of laches. The mill operator sought to enjoin the irrigators from diverting any water from the river, but although he had had notice of the intended appropriation long before the diversion works had been completed, he did not commence his action until well after the irrigation company had substantially constructed its system and obligated itself to the farmers. Under the doctrine of laches, a suitor who makes it impossible to enjoin an act without great injury to his adversary or the public by sleeping on his rights is left to his ordinary legal remedies and is not entitled to an injunction. The irrigation company, after all, was engaged in a work designated by the legislature as being of public interest.

The irrigators had argued, among other things, that the adoption of the 1877 irrigation companies' eminent domain law and the 1889 Rayner Law, now buttressed by the 1895 Akers Law, had abolished the common-law riparian system in Nebraska. They lost that argument. The supreme court pointed out that if the legislature had intended to abolish the common-law riparian system, it could not have done so in a way consistent with the state constitution, unless it paid constitutionally mandated just compensation to all riparians whose vested water rights were terminated by those laws. Just compensation had not been provided in any of the water statutes. Therefore, the mill operator's riparian rights had not been abolished.

Lacking a body of applicable Nebraska case law, the justices relied on treatise writers' descriptions of riparians' water rights and on dicta from one of their own opinions.[31] The court might have looked to California riparian case law precedents because, in the court's words, "[i]t is a well known fact that our irrigation laws are modeled after the statutes of California."[32] However, the court declined to follow California decisions because it thought that Nebraska water law, before the adoption of the Rayner Law, differed from that of California on the issue of privately held land.[33]

Shortly after the turn of the century, in a series of three opinions in one case, *Crawford Co. v. Hathaway,*[34] the supreme court clarified the meaning of the various irrigation laws passed between 1877 and 1895. In this protracted litigation, the appellant irrigation company sought an adjudication of its appropriative rights on the White River as against a downstream mill operator and other landowners claiming common-law riparian rights. Francis G. Hamer, a former district court judge and future supreme court justice, represented the irrigation company in all three appearances in the supreme court.[35] He strove mightily to obtain a declaration that the irrigation legislation of 1877 through 1895 had abolished all riparian rights in Nebraska and then, having failed in that endeavor, sought judicial modification of the state's common-law riparian system to fit the climatic and hydrologic conditions in western Nebraska.

The court refused to accept Hamer's argument that it should, in effect, do away with all riparian rights acquired before 1889. Echoing its earlier decision in *Clark,* the court noted that pre-1889 riparian landowners had vested property rights in the use of the water. Thus, the court could not terminate those rights without taking property from the owners of the land. The Nebraska constitution prohibited the government from taking private property—in this case, water rights—without just compensation.[36] Thus, vested riparian rights remained secure. The court did, however, declare that the adoption of the appropriation statutes had precluded the vesting of new riparian rights.[37] The *Crawford* court initiated use of the 1889 date as the abolition of riparian rights acquisition, a precedent that stood for six decades.[38]

The supreme court also refused to accept Hamer's argument that water law in the western part of the state should be modified. Possibly more important to the court was the fact that very detailed information would be required to establish a boundary between any such eastern and western water law zones. That kind of information generally cannot make its way into the evidence adduced at trial by parties whose cases arise in limited, specific locales. That kind of information *can,* however, be brought before a legislature considering boundary questions. The supreme court pointed out the legislative nature of Hamer's idea, and the justices declined to act as legislators.[39]

The court also declined Hamer's invitation to apply the civil law to riparian rights. Hamer argued that the civil law was applicable because Nebraska had come to the United States through the purchase of the Louisiana Territory, where Spanish and French civil law had been in force. The justices noted that although Spain and France had claimed the lands in question, neither nation's laws had become part of the organic law of the territory or state as later constituted.[40]

By declaring damages an adequate remedy, however, the supreme court did effectively limit appropriators' liability to riparians who could prove that the appropriators had adversely affected their property right to use streamflows.[41] By so doing, the court nearly foreclosed the possibility of riparians' obtaining injunctive relief against appropriators. This interpretation of the 1895 statutes, according to Ralph J. Fischer, Richard S. Harnsberger, and Jarrett C. Oeltjen, had the effect of clothing private appropriators with the power to condemn riparian water rights through the payment of just compensation, a course of action open to the appellant in *Crawford,* an irrigation company vested with eminent domain powers in the 1877 act, which was readopted as part of the 1895 act.[42]

Hamer also argued that because the Crawford Company was under contract to provide water to the village of Crawford for domestic and agricultural purposes, the company held domestic and agricultural use preferences over several of the opposing parties. The court accepted this argument as it related to irrigation. However, the court believed "domestic purposes" as used in the statute carried a meaning far more limited than that for which Hamer contended. In the absence of a statutory definition, the supreme court interpreted domestic purposes to include only those uses recognized by the common law as domestic uses. That meant drinking and cooking purposes and watering of household stock, which take only a small amount of water and do not interfere with streamflow. The court refused to apply the concept of domestic purposes to a village power plant; thus, that use of water could not overcome the stronger claim to the use of the water for agriculture.[43]

On the same day that the supreme court issued its *Crawford III* decision, it also issued its judgment in *Meng v. Coffee,*[44] an opinion written by Commissioner Roscoe Pound.[45] In *Meng,* a lower riparian sought an injunction to prevent upper riparians from diverting all of Hat Creek's water and depriving the lower riparian of any water during times of shortage. The supreme court reversed the district court's denial of an injunction and directed it, in essence, to enjoin the defendants from wasting, unreasonably diminishing, or consuming all of the creek's water. Allen G. Fisher, one of Hamer's cocounsel arguing the inapplicability of the common law in *Crawford,* found himself in the position of arguing in favor of the common law in *Meng.* The supreme court reiterated its position that the common law applied throughout the entire state, despite the different conditions in western Nebraska, and went one step further by setting out its test for reasonable use.[46] The court not only defined the previously undefined term but also provided trial courts with an analytical approach for determining the factual question of whether a use is reasonable. In addition, the *Meng* court described the issue of whether a particular area of Nebraska is arid as a fact question for determination case by case.[47]

Quickly on the heels of *Meng* came the supreme court commission's decision in *McCook Irrigation & Water Power Co. v. Crews,* another opinion by Pound.[48] The supreme court initially accepted the commission's recommendation and reversed the trial court's injunction.[49] Upon rehearing, however, the court vacated its earlier decision and affirmed the injunction.[50] The case involved an upper riparian who had not perfected his riparian right before a lower appropriator had obtained an appropriation from the state board. After finding that the appropriator had an adjudicated priority, the court enjoined the upper riparian from diverting water from the stream but took care to explain: "If this were a case where the riparian owner had actually diverted water to irrigate riparian lands before the rights of an appropriator attached, the case would be entirely different. . . . [T]he appropriator would . . . be compelled to make due compensation before a court would restrain . . . the . . . riparian."[51]

The decisions reviewed thus far have dealt more with legislative omissions relating to the remedies available to parties injured by other streamflow users than with water law itself. Indeed, as James A. Doyle aptly observed, "The value of a substantive right is measured by the relief available for its protection against invasion."[52] Although there were water law questions en route to developing answers to the remedy questions, the former remained, to that extent, subordinate issues. But the flood of appellate litigation rolled on, an occasional substantive issue in the fore.

Kirk v. State Board of Irrigation dealt with the extent of the board's authority to impose conditions in its permit grants.[53] The board granted Kirk a permit to appropriate Niobrara River water for power generating purposes, but conditioned the permit by prohibiting him from selling in South Dakota any of the power generated with the Nebraska water. The Nebraska Supreme Court rejected Kirk's argument that the condition impermissibly burdened interstate commerce, relying on a U.S. Supreme Court ruling that when a state has an interest in or control over property within its borders, it may transfer a qualified ownership interest to others but may also prevent the transfer of the property across state lines.[54] Nebraska, by virtue of the 1895 Akers Law, owns the surface waters of the state in trust for the people: riparian proprietors cannot appropriate surface water without the state's permission. The state, therefore, could withhold its permission to sell across state lines any electric power generated by using Nebraska's surface water. That position remained good law (and then lingered as questionable law) for nearly seventy years before the U.S. Supreme Court corrected it.[55]

Among the substantive questions that the legislature left for the courts were what constitutes an appropriation and what determines the date of priority of a given appropriation. In *Enterprise Irrigation District v. Tri-State Land Co.*, the state board had adjudicated multiple claims of multiple claimants, a number of which were assigned priorities predating the 1889 appropriation statutes.[56] One major issue was whether a canal company that had posted and filed a notice of intention to appropriate a certain quantity of water, but had *actually* appropriated and applied to a beneficial use only a fraction of that quantity, could retain its priority right to the full amount previously adjudicated by the board. The court reasoned that canal companies, as a sort of public service corporation, do not own the water they carry but acquire by appropriation the right to divert the water and to charge a reasonable fee for carrying it through the canals to the land upon which it was designated to be used. The court ruled that under the 1889 act, a canal owner who serves as a carrier of water to be applied to a beneficial use on the lands of others must obtain the application of the water to those lands within a reasonable time in order to retain the right to take the water from the river. The court read into the act both the beneficial use concept from the common law and the reasonable time constraint. Under the 1911 amendments to the 1895 act, a canal owner had a statutorily prescribed time within which to apply the water to beneficial use on customers' land to keep the priority.[57]

In *Kearney Water and Electric Powers Co. v. Alfalfa Irrigation District*,[58] the plaintiff had begun constructing diversion works in 1882 but completed them only in 1886. The 1877 act applied to the claim but contained no procedures whatsoever for determining the validity or vesting of appropriations. The supreme court set a priority date of September 10, 1882, when construction began—no more being required by the law then in force—and applied the reasonable time principle that it had articulated in *Enterprise*. No objection to the appropriation having been made between the commencement of construction and the perfection of the claim by application of the waters so diverted to a beneficial use, the rights of the plaintiff were vested to that extent.

Then, in *Commonwealth Power Co. v. State Board of Irrigation, Highways and Drainage*,[59] the supreme court confronted the need to define "appropriation" in the context of a later application for a permit to divert Loup

River water from nearly the same point as an earlier applicant that had not yet completed its project when the later applicant filed. The water board had decided that the second appropriation, if granted, would be detrimental to the public welfare. The court stated that for purposes of the 1895 act, as amended in 1911,

> [u]sed in its strictest sense . . . the word "appropriation" denotes an appropriation which has been legally initiated by the filing of an application by that body, the construction of the works as specified therein, and the application of the water to a beneficial use within the time limited in the permit or subsequent extensions.[60]

However, in the case of a later conflicting application, a looser use of the term in several sections of the act and in general legal usage allowed the court to adopt a functional meaning:

> An applicant who obtains a permit under the statute acquires thereby a contingent "appropriation" to the extent of his grant which gives him the prior right to the use of this water against all subsequent claimants. It is in effect pledged to him for the period of time fixed by the board within which he may complete and perfect the appropriation, and is an "appropriation" to that extent, but no more.[61]

After reaching that functional definition, the court then determined whether the denial fell within the powers of the board. The second proposed diversion would have used all of the water available in the river at that location. Thus, the court reasoned,

> The object of the law is to encourage and not to hinder the development of the state by the use of its waters for the purposes of agriculture or the generation of power, and the board was entitled to consider whether the allowance of conflicting claims to the same water at practically the same place would tend to accomplish or defeat the legislative purpose.[62]

The supreme court's public policy view in 1913 still emphasized the promotion of economic development through use of the state's surface water resources as an aspect of protecting the public welfare.

In *Kerstenbrock v. Boyes,*[63] decided the next year, the supreme court also upheld the board's power to cancel, after notice and hearing, permits it had previously issued under the 1895 act when the permit holders failed to complete their proposed appropriations. The 1911 amendments to the 1895 act had granted the board the power of cancellation for nonuser, and the court found in the language of the amendments a clear legislative intent that this provision should apply retroactively, not merely prospectively, as plaintiff had argued.

In the later case of *Enterprise Irrigation District v. Willis,* a riparian appropriator with a pre-1889 vested right challenged the attempt to apply the statutory restrictions of the 1895 act to his water use rights.[64] The supreme court relied on that act's express disclaimer of any intention to infringe in any way on pre-1895 vested rights. The old common-law beneficial use requirement, however, still applied to such rights. The legislature continued beneficial use as a key concept in the 1895 act, and the 1920 constitutional amendments (discussed below) did so as well. Unfortunately, neither the 1895 act nor the 1920 constitutional amendments defined "beneficial use." That job fell to the supreme court, of course, and it did what any court in similar circumstances would do: it harkened back to the common law.[65]

Water and the Nebraska Constitutional Convention, 1919–20

The constitutional convention that met from December 1919 until March 1920 sent to the voters a total of forty-one separate proposals to amend the state constitution. One proposal consisting of three related provisions dealt with surface water rights, and one stand-alone proposal dealt with the use and inalienability of surface water for power purposes. The voters approved both by overwhelming margins: 64,353 for and 9,444 against Proposal 35, the water rights proposal, and 69,861 for and 7,377 against Proposal 36, the water power proposal.[66] Obviously, Nebraskans felt strongly about protecting their surface water rights.

The convention published a journal of its proceedings but, unfortunately, did not keep a record of the meetings of its committees.[67] It recorded only the meetings of the convention, both as the convention and as a committee of the whole. To legal minds, an obvious reason for elevating water rights to constitutional status lies in the desire to prevent temporary and shifting legislative majorities from effecting changes in those rights and policies. Only the people themselves retain the capacity to change Nebraska's constitutional water rights provisions. Delegate Claude C.

Flansburg, a lawyer from Lincoln, said: "[T]his entire proposal is but a copy of the Statutes of 1895, and is put in here by the Committee [on Irrigation, Drainage, Water Power, and Natural Resources] for the purpose of preventing any future change by legislative act."[68] No delegates disagreed with him—and this in a session in which a number expressed themselves rather freely on various subjects, albeit politely when seen in print. Other delegates' statements during that session corroborated Flansburg's recital.[69]

But what underlay that obvious purpose remains unexplored. The constitutionalization of these principles was not intended to change Nebraska's water law as of 1919, because it did not alter the prior legislation or the supreme court's precedents. The new constitutional provisions only restated Nebraska's water laws then in force, as adopted by the legislature and elucidated by the supreme court. A committee of the convention worked the adopted amendments into the Nebraska constitution of 1875 and placed the water provisions in article XV, as sections 4 through 7. The differences between the constitutional amendments of 1920 and the 1895 irrigation act are slight at the most, with some important exceptions, such as section 7, which protected the use of water for power purposes, and the addition of water for domestic use to the definition of a natural want in section 4.[70]

The convention's activities as revealed by the journal provide additional points worth noting. Delegate John G. Beeler, a lawyer from North Platte, personally introduced the surface water rights proposal to the convention.[71] The proposal was referred to the Committee on Irrigation, Drainage, Water Power, and Natural Resources, which Beeler himself chaired. His proposal, number 129, became ballot Proposal 35 and eventually article XV, sections 4, 5, and 6, of the Nebraska constitution.[72]

Development of Nebraska Water Law: Groundwater Resources

In the nineteenth century, groundwater remained outside the realm of easy access and capture except for those possessed of windmills and those blessed with a water table high enough to fill their shallow wells. In 1897, the legislature adopted the state's first groundwater law, which regulated the use of artesian wells.[73] Artesian wells run constantly, as long as their aquifer does not become depleted, and their flow will become wasted unless somehow stored or constantly used. To prevent such waste, the statute required that the flow of all artesian wells be controlled.

By 1919, when the constitutional convention assembled, groundwater generally had been used only by the railroads, by settlers for domestic household purposes, and by cities for municipal needs. Pumping technology had not yet developed sufficiently to make groundwater irrigation a major concern.[74] Very little was known about groundwater as a scientific matter, but that was of little import: Nebraska's supply of groundwater was inexhaustible—William Akers had said so. As Kepfield observed, the "apparent abundance of groundwater is crucial in explaining the course of Nebraska groundwater law."[75] As a result, groundwater, unlike surface water, had not yet become a major subject of litigation when the 1919–20 constitutional convention met. The large-scale use of groundwater in irrigation began only after 1929.[76]

The supreme court's first major decision involving groundwater, *Olson v. City of Wahoo,* came out in 1933.[77] Olson contended that the city's pumping from two wells within 3,400 feet of his sand and gravel operation had lowered the water table so severely as to render pumping on his own land impossible. Olson's pumping was prior in time. The ensuing battle of experts ended with the trial judge's finding that Olson had failed to prove that the city had interfered with his operation.

The city of Wahoo argued that the English rule relating to groundwater should apply to the case. That rule granted to the proprietor of land the absolute ownership of all water underlying it and held him harmless for any interference his pumping might cause his neighbors in their use of water below their own land. The supreme court considered the English rule, which nominally applied under Nebraska's common-law adoption statute, and rejected it as inapposite to Nebraska conditions.

Olson argued in favor of an American rule instead—actually a combination of two related but distinguishable principles. American jurisprudence had developed a rule of reasonable use, which allowed the landowner to apply only a reasonable amount of the subterranean water on his overlying land. California's supreme court added a doctrine of correlative rights, which requires an apportionment of groundwater use among neighbors in times of shortage.

The supreme court upheld the trial judge's findings of fact and announced its adoption of the two American rules of reasonable use and correlative rights, though black-letter status would not be conferred for some years.[78] Because the supreme court reached its conclusion in *Olson* by ruling on the sufficiency of the factual evidence, as Harnsberger, Oeltjen, and Fischer explain, everything the court said about the controlling groundwater law in Nebraska was mere dicta.[79] *Olson* eventually did come to matter beyond its own facts, because the supreme court later declared its reasoning to be Nebraska law in cases in which the legal issue, not the factual issue, was decisive.[80]

The need to rely squarely on the *Olson* rule finally reached the supreme court in 1941 in *Luchsinger v. Loup River Public Power District*.[81] The plaintiff in this case owned a tract of land bordering one of the power district's canals. Before the power district dug this particular canal, the plaintiff had benefited from a water table only two to five feet below the surface, which provided subirrigation for his crops. After the power district dug the canal, the water table under plaintiff's field dropped to a depth of twelve to twenty feet below the surface, totally depriving the plaintiff of any subirrigation benefits. The canal, more than 210 feet wide and 36 feet deep, lowered the water table because groundwater drained through the bank and into the canal, a normal thing for groundwater to do. The district defended in part by claiming that the common law did not hold a canal owner liable for seepage damage unless it had caused the damage through negligence or intentional wrongdoing. The state constitution's just compensation clause trumped the common law on that point, however, and the supreme court decided accordingly. Thus, one who damages or interferes with a landowner's right to the use of groundwater can be held liable for damages without proof of negligence or intentional wrongdoing.[82]

Nebraska's period of heavy irrigation development lay just around the corner in the 1950s. Of the state's groundwater law at that juncture, Harnsberger, Oeltjen, and Fischer concluded: "Nebraska began its era of greatest [ground]water development with no legal focus except the judicial rule of reasonable use, an articulated but never applied requirement of sharing in time of shortage, and prohibitions against wasting and polluting."[83] All these rules had come from the supreme court, except the lone statute prohibiting the wasting of artesian water.

At about this time, sprinkler irrigation had become an established and highly effective technology. Center pivots arrived in the mid-1950s, and groundwater irrigation increased dramatically. By 1959, the acreage irrigated by groundwater exceeded that irrigated by surface water. Groundwater depletion also increased dramatically. For the first time, groundwater mining[84] became a reality in Nebraska. Realizing that the groundwater supply might not be inexhaustible after all, the legislature sprang into action and commissioned another study, which produced the *Report of the Nebraska Legislative Council Committee on Ground and Surface Water*, published in

1956.[85] The fruits of that report included a 1957 well registration statute,[86] a well spacing statute,[87] another study published in 1958,[88] and a groundwater preference statute[89] that mirrored the 1895 surface water preference statute and the constitutional surface water preference provision. This last statute, however, contained no enforcement mechanism, did not specify when preferences would apply, did not deal with municipal industrial use, and did not explain the type of preferences created. All that can be said for the statute is that it expressed a legislative concern, saved state senators from having to deal with rural-urban water use conflicts, and gave the courts another problematic law to interpret and apply if and when an appropriate case presented itself.[90]

The 1958 study report[91] led the legislature to enact the Groundwater Conservation Act of Nebraska.[92] This act provided for the creation of groundwater conservation districts, which could be formed only by initiative petition. It authorized the districts to develop measures to ensure proper conservation of groundwater resources in problem areas. The measures adopted were enforceable by actions brought in the district courts. But as of 1963, no groundwater conservation districts had yet been formed.[93]

Transbasin Diversions and the Long Road toward Integrated Management

In 1936, the supreme court, very narrowly interpreting the then current version of the 1895 irrigation act, had ruled in *Osterman v. Central Nebraska Public Power and Irrigation District* that Nebraska law did not allow interbasin or transbasin diversions of surface water.[94] The basins in *Osterman* were unquestionably separate and unrelated. In 1953, the Ainsworth Irrigation District applied for an appropriation to divert water from the Snake River for use on lands located within the district but technically lying outside the Snake River basin, or watershed. The canal was to divert Snake River water across several creek basins and into the lands to be irrigated; the unused water, or return flow, was to drain into the Niobrara River, not back into the Snake. Before the application was acted on, local landowners filed objections, alleging that allowing return flows to drain into the Niobrara would violate the 1895 irrigation act because it was not the stream from which the water had been diverted. The director of water resources heard the application and granted it in 1959. He found, inter alia, that the Snake joined the Niobrara and that they formed a single river basin. Thus, no interbasin transfer was involved. On appeal, in *Ainsworth Irrigation District v. Bejot,* the supreme court accepted the director's finding of fact, rendering the *Osterman* rule inapplicable to the case and the district's diversion permissible.[95]

At about this time, a number of cities whose municipal water systems depended solely on surface water realized that in the near future they would need to augment their sources of supply with groundwater. Several applied for subflow appropriation permits to protect their well fields constructed in alluvial aquifers, but their applications were denied. The supreme court's decision in the *Olson* case indicated that the application of groundwater to uses on nonoverlying lands could be enjoined and suggested that appeals from the permit denials would not have succeeded.[96] Rather than appeal, the cities brought their problem before the 1963 legislature. The legislature's 1962 study report[97] had recommended enactment of a definition of groundwater that would have included underground streams accompanying surface streams, or subflow, and a permit system for the pumping of groundwater within two hundred feet of streams. The 1962 report included no specific recommendation relating to the cities' problem but did provide information for the cities to use in approaching the legislature.

The legislature declined to include subflows in its new statutory definition of groundwater, a refusal that contributed to retarding the development of integrated ground and surface water management in Nebraska by thirty to forty years.[98] The legislature did adopt a permit system[99] for the pumping of irrigation water from pits located within fifty feet of any stream—the lawmakers had reached the limited understanding that pumping within that proximity to a stream could have a negative impact on surface flow. The idea that everything in the hydrologic cycle is connected with everything else in the hydrologic cycle had found a small receptive zone in the legislative collective mind, but the big picture continued to elude them for years to come.

The 1963 legislature also revisited the 1957 groundwater preference act and enacted a definition of "domestic use" for purposes of that act. The amendment defined the term as including all uses required for human needs as related to health, fire control, and sanitation, and specifically the use of groundwater for domestic livestock as related to normal farm and ranch operations.[100] The legislature did not stray far from the supreme court's interpretation of domestic use under the constitutional surface water preference provision.

The concerned municipalities did manage to obtain some legislation favorable to their cause in the 1963 enactment of the City, Village and Municipal Ground Water Permit Act, which allowed for groundwater transfers.[101] Under this act, the Metropolitan Utilities District of Omaha sought a transfer permit allowing it to pump water from a well field located on the bank of the Platte River and on an island in the Platte five miles west of its confluence with the Missouri. Seven percent of the water pumped was to be groundwater, and the remainder induced recharge water from the Platte. Objections came in from riparian owners who alleged that the district, in effect, was seeking to transfer surface water to another basin. When the director granted the permit, the objectors appealed.[102] The record showed that the transfer would cause the objectors no injury: just compensation was not an issue in the case. The supreme court could find no directly applicable legislation within the scanty patchwork of groundwater-related laws on the books that would prohibit the transfer. It looked to the state constitution and found that the general language of article XV, section 4, was the state's only declared public policy that might relate to groundwater in this context. That section declared that water—not surface water, not groundwater, but *water*—is a natural want. If the water was to be used reasonably for a beneficial purpose without waste by a permit applicant, the supreme court could see no cause to deny the permit.[103]

The Natural Resources Districts and the Groundwater Management Act

Through the years since statehood, the legislature, in traditional Nebraska fashion, had created so many single- or special-purpose local governmental entities that not even the lawmakers themselves could easily decide who held the authority to deal with which problems. In 1939, there were 172 special-purpose districts operating in the state. By the late 1960s, there were 500 resource-related special-purpose districts alone. These entities, usually organized along artificial boundaries, included irrigation districts, drainage districts, soil and water conservation districts, watershed districts, rural water districts, watershed planning boards, advisory watershed improvement boards, reclamation districts, mosquito abatement districts, public power and irrigation districts, sanitary improvement districts, and sanitary drainage districts. Their duties and powers were spread across an organizational grid so complex that points of accountability were hard to find.

The 1969 legislature took up the problem and, with considerable political difficulty, created twenty-three[104] Natural Resources Districts (NRDs), each governed by an elected board and organized along natural river basin boundaries instead of artificial political boundaries.[105] On July 1, 1972, 154 special-purpose districts were merged into the NRDs, an event that could not be allowed to pass without the seemingly mandatory filing of litigation to challenge the creation and existence of the new entities. Lancaster County District Court judge William C. Hastings—the future chief justice—initially drew the case. On June 29, 1972, he denied the plaintiffs' request for a temporary injunction that would have prevented the NRDs from coming into operation.[106] District judge Samuel Van Pelt heard the trial and denied a permanent injunction on July 26, 1973.[107] The only constitutional problem Judge Van Pelt found dealt with membership on the state-level Natural Resources Commission. The supreme court affirmed Judge Van Pelt's decision and removed the last obstacle to full NRD operations.[108]

The NRDs are statutorily charged with twelve areas of responsibility: erosion prevention and control; prevention of damage from flood water and sediment; flood prevention and control; soil conservation; water supply for any beneficial uses; development, management, utilization, and conservation of groundwater and surface water; pollution control; solid waste disposal and drainage; drainage improvement and channel rectification; development and management of fish and wildlife habitat; development and management of recreational and park facilities; and forestry and range management. Unlike their predecessor special-purpose districts, they have taxing power, eminent domain power, and all powers necessary or incidental to discharging their responsibilities.[109] They also have the power to adopt all necessary rules and regulations to carry out their purposes.[110]

In 1975, the legislature gave the NRDs broad regulatory authority under the Ground Water Management Act (GWMA).[111] The act empowered the NRDs, with the approval of the director of the Department of Natural Resources, to create groundwater control areas for the enforcement of groundwater withdrawal restrictions, among other things. Three NRDs have done so to date. In a unique dual system, the twenty-three NRDs administer the state's groundwater resources generally independently of each other and free from most state-level control, while the Department of Natural Resources administers the state's surface waters.

The GWMA has been criticized for numerous shortcomings. For example, groundwater control areas could be instituted only after someone in the affected area asked the local NRD board to do so. The NRD, in turn, had to request a hearing before the director of water resources, who could then designate the area. Michael C. Klein, for example, opined that "[t]his type of system, while commendable in that it provides for local formulation of issues and consequent controls, is tantamount to a legislative failure to deal with the problem."[112] The act failed to recognize the hydrological relationship between groundwater and surface water, which by 1975 was scientifically beyond doubt; failed to deal with proprietary interests in groundwater; failed to create any systematic way of dealing with groundwater preferences; and failed to address interbasin transfers, among other deficiencies.[113] Klein also predicted that the GWMA would encourage litigation based on proprietary issues. But Klein did not recognize how far the legislature had come from its earlier do-nothing approach.

While the legislature was creating excitement in the 1970s,[114] the supreme court was not permitted to rest. First, the court dealt with one of the ever-present diffused surface water conflict cases.[115] Then the court invalidated a rural water district's proposed transfer of groundwater from one tract of land to another, nonoverlying tract.[116] One of the decade's big decisions was *Prather v. Eisenmann,*[117] a well interference dispute involving domestic users and irrigation users, in which the supreme court departed for the first time from its traditional reasonable use rule. Domestic water users had drilled wells into an artesian aquifer, the pressure from which forced the water close to the surface and created a shallow water table. Withdrawals from irrigation wells subsequently drilled into the same aquifer reduced the water pressure, caused the water level to drop below the reach of the domestic wells, and resulted in the destruction of the domestic well pumps. Litigation for damages ensued. The district court ruled in favor of the domestic well owners and awarded them damages, relying on both the groundwater preference statute and the test created by the *Restatement (Second) of Torts,* section 858A.[118]

The supreme court used only the preference statute in developing its own two-step approach for trial courts to use in similar situations. David Aiken described the approach this way: first, if groundwater users applying the resource for the same purposes come into conflict, they should be allowed to use only a proportional share of the available groundwater supply; and, second, if a conflict develops between parties using the groundwater for different purposes, then the preference statute will be applied. As Aiken noted, *Prather* demonstrated that well spacing may reduce well interference conflicts but will not necessarily prevent them.[119] Despite its importance, *Prather* was not the major decision of the period.

In its 1936 decision in *Osterman v. Central Nebraska Public Power and Irrigation District,*[120] the supreme court had ruled unanimously that interbasin transfers of surface water were not permitted under section 59 of the 1895 irrigation act, which provided

> The owner or owners of any irrigation ditch or canal shall carefully maintain the embankments thereof so as to prevent waste therefrom, and shall return the unused water from such ditch or canal with as little waste thereof as possible to the stream from which such water was taken or to the Missouri river.

As Oeltjen, Harnsberger, and Fischer have noted, the court simply declared the last phrase, "or to the Missouri river," inapplicable to the issue at hand in *Osterman.*[121] Despite that problem, they believed that most critics of *Osterman* realized that the result may have been correct for its time.[122] A less charitable characterization might point out that the *Osterman* court, in interpreting section 59 the way it did, was thinking extremely narrowly and chose simply to ignore the last phrase—but made it appear that they were not ignoring it by declaring it "inapplicable." In 1980, section 59 of the 1895 irrigation act was still in force, and in the same language, except that "River" had been capitalized. *Little Blue Natural Resources District v. Lower Platte Natural Resources District*[123] (*Little Blue I*) reached the supreme court in that year.

The Little Blue NRD had applied to the department for a permit to appropriate Platte River water and to apply it to lands in the Blue River basin. The basins of the Platte and Blue rivers are not connected in any way. The director determined that sufficient unappropriated water was available but denied the permit, relying on the authority of *Osterman.* On appeal, a unanimous supreme court expressly overruled *Osterman.* The *Little Blue* court found that nothing in the state constitution prohibited interbasin transfers and that it encouraged the application of the waters of every stream to the benefit of all the people of the state, not only to privileged basin residents.[124]

The true importance of the *Little Blue I* decision lies in its making possible the use of transferred surface waters to recharge areas in which groundwater has been mined.[125] Two years later, the supreme court decided *Little Blue II,*[126] ruling that water projects must comply with state endangered species acts and temporarily halting water development in the state.[127]

While the Nebraska Supreme Court was deciding *Little Blue I,* an interstate groundwater transfer case was waiting in the wings, *State ex rel. Douglas v. Sporhase.*[128] The legislature had enacted an interstate groundwater transfers act[129] in recognition of the many landowners whose property lines crossed Nebraska's state borders—and to facilitate Nebraskans' continued use of Kansas groundwater.[130] The act contained a reciprocity clause that allowed interstate transfers of Nebraska groundwater only if the state to which the water was to be transferred had also enacted a similar law. Sporhase and her partner, Moss, bought a tract of land, part of which lay in Nebraska and part of which lay across the border in Colorado. Colorado would not permit Sporhase and Moss to drill a well on the Colorado side, nor did that state have a law that fulfilled the requirements of Nebraska's reciprocity clause. After learning that Sporhase and Moss were transferring Nebraska groundwater to the Colorado side, Nebraska brought suit in state district court. There Sporhase and Moss contended, among other things, that the Nebraska act violated the interstate commerce clause of the federal Constitution.[131]

The state district court upheld the validity of Nebraska's interstate groundwater transfer law, concluding that its effect on interstate commerce did not reach the level of an unreasonable burden. The Nebraska Supreme Court relied on the state constitution, declared Nebraska groundwater not an article of commerce, and so did not reach the question of whether the act impermissibly burdened interstate commerce. The state supreme court's position flowed naturally from the proposition that Nebraska groundwater cannot be reduced to a state of private possession:

> The term "commerce" implies that the commodity must be capable of being reduced to private possession and then exchanged for goods or services of the same or similar value. An analysis of Nebraska case law and statutes demonstrates that Nebraska law has never considered groundwater to be a market item freely transferable for value among private parties, and therefore not an article of commerce.[132]

Analyzing the question of whether the statute deprived Sporhase and Moss of liberty or property without due process, the supreme court concluded that

> conditioning a landowner's right to transfer groundwater either within or without Nebraska does not deprive [that landowner] of

> a property right, since, under Nebraska common law, groundwater may not be transferred off the overlying Nebraska land at all unless the public, owners of the water, grant that right. Not being at liberty to transport groundwater without public consent and having no private property right in water itself, appellants are deprived of neither liberty nor property.[133]

On appeal, the U.S. Supreme Court restricted its review to three constitutional questions: (1) whether groundwater is an article of commerce; (2) whether the Nebraska statute impermissibly burdened interstate commerce; and (3) whether Congress had granted the states authority to regulate groundwater in a way that would be impermissible under the commerce clause without congressional approval.[134] The Court concluded that groundwater *is* an article of commerce, that a state can regulate groundwater within some limits, and that the Nebraska statute did not contravene federal constitutional requirements except in its reciprocity clause. Although the Court ruled that the particular reciprocity clause in Nebraska's statute violated the federal Constitution, it also went to unusual lengths to explain how a state could devise a reciprocity clause that would not violate constitutional requirements.[135] Back in Nebraska, the state supreme court ruled that the reciprocity clause was severable and that the rest of the act was valid.[136] After that, Sporhase and Moss obtained their permit.

Richard C. Harnsberger, Josephine R. Potuto, and Norman W. Thorson reached six major conclusions in their analysis of *Sporhase:* Nebraska groundwater remains publicly owned and can be extensively regulated, even to the point of prohibiting all new well installations and all other new uses. The Court's ruling was "exceedingly narrow" because it invalidated only that particular reciprocity clause, and the effect of the decision on Nebraska water law has been negligible. Although the Court noted that no constitutional obstacles prevent Congress from taking over exclusive management of water resources, the Court still reaffirmed the states' leadership in the area of water law and administration. Finally, in times of severe shortage the Court would allow states to favor their own citizens, albeit only on a showing of substantial evidence connecting any ban on interstate transfers with the stated purpose of conserving and preserving water resources.[137]

The 1984 legislature adopted an instream flow appropriation act[138] that earned a constitutional challenge in *In re Application A-16642.*[139] The Game and Parks Commission applied for an instream flow appropriation to protect trout habitat, and numerous opponents objected. The director partially granted the requested permit, the first ever instream appropriation in the state. On appeal, the objectors argued that the instream flow statutes adopted in LB 1106 (1984) violated the 1920 water amendments to the state constitution: without an actual diversion, an instream flow appropriation could not qualify as the sort of appropriation the constitution authorized. Several states do still call for an actual diversion, basing the requirement on their peculiar appropriative rights histories, especially the practices of early mining communities. But Nebraska had no such mining communities, and after exhaustively reviewing the history of appropriation in Nebraska and contrasting the state constitutions of the jurisdictions that do require actual diversions, the supreme court rejected the objectors' arguments and affirmed the director's decision.[140]

In *Northport Irrigation District v. Jess,*[141] the supreme court was called upon to resolve the issue of whether water that has returned to a natural watercourse by seepage from the ditch into which it was diverted remains subject to the ditch company's appropriation or whether it has returned to its original state and is again subject to state administration. In the course of deciding that the seepage had returned to streamflow, the supreme court taught a brief history lesson drawn from a Montana case:

> The corpus of running water in a natural stream is not the subject of private ownership. "Such water is classed with light and the air in the atmosphere. It is publici juris or belongs to the public. A usufructuary [*sic*] right or right to use it exists, and the corpus of any portion taken from the stream and reduced to possession is private property so long only as the possession continues. These principles were borrowed by the common law from the civil law and in turn were borrowed by the law of appropriation from the common law."[142]

The Montana court had traced the doctrine all the way back to the Institutes of Justinian and asserted that Blackstone had discussed the civil law origins of the law of running water and showed that it was brought into the common law. American state courts rarely advert to the civil law as the source, or as a source, of common-law principles, and when they do, it becomes notable.

The drought of the 1970s had its effect on Nebraska irrigation activities. August 1976 set records for the depth of drought conditions, exceeding even the 1930s Dust Bowl: forty-one Nebraska counties were designated drought disaster areas. The drought conditions brought about a new record in groundwater pumping levels, and water tables fell by 100 to 120 feet in some afflicted areas. Sales of center pivot irrigation units also set a record in 1976 and 1977.[143] Three NRDs established groundwater control areas under the 1975 GWMA; three others tried and failed. The Upper Republican NRD established its control area in August 1977; the Upper Big Blue NRD in December 1977; and the Little Blue NRD in January 1979.[144] The declaration of a control area allowed an NRD to set groundwater withdrawal allocation limits, to check on irrigators to assure compliance, and to seek enforcement in cases of noncompliance.

Bamford v. Upper Republican Natural Resources District,[145] a challenge to the constitutionality of control area withdrawal restrictions, sometimes is described as a takings clause case or a case dealing with just compensation for damages resulting from the NRD's ordered reduction in groundwater withdrawals.[146] It was neither. The appellants failed to raise the issue. As a result, the supreme court refused to entertain the argument, deciding only that this aspect of the case was not properly before the court. *Central Nebraska Conservation Association & Central Platte Natural Resources District v. City of Fremont*[147] is another decision likely to be cited for something that the supreme court did not do. The court did *not* deny a groundwater appropriation for intentional groundwater storage. The appellant corporation initially had applied for an intentional groundwater storage appropriation, but by the time the director heard the application, the company had changed its plans so substantially that the application no longer could be characterized as such. The court affirmed the director's decision, finding that his actions were not arbitrary, capricious, or unreasonable on the basis of the evidence presented.

By 1986, Nebraska had become the nation's leader in both sales and usage of center pivot irrigation units. Kepfield theorized that the 1980s center pivot explosion in the Sandhills region of western Nebraska may have been the catalyst for a major attitudinal change among the indigenous irrigators and ranchers of that region, people who tend to pride themselves on their stewardship of the land without the need for government regulations. So-called outside investors bought up Sandhills land cheaply, installed center pivots, inflated land values, and then sold at a profit and left. Before they left, however, these outside investors cut off hilltops and plowed them into ravines to produce a more level surface for the center pivot units, and this on land classified as highly erodible. When the farm economy turned sluggish in the 1980s, many of these corporate operations failed, and the investors simply left the pivots to rust. The abandoned lands became deserts. The Nebraska water law of the day offered the ranchers little help. It was too weak, and the NRDs were too weak. Then in 1988 there came another drought and another explosion in well irrigation and its concomitant groundwater depletion.[148] The stage was set for real reform.

It took a few more years, a number of small additions to the powers of the NRDs and the state agencies, a new governor, a new chair of the natural resources committee in the legislature, the protracted efforts of the governor's water council, some major educational sessions, pressure from the state of Kansas, multiple compromises, and a victory over a filibuster, but something real finally got done—Nebraska's integrated water management legislation, LB 108 (1996). Too many questions remain, even after ten years, to advance any definitive assessment of its results. However, just getting it passed and seeing the adoption of integrated management plans in three NRDs[149] may constitute success. Nebraska actually may be catching up with the other western water law states. Stephen Mossman, a water council member throughout the LB 108 struggle, expressed this belief:

> The long-term debate, not about the term "conjunctive use" but about integrated management, did not end with the passage of LB 108. However, LB 108 was the greatest step to date. By building upon the Groundwater Management and Protection Act and maintaining local control, LB 108 will hopefully be successful in bringing about equity among Nebraska's water users and protecting Nebraska's irrigated agriculture economy.[150]

Since that time, the legislature has strengthened LB 108 by enacting LB 962 (2004). Under these two statutes, NRDs can declare river basins fully appropriated—or overappropriated—and exercise water marketing authority. In addition,

> [w]hile LB 962 stops short of establishing an explicit tributary groundwater system, it does so implicitly in basins designated as overappropriated. Hydrologically connected groundwater withdrawals may be reduced, new well-drilling stopped, and surface water rights retired. Certainly the DNR and NRDs have a wide range of management alternatives to achieve a more sustainable water system in overappropriated basins.[151]

Such was the state of Nebraska water law by 2004. This chapter stops with the enactment of LB 962 (2004) and very brief mention of the bill. A highly contentious current case has engendered three supreme court decisions before even having reached the trial stage, and LB 962 became involved in the litigation.[152] Because that matter is pending as this book goes to press, this chapter will not address the case in order to avoid the appearance of advocating any particular position or result. Readers wanting to know more may consult law review articles presenting extensive discussion of the case.[153]

Thomas Oliver, an attorney in the *Spear T* case, underscored the reality that human-made law does not tame Mother Nature when he observed: "Nebraska's new water law, passed last year [2004] as Legislative Bill 962, creates a procedure to help manage water disputes but doesn't put water back in streambeds."[154]

Nebraskans have expended considerable legislative, judicial, and administrative efforts in their attempt to control the human activities that affect the water supplies available for beneficial, or even for any, use. To move from no apparent control mechanisms to creation of a legal framework for integrated management of Nebraska's surface and groundwater resources took roughly 140 years. From the highlights of Nebraska's state water law history presented in this chapter, one can predict several things. The Nebraska Supreme Court will remain a major player in Nebraska water law development. When conflicts develop because of unclear or incomplete legislation—and especially in the absence of legislation—the contesting parties will look to the courts for resolution. In the absence of legislative guidance, the courts will continue to look to the common law when necessary. Finally having awakened to the need to act, the legislature likely will continue to do so. But the operations of the hydrologic cycle will not be subjected to human laws. The hydrologic cycle will continue to follow nature's laws. As this chapter has shown, humans' choices can assist or humans' choices can do untold damage. The saga goes on.

Notes

1. The hundredth meridian roughly marks the boundary between the part of the United States that receives an annual average rainfall exceeding twenty inches from the part that receives less than twenty inches. Sam S. Kepfield, "El Dorado on the Platte: The Development of Agricultural Irrigation and Water Law in Nebraska, 1860–1895," *Nebraska History* 75, no. 3 (1994): 232–43; Charles J. Bicak, "The Rigors of

Existence: The Role of Water," and Conrad T. Moore, "Hydrological Drought as a Settlement Inhibiting Factor," both in *Water on the Great Plains: Issues and Policies,* ed. Peter J. Longo and David W. Yoskowitz (Lubbock: Texas Tech University Press, 2002), 3–15 and 16–34, respectively.

2. On the east side of Ohio, annual rainfall averages thirty-nine to forty inches. At Omaha, annual rainfall averages drop to twenty-nine to thirty inches, and at Scottsbluff, annual rainfall averages only fifteen inches. *About.com,* "100th Meridian," http://geography.about.com/od/learnabouttheearth/a/100thmeridian.htm.

3. Kepfield, "El Dorado on the Platte," 240.

4. The western water law states are Arizona, California, Colorado, Idaho, Kansas, Montana, Nebraska, Nevada, New Mexico, North Dakota, Oklahoma, Oregon, South Dakota, Texas, Utah, Washington, and Wyoming. J. David Aiken, "Nebraska Ground Water Law and Administration," *Nebraska Law Review* 59, no. 4 (1980): 918n1.

5. The intersections among Nebraska's water laws and those of other states, Nebraska's interstate compacts relating to water law, and most federal water law lies outside the scope of this chapter. For information on these topics, readers may wish to consult Longo and Yoskowitz, *Water on the Great Plains;* Robert D. Kuzelka and Charles Flowerday, *Flat Water: A History of Nebraska and Its Water* (Lincoln: Conservation and Survey Division, Institute of Agriculture and Natural Resources, University of Nebraska–Lincoln, 1993); J. David Aiken, "The Western Common Law of Tributary Ground Water: Implications for Nebraska," *Nebraska Law Review* 83, no. 2 (2004): 541–95; Aaron M. Popelka, "The Republican River Dispute: An Analysis of the Parties' Compact Interpretation and Final Settlement Stipulation," *Nebraska Law Review* 83, no. 2 (2004): 596–629; J. David Aiken, "Balancing Endangered Species Protection and Irrigation Water Rights: The Platte River Cooperative Agreement," *Great Plains Natural Resources Journal* 3, no. 2 (1999): 119–58; J. David Aiken, "Protecting the Hidden Resource: The Quiet Crisis in Nebraska Pesticide and Ground Water Protection Policies," *Creighton Law Review* 26, no. 3 (1993): 639–96; Eric Pearson and J. David Aiken, "Protecting Public Values in the Platte River," *Creighton Law Review* 20, no. 2 (1987): 361–84; J. David Aiken, "New Directions in Nebraska Water Policy," *Nebraska Law Review* 66, no. 1 (1987): 8–75; J. David Aiken, "Nebraska Ground Water Law and Administration," *Nebraska Law Review* 59, no. 4 (1980): 917–1000; and J. David Aiken, "The National Water Policy Review and Western Water Rights Law Reform," *Nebraska Law Review* 59, no. 2 (1980): 327–44.

6. According to Kepfield, "the need for irrigation came about only as settlers crossed the 100th Meridian into a semi-arid region prone to droughts." Kepfield, "El Dorado on the Platte," 232.

7. For settlers' states of origin, see introduction, this volume, text at notes 5–12.

8. The exact nature of the common law adopted, however, varied from state to state. Connecticut chief judge Jesse Root, for example, rejected the idea that any form of English common law had become part of the law of Connecticut and maintained that the state had its own common law derived from sources independent of England. 1 Root (Conn.) ix–xv (1798).

The first Nebraska Territorial Assembly expressly adopted the common law for the territory on March 16, 1855, in a statute that provided: "So much of the common law of England *as is applicable* and not inconsistent with the constitution of the United States, with the organic law of this Territory, or with any law passed or to be passed by the Legislature of this Territory be and the same is adopted and declared to be law within said Territory" (1855 Laws of Nebraska Territory 328 [italics added]). The italicized language, reflecting the flexibility of the common law, can become critically important to what a court may choose to do with that common law, and it did become critically important in several Nebraska water law cases. The Nebraska constitution of 1866 expressly adopted as state laws all territorial laws in force when the constitution took effect until altered, amended, or repealed (Neb. const. schedule [1866]). The only important changes in the Nebraska common-law adoption statute have been the replacement of the word "territory" with the word "state" and insertion of "State of Nebraska" for "said territory." It remains in effect as this chapter is written.

Whatever else reasonably could be argued, it is crystal clear that the common law did not first apply to Nebraska in 1866, despite any claims to that effect, explicit or implicit. See, e.g., Donald Blankenau, Thomas Wilmoth, and Jaron Bromm, "*Spear T Ranch v. Knaub:* The Reincarnation of Riparianism in Nebraska Water Law," *Creighton Law Review* 38, no. 5 (2005): 1214nn77–82; and Stephen D. Mossman, "Whiskey Is for Drinkin' but Water Is for Fightin' About: A First-Hand Account of Nebraska's Integrated Management of Ground and Surface Water Debate and the Passage of L.B. 108," *Creighton Law Review* 30, no. 1 (1996): 69.

9. Morton Horwitz, *The Transformation of American Law, 1780–1860* (Oxford: Oxford University Press, 1992), 31–53.

10. *Black's Law Dictionary,* 6th ed. (St. Paul, Minn.: West, 1990), s.v. riparianism. See also the foundational American case on riparianism, *Tyler v. Wilkinson,* 24 F. Cas. 472 (C.C.D. R.I. 1827) (No. 14,312). For a historical introduction to riparian doctrine, see A. Dan Tarlock, James M. Corbridge Jr., and David H. Getches, *Water Resource Management: A Casebook in Law and Public Policy,* 5th ed. (New York: Foundation Press, 2002), 62–66, 111–58.

11. 24 F. Cas. at 474.

12. *Black's Law Dictionary,* s.v. appropriation. See also Irwin v. Phillips, 5 Cal. 140 (1855); Tarlock, Corbridge, and Getches, *Water Resource Management,* 75–83, 158–261.

13. The operative principles were stated most pithily in *Coffin v. Left Hand Ditch Co.,* 6 Colo. 443 (1882): "Imperative necessity, unknown to the countries which gave it birth, compels the recognition of another doctrine in conflict [with riparianism]. And we hold that, in the absence of express statutes to the contrary, the first appropriator of water from a natural stream for a beneficial purpose has . . . a prior right thereto, to the extent of such appropriation." For a Nebraska case interpreting the concepts of "beneficial purpose" and "waste" in extreme conditions, see *State ex rel. Cary v. Cochran,* 138 Neb. 163, 292 N.W. 239 (1940).

14. See, e.g., Lux v. Haggin, 69 Cal. 255, 10 P. 674 (1886); Clark v. Cambridge & Arapahoe Irrigation & Improvement Co., 45 Neb. 798, 64 N.W. 239 (1895); Kepfield, "El Dorado on the Platte," 240.

15. Nor does any surviving decision of the Nebraska Territorial Supreme Court (published in 1 Neb. 411–71 [1871]) deal with water or water rights. One case indexed as a "riparian" case, *Lammers v. Nissen,* 4 Neb. 245 (1876), made it to the Nebraska Supreme Court in 1876. However, *Lammers* dealt with the ownership rights of riparian proprietors in accretion lands; it did not deal with riparian water rights.

16. 1877 Laws of Nebraska 168. There were several early attempts at creating viable irrigation systems fed by surface water diversions, but few lasted. Ralph J. Fischer, Richard H. Harnsberger, and Jarrett C. Oeltjen, "Rights to Nebraska Streamflows: An Historical Overview with Recommendations," *Nebraska Law Review* 52, no. 3 (1973): 332n71.

17. Kepfield, "El Dorado on the Platte," 233.

18. Kearney Water & Elec. Powers Co. v. Alfalfa Irrigation Dist., 97 Neb. 139, 149 N.W. 363 (1914), modified, 97 Neb. 779, 151 N.W. 319 (1915).

19. Two cases dealing with other riparian issues did come out of the supreme court during this period: *Culver v. Garbe,* 27 Neb. 312, 43 N.W. 237 (1889) (construction of lease and eminent domain relating to a stream), and *Wiggenhorn v. Kountz,* 23 Neb. 690, 37 N.W. 603 (1888) (accretion). On December 31, 1889, the supreme court released its decision in *Barton v. Union Cattle Co.,* 28 Neb. 350, 44 N.W. 454 (1889) (surface water pollution).

20. 1889 Laws of Nebraska 503. Contrast this position with that of the Illinois Supreme Court when it ruled forty-seven years earlier that the use of streamflow for irrigation constituted an unnatural, artificial, and, therefore, improper use by a riparian proprietor. Evans v. Merriweather, 4 Ill. 492 (1842).

21. 1889 Laws of Nebraska 504.

22. In 1893, the legislature reduced the scope of this limitation to streams not exceeding twenty feet in width. Professor James A. Doyle believed that the 1889 and 1893 acts showed that Nebraskans had come to recognize "the importance of water in the state's economic structure" and a judgment that the "distribution [of water] on the basis of the law of appropriation is more compatible with its complete utility." Doyle, "Water Rights in Nebraska," *Nebraska Law Review* 20, no. 1 (1941): 6.

23. Fischer, Harnsberger, and Oeltjen, "Rights to Nebraska Streamflows," 337–38.

Morrissey v. Chicago, Burlington & Quincy R.R. Co., 38 Neb. 406, 56 N.W. 946 (1893), was the only water case decided in the supreme court between 1889 and 1893, and it was a diffused surface water case (in that period, the court referred to what current practice calls "diffused surface water" as "mere surface water").

24. 1894 also brought the first Nebraska Supreme Court groundwater decision, *Beatrice Gas Co. v. Thomas,* 41 Neb. 662, 59 N.W. 925 (1894) (water quality). The supreme court's second groundwater decision was also a water quality decision, *Lowe v. Prospect Hill Cemetery Ass'n,* 58 Neb. 94, 78 N.W. 488 (1899).

25. 1895 Laws of Nebraska 244. For descriptions of the politics involved in its development and passage, see Kepfield, "El Dorado on the Platte," 238–39, and Fischer, Harnsberger, and Oeltjen, "Rights to Nebraska Streamflows," 347–48. W. R. Akers is identified as the secretary of the State Board of Irrigation and state engineer in *Enterprise Irrigation Dist. v. Tri-State Land Co.,* 92 Neb. 121, 129, 138 N.W. 171, 174 (1912).

26. Fischer, Harnsberger, and Oeltjen, "Rights to Nebraska Streamflows," 348–49.

In 1902, the federal government created the agency that is now the U.S. Bureau of Reclamation. The legislature amended the 1895 act in 1911 Laws of Nebraska 495, in order to allow the federal government to appropriate, develop, and store any unappropriated surface water in connection with reclamation projects. As part of that same amendatory act, the legislature also required the agency administering the act to examine every appropriation annually and, after notice and hearing, to cancel any appropriation that had not been used in the last three years.

27. That agency has carried different names over the years, including State Board of Irrigation; State Board of Irrigation, Highways, and Drainage; Department of Public Works; Department of Roads and Irrigation; Bureau of Irrigation, Water Power, and Drainage; Department of Water Resources; and, currently, Department of Natural Resources. Ashley D. Washburn, ed., *Nebraska Blue Book 2004–05* (Lincoln: State of Nebraska, 2005).

28. The appeals from the DNR, now judicial reviews under the Nebraska Administrative Procedure Act, go first to the district courts, then to the court of appeals, and finally to the state supreme court, if the supreme court accepts them.

29. Peter J. Longo and Robert D. Miewald, "Institutions in Water Policy: The Case of Nebraska," *Natural Resources Journal* 29 (Summer 1989): 751–62.

30. 45 Neb. 798, 64 N.W. 239 (1895).

31. *Eidemiller Ice Co. v. Guthrie,* 42 Neb. 238, 60 N.W. 717 (1894), was a decision that turned on insufficient proof of irreparable damages under injunction law, not at all on water law, but in which the court had included some unnecessary discussion of water law.

32. 45 Neb. at 806, 64 N.W. at 241. On first reading, it seems there is disagreement on the source of the 1895 Akers Law, but the disagreement may be one of emphasis or precision instead of one of fact.

Kepfield concluded that the parentage of Nebraska's irrigation laws of 1877 through 1895 ran through California, Colorado, and Wyoming, in that order. Kepfield, "El Dorado on the Platte," 240. Wilbur F. Bryant, deputy reporter of the Nebraska Supreme Court, appended to the opinion in *Crawford Co. v. Hathaway,* 67 Neb. 325, 93 N.W. 781 (1903) (*Crawford III*), a historical note in which he described the Akers Law as very closely resembling the law of Wyoming and provided citations to the Wyoming statutes he had in mind. 67 Neb. 382–84 (1895) (Bryant's note was not included in the Northwest Reports publication of the case).

The Nebraska Supreme Court itself, in *Crawford III,* referred to the specific sections at issue as borrowed from the statutes of Wyoming. In *Clark,* the supreme court said that Nebraska's irrigation laws, as of September of 1895, were modeled after California's statutes. Fischer, Harnsberger, and Oeltjen said the 1895 irrigation law was copied almost verbatim from Wyoming's statutes. Fischer, Harnsberger, and Oeltjen, "Rights to Nebraska Streamflows," 347.

In his 1941 article, Doyle wrote that the 1895 act was "[a] complete revision of the irrigation laws, taking as a model the Wyoming irrigation code, which adopted the

'Colorado Doctrine' of prior appropriation as the basis of water rights" (footnotes in original deleted). Doyle, "Water Rights in Nebraska," 7.

33. 45 Neb. at 806, 64 N.W. at 241.

34. 60 Neb. 754, 84 N.W. 271 (1900) (opinion by Norval, C.J.); 61 Neb. 317, 85 N.W. 303 (1901) (opinion by Norval, C.J.); and 67 Neb. 325, 93 N.W. 781 (1903) (opinion by Holcomb, J.). In both the 1941 Doyle article and the Fischer, Harnsberger, and Oeltjen, "Rights to Nebraska Streamflows" article, the authors refer to this case as *Crawford County v. Hathaway.* The reports, both Nebraska and Northwest, show the name of this case as *Crawford Company v. Hathaway.*

35. See chapter 3, this volume.

36. 67 Neb. at 342, 93 N.W. at 786.

37. Ibid., 357–58, 93 N.W. at 792.

38. In *Wasserburger v. Coffee,* 180 Neb. 149, 141 N.W.2d 738 (1966), the supreme court rethought that date and reestablished it as the date the 1895 irrigation law was adopted.

39. 60 Neb. at 762, 84 N.W. at 273.

> It is well known that, beginning with the eastern line of the state, the annual amount of rainfall steadily diminishes until the western line of the state is reached. But can any one tell at what particular point in the state the common law rule applicable to riparian owners would cease and the rule said to be better applicable to the less favored portions of the state would begin? Such a rule would merely tend to breed "confusion worse confounded," and would be an assumption of legislative powers by this court, inhibited by the constitution.

40. 67 Neb. at 334–35, 93 N.W. at 783–84.

41. Ibid., 345–47, 93 N.W. at 787–88.

42. Fischer, Harnsberger, and Oeltjen, "Rights to Nebraska Streamflows," 361. See 1895 Laws of Nebraska 260.

43. 67 Neb. at 371–72, 93 N.W. at 797.

44. 67 Neb. 500, 93 N.W. 713 (1903).

45. Future Nebraska Law College dean and Harvard Law School dean. In 1901, the legislature had authorized the appointment of commissioners to assist the three-member supreme court with its overwhelming case load. Pound was one of them. See chapter 15, this volume.

46. 67 Neb. at 515–16, 93 N.W. at 718.

47. Pound's opinion in *Meng* is worth reading for its elegance.

48. 70 Neb. 109, 96 N.W. 996 (1903).

49. The trial judge was George W. Norris, future U.S. senator from Nebraska.

50. McCook Irrigation and Water Power Co. v. Crews, 70 Neb. 115, 102 N.W. 249 (1905).

51. Ibid., 123, 102 N.W. at 252. On the same day it issued its *Crews* decision, the supreme court also issued its decision in *Cline v. Stock,* 71 Neb. 79, 102 N.W. 265 (1905), *rev'g on rehearing* 71 Neb. 70, 98 N.W. 454 (1904), another injunction action—

and another appeal from a decision by Norris—which Fischer, Harnsberger, and Oeltjen in "Rights to Nebraska Streamflows" incorrectly describe as a case in which the court denied a lower riparian manufacturer an injunction against an upper and subsequent appropriator-irrigator (362). As long as the appropriator complied with the conditions of his permit, the lower riparian could not enjoin the appropriator's continuing water use but could seek damages, if any.

The supreme court did no such thing. The supreme court commission would have allowed a trial. The trial court and the supreme court ruled that the plaintiff had failed to allege facts sufficient to qualify for a trial. That result was unfortunate because the plaintiff was a Kansas mill owner suing Nebraska irrigators for their activities in Nebraska that resulted in the total loss of streamflow in the Republican River in Kansas.

52. Doyle, "Water Rights in Nebraska," 19.

53. 90 Neb. 627, 134 N.W. 167 (1912).

54. Geer v. Connecticut, 161 U.S. 519 (1896).

55. Hughes v. Oklahoma, 441 U.S. 322 (1979).

56. 92 Neb. 121, 138 N.W. 171 (1912).

57. 1911 Laws of Nebraska 497.

58. 97 Neb. 779, 151 N.W. 319 (1915), rev'g after rehearing, 97 Neb. 139, 149 N.W. 363 (1914).

59. 94 Neb. 613, 143 N.W. 937 (1913).

60. Ibid., 616, 143 N.W. at 938.

61. Ibid., 618, 143 N.W. at 938.

62. Ibid., 143 N.W. at 938–39.

63. 95 Neb. 407, 145 N.W. 837 (1914).

64. 135 Neb. 827, 284 N.W. 326 (1939).

65. Ibid., 832–33, 284 N.W. at 329.

66. Ashley D. Anderson, ed., *Nebraska Blue Book 2002–03* (Lincoln: State of Nebraska, 2003), 253.

67. Clyde H. Barnard, ed., *Journal of the Constitutional Convention of 1919–20*, 2 vols. (Lincoln, Neb.: Kline, 1921[?]).

68. Ibid., 2:1923.

69. Ibid., exchanges between delegates Beeler and McDonald at the bottom of 2:1917 and between Selleck and Beeler at the bottom of 2:1920.

70. Section 4 provides: "The necessity of water for domestic use and for irrigation purposes in the State of Nebraska is hereby declared a natural want." Compare 1895 Laws of Nebraska ch. 69, § 65, declaring only water for irrigation use a natural want.

71. *Journal of the Constitutional Convention*, 2:1913.

72. According to the record, numerous delegates probed the intended import of Proposal 129. All of them directed their questions to Beeler and inquired as to what his intent—not the committee's intent, but *his* intent—might be with regard to various points. He provided the convention with a great deal of information relating to Nebraska's water law and lengthy, clear explanations of "his" intent and "his" understandings of the meanings of various parts of Proposal 129. His understanding and

explanations of Nebraska water law were accurate and apparently to the liking of the delegates. The convention did amend Proposal 129 in several respects, but generally retained Beeler's format and preferred language. Ibid., 2:1930–31.

73. 1897 Laws of Nebraska 358.

74. Sam S. Kepfield, "The 'Liquid Gold' Rush: Groundwater Irrigation and Law in Nebraska, 1900–93," *Great Plains Quarterly* 13 (Fall 1993): 237–50. Groundwater pumping had made great strides by the 1920s, but the costs involved and the lack of a farm credit system put the more effective irrigation systems out of the reach of most farmers. By the time the Great Depression visited Nebraska, pumping technology was taking off, but the bad times retarded the deep-well irrigation approach from spreading even faster in the farming community. The Dust Bowl of the 1930s proved the need for groundwater irrigation.

The rural electrification program initiated in the 1930s assisted immeasurably with the provision of less expensive power for irrigation. Then World War II intervened. Even the war, with its mechanical innovations and improvements, contributed to the postwar readiness for a surge forward in groundwater irrigation. Scientific knowledge still was limited until 1943.

In that year, the University of Nebraska's Conservation and Survey Division had published the first comprehensive published study and mapping of the state's groundwater resources, a project begun in 1930. Some catalyst was required to get the irrigation boom started. The Little Dust Bowl, the drought of 1952–57, performed that service.

75. Ibid., 241.

76. See Richard S. Harnsberger, Jarrett C. Oeltjen, and Ralph J. Fischer, "Groundwater: From Windmills to Comprehensive Public Management," *Nebraska Law Review* 52, no. 1 (1973): 185–92.

77. 124 Neb. 802, 248 N.W. 304 (1933).

78. Ibid., 811, 248 N.W. at 308. In *Osterman v. Central Nebraska Public Power and Irrigation District,* 131 Neb. 356, 268 N.W. 334 (1936), the supreme court, en route to its decision making transbasin diversions nearly impossible under Nebraska law, used part of its *Olson* preferred rule to support the subirrigators' right to sue: "The owner of land is entitled to appropriate subterranean waters found under his land, but his use thereof must be reasonable, and not injurious to others who have substantial rights in such waters." 131 Neb. at 365, 268 N.W. at 338.

79. Harnsberger, Oeltjen, and Fischer, "Groundwater," 193.

80. See Luchsinger v. Loup River Public Power District, 140 Neb. 179, 299 N.W. 549 (1941), discussed *infra.*

81. 140 Neb. 179, 299 N.W. 549 (1941).

82. Ibid., 181–83, 299 N.W. at 550–51.

83. Harnsberger, Oeltjen, and Fischer, "Groundwater," 196. While the legislature had funded a study of groundwater legal needs in 1940, "Regulation of the Use of Groundwater in Nebraska," *Nebraska Legislative Council Reporter* 14 (November 1940), no legislation resulted. Aiken, "Nebraska Ground Water Law and Administration," 945–48.

84. That is, groundwater withdrawals exceeded recharge capacity of the aquifer.

85. "Report of the Nebraska Legislative Council Committee on Ground and Surface Water," *Nebraska Legislative Council Reporter* 81 (November 1956).

86. 1957 Laws of Nebraska 701.

87. Irrigation well spacing can reduce the likelihood of well interference conflicts and reduce the density of groundwater extraction. Aiken, "Nebraska Ground Water Law and Administration," 950.

88. "Report of the Nebraska Legislative Council Committee on Ground Water," *Nebraska Legislative Council Reporter* 84 (November 1958).

89. 1957 Laws of Nebraska 701. See Aiken, "Nebraska Ground Water Law and Administration," 948–51.

90. Peter J. Longo, "Water Policymaking by the Courts in Nebraska" (Ph.D. diss., University of Nebraska, 1986), 26–27.

91. See note 88, *supra*.

92. 1959 Laws of Nebraska 773.

93. Richard S. Harnsberger, "Nebraska Groundwater Problems," *Nebraska Law Review* 42, no. 4 (1963): 755.

94. 131 Neb. 356, 268 N.W. 334 (1936).

95. 170 Neb. 257, 102 N.W.2d 261 (1960).

96. 124 Neb. 802, 248 N.W. 304 (1933).

97. "Report of the Nebraska Legislative Council Committee on Water Control," *Nebraska Legislative Council Reporter* 114 (November 1962).

98. 1963 Laws of Nebraska 827.

99. 1963 Laws of Nebraska 828.

100. 1963 Laws of Nebraska 835.

101. 1963 Laws of Nebraska 828.

102. Metro. Utils. Dist. of Omaha v. Merritt Beach Co., 179 Neb. 783, 140 N.W.2d 626 (1966).

103. In 1967, one year after *M.U.D.*, the supreme court limited cities' eminent domain powers with respect to water. The city of Beatrice sought to condemn land in order to obtain a water source for a desired industrial development and for no other purposes. The supreme court reaffirmed the city's power to condemn land to obtain water for domestic use but ruled that the intended use in this case was purely private and outside of the realm of the city's eminent domain power. Burger v. City of Beatrice, 181 Neb. 213, 147 N.W.2d 784 (1967). The supreme court reiterated in a 1969 decision that domestic streamflow users have priority over all other users. As a result, an upper appropriator could not dam for agricultural and recreational purposes the flow from two springs to a point that would unreasonably diminish a lower appropriator's streamflow for domestic use. The problem in the case was that the supreme court allocated to the lower appropriator the burden of proving that the upper appropriator would make an unreasonable use of the streamflow to the detriment of the lower appropriator. The lower appropriator failed in that regard because his expert witness's testimony was indefinite and inconclusive on the effects of the proposed dam. Drummond v. Vogel, 184 Neb. 415, 168 N.W.2d 24 (1969).

104. Initially twenty-four, but one was merged into one of the others due to an inadequate tax base, among other reasons.

105. 1969 Laws of Nebraska LB 1357. More than one legislative enactment was involved, but LB 1357 was the primary bill. For a detailed history of the NRDs, see *A History of Nebraska's Natural Resources Districts,* comp. Hazel M. Jenkins and ed. Robert B. Hyer (1975), accessible at http://www.dnr.ne.gov/databank/nrd/histnrd.html.

106. Judge Hastings did grant a temporary injunction relating to the NRDs' finances, which made necessary a difficult bookkeeping system but did not stop the NRDs from operating. Lancaster County District Court, docket 274, page 131, order of June 29, 1972.

107. Ibid., order of July 26, 1973.

108. Neeman v. Nebraska Natural Resources Comm'n, 191 Neb. 672, 217 N.W.2d 166 (1974). The original concept of the promoters of the NRDs envisioned the creation of "a functional vehicle at the local level with not only the authority, but also the ability to achieve the coordination and comprehensive management of the state's land and water resources." Jenkins, *History of Nebraska's Natural Resources Districts,* 21.

109. 1969 Laws of Nebraska 118.

110. Ibid., § 28.

111. 1975 Laws of Nebraska LB 577, § 26.

112. Michael C. Klein, "Groundwater Management in Nebraska without a Legislative Solution: Is There an Alternative?" *Nebraska Law Review* 57, no. 1 (1978): 81.

113. Ibid., 82–85.

114. The 1971 legislature enacted the Nebraska Environmental Protection Act, which created the Nebraska Department of Environmental Control, now the Department of Environmental Quality, with groundwater pollution control authority. 1971 Laws of Nebraska LB 939. The 1972 legislature adopted a requirement that irrigation wells used to apply chemicals to crops be equipped with check valves to prevent agricultural chemicals from polluting the groundwater by siphoning down the wells in cases of well pump failure. The 1976 legislature enacted the Nebraska Safe Drinking Water Act, 1976 Laws of Nebraska LB 821.

115. Peters v. Langrehr, 188 Neb. 480, 197 N.W.2d 698 (1972).

116. McDowell v. Rural Water Dist. No. 2, 204 Neb. 401, 282 N.W.2d 594 (1979).

117. 200 Neb. 1, 261 N.W.2d 766 (1978).

118. Terry T. Uhling, "Groundwater Preferences in Nebraska," *Nebraska Law Review* 59, no. 3 (1980): 833–34.

119. Aiken, "Nebraska Ground Water Law and Administration," 988.

120. 131 Neb. 356, 268 N.W. 334 (1936).

121. Jarrett C. Oeltjen, Richard S. Harnsberger, and Ralph J. Fischer, "Interbasin Transfers: Nebraska Law and Legend," *Nebraska Law Review* 51, no. 1 (1971): 106.

The *Osterman* court said: "It is also obvious that the words 'or to the Missouri river' can have no application to the issue to be determined in the instant case." 131 Neb. at 368, 268 N.W. at 340.

122. Oeltjen, Harnsberger, and Fischer, "Interbasin Transfers," 106.

123. 206 Neb. 535, 294 N.W.2d 598 (1980).

124. Ibid., 544, 294 N.W.2d at 602.

125. See Aiken, "Nebraska Ground Water Law and Administration," 971–72.

126. Little Blue Natural Res. Dist. v. Lower Platte Natural Res. Dist., 210 Neb. 862, 317 N.W.2d 726 (1982).

127. J. David Aiken, "New Directions in Nebraska Water Policy," *Nebraska Law Review* 66, no. 1 (1987): 8–75, discussing effects, aftermath, and responses to *Little Blue II* in depth at pages 55–57 and 72–74. Nebraska adopted its endangered species law primarily, if not solely, to qualify for federal endangered species funds. Ibid., 40.

128. 208 Neb. 703, 305 N.W.2d 614 (1981).

129. 1967 Laws of Nebraska. 761.

130. Richard S. Harnsberger, Josephine R. Potuto, and Norman W. Thorson, "Interstate Transfers of Water after *Sporhase*," *Nebraska Law Review* 70, no. 4 (1991): 764n29.

131. U.S. Const., Art. I, Sec. 8, cl. 3.

132. 208 Neb. at 705, 305 N.W.2d at 616.

133. Ibid., 710, 305 N.W.2d at 619.

134. Sporhase v. Nebraska ex. rel. Douglas, 458 U.S. 941, 943 (1982).

135. Harnsberger, Potuto, and Thorson explain the decision and its ramifications and how to deal with it in detail. The so-called negative commerce clause aspect of the U.S. Supreme Court's *Sporhase* decision has major implications well beyond the world of water law, all of which lie outside the scope of this chapter. Harnsberger, Potuto, and Thorson, "Interstate Transfers of Water after *Sporhase*."

136. State ex rel. Douglas v. Sporhase, 213 Neb. 484, 329 N.W.2d 855 (1983).

137. Harnsberger, Potuto, and Thorson, "Interstate Transfers of Water after *Sporhase*," 773.

138. 1984 Laws of Nebraska LB 1106.

139. 236 Neb. 671, 463 N.W.2d 591 (1990).

140. Ibid., 683, 463 N.W.2d at 600.

141. 215 Neb. 152, 337 N.W.2d 733 (1983).

142. Ibid., 159, 337 N.W.2d at 738, quoting Rock Creek Ditch & Flume Co. v. Miller, 93 Mont. 248, 258, 17 P.2d 1074, 1076 (1933).

143. Kepfield, "'Liquid Gold' Rush," 243–44.

144. Ibid., 247. The NRDs whose control area requests were denied included the North Platte, Lower Platte South, and Lower Loup. Aiken, "Nebraska Ground Water Law and Administration," 962.

145. 245 Neb. 299, 512 N.W.2d 642 (1994) (two cases consolidated on appeal).

146. See, e.g., Kepfield, "'Liquid Gold' Rush," 247; Mossman, "Whiskey Is for Drinkin' but Water Is for Fightin' About," 76, text accompanying note 66.

147. 240 Neb. 117, 480 N.W.2d 709 (1992).

148. Kepfield, "'Liquid Gold' Rush," 243–44.

149. J. David Aiken, "Hydrologically-Connected Ground Water, § 858 and the *Spear T* Decision," *Nebraska Law Review* 84, no. 3 (2006): 978nn78–79.

150. Mossman, "Whiskey Is for Drinkin' but Water Is for Fightin' About," 100.

151. J. David Aiken, "The Western Common Law of Tributary Ground Water: Implications for Nebraska," *Nebraska Law Review* 83, no. 2 (2004): 541–95, 591.

152. Spear T Ranch, Inc., v. Knaub (*Spear T I*), 269 Neb. 177, 691 N.W.2d 116 (2005); Spear T Ranch, Inc., v. Neb. Dep't of Natural Res. (*Spear T II*), 270 Neb. 130, 699

N.W.2d 379 (2005); and Spear T Ranch, Inc., v. Knaub and Cent. Neb. Pub. Power and Irrigation Dist. (*Spear T III*), 269 Neb. 177, 691 N.W.2d 116 (2006).

153. See, e.g., Aiken, "Hydrologically-Connected Ground Water," for a balanced analysis. For a critical review, see Blankenau, Wilmoth, and Bromm, "*Spear T Ranch v. Knaub.*"

154. *Omaha World Herald,* June 30, 2005.

SIX

J. David Aiken

FORECLOSURE MORATORIA AND FARM CREDIT MEDIATION

Nebraska's Legal Response to Two Agricultural Crises

Nebraska and the nation experienced a devastating agricultural economic crisis in the 1920s and 1930s and a difficult agricultural financial crisis in the late 1970s and early 1980s. In responding to the challenges of the Great Depression, lawmakers struggled against the constraints of an often conservative judicial philosophy. That effort to define the proper role of the state resulted in the transformation of American law and government, from a largely common-law system to our modern governmental welfare system administered through state and federal agencies. The existence and widespread acceptance of this social safety net made dealing with the more recent farm financial crisis less traumatic. In its judicial response to the state's Depression-era policy initiatives, the Nebraska Supreme Court lagged behind its state and federal peers. In the more recent farm financial crisis, a more moderate Nebraska Supreme Court played no constraining role whatsoever, reflecting judicial acceptance of a broader government role in dealing with economic crises.

The predominant judicial philosophy regarding the role of government in economic and social affairs prior to the New Deal was the substantive due process doctrine. Under this doctrine, state and federal exercise of the police power would be restrained if legislation interfered too greatly with vested rights. American legal historian Kermit Hall has identified two principal consequences of the substantive due process doctrine. First, it protected the rich from the political demands of the poor by restricting governmental policies, such as minimum wage or maximum workweek legislation, that sought to shift more of the costs associated with industrialization onto business and capital. Second, it invalidated legislation that explicitly favored one group over another, for example, statutes creating occupational monopolies. In this regard, substantive due process often hindered the economically privileged.[1] But on balance, substantive due process did slow state and federal efforts to deal with the economic crisis posed by the Great Depression.

The Great Depression began with the stock market crash of October 1929. Economic conditions were already precarious because of unbridled stock speculation in the United States and the European war reparations financial crisis. The stock market crash, however, set off an economic chain reaction, and the U.S. economy went into a tailspin. The high living of the Roaring Twenties financed by the stock bubble came to an abrupt end when Wall Street crashed, and the United States faced its gravest domestic crisis since the Civil War. At the depth of the Depression, one in four workers was unemployed. Businesses failed, banks collapsed, and people lost their jobs, their savings, their homes, their farms, and ultimately their hope for a better future. People were evicted from their homes and camped in the streets in what were bitterly called "Hoovervilles," shantytowns named for the president on whose watch the economic calamity began. In the chilling words of American legal historian Lawrence Friedman, "hunger and misery stalked the land."[2]

Farmers had been in an agricultural depression since 1920, well before the 1929 stock market crash. When World War I disrupted food production in Europe, American farmers rushed to meet the wartime demand. Farm commodity prices rose during the war, peaking in 1919 at 230 percent of the 1909–14 average. Farmland prices also rose, and new farmland was brought under cultivation to meet European food demand. At the end of the war, however, commodity prices and subsequently farmland prices crashed. In 1920, crop prices fell by two-thirds from their 1919 peak and in the early 1920s, nearly one-quarter of American farmers faced foreclosure or bankruptcy.[3]

The farm depression of the 1920s hit Nebraska hard. Farmers who had taken out mortgages to purchase high-priced land during the World War I farm boom faced falling crop prices and falling mortgage collateral values.

Farm foreclosures rose, and rural banks failed: nearly 100 in 1924, 400 in 1928, and 106 in 1929.[4] The Nebraska Legislature responded in the 1930 special session with a bank guarantee statute funded by levying assessments upon solvent banks for the benefit of the depositors of insolvent banks. The Nebraska Supreme Court showed its conservative mettle by ruling in 1932 that this statute deprived plaintiffs of property without due process of law by creating an invalid classification for the benefit of depositors of failed banks.[5]

The years 1929 through 1932 were some of the worst: Nebraska corn prices fell from sixty-seven cents a bushel in 1929 to thirteen cents in 1932, a decline of more than 80 percent. While federal agricultural programs began to provide much-needed financial relief after 1932, Nebraska farmers suffered a drought of historic proportions that created the Dust Bowl. Between 1931 and 1937, only in one year—1934—did Nebraska farmers receive normal precipitation.[6] "The dry, powdered soil began to blow, as Nebraska and all the plains states experienced a series of heavy dust storms that blotted out the sun and hope."[7] Hard times created a desperation among financially strapped farmers in the Midwest that led to the creation of America's most violent farm organization, the Farmers' Holiday Association.[8]

In response to the wave of farm foreclosures of the 1920s and early 1930s, radical Farmers' Union members began to feel that direct, self-help action was needed. By February 1932, this discontent had coalesced into a proposal for a farm holiday (not unlike President Franklin D. Roosevelt's 1933 bank holiday), during which farmers would neither buy nor sell. Organizers hoped that this withholding action would close food processing plants, empty grocery stores, and lead to federal farm assistance. In May 1932, the Farmers' Holiday Association was organized in Des Moines to implement the farm holiday. In August, member dairy farmers blockaded roads into Sioux City to raise milk prices. The strike quickly spread throughout Iowa and Nebraska, and resulted in bloody clashes between striking farmers and law enforcement officials. But the strike ended in late August, as farmers realized that they could no longer afford to withhold their products from market.[9]

Association leaders urged members to refrain from additional withholding actions until after the November 1932 presidential election, in which they hoped Franklin D. Roosevelt would be elected and would establish federal farm assistance programs. In October 1932, however, the association began its penny auction actions, in which members made bids of less than a dollar on behalf of the farmer-debtor and intimidated other potential bidders.[10] In Pennsylvania, a sheriff's sale of livestock brought bids of only three to six cents per animal and realized a total of $1.18. The livestock was then resold to the original owner for one dollar. In Illinois, a farm encumbered by a $2,750 debt was bought for $4.96 and returned to the original owner.[11] The penny auction was the most visible and widespread of the association's activities.[12]

Penny auction tactics reached Nebraska, as well. On March 14, 1933, a group of Farmers' Holiday Association members prevented a Lancaster County sheriff's sale of a farm by locking the sheriff in his office and disconnecting his telephone so that he was unable to conduct the sale or to call for assistance. The protesters were finally dispersed with tear gas, and the defendants were punished for contempt.[13]

In Nebraska, the farmers' financial distress had significant economic ripple effects,[14] more so than it would today. Farmers who couldn't pay their mortgages also had trouble paying their real estate taxes. In 1935, more than $46 million in real estate taxes were delinquent in Nebraska. In 1934, the total real estate tax levy came to just less than $31 million, so the arrears equaled nearly 150 percent of the annual levy.[15] Urban economic distress existed as well. In a rare but appropriate display of sympathy, the Nebraska Supreme Court in 1936 recognized the seriousness of the plight of destitute Nebraskans in Omaha and Douglas County:

> It is asserted in argument, and the record supports the contention, that an emergency exists unlike any previous situation. The relator is unquestionably in a deplorable situation. Social workers retail a story of poverty, want, and need of cases numerous enough to depress and sadden any one who has any sympathy and concern for his fellow men. Various governmental agencies have spent vast sums of money for the relief of those distressed by the economic conditions. It is said that there were 4,500 families in dire need at the time of the trial. Of course, before granting relief to any, the board of county commissioners is required to satisfy themselves that each comes within the purview of the statute providing for relief. However, it is estimated that it would require at least $130,000 a month to meet the responsibility. This would amount to approximately $ 1,560,000 a year. The emergency, as serious as it appears to be, does not empower the county commissioners to do anything except what they are empowered by law to do.[16]

In this case, Douglas County had exhausted its mill levy authority for poor relief and was petitioning the court for emergency authority to exceed its levy authorization and go into debt, which the court reluctantly, in view of the dire circumstances, nonetheless declined to do. The case graphically illustrated the necessity for federal assistance for the unemployed and destitute.

States sought to deal with the deepening economic crisis by adopting minimum price regulations, relief programs, minimum wage and maximum workweek legislation, and mortgage foreclosure moratoria.[17] These state actions to relieve human suffering associated with the Depression were threatened by the U.S. Supreme Court's substantive due process doctrine. The Court invalidated legislation on maximum hours[18] and minimum wages[19] but ultimately abandoned substantive due process in a 1937 decision approving minimum wage legislation for women.[20] The Court did, however, uphold Minnesota's two-year foreclosure moratorium statute in 1934 in *Blaisdell v. Home Building and Loan Association.*[21] The *Blaisdell* decision was surprising in light of unanimous state court disapproval of previous state moratoria statutes,[22] and it resulted in the survival of Nebraska's own 1933 moratorium statute in at least limited form until its invalidation by the Nebraska Supreme Court in 1938.

In order to understand the 1933 Nebraska foreclosure moratorium statute, one must first briefly review the then-extant Nebraska mortgage foreclosure procedures. The mortgagee filed the foreclosure lawsuit in district court.[23] The court was then authorized to order a sale of the mortgaged property.[24] The court could also grant a deficiency judgment.[25] The debtor could redeem the property by paying all amounts due before the property was sold.[26] If the loan had an acceleration clause, the entire mortgage balance would be due, which would require the debtor to refinance the entire debt, plus interest and unpaid taxes, if any. The debtor could request a nine-month stay before the property was sold.[27]

The 1933 moratorium statute altered this sequence by staying until March 1, 1935, any pending or future mortgage foreclosures upon the request of the debtor, except upon a showing of good cause to the contrary.[28] The debtor had to pay rent, and income from the property was applied against taxes, insurance, maintenance, and upkeep under the court's supervision.[29] The moratorium legislation reflected the economic emergency and particularly the collapse of Nebraska real estate values.[30] In 1935, the legislature extended the stay through March 1, 1937.[31] The 1935 act added a new section 20-21,165, which excepted from the moratorium mortgages executed after March 1, 1934.[32] The moratorium was extended again in 1937 to March 1, 1939.[33]

The 1933 foreclosure moratorium received its initial challenge in 1934, in *Bell v. Niemann.*[34] The mortgagee had foreclosed on plaintiff's two hundred acres of farmland in Seward County in 1932; the nine-month stay had run its course, and the land was sold in 1933. Before the sale could be confirmed, however, the debtors filed for a stay until March 1, 1935. The creditor objected on the grounds that § 20-21,159 impaired the obligation of contracts in violation of Article I, Section 10, of the U.S. Constitution. The Nebraska Supreme Court determined that the federal constitutional issue had been dealt with by the U.S. Supreme Court in *Blaisdell* and so rejected the creditor's argument. The court then made two interesting comments. First, the justices signaled their disagreement with the outcome in *Blaisdell* by stating, "*Whatever may be thought of that decision,* it is binding on the supreme court of Nebraska [regarding the federal contract clause issue]."[35] The court then invited future litigants to raise the impairment of contracts argument under the Nebraska constitution: "Whether the Nebraska moratory act violates the Nebraska Constitution is a question not presented to the district court in this case and consequently it is not determinable in the supreme court on an appeal in the same case, but is left open for future consideration."[36] The court clearly disagreed with *Blaisdell* and wanted to invalidate the foreclosure moratorium under the state constitution.

While it waited for that opportunity, the court significantly narrowed the reach of § 20-21,159 in 1935, ruling in *Clark v. Hass* that a debtor must have an equity interest in the mortgaged property in order to qualify for the statutory stay.[37] Section 20-21,159 required the court to grant the stay "unless . . . good cause is shown to the contrary" but did not define what constituted "good cause." The court found the debtor's lack of equity in the property to be good cause to deny the stay.[38] The court did little to justify its conclusion, although it did cite a concurrence to the Minnesota Supreme Court's decision in *Blaisdell,* which suggested that a mortgagor who had no equity in the property would not be entitled to a stay.[39] Whatever the court's rationale, the effect of its ruling was to extend the life of § 20-21,159, although the court significantly narrowed its scope. If the court had allowed mortgagors like Hass, having little or no equity, to claim the § 20-21,159 stay, creditors like Clark would have been able to raise the state constitutional issue at an earlier date. As it happened, no mortgagor with an equity stake in the mortgaged property came before the court until 1938, allowing § 20-21,159 to remain in effect and perhaps to provide some incidental foreclosure relief along the way.

The court interpretation in *Clark* made it difficult for creditors to respond to the court's invitation in *Bell* to challenge the moratorium's constitutionality under state law. The court had another opportunity to strike down the moratorium law in 1936 but refrained from doing so because it was not necessary to reach the issue of constitutionality in order to decide the case, the debtor having no equity in the mortgaged property.[40] The creditor in that case had argued, inter alia, that § 20-21,159 violated both the state and federal constitutions. The court found that "[t]his [case] provides interesting and attractive questions for consideration. We must, however, brush aside the temptation to indulge in such a discussion because the rule is well established . . . that a statute will not be declared unconstitutional unless necessary for a proper disposition of the pending case."[41]

Finally, in 1938, the court found what it had been waiting for—a mortgagor with an equity interest in the mortgaged property.[42] This meant that the debtor could lawfully claim a § 20-21,159 stay and, therefore, that the creditor could raise the state constitutional issue. In *First Trust Co. v. Smith,* the court found that the emergency originally contemplated in 1933 had run its course and had been replaced by a "continued depression."[43] The court might have been open to the suggestion that some sort of emergency powers might possibly be justified in a short-run emergency but not in a long-term one—an odd distinction at best (one wonders what the *First Trust* court might have done in wartime). The justices seemed to take comfort in the fact that farm debtors by 1938 had more debt relief options available to them than they did in 1933, such as favorable Federal Land Bank loans, a more stable banking industry, and federal farm bankruptcy legislation that included a five-year bankruptcy stay.[44]

These changed circumstances may have allowed the *First Trust* majority the luxury of making what it must have felt to be an otherwise inappropriate decision because it would not have to face the consequences. In any event, the court concluded that debtors had other remedies available to them and that the "temporary emergency" that had formed the factual basis for the state and federal *Blaisdell* decisions was "disapproved" by the court.[45] What exactly was being disapproved was unclear—possibly the court was attempting to distinguish the temporary economic emergency that had faced the *Blaisdell* court in 1933 from the ongoing depression that, in the estimation of the *First Trust* court in 1938, was not temporary. The court did not address the significance of the appellation "temporary," beyond its providing a legalistic basis for distinguishing the two sets of circumstances.

The court then reserved to itself the sole authority to interpret the Nebraska constitution, regardless of how the U.S. Supreme Court had ruled on essentially the same language in the U.S. Constitution.[46] The *First Trust* court ruled that § 20-21,159 did impair mortgage contracts and violated article I, section 16, of the Nebraska constitution.[47] The court further ruled that the meaning of the constitution did not change with changing circumstances and that constitutional rights could not be impaired under any circumstances by an exercise of the police power.[48]

A vigorous dissent by Justice Bayard H. Paine contended that the crisis had not yet passed and that current economic conditions more than adequately justified § 20-21,159. Citing numerous opinions in which similar legislation had been found to be a constitutional exercise of the police power, Justice Paine castigated his colleagues for hiding their heads in the sand.[49] A student note in the *Nebraska Law Bulletin* echoed Justice Paine in concluding that for the majority "not even self-preservation of the government would warrant any legislation which impaired a contract to the slightest degree" and concluded that the court's opinion could not be reconciled with *Blaisdell*.[50]

First Trust was a telling moment for the Nebraska Supreme Court, one in which the court came up short. The *First Trust* court had the choice to cling—as it did—blindly to the fading judicial doctrines of the past or to follow the lead of an admittedly closely divided U.S. Supreme Court into the future with *Blaisdell*. The *First Trust* majority chose to align itself with the *Blaisdell* minority and to look backward.

At the same time, one must bear in mind that the U.S. Supreme Court had split 5 to 4 in the *Blaisdell* decision. Decades passed before the shadow cast over progressive state and federal legislation by substantive due process doctrine would diminish. Decades passed before the U.S. Supreme Court clearly repudiated substantive due process for good. Although the doctrine remained viable in the states, even there its strength diminished over time. So, although the *First Trust* court was hardly in the progressive vanguard, its behavior was not out of the legal mainstream at the time. Nonetheless it is disappointing that only one of seven Nebraska Supreme Court justices seemed able to realize, as late as 1938, that clinging to the legal doctrines of the past was inexcusable in the face of widespread and obvious human suffering—particularly when the U.S. Supreme Court and state supreme courts around the country were trying to accommodate legislative policies and a larger governmental role in economic affairs to deal with a long-term economic depression.

Nebraska, like most other states, was unable to do much for its destitute citizens, on or off the farm, nor would it have been able to do much more even had its supreme court been more supportive of change. In the end, federal programs made the most difference in improving the economic lot of the unemployed and destitute.[51] In 1933, President Franklin Roosevelt and the Congress provided federal loans to help refinance farm debt.[52] Under the Agricultural Adjustment Act (AAA), farmers received federal payments for reducing crop and livestock production, subsidies financed through a tax on agricultural processors.[53] The U.S. Supreme Court invalidated this feature of the AAA in 1936,[54] ruling that the tax was a mere pretext used to regulate agricultural production, something the federal government had no authority to do.[55] The AAA was the second major piece of New Deal legislation to be invalidated by the Court, the National Industrial Recovery Act having been the first in 1935.[56] These were two of the judicial defeats that led FDR to formulate his court-packing plan. Although the plan was not adopted, the Court ultimately did cast off from its conservative moorings.[57] In 1938, Congress enacted a revised AAA, which paid farmers for planting soil-conserving crops on what the original AAA would have designated as set-aside acres. The Supreme Court upheld the constitutionality of the revised AAA in 1942, a complete reversal of its earlier ruling.[58] The revised act became the foundation for the current federal farm aid program.[59]

The federal government attempted to help farm debtors by adding the Frazier-Lemke agricultural bankruptcy option to federal the bankruptcy statutes in 1934.[60] Frazier-Lemke, which included a five-year bankruptcy stay,[61] was unanimously invalidated by the U.S. Supreme Court in 1935 for unduly interfering with the rights of creditors.[62] Congress quickly adopted a revised Frazier-Lemke farm bankruptcy statute in 1935,[63] and the Supreme Court unanimously upheld its constitutionality in 1937.[64] Frazier-Lemke expired in 1949, and permanent farm bankruptcy legislation remained an unresolved issue until the adoption of chapter 12 family farm bankruptcy legislation in 1986.[65] Financially distressed farmers had other options in addition to bankruptcy: the 1933 Farm Credit Act, for example, contained a voluntary farm debt conciliation program, under which committees of local farmers and creditors could propose what we would call today farm workout plans or restructuring plans to avoid foreclosure and bankruptcy.[66] This voluntary debt adjustment program foreshadowed the Nebraska farm credit mediation program adopted in 1986.

Farmers enjoyed generally better prices during World War II, and federal price supports helped prevent a recurrence of the agricultural depression of the 1920s and 1930s.[67] The farm program safety net worked well in Nebraska, where farmers did not face a severe financial crisis until the 1980s.[68] This crisis had its origins in the USSR's major wheat purchase in

1972. Up to this time, a major USSR policy objective had been agricultural self-sufficiency, the ability to feed the population without large foreign agricultural imports. However, inefficient agricultural practices plus several crop failures led to the decision to secretly purchase wheat on the world market. The Soviets were very clever in approaching the market, well understanding that if their interest in purchasing large quantities of wheat were known, wheat prices would rise significantly. The Soviets played the game well and purchased their wheat at the then-prevailing world price.[69] Wheat prices soared, not to return to their original level for several years.[70] High agricultural commodity prices were soon incorporated into higher farmland prices, and domestic inflation served to keep both land and crop prices up.

This train of events came to an abrupt halt after Ronald Reagan became president. Reagan's Federal Reserve Board raised interest rates in an effort to wring inflation out of the economy. Prime lending rates soared to more than 18 percent, rates usually charged only by credit card companies and loan sharks. As interest rates rose, farmland prices dropped. In Nebraska, the land boom that had begun in 1973 came to an end in 1981. The price of Nebraska farmland increased by 92 percent from 1972 to 1981, and fell by 68 percent from 1981 to 1987.[71] As land values fell, farm collateral values fell as well, and farm real estate lenders went from being oversecured to undersecured.[72] This loss of value led to a wave of farm foreclosures and rural bank failures.[73] In the fall of 1977, Congress enacted another farm bill that ensured four more years of crop prices below the farmers' cost of production, leading to the rise of the American Agriculture Movement, which protested the rising numbers of farm foreclosures and looked to Washington for relief.[74] This relief was slow in coming.[75] The 1985 federal farm bill did little to stem the flow of red ink on the balance sheets of highly leveraged farmers.[76] In 1986, Nebraska and federal legislation finally began to provide some legal relief to debt-stressed farmers. The new chapter 12 family farmer bankruptcy statute became law in October 1986,[77] and Nebraska adopted homestead redemption legislation in November of that year. In 1988, Nebraska followed the lead of Iowa and Minnesota by adopting farm credit mediation legislation, which led in 1991 to a more general mediation program.[78]

Chapter 12 was designed in part to allow farmers who had too much debt to qualify for chapter 13 bankruptcy to have at least a chance to reorganize. Farmers often had difficulty meeting the requirements for a successful chapter 11 reorganization,[79] and chapter 12 was largely a response to those difficulties.[80] The chapter 12 automatic stay allowed the farmer to avoid foreclosure and provided time to prepare and submit a bankruptcy reorganization plan, the same sort of breathing space that had been the objective of the 1930s foreclosure moratoria.[81]

In the 1986 regular session, the Nebraska Legislature enacted LB 999, which established a right to cure default on a mortgage or trust deed without acceleration of the loan.[82] Loan agreements typically include an acceleration clause that automatically makes the entire loan balance due upon default. The debtor can prevent the sale of the property only by refinancing the entire balance. If the debtor is unable to find a new loan to pay off the outstanding balance, then he or she loses the collateral—even if sufficient money is available to make the overdue payment and bring the loan current. LB 999 required creditors foreclosing on agricultural land to provide notice of default that identified the delinquent amount prior to acceleration; notice that the debtor had sixty days to pay the delinquent amount to reinstate the loan; and an indication whether the creditor would accept a lesser amount to reinstate the loan.[83] If the debtor complied with the conditions stated in the notice of default within sixty days, the loan would be reinstated.[84] This was a significant benefit, as it was in many cases easier to find new money (from new junior lenders, or—more often—from family) to make up delinquent payments than to refinance the entire loan.[85]

Homestead redemption was also part of LB 999. Family farm advocates, notably Nebraska's Center for Rural Affairs,[86] contended that many farmers facing financial distress wished to remain in farming and to live on the farm, even if they lost the rest of their assets. The notion was that if the family could remain on the farmstead, they had a base from which they might be able to get back into farming (for example, by renting land or by custom farming for others). At a minimum, they might be able to remain in the country, perhaps by finding an off-farm job nearby. LB 999 increased the homestead exemption from $6,500 to $10,000[87] and provided a procedure for redemption.[88] Redemption of up to 160 acres, including the farm homestead, was accomplished by the debtor's paying the appraised value of the property redeemed. If the debtor had sufficient equity in the entire property to redeem the homestead, he or she could obtain an equity homestead redemption if the remaining debt did not exceed 85 percent of the appraised value of the excess property.

LB 999 became part of LB 3, the 1986 special session Farmstead Protection Act.[89] Farm homestead redemption was the major new feature of LB 3.[90] Agricultural lenders took careful note of the LB 999 homestead redemption process and were successful in establishing a process more favorable for lenders in LB 3. The act provides two methods of homestead redemption: one for mortgages or trust deeds recorded on or before LB 3's effective date of November 21, 1986, and another for post-LB 3 mortgages and trust deeds.

Under LB 999, the debtor could redeem the homestead by paying its appraised value or through an equity redemption. This approach is used for post-LB 3 mortgages or trust deeds. However, a two-sale method is used for pre-LB 3 mortgages and trust deeds.[91] The effect of the two-sale method is to require the debtor to pay the current market value of the homestead plus any loan deficiency on the entire tract in order to redeem the homestead. In the first sale, the lender can bid the entire loan amount, which may greatly exceed the tract's current market value. In the second sale, the entire tract less the homestead is sold first, and the homestead is sold separately. If the lender does not bid at the second sale, which is the usual case, the tract minus the homestead is sold at its market value. To redeem the homestead, the debtor must pay the difference between the two sales—in effect, the homestead's market value plus any loan deficiency, if the lender bids the debt at the first sale. The LB 3 homestead waiver provision also gives creditors the opportunity to require debtors, especially low-equity debtors, to give up their homestead redemption rights as a condition of receiving the loan. Thus, it is doubtful that many farm families facing financially stress and foreclosure were able to redeem their homesteads under LB 3. Nonetheless, the statute was a worthy and helpful response to financially distressed farmers, and some have probably benefited from it.

The last important Nebraska statute enacted in response to the 1980s farm financial crisis was LB 664, the Farm Mediation Act, passed in 1988.[92] Several farm states enacted farm credit mediation legislation: Minnesota and Iowa, for example, adopted mandatory farm mediation statutes in 1986.[93] Under mandatory mediation programs, creditor participation in mediation or waiver of mediation by the debtor is a prerequisite to foreclosure.[94] Nebraska, in contrast, chose voluntary farm mediation programs.

Under the Nebraska statute, agricultural creditors must notify debtors of the availability of mediation thirty days before initiating foreclosure proceedings on a farm debt of at least $40,000.[95] Creditors need not delay foreclosure proceedings, however, even if the farmer requests mediation. Farmers involved in mediation are eligible for free financial counseling to assist them in preparing for mediation.[96] If no creditor agrees to mediate, the process stops at that point.[97] If at least one creditor agrees to mediate, the Nebraska Department of Agriculture farm mediation service will arrange the mediation session.[98] If creditor and debtor are able to come to terms, the mediator prepares a draft workout agreement for signature by the parties. The parties then have two weeks to review the draft. If no objection is received within that period, the signed draft agreement becomes final, a binding legal contract.[99] Under the federal Agricultural Credit Act of 1987, federal farm lenders must participate in a USDA-approved state mediation program if the debtor wishes to mediate.[100] Because this federal requirement to mediate applies to the Farm Credit System (formerly the farmer-owned Federal Land Bank Association and Production Credit Association), the USDA Farm Services Agency (FSA, formerly the Farmers Home Administration), and banks with FSA loan guarantees, Nebraska's voluntary mediation program is, in effect, mandatory for most farm creditors.

Although the Nebraska legislature enacted three significant statutes to help ease the plight of debt-stressed farmers, federal legislation provided the most real relief, as was the case in the 1930s. The Nebraska Supreme Court played no significant role in the 1980s farm financial crisis, at least not in terms of deciding the constitutionality of state debtor relief legislation. Perhaps none of the 1980s statutes were as bold as the 1933 foreclosure moratorium. Perhaps the legal sea change that occurred in the 1930s prompted the Nebraska Supreme Court to modify its judicial outlook. Although perhaps 20 to 25 percent of Nebraska farmers faced severe financial distress during the 1980s, a far greater number suffered during the Depression. In addition, the safety net created by the federal farm program largely succeeded in preventing the privation faced in the 1920s and 1930s. The degree of human suffering was much greater in the 1930s than in the 1980s, which is why the later event is usually referred to as a farm *financial* crisis instead of a farm crisis. The state and federal governments faced far greater economic and judicial challenges in the 1930s. State judicial conservatism would have doomed meaningful state response to the financial crisis in the 1930s, but that result was largely mooted by the ultimately more successful federal response.

The more finely tuned debt relief statutes of the 1980s could focus on the particular issues facing financially overextended farmers and probably did so as effectively as such state legislation could. The federal bankruptcy and farm credit legislation went further in providing an opportunity for effective debt restructuring for those farmers able to work their way out of their financial difficulties. The positive experience with farm credit mediation doubtless made the later implementation of a more general state mediation program much easier. And that may be the most important legacy of all.

Notes

1. Kermit L. Hall, *The Magic Mirror: Law in American History* (New York: Oxford University Press, 1989), 232. Regarding substantive due process and pre–New Deal economic regulation, see ibid., 231–38; regarding the impact of substantive due process on pre–New Deal labor legislation, see ibid., 238–45; regarding the legal struggle over the proper role of government and the decline of substantive due process during the New Deal, see ibid., 271–85.

2. Lawrence M. Friedman, *American Law in the Twentieth Century* (New Haven, Conn.: Yale University Press, 2002), 151.

3. H. C. M. Case, "Farm Debt Adjustment during the Early 1930s," *Agricultural History* 34, no. 4 (1960): 173–81; Alan Brinkley, *American History: A Survey,* 10th ed. (New York: McGraw-Hill, 1999), 848–50; R. Douglas Hurt, *American Agriculture: A Brief History,* rev. ed. (West Lafayette, Ind.: Purdue University Press, 2002), 221–22, 231–35; James C. Olson and Ronald C. Naugle, *History of Nebraska,* 3d ed. (Lincoln: University of Nebraska Press, 1997), 285–87, 305–9.

4. Olson and Naugle, *History of Nebraska,* 308.

5. Hubble Bank v. Bryan, 124 Neb. 51, 245 N.W. 20 (1932); noted, *George Washington Law Review* 1, no. 3 (1933): 402–3.

6. Olson and Naugle, *History of Nebraska,* 309–10.

7. Ibid., 310.

8. Hurt, *American Agriculture,* 264. Regarding earlier farm protests, see ibid., 203–13, 260–66. Regarding Nebraska farm protests, see Olson and Naugle, *History of Nebraska,* 175–80, 216–36.

9. Hurt, *American Agriculture,* 264–65.

10. Ibid., 265.

11. Case, "Farm Debt Adjustment during the Early 1930s," 176. More disturbingly, a Kansas real estate agent was shot and killed along the highway the same day he had handled a farm foreclosure. Ibid.

12. Hurt, *American Agriculture,* 265.

13. Lux v. State, 126 Neb. 133, 252 N.W. 897 (1934).

14. Olson and Naugle, *History of Nebraska,* 312–13.

15. Steinacher v. Swanson, 131 Neb. 439, 456, 268 N.W. 317, 326 (1936) (Paine, J., dissenting). In this case, the court ruled that legislation to allow additional time to pay delinquent property taxes was unconstitutional.

16. State ex rel. Boxberger v. Burns, 132 Neb. 31, 37, 270 N.W. 656, 660 (1937); noted, *Nebraska Law Review* 18, no. 3 (1939): 341–42.

17. Hall, *Magic Mirror,* 272; Friedman, *American Law in the Twentieth Century,* 173–76.

18. Lochner v. New York, 198 U.S. 45 (1905) (5–4 decision).

19. Adkins v. Children's Hospital, 261 U.S. 525 (1923) (5–3 decision).

20. West Coast Hotel Co. v. Parrish, 300 U.S. 379 (1937) (5–4 decision).

21. Blaisdell v. Home Bldg. & Loan Ass'n, 290 U.S. 398 (1934) (5–4 decision). See Hall, *Magic Mirror,* 277–85.

22. Note, *George Washington Law Review* 2, no. 4 (1934): 486–94.

23. Neb. Comp. Stat. § 20-2139 (1930).

24. Ibid., §§ 20-2140 through 20-2146. Regarding the sheriff's foreclosure sale process, see ibid., §§ 20-1501 through 20-1552.

25. Ibid., § 20-2141. The deficiency could not be recovered until after the property had been sold. Ibid., § 20-2142.

26. Ibid., §§ 20-1530 through 20-2151.

27. Ibid., § 20-1506.

28. 1933 Laws of Nebraska ch. 65, §1, codified at 1929 Neb. Comp. Stat. § 20-21,159 (Cum. Supp. 1933). Section 20-21,159 applied to real estate mortgages, deeds of trust, land sale contracts, and notes secured thereby. If creditors did not demonstrate good cause why the § 20-21,159 stay should not be granted, the debtor was entitled to the stay. Howarth v. Becker, 128 Neb. 580, 259 N.W. 505 (1935). On remand, the creditor subsequently proved that the debtor had no equity in the mortgaged property and was not entitled to the § 20–21,159 stay. Howarth v. Becker, 131 Neb. 233, 267 N.W. 444 (1936).

29. Neb. Comp. Stat. § 20-21,159 (Cum. Supp. 1933).

30. Ibid., § 20-21,163.

31. Ibid., § 20-21,159 (Cum. Supp. 1935).

32. Accord, Neble v. Marshall, 134 Neb. 280, 278 N.W. 489 (1938).

33. Neb. Comp. Stat. § 20-21,159 (Cum. Supp. 1937).

34. Bell v. Niemann, 127 Neb. 762, 257 N.W. 69 (1934).

35. Ibid., 764, 257 N.W. at 70 (emphasis added).

36. Ibid.

37. Clark v. Hass, 129 Neb. 112, 260 N.W. 792 (1935).

38. Ibid., 114, 260 N.W. at 793.

39. Ibid., 114–15, 260 N.W. at 793, referring to *Blaisdell v. Home Bldg. & Loan Ass'n,* 189 Minn. 422, 434, 249 N.W. 334, 339 (1933). In fact, similar language is found in the majority opinion: "The law is challenged because of its title. Attention is called to the word 'inequitable' therein. The word may be disregarded. It adds nothing except to suggest that perhaps there may be certain foreclosures where no equity whatever remains in the mortgagor, and hence those cannot be said to be inequitable so as to call for the interposition of relief." 189 Minn. at 433, 249 N.W. at 338.

40. First Trust v. Stenger, 130 Neb. 750, 266 N.W. 642 (1936).

41. Ibid., 752, 266 N.W. at 644.

42. First Trust Co. v. Smith, 134 Neb. 84, 277 N.W. 762 (1938); noted, *Nebraska Law Bulletin* 19, no. 1 (1940): 58–62.

43. 134 Neb. at 99, 277 N.W. at 770.

44. Ibid., 98–100, 277 N.W. at 770–71.

45. Ibid., 101, 277 N.W. at 771.

46. Ibid., 102–5, 277 N.W. at 771–73.

47. Ibid., 105–13, 277 N.W. at 773–77.

48. Ibid., 113–16, 277 N.W. at 777–78.

49. Ibid., 116–25, 277 N.W. at 778–82.

50. Note, *Nebraska Law Bulletin* 19, no. 1 (1940): 61.

51. Hall, *Magic Mirror,* 272–85; Friedman, *American Law in the Twentieth Century,* 151–62; Brinkley, *American History,* 875–82; Olson and Naugle, *History of Nebraska,* 317–24; Hurt, *American Agriculture,* 287–95, 300–306, 320–25.

52. Olson and Naugle, *History of Nebraska,* 318; Case, "Farm Debt Adjustment during the Early 1930s," 174–75.

53. Olson and Naugle, *History of Nebraska,* 318–20; Brinkley, *American History,* 876–77; Hurt, *American Agriculture,* 288–91.

54. U.S. v. Butler, 297 U.S. 1 (1936).

55. Friedman, *American Law in the Twentieth Century,* 159; Hall, *Magic Mirror,* 280–81.

56. Schechter Poultry Corp. v. U.S., 295 U.S. 495 (1935).

57. Brinkley, *American History,* 892; Friedman, *American Law in the Twentieth Century,* 158–62; Hall, *Magic Mirror,* 281–84.

58. Wickard v. Filburn, 317 U.S. 111 (1942). See Friedman, *American Law in the Twentieth Century,* 161–62, Hall, *Magic Mirror,* 282–83.

59. Hurt, *American Agriculture,* 291.

60. Note, *George Washington Law Review* 3, no. 1 (1934): 86–97; note, *George Washington Law Review* 5, no. 1 (1936): 80–89.

61. 48 Stat. 1289 (1934).

62. Louisville Joint Stock Land Bank v. Radford, 295 U.S. 555 (1935).

63. Note, *George Washington Law Review* 4, no. 1 (1935): 105–14; 49 Stat. 942 (1935). See John Hanna, "Adjustment of Farmers' Debts in Bankruptcy," *Nebraska Law Bulletin* 12, no. 3 (1934): 231–46.

64. Wright v. Vinton Branch of Mountain Trust Bank, 300 U.S. 440 (1937).

65. Ernest Feder, "What Kind of Bankruptcy Legislation for Farmers?" *Nebraska Law Review* 35, no. 1 (1955): 39–75; J. David Aiken, "Chapter 12 Family Farm Bankruptcy," *Nebraska Law Review* 66, no. 4 (1987): 632–94, 663–71.

66. Case, "Farm Debt Adjustment during the Early 1930s," 173–81.

67. Hurt, *American Agriculture,* 320–25, 352–57.

68. Olson and Naugle, *History of Nebraska,* 380–81, 386–87. But regarding farm financial difficulties in the 1960s, see John T. Schlebecker, "The Great Holding Action: The NFO in September, 1962," *Agricultural History* 39 (October 1965): 204–13.

69. Bruce L. Gardner, *American Agriculture in the Twentieth Century* (Cambridge, Mass.: Harvard University Press, 2002): 150–51.

70. Kenneth L. Peoples, David Freshwater, Gregory D. Hanson, Paul T. Prentice, and Eric P. Thor, *Anatomy of an American Agricultural Credit Crisis: Farm Debt in the 1980s* (Lanham, Md.: Rowman and Littlefield, 1992), 6–9, 31–33, 48–67; Steve H. Murdock and F. Larry Leistritz, eds., *The Farm Financial Crisis* (Boulder, Colo.: Westview, 1988), 15–17.

71. Aiken, "Chapter 12 Family Farm Bankruptcy," 634n5.

72. Ibid., 635.

73. Olson and Naugle, *History of Nebraska,* 391–93.

74. William P. Browne and John Dinse, "The Emergence of the American Agricultural Movement, 1977–1979," *Great Plains Quarterly* 5 (Fall 1985): 221–35; Hurt, *American Agriculture,* 369.

75. Neal E. Harl, *The Farm Debt Crisis of the 1980s* (Ames: Iowa State University Press, 1990).

76. Hurt, *American Agriculture,* 356.

77. Aiken, "Chapter 12 Family Farm Bankruptcy," 663–71. Regarding the economic and legal events leading up to the adoption of chapter 12, see ibid., 634–63.

78. Neb. Rev. Stat. §§ 25-2901 through 25-2920 (1995 Supp.).

79. Aiken, "Chapter 12 Family Farm Bankruptcy," 652–59.

80. Ibid., 663–71.

81. Ibid., 679–82.

82. 1986 Laws of Nebraska LB 999; codified at Neb. Rev. Stat. §§ 40-101, 40-110, 76-1008, 76-1012, 76-1518, 76-1519 (1986).

83. Neb. Rev. Stat. § 76-1518(1), (2) (1986); repealed, 1986 Laws of Nebraska, 3d special session, LB 3, § 21. If the default was for nonmonetary reasons, the notice would specify what actions the debtor needed to take to cure the default. Neb. Rev. Stat. § 76-1518(2) (1986); repealed, 1986 Laws of Nebraska, 3d special session, LB 3, § 21.

84. Neb. Rev. Stat. § 76-1518(3) (1986); repealed, 1986 Laws of Nebraska, 3d special session, LB 3, § 21.

85. Of course, if there were a significant deficiency, the farm debtor was better off to allow the foreclosure to proceed, especially if he or she could get a deficiency release from the lender. For many financially stressed farmers, the only hope to work their way out of debt was to have significant debt write-off or write-down. If losing some land to foreclosure meant that the total debt was lowered to a level that the farmer could service, partial liquidation could save the rest of the farm. Finding this solution was the object of voluntary debtor-creditor farm workout agreements.

86. The Center for Rural Affairs has championed many rural and family farm issues in Nebraska and throughout the Midwest, including the Nebraska Initiative 300 corporate farming amendment, the Nebraska Farm Homestead Protection Act, and the Nebraska farm credit mediation statute. The center continues to work on behalf of family farms and rural communities. The center's Web site is http://www.cfra.org/.

87. Neb. Rev. Stat. §§ 40-101, 40-110 (1984 and 1986).

88. Ibid., § 76-1519 (1986); repealed, 1986 Laws of Nebraska, 3d special session, LB 3, § 21.

89. Neb. Rev. Stat. §§ 76-1901 through 76-1916 (1987 Cum. Supp.).

90. LB 3 allows debtors to waive or disclaim their homestead redemption rights in writing. Neb. Rev. Stat. § 76-1904(3) (1987 Cum. Supp.). In cases in which creditors want to be able to foreclose on the homestead, low-equity debtors will have little choice but to waive their homestead redemption rights if they wish to obtain the loan. Debtors may also defer their homestead redemption decision until foreclosure. Ibid., § 76-1904(2).

91. Ibid., §§ 76-1912 and 76-1913.

92. Ibid., §§ 2-4801 to 2-4816 (1997).

93. Minn. Stat. Ann. §§ 583.20 through 583.32 (West 2000 and 2006 Supp.); Iowa Code Ann. §§ 654A.1 through 654A.17 (West 1995 and 2006 Supp.).

94. Minn. Stat. Ann.§§ 583.26 (West 2000); Iowa Code Ann. §§ 654A.6 (West 1995); S.D. Comp. Laws §§ 54-13-10 (2004).

95. Neb. Rev. Stat. § 2-4807 (1997).

96. Ibid., §§ 2-4804 and 2-4805.

97. Ibid., § 2-4808.

98. Ibid., § 2-4809. The farm mediation service's Web site is at http://www.agr.ne.gov/division/med/med.htm.

99. Neb. Rev. Stat. § 2-4811 (1997).

100. 7 U.S.C. §§ 5101 through 5103 (1999 and 2005 Supp.).

SEVEN

James W. Hewitt

NEBRASKA'S UNICAMERAL LEGISLATURE

Situated out on the plains, with no mountains, no natural lakes of any size, and no striking geographic features, Nebraska may seem to some an uninteresting, nondescript, run-of-the-mill backwater. But when the focus is on government, on the essential relationship between the governors and the governed, on the social contract whereby citizens yield some of their freedom to an entity that will aid and protect them, Nebraska takes a backseat to no one.

Two of the nation's most striking governmental features are found in the Cornhusker State. One is the magnificent state capitol building, which occupies a four-square-block area in downtown Lincoln and which the American Institute of Architects has designated a modern architectural wonder of the world. The building, which features a four-hundred-foot-high domed tower crowned by a nineteen-foot bronze depiction of a sower, dominates the skyline for miles around the capital city. Designed by Bertram Goodhue, winner of a competition to select the most artistic and representative plan, the structure was built over a ten-year period in the 1920s and 1930s and was paid for when completed. No bonded indebtedness here. The beautiful designs, inside and out, the iconography and the symbolism attendant to the murals, tile work, and carvings make the building one of the most striking venues in the entire world.

Occupying a good portion of the magnificent capitol is the second of Nebraska's governmental innovations, the unicameral legislature. Although unicamerals, or one-house legislatures, are not unknown throughout the world, Nebraska has the only one-house state legislature in the United States. It held its first session in 1937, seventy years after Nebraska became a state—seventy years after a bicameral legislature had revealed its inadequacies and its lack of attention to public concerns. How and why the embattled farmers of Nebraska decided to go it alone makes a fascinating story.

During the 1890s, Nebraska, like other states on the Great Plains, was a hotbed of Populism. The Populists, or People's Party, were an energetic and aggressive coalition of farmers, immigrants, and the economically disadvantaged. They felt, with some justification, that the "interests," and especially the railroads, preyed upon them, ignored their economic welfare, and made life much more difficult than it should be. Their response came at the polls, where they elected legislators and other state officers to speak for them. Their power began to wane, however, when William Jennings Bryan, the pride of the plains and the boy orator of the Platte, subsumed their organization and their concerns into the Democratic Party in the presidential election of 1896, an election Bryan lost to William McKinley and the Gold Bugs of the Republican Party.

After a brief hiatus at the turn of the twentieth century, these disaffected segments of society, along with others of like mind, turned to the Progressive movement for succor and demanded political reform. A joint committee of Nebraska's Senate and House made several recommendations in 1913 to the legislature that was to meet in 1915. Among them was a proposal to establish a unicameral.[1] The recommendations died a-borning.

John Norton, of Osceola, a member of the House of Representatives in Nebraska's bicameral system, was an ardent advocate of unicameralism. In 1917, Norton introduced a joint resolution to put forth a constitutional amendment to create a one-house legislature with a membership of sixty.[2] Although the proposal made it out of committee, it was never passed by either house.

Norton remained undaunted. In 1919, Nebraska convened a constitutional convention, which lasted into 1920. The convention considered junking Nebraska's 1875 constitution, largely modeled upon that of Illinois, but decided instead to submit to the voters some forty-one amendatory proposals. All were ratified by the electorate. Norton's proposal for a unicameral legislature, to have at least 100 members but not more than 133, did not make it to the ballot, having been laid to rest by the convention delegates on a 43-to-43 vote.[3] Norton continued to plump for a unicameral, but he took no overt action for a number of years.

The idea of unicameralism did not go away, however. In 1923, an initiative campaign to place the matter on the 1924 ballot failed to garner sufficient signatures. A bill introduced in the legislature to establish a single legislative chamber of no more than a hundred members was indefinitely postponed, a procedural kiss of death. Nothing more happened until 1933, when a bill was introduced in the state Senate to create a legislature comprising only a House of Representatives. It lost by one vote, several senators abstaining from voting on the measure.

Although initiative and legislative efforts to convert the legislature to a single house consistently failed, the cause of unicameralism found a champion in George W. Norris, senior U.S. senator from Nebraska. Norris, one of the nation's leading Progressives, had been a member of the U.S. House of Representatives before his election to the Senate in 1912. There he had successfully challenged Speaker Joseph "Uncle Joe" Cannon in reforming House rules. He also led the charge to enact the so-called lame-duck amendment to the U.S. Constitution, changing the date of presidential inauguration from March to January. Norris, a self-styled fighting liberal, was held in high esteem by the great majority of Nebraskans. He was an ardent believer in unicameralism.

For years, Norris had railed against what he believed to be the worst aspect of bicameralism, the conference committee.[4] Norris felt that it was highly secretive, and one of his primary goals throughout his career was to make government open and easily understood by the constituency. The conference committee consisted of members from both houses of the bicameral legislature and was charged with reconciling the differences between Senate and House when each body had passed bills on the same subject that differed in form. The conference committee met in secret, kept no written record of its proceedings, traded horses with vigor in order to get some acceptable legislation passed, and came back to each house with a take-it-or-leave-it result that had to be accepted without amendment. The public—and, often, many legislators—had no real voice in what had been hammered out behind closed doors by the committee members.

In a widely read and thoughtful article that appeared in the *New York Times* on January 28, 1923, Norris set forth his arguments against the conference committee and in favor of unicameralism.[5] His thesis was that the public should be able to place responsibility for the success or failure of legislation and that such answerability was impossible to attain in a two-house body dominated by the conference committee. His presentation started a number of intellectual discussions but did not bear immediate fruit.

The United States plunged into the throes of an awful depression in 1929, a depression that lasted until the country became embroiled in the chaos of World War II. In Nebraska, the worst years of the depression occurred between 1930 and 1935. Money was scarce, jobs were few, and Mother Nature added to the anguish by virtually stopping rainfall. Crops failed, milk was poured in roadside ditches because no market existed, and farmers marched to the Statehouse to cow legislators into enacting a moratorium on farm mortgage foreclosures.

In 1932, Franklin D. Roosevelt swept into the presidency by a huge margin over Herbert Hoover, whom many Americans blamed for the depression and the federal government's policy of nonintervention in the workings of the capitalist economy. Nebraska was heavily in the Roosevelt column, an aberrant result for such a strongly Republican state. As voters cast their ballots for a new broom in Washington, they also swept away many of the state's more experienced legislators, sending to the capital many new lawmakers pledged to assist Roosevelt and his New Deal.

Roosevelt's minions in Washington, however, proved far more able than those who rallied to his banner in Nebraska.[6] The legislators elected in Nebraska in 1932 proved to be as inept a lot as one could find in the Cornhusker State. Their lack of experience, foresight, and ability resulted in a dismal record. When the legislature adjourned in 1933, there was a widespread outpouring of dissatisfaction at the meager accomplishments of the inexperienced solons.

Fueled by the continuing efforts of Norris and Norton, and abetted by the academic expertise of University of Nebraska political scientist John Senning, a machine began to take shape to reconsider the issue of a unicameral legislature. A citizens' committee, called the Model Legislative Committee, began in 1933 to draft a constitutional amendment for the establishment of a one-house legislature. The committee decided that its work product should be a broad and general exposition of what a new legislature should look like, not a highly detailed, multipage document that would overwhelm voters with minutiae.[7]

Several issues did need to be decided, however. How large should the body be? Would the lieutenant governor continue to be the presiding officer? What should be the term of office of the legislators? How much should they be paid? Should it be a nonpartisan body?

Norris favored a legislature of twenty-one members. Earlier legislative bills had suggested a membership of not more than a hundred. Some felt that the proposal should not dictate the exact number but should leave it to the 1935 legislature to select between a prescribed minimum and maximum. The suggestion to let the legislature make the determination won out; the proposed amendment provided that the unicameral should consist of no fewer than thirty and no more than fifty members.[8]

Because the lieutenant governor had been the presiding officer of the Senate in the bicameral legislature, he or she was to be awarded the same post in the new unicameral. One rather pragmatic reason for this designation was that, but for these duties as presiding officer, the lieutenant governor would have virtually nothing to do except to serve as acting governor on those rare occasions when the governor left the state.

The term of office for legislators was established at two years. Norris was a firm advocate of paying a fair salary, so that the office would attract suitable candidates. He proposed an annual salary of $2,400, but the committee was of the opinion that the salary total should not exceed $50,000 per year, a figure that it ultimately lowered to $37,500 as the depression wore on and the state's fiscal condition worsened.[9] Thus, if there were thirty members in the body, each would receive a salary of $1,250 per year, whereas if there were fifty members, each would receive only $750. The salary figure was set forth in the amendment, which proved to be a mistake of major proportions. Every time the legislature seeks a pay raise, the public must vote on amending the constitution to allow the proposed raise. Legislative salaries, as of 2007, are set at $12,000 per year.

The most controversial decision reached by the committee was to make the legislature nonpartisan. Norris was vehement in his espousal of nonpartisanship. Many on the committee—as well as politicians of every stripe—felt that to include nonpartisanship in the proposed amendment might jeopardize its ratification. Many felt that voters would be confused without an indication of a candidate's party affiliation. Norris maintained that most legislators voted more in keeping with economic self-interest than in conformity with any political party platform. His unrelenting refusal to yield on this issue finally prevailed. The fact that the legislature is nonpartisan has been the single most controversial issue surrounding the body.

Nebraska law at that time required initiative petitions to amend the constitution to be signed by a number of registered voters equal to 10 percent of the total number of votes cast for governor at the general election next preceding the filing of the initiative petition (in this instance, the election of

1932). Based on the 1932 gubernatorial vote, the committee needed to collect 57,000 signatures. It collected 95,000.[10]

Norris presented a speech on a model legislature to a huge throng in Lincoln in February 1934, and this speech formed the basis for much of the 1934 campaign to pass the amendment. But Norris was not content to rest on his laurels. He spent all of October 1934 driving around Nebraska, speaking in all of the state's population centers and reaching out to rural voters by radio.[11] Norris reiterated his dislike of the conference committee, and other proponents of the measure talked about how much money a unicameral would save in salary and expenses.

Not everyone viewed the amendment as a panacea for Nebraska's ills. There was determined opposition, much of it from past and present legislators and from the most conservative elements of state society. The principal argument advanced by the opponents was that the people would be deprived of the services of three-fourths of their elected legislators. Many party officials and partisans decried the move to make the legislature nonpartisan.

Nebraska's press was almost unanimous in its opposition to the amendment. Among the dailies, only the *Lincoln Star* and the *Hastings Tribune* favored the unicameral proposal. Most of the opposition was directed at Norris, claiming that the unicameral was really only a whim of his, that the bicameral legislature was good enough for Congress and the rest of the country, and that it should be good enough for Nebraska, as well.[12]

In the crucial election of November 1934, there were two other constitutional amendments on the ballot that excited a great deal of public interest. Most compelling was a proposal to repeal Nebraska's constitutional provision prohibiting the sale or dispensation of alcoholic beverages. The other was to allow pari-mutuel betting on horse races in Nebraska, a move favored by the moneyed nabobs of Omaha and its civic organization, Ak-Sar-Ben. Political pundits engaged in an orgy of speculation as to how the three propositions would interact and whether one might affect the chances of passage of the others.

Nebraskans went to the polls in droves in November 1934 and passed all three major ballot issues. The unicameral amendment received 286,086 votes in favor and 193,152 votes against, a margin of 92,934 votes. The pari-mutuel amendment passed by a vote of 251,111 to 187,455, a margin of 63,656. The repeal of prohibition received the most interest by far, with 328,074 votes in favor and 218,107 votes against, a margin of 109,967 votes.[13] The stage was now set for the necessary legislative steps to transform Norris's grand dream into reality.

The 1935 legislature did not, as Dylan Thomas wrote, "go gentle into that good night," and it was no easy task to fix the number of senators who would open the first unicameral in January 1937. Most, if not all, of the existing legislators wanted to be in the unicameral body, and for those who were dispossessed, it was truly a traumatic experience. Finally, though, they fixed the number of senators in the new body at forty-three. John Senning, of the university's political science department, aided the legislators by preparing a number of potential district maps and attempting to reach an equitable distribution of seats across the state with an approximately equal distribution of population among districts.[14]

In 1965, the legislature voted to increase the number of senators from forty-three to forty-nine and attempted to include an area factor in redrawing the districts. The attempt was vitiated by a three-judge panel of the U.S. District Court for the District of Nebraska, which followed the mandate of the U.S. Supreme Court in *Reynolds v. Sims* and *Baker v. Carr* and adhered to the new mantra of "one man, one vote."[15]

In 1962, the voters had approved a change in the length of legislative terms, expanding them from two years to four. In 1970, they approved an amendment providing for annual sessions of the legislature: the body was to meet for ninety legislative days (as opposed to calendar days) in odd-numbered years and for sixty legislative days in even-numbered years.[16]

There have been no significant challenges to unicameralism since the 1934 election, although a few unsuccessful efforts have been made. A petition drive in 1954 that would have restored a two-house partisan legislature failed to garner enough votes to place the measure on the ballot. But that does not mean that the citizenry no longer cares about what the legislature is doing. Since 1992, voters have passed three different constitutional amendments restricting the length of legislative terms. The initiatives of 1992 and 1996 were jettisoned by the Nebraska Supreme Court, but an amendment adopted in 2000, which limits the length of legislative service to two four-year terms, has withstood judicial scrutiny. As a result, the general election in 2006 saw the replacement of almost one-half of the legislative cadre.

One reason for the lack of any real, concerted effort to return to bicameralism lies in the position taken by the U.S. Supreme Court. Because both houses of a bicameral legislature must be elected from districts of relatively equal population, both houses represent the same constituencies. Thus, it seems unnecessary to have two houses in a state legislature if they cannot represent divergent segments of society.[17]

Students of the legislature have evaluated its efficacy and have interviewed many legislative leaders on the issues of legislative rules providing for the openness that Norris coveted, especially on the issue of partisanship. Their conclusions are quite consistent.

In 1961, the University of Nebraska College of Journalism produced a thirty-six-page report on the unicameral and interviewed a number of past and serving senators about such issues as partisanship and relationships between the legislature and the governor. A great majority of the sixty-eight senators interviewed believed strongly that the nonpartisan aspect of the Nebraska Legislature was a significant strength. Senators also believed that nonpartisanship gave them a sense of independence in dealing with partisan governors. The governors interviewed for the report differed rather strongly, believing that there was a significant lack of leadership in the legislature, as in an army in which all the soldiers hold the rank of general.[18]

Legislative rules require that all but the most mundane and technical matters in proposed legislation receive a public hearing before the committee to which the bill has been referred. This requirement is in keeping with Norris's view that all public business should be publicly transacted. It is a rule unique among American legislatures. When bills are scheduled for hearing, notice is given to the public a week in advance. Witnesses may appear and testify on a bill without having scheduled an appearance.

Bills are disposed of only at regularly scheduled committee hearings. No clandestine conversations among committee members can determine the fate of proposed legislation. Bills receive up or down votes at scheduled meetings of the various committees, and although the public is excluded from executive committee sessions, the press is not. Senators' votes on each bill are recorded, and the press reports to the public how each senator voted on each piece of proposed legislation. Again, the emphasis is on keeping the law-making process open for all to see.

Senators regularly speak favorably about the openness of the process but consistently acknowledge that the requirement adds a great deal to the legislative workload. That time commitment and the problems of redistricting the legislature based on the federal decennial census seem to consume the greatest amount of legislative time and effort.[19]

The western and central portions of the state were well represented in the original unicameral, as initial efforts to outline legislative districts attempted to ensure that Nebraska's agricultural industry received its fair share of representation. But in the years since *Reynolds v. Sims* and *Baker v.*

Carr, eastern Nebraska—and especially the city of Omaha—has come to dominate the legislative body.

Nebraska has a current population of approximately 1.7 million people, more than half of whom live in the state's two metropolitan areas, Omaha and Lincoln. The forty-nine senatorial seats are allocated to smaller and smaller geographic areas in eastern Nebraska, whereas in the sparsely populated western portion of the state, one legislative district comprises 16,000 square miles and includes all or part of thirteen counties. As of 2006, Omaha and Sarpy County had twelve seats, and Lincoln had eight, together making up slightly more than 40 percent of the total legislative membership.

Federal law dictates the makeup of the districts, and although the agricultural interests in central and western Nebraska decry their lack of legislative clout, little can be done to alleviate their distress. The people live in the east, and that is where the senate seats have gone. There have been some unforeseen consequences to such redistricting, one of which is the denial to the legislature of the leadership that for years was a product of nonmetropolitan Nebraska.

There's an old saw in the Cornhusker State that says, while many ranchers and farmers may seem a bit slow to the casual observer, very few of them are in need of a guardian. Such legislative leaders as George Gerdes, of Alliance; Elvin Adamson, of Nenzel; Maurice Kremer, of Aurora; Richard Marvel, of Hastings; Jules Burbach, of Crofton; C. W. Holmquist, of Oakland; Cecil Craft, of North Platte; and Rick Budd, of Nebraska City, all came from outlying areas of the state. Kathleen Foote, of Axtell, was the first woman elected to serve in the legislature. George Danner and Ernie Chambers, of Omaha, represented African American interests with skill and passion.

C. Petrus Peterson, Fern Hubbard Orme, Shirley Marsh, Roland Luedtke, Chris Beutler, David Landis, and the nonpareil Jerome Warner represented Lincoln, while Sam Klaver, Gene Mahoney, George Syas, and Bill Skarda were all effective partisans for Omaha. Talent, effectiveness, and acceptance by their peers were hallmarks of the legislative leadership of the senators listed above. Whatever idiosyncrasies they may have possessed, their colleagues were willing to accept their direction—direction that was both enlightened and, for the most part, selfless. Nebraska's best interests were paramount in their pantheon of values.

Seats on the legislature's committees are allocated, to a significant degree, on a geographic basis among four diverse areas of the state: Omaha, northeast, southeast, and west. Individual requests for committee seats are accommodated to the extent possible, but the controlling criterion is geography.[20]

The legislature has worked consistently to make its actions and its processes open and accessible to the public. Since 1971, Nebraska educational television has broadcast coverage of the sessions on the floor of the legislature. Committee hearings are not covered, but when the legislature is in session as a whole, the red lights of television cameras signal that every word, every gesture, every nuance of argument, is open to scrutiny. Much of what is delivered is boring beyond belief. But on the rare occasions when tempers flare or ideas spark or matters of great significance are at issue, the viewing public has a ringside seat, even if four hundred miles away from the scene of action.

Senators have tried a number of remedies to cure the ills of long hours and a heavy workload, while retaining the openness for which the unicameral is justly celebrated. In 1971, the body decided that it was considering too many bills, and after much debate, it instituted a limit on the number of bills that each senator could introduce. Ten was the magic number.[21] Ten times forty-nine is 490 bills, a very adequate workload. But those who had a desire to foster more legislation found an easy way to evade the stricture: by prevailing upon committees, which operated under no such numerical limitation, to introduce those bills a senator needed to placate important constituents. The methods of evasion proved so effective that the ten-bill limit was scrapped in 1981.

To ensure that the session does not become bogged down with a number of mundane but time-consuming bills, the Speaker of the legislature has been invested with the power to set the agenda and to determine the order in which bills will be heard. Senators have worried about how much power they have given the Speaker, and they debated the issue at great length before allowing the Speaker, with the blessing of the executive board, to designate certain bills as priority agenda items. There is a great deal of angst in the legislature over which is more important—the Speaker's ability to move legislation along or the fact that all senators stand on an equal footing.[22]

One of the problems that virtually every legislature faces, and one that is quite unique in the unicameral, is that of lobbyists. George Norris viewed lobbyists with the sort of distaste that he usually reserved for the conference committee. He felt that the two operated hand in glove to keep the public in the dark about their nefarious machinations and to produce legislation that benefited no one but the conferees and lobbyists. Norris, however, did not propose any overt regulation of lobbyists, apparently believing that a small, one-house, nonpartisan body would be sufficient to deal with the problem. For the most part, it has been sufficient.

Especially helpful in regulating the lobby has been the lack of party leadership. A lobbyist wanting to pass or to torpedo legislation does not have the luxury of dealing with only a party leader or a party whip. He has to deal with enough senators to guarantee a majority of the body, some twenty-five votes, and the coalitions for and against passage may change at various stages of the bill's career.[23]

Such difficulty has not deterred lobbyists from approaching the legislature, however. In the initial 1937 unicameral session, there were 187 registered lobbyists for 43 senators. By 2002, when the number of senators had increased to 49, the number of registered lobbyists had climbed to 265.[24]

Legislators and lobbyists alike agree that, Norris's animadversion notwithstanding, lobbyists perform a necessary role in any legislature. Viewed in the most charitable light, lobbyists aid groups with related interests in exercising their First Amendment right to petition their government for the redress of grievances. They are sources of information on the policy behind proposed legislation and of factual reasons why the bill should be advanced or laid to rest. But because the general public is suspicious of their access, their funds, and their power, some form of regulation of their activity is necessary, if only to placate the public perception.

When the unicameral first convened, it occupied the legislative chamber originally designed for the House of Representatives in Nebraska's bicameral system. That body had had a hundred members, and thus the forty-three members of the unicameral rattled around in a largely empty room. Lobbyists, tipstaffs, and other assorted hangers-on occupied seats on the floor toward the rear of the chamber.

Things have changed over the intervening years. Lobbyists were relegated to standing in the rear of the room, under the balcony, and then were shunted into the rotunda of the capitol, where they sit and wait to buttonhole senators leaving the chamber or to discuss strategy with senators whose interests parallel their own on certain bills.[25] The whole picture reminds one of sparrows sitting on telephone wires.

Lobbyists must register with the clerk of the legislature and pay a fee for each client whom they represent. They must report who has hired them and for what purpose, and at the end of each legislative session they must file a report setting forth all bills they advocated or opposed. Lobbyists can entertain senators but must report their expenditures in detail. They can give legislators gifts up to fifty dollars in value but must report those gifts. They are allowed to make financial contributions to a legislator's election or reelection campaign. The emphasis is on disclosure of lobbying activities, not on restricting those activities. And both legislators and lobbyists seem to feel the system works.

Nebraska has had its unicameral legislature for seventy years as this is written. It came about because of the efforts of Populists and Progressives, experienced politicians and political scientists, and ordinary citizens, all of whom felt the existing bicameral legislature had failed to respond to the needs and desires of the citizenry. It was designed to be more open, more accessible, more efficient, and more economical, than its predecessor. It has been a noble experiment, and for the most part, it has achieved the hopes of its designers.

Business is done openly. Votes on the floor and in committee are recorded. Any citizen can find out how any legislator voted on any issue at any stage of consideration. There is no conference committee reaching a secretive compromise in a closed room.

The legislature is small—only forty-nine members—and it is readily accessible. Every bill must have a public hearing, and anyone, for any reason, can walk into the hearing and testify. Every member of the body has a voice on every issue, even though a desire for efficiency has led in recent years to the conferring of more power to the Speaker of the legislature to set the agenda and move legislation along.

The legislature continues to be a model of economy. It remains the smallest legislature in the United States and one of the worst-paid. In recent years, some money has been spent on hiring staff, remodeling offices, and providing secretarial assistance and the other accoutrements of any successful institution; but all in all, the citizens of Nebraska are getting a fiscal bargain, and they seem to know it.

Nebraskans appear to be quite content with the unicameral. No really serious effort to revert to bicameralism has been made. No political groundswell to change to a partisan body exists—neither of the major political parties makes legislative change a part of its platform. The public appears satisfied with legislative term limits, and efforts to abolish them have come from legislators unwilling to yield up their seats rather than from the public itself. All in all, the goals of Norris and his colleagues have been met, and Nebraska's voters have said, emphatically and frequently, "It works for me."

Notes

1. John P. Senning, *The One-House Legislature* (New York: McGraw-Hill, 1937), 43.

2. Ibid., 44.

3. Ibid., 45.

4. George W. Norris, *Fighting Liberal: The Autobiography of George Norris* (New York: Macmillan, 1945), 353.

5. *New York Times,* January 28, 1923, 12.

6. Senning, *One-House Legislature,* 51.

7. Ibid., 53.

8. Ibid., 54–55.

9. Ibid.

10. Ibid., 56.

11. Charlyne Berens, *One House: The Unicameral's Progressive Vision for Nebraska* (Lincoln: University of Nebraska Press, 2005), 36–37.

12. Senning, *One-House Legislature,* 59.

13. Ashley D. Washburn, ed., *Nebraska Blue Book, 2000–01* (Lincoln: State of Nebraska, 2000), 260.

14. Senning, *One-House Legislature,* 67–73.

15. League of Nebraska Municipalities v. Marsh, 253 F. Supp. 27 (D. Neb. 1966). Reynolds v. Sims, 377 U.S. 533 (1964); Baker v. Carr, 369 U.S. 186 (1962). *Baker v. Carr* held that the federal courts had jurisdiction to consider whether or not state efforts to redistrict legislative and congressional districts were constitutional. *Reynolds v. Sims* held that representation in state legislatures must be based on population. Chief Justice Earl Warren, author of the majority opinion, wrote, "Legislators represent people, not trees or acres."

16. Berens, *One House,* 55.

17. Washburn, *Nebraska Blue Book 2000–01,* 290.

18. University of Nebraska School of Journalism, *Behind These Doors Is the Story of Nebraska's Unicameral Legislature* (Lincoln: University of Nebraska School of Journalism, 1961), 17.

19. Ibid., 19.

20. Robert Sittig, *The Nebraska Unicameral after Fifty Years* (Lincoln: Department of Political Science, University of Nebraska–Lincoln, 1986), 22.

21. Berens, *One House,* 55.

22. Ibid., 86–89.

23. Ibid., 164.

24. Ibid., 160.

25. Ibid., 156–57.

EIGHT

John M. Gradwohl

ACCIDENTAL JURISTS

The Nebraska Commission of Industrial Relations

The Jurists

The Nebraska Commission of Industrial Relations (CIR) deals with public employment collective bargaining and impasse resolution.[1] It has authority to decide representation and negotiations issues and to establish rates of pay and conditions of employment for public employees. The CIR is composed of five part-time judges appointed by the governor, with consent of the legislature, to "be representative of the public." The statutes provide that the judges "shall not be appointed because they are representatives of either capital or labor, but they shall be appointed because of their experience and knowledge in legal, financial, labor and industrial matters." All but one of the thirty-five judges who have served since its inception in 1947 have been lawyers.[2]

In exercising their distinctive jurisdiction, the commission members function more like district court judges than like administrative law judges, hearing officers, or arbitrators. CIR proceedings are required to "conform to the code of civil procedure applicable to the district courts," although the commission also has authority to adopt its own procedural rules. The code governing taking of evidence in civil trials also applies to proceedings before the CIR. The CIR is not subject to the Administrative Procedure Act. Appeals from final orders are taken in the same manner as appeals from decisions of district courts.[3]

The present contours of the CIR have been shaped by a series of unrelated historical circumstances, beginning with the Nebraska constitutional convention of 1919–20. The commission's judicial characteristics are more the product of historical happenstance than of comprehensive legislative design.

Historical Happenstances

Nebraska Constitutional Convention of 1919–20

The constitutional convention met at a time of postwar labor unrest, both national and local.[4] Establishment of constitutional authority for an industrial commission was one of the most thoroughly considered topics.[5] On February 20, 1920, the Committee on Industrial Conditions reported Proposal 329 to the floor of the convention.[6] Proposal 329 was a substitute for four initial proposals referred to the committee for consideration.

Proposal 329 was first discussed on the afternoon of February 25. Near the end of that session, delegate C. Petrus Peterson, a young Lincoln lawyer, delivered lengthy remarks in support of an industrial commission: "It begins to look as though the Convention ha[s] really arrived at a point that would justify its having been called. So far we have dealt with our old questions and we have polished up our old machinery a little here and a little there. This question brings us to a really new field that justifies consideration which was not before the Convention that preceded this."[7]

The next afternoon, Governor Henry J. Allen, of Kansas, gave a major address to the convention. After stating that not more than possibly 25 percent of Governor Samuel R. McKelvie's "very kind" introductory remarks were deserved, Allen told the delegates: "I think that possibly I could not present to you anything that would be of more immediate interest than that which we have just accomplished in Kansas, because I am told by the distinguished President of this Convention that you have been giving some consideration to industrial affairs." The balance of Allen's formal remarks dealt with a coal strike in Kansas, the surrounding circumstances, and the resulting legislation. In the question and answer period following his speech, Allen explained the Kansas legislation: "Technically under the

Constitution it is a commission, but it has the powers of a court. . . . We realized, when we call it a Court of Industrial Relations, that in the general application of the court, that is a misnomer, because really we have made it a commission which we have done to give it an elasticity of jurisdiction. . . . We call it a court because we have to make it as nearly a court of justice as we can."[8]

The convention met for a half day on February 27, dealing with other topics, and then adjourned until March 3. On March 3, when the convention again took up Proposal 329, Peterson stated: "At the last session, when we were considering this subject, I tried to map out some of the lines which appeared to me to be the basis on which we ought to build our constitutional provision. Since that time, I have had the opportunity of spending two or three days in Kansas, and I have gone over with some care the theory of the gentlemen down there who have established the first industrial court in the country."[9]

From then on, Peterson championed a constitutional provision allowing the legislature to establish an industrial commission. After extensive consideration and maneuvering, Proposal 329 was combined with proposals dealing with unfair trade practices into Proposal 333. Proposal 333 was adopted by the convention, approved by the electorate, and is now article XV, § 9, of the Nebraska constitution: "Laws may be enacted providing for the investigation, submission, and determination of controversies between employers and employees in any business or vocation affected with a public interest and for the prevention of unfair business practices and unconscionable gains in any business or vocation affecting the public welfare. An Industrial Commission may be created for the purpose of administering such laws, and appeals shall be as provided by law."[10]

It seems likely that article XV, § 9, would not be part of the Nebraska constitution today were it not for the fortuitous timing of the Kansas coal strike, Allen's address to the constitutional convention of 1919–20, and the considerable interest of Peterson in providing constitutional authority for an industrial commission. The legislature has not implemented the business practices portion of article XV, § 9, but the labor dispute authorization has had an interesting legislative and judicial journey.

Supreme Court of the United States, 1923 to 1934

In 1923, the federal Supreme Court found the Kansas Court of Industrial Relations Act unconstitutional on Fourteenth Amendment substantive due process grounds in *Wolff Packing Co. v. Kansas Court of Industrial Relations.*[11] C. Petrus Peterson wrote in an article published in the 1925 *Nebraska Law Bulletin* that the Nebraska constitutional provisions were "fundamentally different from the Kansas Legislation" and not necessarily nullified by the decision. He contended "that the provisions of the Nebraska constitution remain valid to the extent that legislation may be enacted under it to protect the public against interruption of a business or vocation affected with a public interest while the Kansas legislation falls, at least to the extent that it undertakes to enter the broader field."[12]

Peterson's analysis was vindicated by the landmark 1934 Supreme Court decision in *Nebbia v. New York,* which upheld the power of the New York Milk Control Board to set the price of milk. The Court distinguished *Wolff Packing Co.* on the grounds that the Kansas statutory designation of businesses "affected with a public interest" had created a "closed class or category of businesses affected with a public interest, and the function of courts in the application of the Fifth and Fourteenth Amendments is to determine in each case whether circumstances vindicate the challenged regulation as a reasonable exertion of governmental authority or condemn it as arbitrary or discriminatory."[13]

In 1935, Congress passed the National Labor Relations Act, which recognizes the rights of private sector employees to organize, bargain collectively, and strike. This private sector federal legislation operates on an underlying theory that the economic marketplace, not an industrial commission, will determine the level of wages and working conditions.

Nebraska Legislature, 1947

The 1947 Nebraska Legislature met in economic circumstances similar to those in which the constitutional convention had assembled in 1920. By then, C. Petrus Peterson had become a luminary and was a senator in the unicameral. Early in the session, he introduced LB 349 to "make operative the provisions of Section 9, Article XV, of the Constitution of Nebraska." Peterson's LB 349 would have applied to "a business or vocation affected with a public interest," to a private business if there is a written contract of employment or a collective bargaining agreement, and to jurisdictional disputes between unions. It also stated, "The Court of Industrial Relations shall have no jurisdiction with reference to employment in governmental service."[14] Both employers and unions strongly opposed LB 349 at its hearing before the Labor and Public Welfare Committee on March 28, 1947.

On April 7, 1947, Governor Val Peterson, no relation to Senator C. Petrus Peterson, appeared before the legislature and stated: "Because we face today, and apparently must expect to continue to face for an indefinite future period, industrial disturbances fraught with serious consequences to all governmental services and our citizenry generally, I am appearing here today with a legislative proposal for the first time. This morning we are in the opening stages of a telephone strike. . . . [W]e are unable to foresee the serious effects which disruption of this service may have to the public health and safety."[15]

Senator John P. McKnight, an Auburn lawyer, introduced LB 537 on behalf of the governor. The bill, as introduced, applied to "disputes involving employees in governmental service or of public utilities." It did not include private businesses other than public utilities "which carry on an intrastate business in this state and over which the government of the United States has not assumed exclusive regulation and control."[16] LB 537 was supported by private business employers and opposed by union representatives at a hearing of the Labor and Public Welfare Committee on April 14, 1947.

Committee amendments on April 16 changed "governmental service" to "governmental service in a proprietary capacity." The term "proprietary capacity" meant "a commercial or business enterprise, which is owned, managed or operated by the State of Nebraska [or] any political or governmental subdivision thereof."[17] The committee amendments also refined the statutory standards upon which the Court of Industrial Relations could set wages and conditions of employment, based in large part on an Indiana public utilities employment statute that had become effective on March 14, 1947.[18] A later substitute LB 537, expressly "correlated with Legislative Bill 349 introduced by C. Petrus Peterson," reinstated the language of LB 349 that provided, "The Court of Industrial Relations shall have no jurisdiction with reference to employment in government service."

Substitute LB 537 clearly reflected the thinking of Peterson and his persistence in implementing the provisions from the constitutional convention of 1920, particularly the judicial framework of an industrial commission. Nebraska joined a number of other states in enacting legislation in 1947 to deal with public utility employment disputes. But Nebraska was the only state to designate its industrial commission a "court" to endow it with predominantly judicial characteristics. There have been important legislative changes to the 1947 enactment, but the dispute resolution mechanism envisioned by Peterson during the constitutional convention of 1920 and implemented with his active participation as a senator in 1947 has remained relatively unchanged.

Supreme Court of the United States, 1951

Wisconsin was one of the states that enacted public utility employment dispute legislation in 1947. It outlawed strikes and authorized an arbitrator, rather than a court of industrial relations, to set wages and conditions of employment on the basis of comparability of overall compensation, much like the standard specified in the Nebraska statutes.[19]

Wisconsin courts enjoined strikes at two local public utilities, a gas company and a streetcar company, that provided services solely within the state of Wisconsin. The U.S. Supreme Court invalidated the Wisconsin legislation in *Amalgamated Ass'n of Street, Electric Railway & Motor Coach Employees v. Wisconsin Employment Relations Board,* holding that "Congress occupied this field and closed it to state regulation."[20] This decision precluded application of the Nebraska statutes to privately owned telephone companies, the industry whose labor difficulties largely had precipitated the creation of the Court of Industrial Relations in 1947.

In 1959, Congress slightly relaxed the preemption of the National Labor Relations Act by allowing states to act when the National Labor Relations Board declines "to assert jurisdiction over any labor dispute involving any class or category of employers, where, in the opinion of the Board, the effect of such labor dispute on commerce is not sufficiently substantial to warrant the exercise of its jurisdiction."[21] That left the scope of the Nebraska Court of Industrial Relations jurisdiction limited to very small public utilities, such as local taxicab companies, and governmental service in a proprietary capacity. The federal law does not apply to "any state or political subdivision thereof."[22] The Nebraska statutes, however, continued to deny the court "jurisdiction with reference to employment in governmental service."

Nebraska Legislature, 1969

In 1969, the Nebraska Legislature made Court of Industrial Relations procedures applicable to establishing wages and conditions of employment for Nebraska public employees. What began as a proposal "to establish a public employees' fair employment practices act," and contained no binding impasse resolution mechanism, ended up making the court's wage-setting provisions applicable to "all disputes involving governmental service."

Senator Terry Carpenter introduced LB 15 on the second day of the legislative session.[23] LB 15 was modeled on the New York Public Employees' Fair Employment Act (popularly known as the Taylor Act) passed in 1967.[24] It recognized the rights of public employees to organize and to be represented by unions in collective bargaining. It provided authority for governmental units to recognize and to bargain with unions and required public employers to negotiate collectively with certified or recognized bargaining representatives.

The Nebraska Supreme Court had held in 1965 that "a public agency or governmental employer has no legal authority to bargain with a labor union in the absence of express statutory authority."[25] In response, in 1967, the Nebraska Legislature enacted a so-called meet and confer law, the Nebraska Teachers' Professional Negotiations Act, applicable to class III, IV and V school districts.[26] The initial purpose of LB 15 was to provide general statutory authority for collective bargaining in the public sector.

As introduced, LB 15 called for the establishment of a new Public Employment Relations Board to determine representation issues, to conduct research, to provide studies, to resolve bargaining process issues, and to support mediation, fact-finding, and other voluntary dispute resolution procedures. The proposal called for broad disclosures of factual matters surrounding the controversy and recommendations from a fact-finding board. There was no authority for the Public Employment Relations Board to establish wages and conditions of employment. That power remained with the legislative body of the government involved. The bill was similar in concept to legislation enacted in 1965, which applied to some cities and provided for public fact finding, recommendations, and conciliation efforts but lacked any impasse resolution mechanism binding upon the governmental entity.[27]

The labor committee reported LB 15 to the floor of the unicameral on February 3 with just a single amendment. The pay of the two part-time members of the proposed Public Employment Relations Board was reduced from $100 to $50 dollars per day of service.[28]

The bill came up for consideration on General File two days later. Several amendments were adopted, and the bill was laid over to the next day. On February 6, a motion to kill LB 15 was defeated: twelve senators voted to "indefinitely postpone" the bill, twenty-eight voted against postponement, and nine did not vote. It then was advanced from General File without further amendment by the bare twenty-five votes required, with eleven votes against and thirteen abstentions.[29]

At that point, LB 15 simply created a new state Public Employment Relations Board applicable to public employers. It contained no binding impasse resolution provisions and did not amend any of the statutes pertaining to the Court of Industrial Relations. Those statutes remained as written in 1947, including the limitation on "jurisdiction with reference to employment in governmental service."

The bill was laid over when it came up on the Select File agenda on February 11. On February 12, it was laid over again until February 17 at Carpenter's request. On February 17, Senator Henry F. Pedersen Jr., an Omaha lawyer, proposed a comprehensive substitute LB 15, and the bill was again laid over.[30] Pedersen's substitute struck the entire LB 15 as it had been introduced, considered by the Labor Committee, and advanced to Select File. It amended six sections of the Court of Industrial Relations statutes and added one new section recognizing the rights of public employees to association and representation in collective bargaining activities.

Pedersen's substitute amendment made the Court of Industrial Relations legislation applicable to "all disputes involving governmental service, service of a public utility, or other disputes as the Legislature shall provide" eliminating the jurisdictional limitation with reference to governmental service. The amendment increased the number of judges from three to five and required that "[s]uch judges . . . be representative of the public." It also prohibited retaliatory action against employees who invoked the statutes, broadened the authority of the court to conduct studies, and inserted language to support the same sort of mediation and fact-finding activities that the introduced version of LB 15 would have authorized the Public Employment Relations Board to conduct.

Additionally, Pedersen's amendment made a very important change in the statutory standard by which the Court of Industrial Relations could "establish or alter the scale of wages, hours of labor, or conditions of employment, or any one or more of the same." Left intact was the lodestar of "overall compensation" that is "comparable to the prevalent wage rates paid and conditions of employment maintained for the same or similar work of workers exhibiting like or similar skills under the same or similar working conditions." Stricken was the requirement that wage orders of the Court of Industrial Relations "bear a generally comparable relationship to wage rates paid and conditions of employment maintained by all other employers in the same labor market area," a provision that had seemed well suited to privately owned public utilities in 1947 but would not have carried over well to wage setting in the public sector.

The record of legislative floor debate does not reflect a focused, analytical discussion of the dramatic changes proposed by Pedersen. Carpenter explained that Pedersen had come to him in an effort to effect a compromise. When another senator asked Pedersen with whom he had consulted, he replied: "I talked to my wife. I drew up the amendment and then gave copies out to Senators Carpenter, Bloom and I don't know who got a copy of it. I had visited with a number of people including a number of men [lobbyists] in the rear of the room who looked at it but it was my own work product."[31] Carpenter felt that compromise was necessary to achieve passage of LB 15. He said, "It is my added opinion that we get this or nothing. It's that simple. We may not even get this. . . . I found, from experience, that when you get in a position like this, you have to compromise."[32]

The Pedersen substitute LB 15 was adopted by unanimous consent on February 19 and the bill advanced from Select File without amendment. It appeared for Final Reading as written by Pedersen, with only technical amendments of form. But it was returned to Select File for an amendment providing that the Court of Industrial Relations would have no jurisdiction over public school districts until the provisions of the Nebraska Teachers' Professional Negotiations Act have been exhausted without resolution of the dispute. Another amendment inserted language from the original version of LB 15 allowing the parties to agree to a secret ballot representation election; providing express statutory authority for public employers to recognize, negotiate, and enter into collective bargaining agreements with employee organizations; and obligating public employers to negotiate collectively with employee organizations that have been certified or recognized. A further amendment required that agreements with state agencies coincide with the biennial state budgeting period.

LB 15 advanced to Final Reading for a second time. It was passed by the unicameral on April 28, 1969, by a vote of 27 to 19 and was signed by Governor Norbert T. Tiemann the next day.[33] LB 15 thus expanded the wage-setting impasse resolution jurisdiction of the Court of Industrial Relations to all Nebraska governmental entities, made important substantive changes in the statutes, and left the procedural features of the Court of Industrial Relations unchanged.

Nebraska Supreme Court, 1972–79

It is understandable that the Nebraska Supreme Court would have difficulty in deciding issues relating to the Court of Industrial Relations following the 1969 legislation. The constitutional convention of 1919–20 had focused primarily on private sector issues, although it is clear that concerns about public work stoppages also had lurked in the background.[34] In addition to issues concerning the interpretation and application of the substantive provisions of the statutes, the Nebraska Supreme Court was uncharacteristically and bitterly divided over whether article XV, § 9, applied to governmental employers and employees; whether the Court of Industrial Relations could possess mixed judicial, legislative, and executive powers apart from Nebraska's constitutional separation of powers article and how closely the Court of Industrial Relations was required to adhere to formal judicial procedures.[35] After a fierce struggle, these issues eventually were dissipated rather than resolved by judicial decisions.

The first impasse resolution and wage determination case to reach the Nebraska Supreme Court on appeal from the Court of Industrial Relations involved the Seward School District and Education Association in 1972.[36] A four-judge majority held that article XV, § 9, is not subject to the Nebraska constitution's separation of powers article, which prohibits any branch of the state government from exercising a power belonging to another branch except as "expressly directed or permitted" by the constitution.[37] One of the three dissenting judges also agreed with this conclusion.

With respect to the authority of the legislature to make LB 15 applicable to public school districts, however, the four-judge majority opinion relied upon the legislature's "plenary power and control over school districts" rather than article XV, § 9. It reasoned that "[i]f the Legislature has such complete control over public school districts, it follows, by the enactment of L.B. 15, Laws 1969, chapter 407, page 1405, it was exercising that control."[38] The fifth judge, who agreed on the scope of article XV, § 9, as an exception to the separation of powers requirements, dissented from the rest of the majority holding. He reasoned that if the plenary power of the legislature over school districts—rather than article XV, § 9—was the source of authority relied upon to enact LB 15, then the jurisdiction given the Court of Industrial Relations was a violation of the separation of powers article. The other two dissenters concluded that the legislature lacked authority to deprive "local political subdivisions of the right to manage their own affairs in regard to employment practices."[39]

The issue of whether article XV, § 9, directly applies to public school districts and employees was not clearly raised by the parties or clearly decided by the court. Two of the four judges joining in the majority opinion wrote a separate concurrence stating "it would appear that the terms business or vocation were used in an alternative sense and that legislation relating to controversies between employers and employees under this section is not limited to a business affected with a public interest."[40] But the three dissenting judges were all of the view that article XV, § 9, did not apply to governmental employers and employees.

Three years later, the supreme court again held that the jurisdiction of the Court of Industrial Relations to set public school teacher salaries and conditions of employment stemmed from the plenary power of the legislature and not from article XV, § 9.[41] The five-judge majority opinion stated: "One may be willing to concede the validity of the contention that [article XV, § 9] was intended to apply only to the regulation of public utilities. However, this does not answer the question of whether the Legislature otherwise has power to devise methods for dealing with the labor relations of governmental entities and departments."[42] With respect to the constitutional issues of separation of powers and the delegation of jurisdiction to the Court of Industrial Relations, the opinion held that "[t]he function it exercises is a legislative one; its quasi-judicial powers are purely incidental."[43] One judge concurred in the result without a written opinion. Judge John E. Newton dissented, asserting that article XV, § 9, does not apply to governmental entities. The author of the majority opinion wrote an additional opinion styled "respondente" in which he said: "Judge Newton, in his dissent, accused this court of undertaking a legislative or constitutional function on policy grounds. This assertion is so serious that it cannot go unanswered. . . . The dissent contends that, because the Constitution authorized the Legislature to create an industrial commission for the purpose of dealing with certain labor relations problems, that constitutional provision restricts the Legislature from ever after entrusting to that same commission, later created by it, authority to deal with, in such manner as the Legislature shall direct, the labor relations of governmental subdivisions. Such a construction is contrary to the fundamental nature of the state legislative power under our system of government."[44]

The controversy within the supreme court continued. In 1976, a three-judge per curiam decision stated that the Court of Industrial Relations had jurisdiction as to the Nebraska Department of Public Institutions by virtue of the constitutional provision that "[t]he general management, control and government of all state . . . institutions shall be vested as determined by the Legislature."[45] Two judges concurred in the result without a written opinion. Two judges dissented on the ground that the constitution does not give the legislature "complete control" over the Department of Public Institutions.

Similarly, in 1978, a four-judge majority held that the legislature's authority over the Nebraska Department of Roads provided a jurisdictional basis for the Court of Industrial Relations.[46] One judge concurred in the result without a written opinion. Two judges dissented in an opinion written by Judge Harry A. Spencer, who had authored the opinion in the threshold *Seward* litigation: "I am now convinced that in adopting Article XV, section 9, Constitution of Nebraska the Constitutional Convention of 1920 clearly intended to exempt the state and its political subdivisions from the operations of the Court of Industrial Relations. We have opened a Pandora's box, by judicial construction, which can ultimately destroy and nullify Article II, section 1, Constitution of Nebraska [the separation of powers article]."[47]

The next year, the two dissenters were no longer on the court, and the court ruled unanimously that the University of Nebraska was subject to the legislation conferring jurisdiction on the Court of Industrial Relations.[48] The opinion invokes the authority of article XV, § 9, in addition to that of article VII, § 10, which provides that "[t]he general government of the University of Nebraska shall, under the direction of the Legislature be vested in . . . the Board of Regents." The opinion recognized the primary authority of the board of regents to set wages and terms of employment, but, analogizing to workers' compensation and unemployment compensation laws, the court also stated:

> If however, a controversy between UNL and its employees arises, the Constitution grants to the Legislature authority to enact laws to resolve that controversy. This is really nothing other than simply prescribing a forum wherein controversies involving a public employer and its employees may be arbitrated [*sic*]. Certainly UNL would not argue that their authority is so absolute that an employee could have no recourse anywhere if a dispute existed between the employer and the employee.[49]

The judicial character of proceedings before the Court of Industrial Relations persisted throughout this period. In 1979, for example, a four-judge majority of the state supreme court, with one concurrence and two dissents, held that the moving party must make a prima facie case under the statutory rules of evidence before the Court of Industrial Relations may "go out in the first instance and conduct an investigation as to whether a particular wage is comparable to the prevalent."[50] Proceedings in the Court of

Industrial Relations continue to fit more closely the mold of traditional civil litigation than that of typical administrative agency determinations.

Nebraska Legislature, 1979

The 1979 legislature engaged in some cosmetic surgery that placed the previous disagreements about the jurisdiction and procedures of the court in a more favorable perspective. Most importantly, the legislature changed the body's name from "Court of Industrial Relations" to "Commission of Industrial Relations" (though the term "judge" was retained throughout the statutes). The amendments also increased the judges' pay from $120.00 to $150.00 per day and provided that the judges "may be removed by the Governor for the same causes as a judge of the district court." The presiding judge was authorized to appoint hearing officers to take evidence and to make recommended findings and orders when necessary to expedite the determination of cases.[51]

The code of civil procedure continued to apply to CIR proceedings, as did the statutory exemption from the Administrative Procedure Act. The appeals process remained the same, except that bargaining unit determinations were not appealable until after representation elections were held.

Other provisions dealt with the authority of the CIR to make temporary findings and orders, require good faith collective bargaining, conduct investigations, and protect the statutory rights of employees. There was no alteration of the statutory criteria for CIR orders fixing wages and working conditions and no change in the manner in which wage orders are determined.

Since 1979

The philosophical differences among Nebraska Supreme Court judges concerning the constitutional nature of the CIR have manifested themselves only once since 1979. In 1981, in a three-judge opinion, the court held that the CIR did not have authority to award prejudgment interest.[52] The plurality reasoned that the CIR, as an administrative agency, had no express statutory authority to do so. It expressed frustration with the basic statutory system: "The instant case once more points up the difficulty of attempting to operate under the current statutory provisions for resolving public employer-public employee disputes. Each case coming to this court makes those deficiencies even more apparent. Courts, however, are not designed to fill statutory gaps and should not seek to replace the legislative branch of government."[53]

Two judges concurred in the result without a written opinion. Two judges joined in a vigorous dissenting opinion:

> Many of the difficulties referred to in the opinion of the court would be eliminated if this court would follow its earlier decisions . . . [that] "Article XV, section 9, Constitution of Nebraska, obviously was intended to be an exception to Article II of the Constitution." . . . The report of the joint committee that it was authorizing a commission with combined administrative, legislative, and judicial powers clearly indicates the type of commission or agency the Constitutional Convention was authorizing. . . . Although the jurisdiction of the commission is necessarily limited to resolving matters related to labor disputes, I believe the better rule is that the commission exercises all three functions of government in resolving the disputes within that area which are brought before it.[54]

The attitude of the Nebraska Supreme Court toward the CIR seemingly mellowed with the addition of Judge John T. Grant in September 1983. Grant had been a judge of the Court of Industrial Relations from 1972 to 1974 and was instrumental in revising its rules of procedure. He served as a district court judge from 1974 until his appointment to the supreme court.

The legislature has significantly enhanced the statutes since then. Legislation has added criteria for determination of appropriate bargaining units in some situations, clarified and improved the CIR's authority to conduct investigations and surveys, added optional special master proceedings in some circumstances, and detailed prohibited practices. Nonmandatory statutory time frames were refined in 1984 for hearings on requests for temporary relief, hearings on the merits, and the issuance of final orders. A provision was added for a posttrial conference if requested by a party before a wage order becomes final. The 1987 legislature adopted a separate State Employees Collective Bargaining Act, creating twelve bargaining units and special procedures for all state agencies except the University of Nebraska, state colleges, and other constitutional offices. The Nebraska Teachers' Professional Negotiations Act was repealed in 1987, making the CIR statutes applicable to public school districts from the outset of disputes.

The CIR today gives the general impression of a modern administrative agency. But it still has judges who serve in a manner comparable to Nebraska judicial branch judges. The statutory collective bargaining impasse resolution criteria for setting wages and conditions of employment for public employees have remained largely unchanged since C. Petrus Peterson and others envisioned their application by a Court of Industrial Relations. Despite historical happenstances, philosophical differences, and jumbled supreme court decisions, the CIR judges exercise the healthy mix of traditional judicial jurisdiction and other decision-making authority intended by the delegates to the constitutional convention of 1919–20 and the 1947 Nebraska Legislature in providing for a court, now the Commission of Industrial Relations.

Notes

1. The statutes referred to throughout this article are the Industrial Relations Act, Neb. Rev. Stat. §§ 48-801 through 48-838 (Reissue 2004), unless otherwise noted.

2. Judge Walter Nielsen, a North Platte businessman, served from 1970 to 1974. The accidental jurists are still accidental jurists, but they are now known as "commissioners" rather than "judges." On March 7, 2007, the governor signed LB 472, making the name change but leaving the basic judicial trappings of the CIR intact. 2007 Laws of Nebraska 1374.

3. Neb. Rev. Stat. § 48-812 (Reissue 2004).

4. For a discussion of the major Omaha Riot of 1919, of which "labor problems were one source of trouble," see Steven L. Willborn, "The Omaha Riot of 1919," *Nebraska Lawyer* (December 1999–January 2000): 56–61.

5. For a comprehensive discussion of the formation of the Nebraska Court of Industrial Relations, see David George Wagaman, "Public Employee Impasse Resolution: A Historical Examination of the Nebraska Experience with Some Comparisons to the New York Experience" (Ph.D. diss., University of Nebraska, 1977). For a discussion of article XV, § 9, adopted by the constitutional convention of 1919–20, see John M. Gradwohl, "Labor-Management Relations and Nebraska Constitutional Revision," *Nebraska Law Review* 40, no. 4 (1961): 648–96, discussed at 652–86. Portions of this article are used or relied upon in this chapter with permission of the *Nebraska Law Review.*

6. Clyde H. Barnard, ed., *Proceedings of the Nebraska Constitutional Convention, 1919–1920* (Lincoln: Kline, 1921[?]), 2:1318.

7. Ibid., 2:1563–66.

8. Ibid., 2:1618–29, 2:1635–37.

9. Ibid., 2:1694–95 ("I want to suggest to the Committee the advisability, when we set up an industrial court, of including within the same realm this other subject of business regulation ordinarily referred to as profiteering. Manifestly, any attempt to handle the question of fair wages will have to deal with the element of the relative costs of living. No two subjects are more closely related.").

10. The 1920 provision stated, "[A]nd appeals shall lie to the Supreme Court from the final orders and judgments of such commission." This was changed by 1990 constitutional amendments allowing the creation of a court of appeals.

11. 262 U.S. 522 (1923).

12. C. Petrus Peterson, "Industrial Courts," *Nebraska Law Bulletin* 3, no. 4 (1925): 498–99.

13. Nebbia v. New York, 291 U.S. 502, 536 (1934).

14. For a discussion of the 1947 legislative history, see John M. Gradwohl, "Historical Explanation of the Nebraska Public School District Bargaining Impasse Resolution Mechanism," *Nebraska Law Review* 79, no. 4 (2000): 1020–24. Portions of this article are used or relied upon in this chapter with permission of the *Nebraska Law Review.*

15. *Journal of the Nebraska Legislature* (60th Gen. Sess.) 957–59 (April 7, 1947).

16. LB 537 as introduced and amended and its correlation with LB 349 in a mimeographed substitute bill can be found in the bound copy of 1947 Legislative Bills, 60th Session (Nebraska Legislative Council 1947).

17. 1947 Laws of Nebraska, ch. 178, LB 537, § 1(3).

18. 1947 Acts of Indiana 1355, 1358–59.

19. 1947 Laws of Wisconsin 713–19 (approved July 22, 1947).

20. 340 U.S. 383, 390 (1951), quoting Automobile Workers v. O'Brien, 339 U.S. 454, 457 (1950).

21. 29 U.S.C. § 164(c) (2000).

22. 29 U.S.C. § 152(2) (2000).

23. The 1969 legislative session is also discussed in Gradwohl, "Historical Explanation," 1024–28.

24. 1967 N.Y. Laws 1102.

25. IBEW v. City of Hastings, 179 Neb. 455, 138 N.W.2d 822 (1965).

26. 1967 Laws of Nebraska 1738 (repealed in 1987).

27. 1965 Laws of Nebraska 826 (repealed in 1969).

28. *Journal of the Nebraska Legislature* (80th Gen. Sess.) 344 (February 3, 1969).

29. Ibid., 426–27 (February 6, 1969).

30. Ibid., 607–12 (February 17, 1969).

31. Record of legislative floor debate, Nebraska Legislature, February 19, 1969 (unnumbered transcription available at the Office of the Clerk of Legislature or the University of Nebraska Law College Library).

32. Ibid.

33. *1969 Nebraska Legislative Journal,* 1684–85 (April 28, 1969), 1734 (April 29, 1969).

34. See Peterson, "Industrial Courts," 489–92.

35. These issues are also discussed in Gradwohl, "Historical Explanation," 1013–20.

36. School Dist. of Seward Educ. Ass'n. v. School Dist. of Seward, 188 Neb. 772, 199 N.W.2d 752 (1972).

37. Neb. const. art. II, § 1. The section upon which the court relied in its opinion was amended slightly in 2006, but the meaning was not materially altered.

38. Ibid., 779, 199 N.W.2d at 757.

39. Ibid., 785–86, 199 N.W.2d at 760.

40. Ibid., 797–98, 199 N.W.2d at 766.

41. Orleans Educ. Ass'n v. School Dist. of Orleans, 193 Neb. 675, 229 N.W.2d 172 (1975).

42. Ibid., 680, 229 N.W.2d at 175–76.

43. Ibid., 685, 229 N.W.2d at 178.

44. Ibid., 691–92, 229 N.W.2d at 181.

45. AFSCME v. Dep't of Public Institutions, 195 Neb. 253, 237 N.W.2d 841 (1976).

46. AFSCME v. State Dep't of Roads, 200 Neb. 171, 263 N.W.2d 643 (1978).

47. 200 Neb. at 180–82, 263 N.W.2d at 648–49.

48. Univ. Police Officers Union v. Univ. of Nebraska, 203 Neb. 4, 277 N.W.2d 529 (1979).

49. Ibid., 11, 277 N.W.2d at 534.

50. Gen. Drivers and Helpers Union v. City of West Point, 204 Neb. 238, 281 N.W.2d 772 (1979).

51. 1979 Laws of Nebraska 1235.

52. IBEW v. Omaha Pub. Power Dist., 209 Neb. 335, 307 N.W.2d 795 (1981).

53. Ibid., 342, 307 N.W.2d at 799.

54. Ibid., 342–44, 307 N.W.2d at 799–800.

NINE

Brian H. Bornstein, Richard L. Wiener, and Evelyn M. Maeder

PIONEERS IN INTERDISCIPLINARY LEGAL EDUCATION

A History of the UNL Law and Psychology Program

Nebraska has long been noted for its pioneer spirit. Thus, it should come as no surprise that the University of Nebraska–Lincoln (UNL) pioneered the first joint interdisciplinary education program in law and psychology. This chapter will describe the founding of the Law and Psychology Program (LPP), the program's evolution over the years, and its relationship to law-psychology training more broadly.

The Program's Founding

In 1973, when members of the UNL Department of Psychology saw a need for a program that fully integrated graduate psychological and legal training (Ph.D., J.D.), no such programs existed in the United States.[1] David Levine, Psychology Department chair, and Bruce Sales, then an assistant professor at UNL with training in both psychology and law, led the effort. They proposed the program to the psychology and law faculties during the fall of 1973, and both units unanimously approved it. The University of Nebraska Board of Regents followed suit in the spring of 1974. Sales then applied for and obtained a five-year training grant ($200,000) from the National Institute of Mental Health's Center for Studies of Crime and Delinquency to support the program. The nation's first law-psychology training program enrolled its first graduate students in 1974.

As stated in the proposal,

> The primary objective of this program is to produce lawyer-psychologists whose training will provide them with all the necessary skills to do basic and applied research and writing on issues and problems in our legal system. . . . In order for the integration and application of psychological and legal knowledge to occur in a cohesive unified direction, it is essential that scholars be fully trained and qualified in both disciplines. The students graduating from this program will be so qualified and will be encouraged to take Bar Exams and to function as a psychologist fully trained in theory and methodology.[2]

The goal of the LPP was to develop professionals with the training and skills necessary to test the law's assumptions about human behavior in order to improve the functioning of the legal system and the legal process.

The proposed joint degree program required a minimum of five academic years and three summers to complete. With the exception of the first-year law curriculum, taken in its entirety because it was deemed "essential to the students' immersion into legal thought and socialization into the legal profession,"[3] the program of study fully integrated law and psychology courses into students' schedules.[4] Regular faculty taught the traditional classes in both disciplines, and Sales taught several newly created interdisciplinary courses (for example, Law and Social Science, Law and Psychology).

On the research side, interdisciplinary interests developed within each unit, including studies of correctional law and practices, aberrant sexual behavior, substance abuse, and institutionalization of the mentally ill, among others. The proposal captured this move toward integration:

> We feel that the joint degree program is the logical outgrowth and synthesis of the Law School's and Psychology Department's prior scholarly direction. As such it will provide the necessary interdisciplinary integration that the faculty and university want and that the study of the legal system and legal process need.[5]

To some degree, the law and psychology movement and a growing understanding of the intersection of law and social science, more broadly, were "in the air" in the late 1960s and early 1970s because of a combination of factors: the legal realist and sociological jurisprudence movements, high-profile cases that were amenable to social science data (for example, discrimination, obscenity), shifts in academic institutions toward greater interdisciplinarity, and the availability of both public (for example, National Science Foundation, National Institutes of Health) and private (for example, Russell Sage Foundation) funding, among others.[6] This zeitgeist doubtless contributed to the emergence and early success of the UNL program.

An administrative committee composed of two psychology faculty members, two law faculty members, and the program director, Bruce Sales, addressed the challenge of integrating the different administrative structures, pedagogical styles, and organizational cultures of the College of Arts and Sciences, where the Psychology Department was (and still is) housed, and the College of Law.[7] Melvin George, vice president for academic affairs at the University of Missouri, identified the early strengths and problems of the young program in a 1976 report that was essentially the program's first outside evaluation:

> It seems important to state right away that the program . . . has exceeded the expectations that I had for it when it was first conceived and planned. The students appear to be exceedingly bright, well-trained, thoughtful, committed, and energetic. Bruce Sales and those who have worked with him in the program share those same qualities.[8]

Nonetheless, the report identified four problems. First, "[t]here is the critical question of support for the program in the College of Law."[9] This problem apparently arose from the retirement of Law College dean Henry Grether, which created uncertainty in leadership, and the departure around this time of Harvey Perlman and Wallace Rudolph (the two law faculty members on the administrative committee). As a result, the psychology faculty carried most of the teaching and administrative burden, and there was little interaction between the psychology and law faculties.[10]

Second, the financial support for students was inadequate, leading George to recommend increasing the assistantship pool available to the Psychology Department.[11] Third, "[t]he perceptions of the program in the Department of Psychology are varied."[12] Concerns included the further spreading of limited resources, and some older department members' envy of the program's success and perceived preferential treatment.[13] Fourth, the report expressed concern that Sales was overextended and that he consequently could not give students the necessary amount of "personal attention and psychic support."[14] The report noted that the recent hiring of another faculty member in psychology (Jay Hook) would help alleviate this last problem.

From the very beginning, in addition to providing interdisciplinary training, the program has contributed to traditional legal and psychological graduate education (that is, for students not pursuing dual degrees) as well as to undergraduate education. The LPP's interdisciplinary courses were and are open to traditional J.D. and Ph.D. students, and from the outset they have been popular in both groups. For example, by the end of the LPP's second year of operation, 25 percent of the traditional Ph.D. students in psychology had chosen a law and psychology minor.[15] Program faculty also created a new undergraduate course in law and psychology, which remains one of the more popular upper-level courses in the undergraduate major.

At the time the program was founded, and for many years thereafter, it was the only one of its kind.[16] Students at various other institutions pursued both the Ph.D. and J.D., but generally on an ad hoc basis.[17] Thus, to a large extent, UNL set the pattern for future training in psychology and law.[18]

The LPP quickly established itself as a force to be reckoned with in the academic community by attracting, and continuing to attract, high-quality students and faculty who have brought recognition to the program by conducting research, presenting findings at national conferences, and publishing papers in top-tier journals. Furthermore, Sales almost immediately developed a new interdisciplinary journal, *Law and Human Behavior,* which began publication in 1977. *Law and Human Behavior* has long had a strong Nebraska flavor: in addition to Sales, the current director of the LPP, Richard Wiener, served as journal editor from 1996–2005.

Finally, the LPP began to host conferences on important psycholegal issues. Sales chaired the first such conference, "Selected Issues in Our Criminal Justice System," in October 1975. Several distinguished speakers, Norval Morris, Saleem Shah, and David Wexler, presented talks on such topics as who should go to prison, obscenity, dangerousness, and criminal commitment.[19] These conferences exposed prominent scholars to the LPP and reached a much larger audience through their published proceedings.

Thirty Years of Law and Psychology in Nebraska: A Program's Evolution

In the years since its founding, the LPP has grown through a series of stages, each corresponding to the personality and research interests of the program director at the time. Throughout the program's existence, the LPP's director has always been a leading scholar-researcher who has brought renown to UNL by virtue of his scholarly efforts and professional standing in the psychology-law community. The prior program directors whose academic interests helped define each stage of program development were Bruce Sales (1974–81), Gary Melton (1982–93), and Steven Penrod (1995–2001). The current program director is Richard Wiener, who has been at the helm since 2002.

The Sales Years

Sales came to UNL, with both a Ph.D. and a J.D., as an assistant professor of psychology and law in 1973.[20] As noted above, Sales was instrumental in creating the joint degree program in law and psychology and obtained a training grant from the National Institute of Mental Health that contributed to the program's support for many years. Other faculty in both the Psychology Department and the Law College assisted Sales, but in its early years, the program was largely a one-man operation. During his tenure at UNL, Sales and his students conducted research and published articles on (among other topics) children's conception of intentionality in criminal situations, jury selection, child abuse reporting laws, civil commitment laws, sexual offenders, witness credibility, and forensic training.[21]

Sales became known during this period for his work on the comprehensibility of jury instructions and the rights of mentally disabled persons. His research on jury instructions showed that jurors' understanding of them is generally less than what the law assumes but that rewriting the instructions on the basis of psycholinguistic principles improves comprehensibility.[22] It culminated in a widely cited book on the topic.[23] As project director of the Developmental Disabilities State Legislative Project, Sales was one of the first scholars to call attention to the legal rights of institutionalized persons. He coauthored legislation on the commitment of mentally ill dangerous people, which was enacted by the Nebraska Legislature,[24] and edited a volume on mental disability law in Nebraska.[25] This volume has become a model for similar volumes in other states. A number of courts have cited Sales's research on jury instructions.[26] Thus, from its inception, the LPP has been a force in influencing legal policy in the state of Nebraska and beyond, a tradition that continues to this day.

In summary, it would be hard to overestimate Sales's influence on the field of psychology and law as a whole. He edited some of the earliest monographs in the discipline while at UNL, and he was the founding editor of *Law and Human Behavior,* the official journal of the American Psychology-Law Society (AP-LS) and another example of his extensive work in the integrative field of psychology and law.[27] Sales served as the society's president and provided the organization with a new mission and purpose.[28] So significant was his contribution, in fact, that "many . . . probably assumed that he founded the Society."[29] Sales restructured the AP-LS to incorporate all viable relationships between psychology and the law. As a result of his work, the society "came to represent psychology and law itself."[30] He contributed immensely to the society, bringing it recognition through his publication of books, papers, and journals (for example, *Psychology in the Legal Process,*[31] *Law and Human Behavior,*[32] and *Perspectives in Law and Psychology*[33]). Sales used his influence and ideology to bring the society into a new era of development, which "would ensure its vitality and influence on psychology and society for many years."[34] His contributions to AP-LS were later recognized when he was elected the first president of the re-formed society after it merged with the American Psychological Association (APA) to form Division 41 of the larger APA organization.[35]

The Melton Years

Gary Melton, a clinical psychologist with interests in child welfare and children's rights, came to UNL in 1982 to direct the LPP.[36] During the Melton era, the program's concentration on mental health law policy and advocacy grew, facilitated by the hiring of Alan Tomkins in 1986. Melton, Tomkins, and their students researched and wrote a great deal about issues related to the well-being and welfare of children and families. Their work favored a perspective of the law as an instrument for improving the social and psychological health of families.[37] This pioneering work drew the attention of the field toward studying and improving the lives of children and families in such areas as ethics in advocacy,[38] children's competencies,[39] and children's rights in the law.[40] Melton edited a volume of essays that suggested ways to make research relevant to judges, legislators, and practicing attorneys.[41]

The LPP generated papers, books, and conference reports that favored a more general advocacy approach to social science. While at UNL, Melton organized two meetings of the Nebraska Symposium on Motivation, a conference and book series hosted annually by the UNL Psychology Department since 1953 and the longest continually running symposium series in psychology. The 1985 symposium, "The Law as a Behavioral Instrument," produced a volume of papers on the manner in which forces outside the law shape doctrine, the psychological meaning of law and legal process, and the way in which the law influences the behavior of individuals, groups, and whole communities.[42] The 1994 symposium, "The Individual, the Family, and Social Good: Personal Fulfillment in Times of Change,"[43] reflected Melton's interest in family welfare and advocacy.

The LPP model of advocacy research pinpointed emerging legal issues of importance, such as adolescent abortion,[44] gay rights,[45] and the incipient AIDS crisis.[46] Melton crystallized his own approach to law and psychology—if not necessarily that of the LPP—in a paper justifying the American Psychological Association's opposition to the nomination of Robert Bork to the U.S. Supreme Court in 1989 on grounds that Bork's views were more consistent with values of wealth maximization than with values of social community founded in respect for human dignity.[47] In the later years of Melton's tenure, these community values became paramount in the scholarship of the program. This work targeted policy about children and families in the United States[48] as well as the values that support the well-being of children internationally.[49]

During this stage of its development, the LPP also produced scholarly papers analyzing the role that mental health practitioners should play in the legal arena. LPP scholars and their colleagues published a series of empirical investigations of the assessment and treatment of violence and serious offending in juveniles.[50] Perhaps most noteworthy was the now classic book, *Psychological Evaluations for the Courts,*[51] which subsequently became a standard text for mental health practitioners at all levels in the legal system.

The LPP's work in the area of mental health became more diversified when Robert Schopp joined the faculty in 1989. Schopp expanded the program's focus on mental health policy, writing extensively about therapeutic jurisprudence, which encourages the development of law and legal rules to promote the therapeutic mission of the mental health system.[52] Schopp also started writing about the justification of punishment in the criminal law.[53]

Melton founded the Center on Children, Families, and the Law (CCFL) at UNL in 1987. The CCFL is "a home for interdisciplinary research, teaching and public service on issues related to child and family policy and services."[54] During these years, the CCFL joined several amicus briefs submitted to appellate courts. In fact, one brief that Melton had a considerable role in writing was cited heavily in *Maryland v. Craig*,[55] the Supreme Court case that allowed closed circuit video examinations of child witnesses.

The LPP's impact on academics and policy grew during Melton's tenure. Melton served as president of the AP-LS in 1990,[56] during which time he "took the helm of an association that had grown to about 1,400 members" and brought the society into adulthood.[57] Melton was very influential in law and psychology, moving the field into new and exciting directions. Also beginning during this period, Tomkins served as editor of *Behavioral Sciences and the Law*, an influential interdisciplinary journal, from 1989 to 2001.

The CCFL has been very influential in setting policies related to children and families, especially within the state of Nebraska. The CCFL's size, the scope of its activities, and its sphere of influence have continued to expand since Melton's departure in 1993. Brian Wilcox, the current director, has continued the CCFL's advocacy efforts on behalf of children while adding program evaluation to the center's professional contributions. For example, he led efforts to evaluate the Early Head Start program in Lincoln/Lancaster County and abstinence education programs in Georgia. Wilcox oversaw the transition of the CCFL from a part of the Law-Psychology Program to an autonomous unit within the College of Arts and Sciences at UNL.

The Penrod Years

Steven Penrod assumed leadership of the LPP in 1995.[58] There were four important developments during Penrod's tenure as program director. First, the program's research emphasis became more heavily experimental.[59] Second, although support for graduate and postdoctoral students continued to come primarily from the NIMH training grant, there was a growing emphasis on obtaining project-specific extramural funding from agencies like the National Science Foundation. Third, the LPP created an in-house trial consulting organization. Fourth, the university created the Public Policy Center under founding director Alan Tomkins.

Before coming to UNL, Penrod had established himself as one of the leading researchers on eyewitness memory and jury decision making.[60] Thus, while continuing to produce scholarship on mental health policy, the program also acquired a reputation for conducting experimental psycholegal research on eyewitness lineups, expert testimony, and jury simulations. This emphasis was reflected in the research efforts of graduate students, as well as in the hiring of new faculty (Mario Scalora in 1997, Jennifer Hunt in 2000, and Brian Bornstein in 2001).

Among Penrod's policy contributions was his participation, with a group of other scholars, in developing a white paper published by the U.S. Department of Justice, which made recommendations for conducting lineups and photospreads.[61] He was involved in an amicus brief in *Kumho Tire v. Carmichael,* one of the U.S. Supreme Court cases that redefined the standards for expert testimony.[62] Finally, appellate courts have cited his research in numerous decisions.[63]

While at UNL, Penrod was one of the first investigators to apply the techniques of Web-based data collection, complex research designs, and meta-analysis to the field of psychology and law.[64] These efforts further solidified the LPP's standing as a cutting-edge research institution in both psychology and law. Penrod also maintained the LPP's prominent role in the American Psychology-Law Society, serving as president of the society (2000–2001) while at UNL.

Penrod secured multiple grants from the National Science Foundation to support research on topics as varied as decision making in death penalty cases, the reliability of interviews in child sexual abuse cases, the effects of *Kumho* on judicial decisions, and meta-analyses of important psycholegal issues. LPP faculty continued their success in obtaining federal grant funding (especially from the NSF), as well as contracts with various state agencies (for example, Medicaid), which further the program's research mission and provide opportunities to influence legal policy in the state.

As a result of Penrod's research efforts on the impact of pretrial publicity on juror decisions, several attorneys asked him to consult on cases involving change of venue motions.[65] For example, Penrod and his students conducted an extensive analysis of media coverage before the trial of Timothy McVeigh, the defendant in the Oklahoma City bombing. In the course of doing this work, Penrod created, with the university's approval, a nonprofit trial consulting organization called Sci-Jur, which has since been renamed Scientific Resources for the Law (SRL). SRL provides graduate students with the opportunity to gain experience in a variety of trial consulting activities, such as posttrial interview of jurors, focus groups, and witness preparation. The development of the student-run and faculty-advised SRL was a natural transition for the LPP, which had long trained students with interests in trial consulting.[66]

The last major change during the Penrod years was the creation of the University of Nebraska Public Policy Center (PPC), established by the board of regents in 1998. Alan Tomkins took a leave of absence from the LPP to become the PPC's founding director, a position that he now occupies on a permanent basis. The PPC's mission is to conduct "analytic studies that address new or ongoing public policy issues of importance to Nebraskans."[67] It has been "involved in a variety of projects and activities affecting human services, mental health, government, agriculture, communities, and other facets of Nebraska life."[68] The PPC's advocacy work includes such diverse areas as business and economics (for example, promoting competitive employment for persons with disabilities), community development (for example, working with faith-based community organizations to improve access to behavioral health services), education, and government administration. Although the PPC is relatively young, it has been a boon to the University of Nebraska's research and outreach agendas and to the state of Nebraska in general.

The Wiener Years

In 2002, Richard L. Wiener returned to UNL to become the director of the program.[69] Wiener, trained as a social psychologist,[70] has published extensively on applications of social cognition, especially judgment and decision making, to law and the legal process. Before coming to the LPP, Wiener had gained a scholarly reputation in the study of judgment and decision making as applied to juries,[71] the death penalty,[72] sexual harassment,[73] negligence determinations,[74] end-of-life judgments,[75] and the relationship of social science to the law.[76] Wiener and his students write and research from an approach to law and social science that they call *social analytic jurisprudence.* It begins with the proposition that social scientists can and should influence law and legal policy.[77] These researchers use the psychological literature to posit answers to legal questions in the form of research hypotheses and then conduct empirical studies to test the hypothesized answers that they find in the social science literature. Through this process, the empirical scientist exposes the assumptions made in law and tests those assumptions against the accumulated results of scientific testing.[78]

The emerging emphasis in the LPP program is the application of legal decision making both as a tool for investigation and as a model for consultation and program evaluation. Since arriving at UNL, Wiener has continued his work on the death penalty,[79] sexual harassment,[80] and generic prejudice with grant support from NSF's Law and Social Science Program.[81] For example, Wiener and his students are continuing prior work in sexual harassment and expanding the application of models of judgment and decision making in juries to determine whether there are certain types of cases (for example, sexual assault or homicide) that jurors are unable to decide impartially. Wiener and his students are applying judgment and decision making models to additional areas, such as the effect of bankruptcy reform on consumer behavior.[82]

Other members of the LPP faculty (and students) have examined decision making in other areas of law. For example, Brian Bornstein, associate director of the LPP, applies models of judgment and decision making to problems in civil jury litigation and eyewitness identification. Bornstein has strong interests in applied decision making, especially in civil and criminal law. Bornstein, his colleagues, and his students have published a number of papers on jury decision making in liability judgments[83] and damage decisions[84] in civil litigation. In addition, Bornstein coauthored a volume reviewing research on how jurors award damages in civil cases.[85] This part of Bornstein's work[86] relies heavily on models of judgment and decision making, as does his other work on jurors' perceptions of eyewitness testimony,[87] sexual predator laws,[88] medical decision making,[89] and the government's regulation of drug testing for pregnant women.[90]

Robert Schopp is more centrally affiliated with the UNL College of Law than with the Psychology Department, although he holds appointments in both areas. As a clinical psychologist, philosopher, and law professor, Schopp is uniquely qualified to expose the assumptions that courts and legislatures make (sometimes unwittingly) about human conduct. Schopp's scholarship has important implications for how legal and psychological practitioners make legally relevant decisions. For example, his recent work concerning the duty of psychiatric professionals to protect foreseeable victims from harm by outpatients has far-reaching implications for judgment and decision making approaches to the standard of care.[91] Schopp is most interested in the philosophic underpinnings of punishment in the criminal justice system and has written extensively on this topic.[92]

Relationship to Law-Psychology Training More Broadly

Training programs in law and psychology provide graduates with the tools to apply psychological theories to legal practices so that they can conduct psycholegal research, work in mental health law and public policy programs, or practice as attorneys or psychologists.[93] Graduates of dual-degree programs obtain the best of both worlds, which allows them to apply their knowledge in a variety of settings[94] as well as to communicate with professionals in both law and psychology.[95]

Dual degrees may open doors that would otherwise remain closed, allowing students to pursue careers that single-degree students would find difficult to enter.[96] Furthermore, the joint training can serve as a bonus (for example, higher salary) once employment is obtained.[97] The experience of the LPP program in recent years shows that students with dual degrees do enjoy an advantage at least in the academic marketplace, if for no reason other than their qualification for a larger number of positions: J.D./Ph.D. students are eligible for careers in law, psychology, criminal justice, and other assorted social science departments.[98]

The LPP has been recognized since its founding in 1974 as a top program for training scholars in both basic and applied psycholegal research.[99] Students select one of three degree tracks: J.D./Ph.D., Ph.D./M.L.S., or J.D./M.A. All graduates in the program finish with at least a master's degree level of knowledge in the secondary field of study.[100] J.D./Ph.D. students receive full training and the highest degree in both disciplines. The LPP is one of only two programs in North America that offers the joint Ph.D./M.L.S. (master of legal studies) option.[101] This track serves students who are not interested in practicing law but who would like to develop an understanding of legal issues and procedures for use in their psychological research or practice.[102]

Alumni of the program have excelled in a number of ways. Recent graduates and current students have clerked for justices of the Nebraska Supreme Court and for U.S. district court judges. Other graduates have served as trial consultants on some of the highest-profile cases in recent history, including the Rodney King, O. J. Simpson, and Timothy McVeigh trials. A number of the program's graduates have used their interdisciplinary training to better their performance as attorneys.[103]

The Law-Psychology Program at UNL has also held conferences in which top legal and psychological scholars present lectures and lead discussions of specific psycholegal issues.[104] In sum, the Law-Psychology Program has been one of the most influential programs of its kind. Its rich history and successful alumni have allowed it to emerge as one of the most well-respected programs for psycholegal research.[105]

It is clear that the interests, skills, and academic characteristics of the faculty members at any given time determine the tenor of the training and scholarship in the program. Yet the hallmark feature of the LPP has been, and will continue to be, the interdisciplinary nature of training, research, and practice. Collaboration between the psychology and law faculties is strong at the graduate and professional levels, as exemplified by the dual-degree programs, and at the undergraduate level, as shown by a recent NSF award for a Research Experience for Undergraduates program.[106] This program, which also receives support from the UNL College of Arts and Sciences, Research Office, and Office of Undergraduate Studies, brings ten undergraduate students interested in studying psychology and law to our campus for each of three years (2005–8). The program emphasizes participation from a student body diverse in ethnic, cultural, and geographic respects.

In the last several years, the LPP has procured contracts with state, local, and federal government agencies to conduct program evaluation and applied research projects. These projects vary from developing violence prediction strategies for the U.S. capital police, to conducting needs assessment with regard to drug use for the Nebraska Medicaid Office, and to studying juvenile court performance with collaborators from the National Council of Juvenile and Family Court Judges. The LPP's long-range plan includes continued growth and improvement in the policy and program evaluation wing of the LPP program to train students for careers in policy analysis.

Over the next decade, the LPP scholarship agenda will likely become even broader to encompass a mature vision of law and psychology in all its areas. The future is bright and exciting for the Law and Psychology Program at the University of Nebraska, as it continues to play a unique and interesting role in the landscape of legal education in the state. After thirty years of existence, the program has become well-established, but its pioneering spirit survives.

Notes

We are grateful to Peterson Brink of the University of Nebraska Archives for his assistance in locating historical documents and to Dick Dienstbier and Harvey Perlman for sharing their memories of the law-psychology program's early days. We also thank Alan Tomkins and an anonymous reviewer for suggesting several relevant sources.

1. Much of the material in this section comes from (author unknown), "A Selected Review of the Development of the Law-Psychology Graduate Training Pro-

gram," unpaginated; and Bruce D. Sales, "Proposal for a Joint J.D.-Ph.D. Program in Law and Psychology," (Grant Proposal, October 1973), unpaginated [hereinafter "Proposal"], both in the University Archives/Special Collections, Love Library, University of Nebraska–Lincoln.

2. Proposal, 1; see generally Michael J. Saks, "Legal Policy Analysis and Evaluation," *American Psychologist* 44, no. 8 (1989): 1110–17.

3. Proposal, 6.

4. The proposal describes the full curriculum in detail. Ibid., 6–16. The curriculum has changed remarkably little over the years. For a current sample curriculum, see the LPP's Web site, http://psycweb.unl.edu/psylaw/.

5. Proposal, 22.

6. It is beyond the scope of the present work to treat the history of the larger law-psychology movement in depth, but several good sources exist. See, e.g., June L. Tapp, "Psychology and the Law: An Overture," *Annual Review of Psychology* 27 (1976): 359–404; Thomas Grisso, "A Developmental History of the American Law-Psychology Society," *Law and Human Behavior* 15, no. 3 (1991): 213–31; James R. P. Ogloff, Alan J. Tomkins, and Donald N. Bersoff, "Education and Training in Psychology and Law/Criminal Justice: Historical Foundations, Present Structures, and Future Developments," *Criminal Justice and Behavior* 23, no. 1 (1996): 200–235; Donald N. Bersoff, "Preparing for Two Cultures: Education and Training in Law and Psychology," in *Psychology and Law: The State of the Discipline,* ed. Ronald Roesch, Stephen D. Hart, and James R. P. Ogloff (New York: Kluwer Academic/Plenum Publishers, 1999), 375–401; James R. P. Ogloff and David Finkelman, "Psychology and Law: An Overview," in *Psychology and Law: The State of the Discipline,* ed. Ronald Roesch, Stephen D. Hart, and James R. P. Ogloff (New York: Kluwer Academic/Plenum Publishers, 1999), 1–20; Jeremy A. Blumenthal, "Law and Social Science in the Twenty-first Century," *Southern California Interdisciplinary Law Journal* 12, no. 1 (2002): 1–53.

7. The initial members of the committee were James Cole (psychology); David Levine (psychology); Harvey Perlman (law, currently chancellor of UNL); and Wallace Rudolph (law).

8. Melvin George, "Evaluation of Law-Psychology Graduate Program, University of Nebraska–Lincoln, April 13–14, 1976," 1, University Archives/Special Collections, Love Library, University of Nebraska–Lincoln. This evaluation was almost certainly a requirement set in place at the program's inception. Dr. George served as dean of the College of Arts and Sciences, University of Nebraska–Lincoln, from 1970 to 1975, during the LPP's planning and creation.

9. Ibid., 2.

10. To address this issue, George recommended appointing someone on the College of Law faculty to serve as the contact between the college and the LPP. Various individuals have, either formally or informally, filled this role over the years. Bob Schopp has performed this function since he joined the College of Law faculty in 1989.

11. This situation has stabilized considerably over the years. The LPP admits only those students whom it can support financially.

12. George, "Evaluation of Law-Psychology Graduate Program," 3.

13. This sort of concern is inevitable with the creation of any new program; today the LPP is a well-integrated unit within the Psychology Department.

14. George, "Evaluation of Law-Psychology Graduate Program," 4.

15. From "A Selected Review of the Development of the Law-Psychology Graduate Training Program," UNL Archives, 1, University Archives/Special Collections, Love Library, University of Nebraska–Lincoln.

16. Tapp, "Psychology and the Law." Tapp notes that a similar program was launched at Stanford University in 1972, but this program was, and continues to be, considerably smaller than the UNL program. Ibid., 368. See also Gary B. Melton, "Realism in Psychology and Humanism in Law: Psycholegal Studies at Nebraska," *Nebraska Law Review* 69, no. 2 (1990): 251–77. Bersoff observes, "Although there appears to have been a plan to develop a joint J.D./Ph.D. program in law and the social sciences at Northwestern University in the early 1970s . . . it is acknowledged that the first law and psychology program began at the University of Nebraska." Bersoff, "Preparing for Two Cultures," 388.

17. Tapp, "Psychology and the Law"; Alan J. Tomkins, "Introduction: Training and Career Issues," *Behavioral Sciences and the Law* 8, no. 3 (1990): 193–96.

18. See sources cited in note 17, *supra*. Additional material on the current state of law-psychology training is provided in the last section of this chapter, *infra*.

19. Program for "Law-Psychology Research Conference: Selected Issues in Our Criminal Justice System, October 16–17, 1975," University Archives/Special Collections, Love Library, University of Nebraska–Lincoln. This conference took place just a year after the first AP-LS conference in June 1974. Tapp, *supra* note 7, at 363.

20. Sales received his Ph.D. in psycholinguistics from the University of Rochester and his J.D. from Northwestern University School of Law.

21. See, e.g., Charles B. Keasey and Bruce D. Sales, "An Empirical Investigation of Young Children's Awareness and Usage of Intentionality in Criminal Situations," *Law and Human Behavior* 1, no. 1 (1977): 45–61; David L. Suggs and Bruce D. Sales, "Juror Self-Disclosure during the Voir Dire: A Social Science Analysis," *Indiana Law Journal* 56, no. 2 (1981): 245–71; Joseph S. Swoboda, Amiram Elwork, and Bruce D. Sales, "Knowledge of and Compliance with Privileged Communication and Child Abuse Reporting Laws," *Professional Psychology: Research and Practice* 9, no. 3 (1978): 448–57; Lynn R. Kahle and Bruce D. Sales, "The Attitudes of Clinical Psychologists toward Involuntary Civil Commitment Law," *Professional Psychology: Research and Practice* 9, no.3 (1978): 428–39; and Bruce D. Sales and Amiram Elwork, "Issues in the Forensic Training of Psychologists," in *Readings in Forensic Psychology,* ed. G. Cooke (Springfield, Ill.: Charles C. Thomas, 1980), 16–25.

22. See, e.g., Bruce D. Sales, Amiram Elwork, and James J. Alfini, "Improving Comprehension for Jury Instructions," in *The Criminal Justice System,* ed. Bruce D. Sales (New York: Plenum, 1977): 23–90.

23. Amiram Elwork, Bruce D. Sales, and James J. Alfini, *Making Jury Instructions Understandable* (Charlottesville, Va.: Michie, 1982).

24. 1976 Nebraska Laws LB 806 (An Act for the Commitment of Mentally Ill Dangerous People).

25. Bruce D. Sales, *Mental Disability Law in Nebraska* (Lincoln: Nebraska State Bar Association, 1977).

26. See, e.g., Gacy v. Wellborn, 994 F.2d 305 (7th Cir. 1993) (John Wayne Gacy's appeal of his death sentence), and State v. Butler, 951 S.W.2d 600 (Mo. 1997). Courts and legislatures have often been criticized for their reluctance to consider social science data; see, e.g., Bruce Sales and Gary vanden Bos, *Psychology in Litigation and Legislation* (Washington, D.C.: American Psychological Association, 1994); John Monahan and Laurens Walker, *Social Science in Law: Cases and Materials,* 5th ed. (New York: Foundation Press, 2002). It is impossible to document whether the empirical efforts of Sales and others affiliated with the UNL program have been unusually successful in this regard; but such attention from law- and policy-making bodies is clearly not the norm.

27. *Law and Human Behavior* is highly respected in the field and has a consistently high impact factor (1.135 for 2006). Other journals in which law-psychology faculty members frequently publish also have high impact factors, e.g., *Behavioral Sciences and the Law* (1.793) and *Journal of Applied Psychology* (2.892).

28. Thomas Grisso, "A Developmental History of the American Law-Psychology Society," *Law and Human Behavior* 15, no. 3 (1991): 213–31.

29. Ibid, 224.

30. Ibid.

31. Bruce Sales, *Psychology and the Legal Process* (New York: Spectrum, 1977).

32. See note 27, *supra.*

33. A book series published first in 1977.

34. Grisso, "Developmental History," 225.

35. Ibid., 213–31.

36. Dick Dienstbier, a social-personality psychologist and former chair of the Psychology Department, served as interim director from 1981 to 1982 after Sales left UNL. Melton received his Ph.D. from Boston University.

37. See, e.g., Gary B. Melton, "Bringing Psychology to the Legal System: Opportunities, Obstacles, and Efficacy," *American Psychologist* 42, no. 5 (1987): 488–95.

38. Gary B. Melton, "Children, Politics, and Morality: The Ethics of Child Advocacy," *Journal of Clinical Child Psychology* 16, no. 4 (1987): 357–67.

39. Gary B. Melton, "Children's Competency to Testify," *Law and Human Behavior* 5, no. 1 (1981): 73–85; Gary B. Melton, "Psychological Issues in Juveniles' Competency to Waive Their Rights," *Journal of Clinical Child Psychology* 10, no. 1 (1981): 59–62.

40. Gary B. Melton, "Toward 'Personhood' for Adolescents: Autonomy and Privacy as Values in Public Policy," *American Psychologist* 38, no. 1 (1983): 99–103.

41. Gary B. Melton, *Reforming the Law: Impact of Child Development Research* (New York: Guilford, 1987).

42. Gary B. Melton and Michael J. Saks, "The Law as an Instrument of Socialization and Social Structure," *Nebraska Symposium on Motivation* 33 (1985): 235–73.

43. Gary B. Melton, ed., *The Individual, the Family, and Social Good: Personal Fulfillment in Times of Change,* Nebraska Symposium on Motivation 42 (Lincoln: University of Nebraska Press, 1995).

44. Gary B. Melton, "Legal Regulation of Adolescent Abortion: Unintended Effects," *American Psychologist* 42, no.1 (1987): 79–83.

45. Gary B. Melton, "Public Policy and Private Prejudice: Psychology and Law on Gay Rights," *American Psychologist* 44, no.6 (1989): 933–40.

46. See, e.g., Gary B. Melton, Robert J. Levine, and Gerald P. Koocher, "Community Consultation in Socially Sensitive Research: Lessons from Clinical Trials of Treatment for AIDS," *American Psychologist* 43, no. 7 (1988): 573–81.

47. Gary B. Melton, "Law, Science, and Humanity: The Normative Foundation of Social Science in Law," *Law and Human Behavior* 14, no. 4 (1990): 315–32.

48. Gary B. Melton and Brian Wilcox, "Changes in Family Law and Family Life: Challenges for Psychology," *American Psychologist* 44, no. 9 (1989): 1213–16.

49. Gary B. Melton, "Socialization in the Global Community: Respect for the Dignity of Children," *American Psychologist* 46, no. 1 (1991): 66–71.

50. E.g., Scott W. Henggeler, Gary B. Melton, and Linda A. Smith, "Assessing Violent Offending in Serious Juvenile Offenders," *Journal of Abnormal Child Psychology* 21, no. 3 (1993): 233–43.

51. Gary B. Melton, John Petrila, and Norman G. Pothress, *Psychological Evaluations for the Courts: A Handbook for Mental Health Professionals and Lawyers* (New York: Guilford, 1987).

52. Robert F. Schopp, "Therapeutic Jurisprudence and Conflicts among Values in Mental Health Law," *Behavioral Sciences and the Law* 11, no. 1 (1993): 31–45.

53. E.g., Robert F. Schopp, "Punishment as Treatment and the Obligations of Treatment Providers," *International Journal of Law and Psychiatry* 7, no. 2 (1984): 197–205.

54. From the center's Web site, http://ccfl.unl.edu/about.

55. Maryland v. Craig, 497 U.S. 836 (1990). See Gary B. Melton and Susan Limber, "Psychologists' Involvement in Cases of Maltreatment: Limits of Role Expertise," *American Psychologist* 44, no. 9 (1989): 1225–33; Gary B. Melton, "Sexually Abused Children and the Legal System: Some Policy Recommendations," *American Journal of Family Therapy* 61, no. 1 (1985): 61–67.

56. Thomas Grisso, "A Developmental History of the American Law-Psychology Society," *Law and Human Behavior* 15, no. 3 (1991): 213–31.

57. Ibid., 229.

58. J.D., Ph.D., Harvard University.

59. This is not to say that work on mental health policy and advocacy lapsed during Penrod's tenure. These ongoing efforts included conferences hosted by the LPP in November 1996 on Therapeutic Jurisprudence and in April 1999 on HIV-AIDS: Issues in Treatment, Stigma, and Policy, both of which attracted internationally prominent scholars (e.g., David Carson, Jane Goodman-Delahunty, Thomas Grisso, Gregory Herek, Ronald Roesch, and David Wexler).

60. See, e.g., Reid Hastie, Steven Penrod, and Nancy Pennington, *Inside the Jury* (Cambridge, Mass.: Harvard University Press, 1983); Brian Cutler and Steven Penrod, *Mistaken Identifications: The Eyewitness, Psychology, and Law* (New York: Cambridge University Press, 1995).

61. See Gary L. Wells, Mark Small, and Steven D. Penrod, "Eyewitness Identification Procedures: Recommendations for Lineups and Photospreads," *Law and Human Behavior* 22, no. 6 (1998): 603–47.

62. Kumho Tire Co., Ltd. v. Carmichael, 526 U.S. 137 (1999). The amicus brief in *Kumho* has been published as Neil Vidmar, Richard O. Lempert, and Shari S. Diamond, "Amicus Brief: *Kumho Tire v. Carmichael*," *Law and Human Behavior* 24, no. 4 (2000): 387–400.

63. See, e.g., Medina v. People, 114 P.3d 845 (Colo. 2005); U.S. v. Smithers, 212 F.3d 306 (6th Cir. 2000).

64. See, e.g., Kevin M. O'Neil, Steven D. Penrod, and Brian H. Bornstein, "Web-Based Research: Methodological Variables' Effects on Dropout and Sample Characteristics," *Behavioral Research Methods, Instruments and Computers* 35, no. 2 (2003): 217–26; Dennis P. Stolle and Jennifer K. Robbennolt, "Fractional Factorial Designs for Legal Psychology," *Behavioral Sciences and the Law* 20, no. 1–2 (2002): 5–17; and Siegfried Sporer, Steven Penrod, Don Read, and Brian Cutler, "Choosing, Confidence, and Accuracy: A Meta-analysis of the Confidence-Accuracy Relation in Eyewitness Identification Studies," *Psychological Bulletin* 118, no. 3 (1995): 315–27.

65. See, e.g., Christina A. Studebaker, Jennifer K. Robbennolt, and Maithilee Pathak-Sharma, "Assessing Pretrial Publicity Effects: Integrating Content Analytic Results," *Law and Human Behavior* 24, no. 3 (2000): 317–37.

66. At the time of this writing, Dan Wolfe, an LPP graduate, was the current president of the American Society of Trial Consultants.

67. Taken from the PPC website, http://ppc.unl.edu.

68. Ibid.

69. Wiener was, coincidentally, the first student to graduate from the LPP with a master of legal studies (MLS) degree, having come to UNL while on a sabbatical from St. Louis University.

70. Ph.D., University of Houston.

71. E.g., Richard L. Wiener, Kristen Habert, and Gina Shkodriani, "The Social Psychology of Jury Nullification," *Journal of Applied Social Psychology* 21, no. 17 (1991): 1379–1401.

72. Richard L. Wiener, Linda E. Hurt, and Susan L. Thomas, "The Role of Declarative and Procedural Knowledge in Capital Murder Sentencing," *Journal of Applied Social Psychology* 28, no. 2 (1998): 124–44.

73. E.g., Richard L. Wiener and Linda E. Hurt, "How Do People Evaluate Social Sexual Conduct at Work? A Psychological Model," *Journal of Applied Psychology* 85, no. 1 (2000): 75–85.

74. E.g., Richard L. Wiener, Mauricio Gaborit, Christine C. Pritchard, and Erin M. McDonough, "Counterfactual Thinking in Mock Juror Assignments of Negligence: A Preliminary Investigation," *Behavioral Sciences and the Law* 12, no. 1 (1994): 89–102.

75. E.g., Richard L. Wiener, David Eton, Vincent P. Gibbons, Jesse A. Goldner, and Sandra Johnson, "A Preliminary Analysis of Medical Futility Decisionmaking: Law and Professional Attitudes," *Behavioral Sciences and the Law* 16, no. 4 (1998): 497–508.

76. E.g., Richard L. Wiener, "Social Analytic Jurisprudence in Sexual Harassment Litigation: The Role of Social Framework and Social Fact," *Journal of Social Issues* 51, no. 1 (1995): 167–80.

77. Richard L. Wiener and Linda E. Hurt, "An Interdisciplinary Approach to Understanding Social Sexual Conduct at Work," *Psychology, Public Policy and Law* 5, no. 3 (1999): 556–95.

78. Richard L. Wiener, "Social Analytic Jurisprudence and Tort Law: Social Cognition Goes to Court," *St. Louis University Law Journal* 37, (Spring 1993): 503–51.

79. E.g., Richard L. Wiener and Craig Haney, "The Death Penalty in the United States: A Crisis of Conscience," *Psychology Public Policy and Law* 10, no.4 (2004): 618–21, and Richard L. Wiener, "Death Penalty Research in Nebraska: How Do Judges and Juries Reach Penalty Decisions?" *Nebraska Law Review* 81, no. 2 (2002): 757–76.

80. E.g., Richard L. Wiener, Ryan Winter, Melanie Rogers, and Lucy Arnot, "The Effects of Prior Workplace Behavior on Subsequent Sexual Harassment Judgments," *Law and Human Behavior* 28, no. 1 (2004): 47–67.

81. Richard L. Wiener, "The Effects of Observed Conduct, Legal Standards, and Investigative Interviews on Sexual Harassment Judgments," *National Science Foundation, Law and Social Sciences Program* (grant proposal, 2001–5), n.p.; "Comprehensibility of Penalty Phase Instructions: Motivation of Jurors and Quality of Instructions," *National Science Foundation, Law and Social Sciences Program* (grant proposal, 2004–6), n.p.; "Jury Bias in Criminal Cases: Sexual Assault, Homicide, and Generic Prejudice," *National Science Foundation, Law and Social Sciences Program* (grant proposal, 2005–7), n.p., on file with the author.

82. E.g., Richard L. Wiener, Susan Block-Lieb, Karen Gross, and Corinne Baron-Donovan, "Unwrapping Assumptions: Applying Social Analytic Jurisprudence to Consumer Bankruptcy Law," *American Bankruptcy Law Journal* 79, no. 2 (2005): 453–83.

83. E.g., Brian H. Bornstein, "The Impact of Different Types of Expert Scientific Testimony on Mock Jurors' Liability Verdicts," *Psychology Crime and Law* 10, no. 4 (2004): 429–46.

84. E.g., Susan Poser, Brian H. Bornstein, and Kiernan E. McGorty, "Measuring Damages for Lost Enjoyment of Life: The View from the Bench and the Jury Box," *Law and Human Behavior* 27, no. 1 (2003): 53–68 and Brian H. Bornstein, Lahna M. Rung, and Monica K. Miller, "The Effects of Defendant Remorse on Mock Juror Decisions in a Malpractice Case," *Behavioral Science and the Law* 20, no.11 (2002): 393–409.

85. Edie Greene and Brian H. Bornstein, *Determining Damages: The Psychology of Jury Awards* (Washington, D.C.: American Psychological Association, 2003).

86. E.g., Brian H. Bornstein, Brooke L. Whisenhunt, Robert J. Nemeth, and Deborah L. Dunaway, "Pretrial Publicity and Civil Cases: A Two-Way Street?" *Law and Human Behavior* 26, no. 1 (2002): 3–17.

87. E.g., Brian H. Bornstein and Stephanie L. Muller, "The Credibility of Recovered Memory Testimony: Exploring the Effects of Alleged Victim and Perpetrator Gender," *Child Abuse and Neglect* 25, no. 11 (2001): 1415–26.

88. Cynthia C. Mercado, Robert F. Schopp, and Brian H. Bornstein, "Evaluating Sex Offenders under Sexually Violent Predator Laws: How Might Mental Health Professionals Conceptualize the Notion of Volitional Impairment?" *Aggression and Violent Behavior* 10, no. 3 (2003): 289–309; Cynthia C. Mercado, Brian H. Bornstein, and Robert F. Schopp, "Decision-Making about Volitional Impairment in Sexually Violent Predators," *Law and Human Behavior* 30, no. 5 (2006): 587–602.

89. E.g., Brian H. Bornstein, A. Christine Emler, and Gretchen B. Chapman, "Rationality in Medical Treatment Decisions: Is There a Sunk-Cost Effect?" *Social Science and Medicine* 49, no. 2 (1999): 215–22.

90. Brian H. Bornstein, "Pregnancy, Drug Testing, and the Fourth Amendment: Legal and Behavioral Implications," *Journal of Family Psychology* 17, no. 2 (2003): 220–28.

91. E.g., Michael R. Quattrocchi and Robert Schopp, "Tarasaurus Rex: A Standard of Care That Could Not Adapt," *Psychology Public Policy and Law* 11, no. 1 (2005): 109–37.

92. E.g., Robert F. Schopp, *Competence, Condemnation, and Commitment* (Washington, D.C.: American Psychological Association, 2001). See also *Nebraska Law Review* 81, no. 2 (2002–3), which contains papers from a symposium organized by Schopp.

93. See Bette Bottoms, Mark Costanzo, Edie Greene, Allison Redlich, Jennifer Woolard, and Patricia Zapf, "Careers in Psychology and the Law: A Guide for Prospective Students," American Psychology-Law Society, http://www.ap-ls.org/students/careers%20in%20psychology.pdf.

94. Thomas L. Hafemeister, James R. P. Ogloff, and Mark. A. Small, "Training and Careers in Law and Psychology: The Perspective of Students and Graduates of Dual Degrees," *Behavioral Sciences and the Law* 8, no. 3 (1990): 263–83.

95. Gary Melton, "Training in Psychology and the Law," in *Handbook of Forensic Psychology,* ed. Allen K. Hess and Irving B. Weiner (New York: John Wiley and Sons, 1987), 700–20; Alan J. Tomkins and James R. P. Ogloff, "Training and Career Options in Psychology and Law," *Behavioral Sciences and the Law* 8, no. 3 (1990): 205–16; Bersoff, "Preparing for Two Cultures."

96. Donald N. Bersoff, Jane Goodman-Delahunty, and Thomas J. Grisso, "Training in Law and Psychology: Models from the Villanova Conference," *American Psychologist* 52, no. 12 (1997): 1301–10.

97. Alan J. Tomkins and James R. P. Ogloff, "Training and Career Options in Psychology and Law," *Behavioral Sciences and the Law* 8, no. 3 (1990): 205–16.

98. Ibid.

99. See, e.g., Tapp, "Psychology and the Law"; Bersoff, "Preparing for Two Cultures."

100. University of Nebraska–Lincoln, Law and Psychology Program, http://psycweb.unl.edu/psypage/dynamic.asp?dir=grad&page=lawpsych.htm.

101. "Forensic Psychology Programs," http://www.psywww.com/careers/forensic.htm. Stanford University has the other MLS program.

102. "Information for Prospective Students," Psychology-Law Program, University of Nebraska–Lincoln, http://psycweb.unl.edu/psylaw/prospective_students.htm.

103. E.g., Dennis Stolle, an attorney and trial consultant with Barnes & Thornburg LLP, recently published a textbook on therapeutic jurisprudence. Dennis P. Stolle, David B. Wexler, and Bruce J. Winick, *Practicing Therapeutic Jurisprudence: Law as a Helping Profession* (Durham, N.C.: Carolina Academic Press, 2000).

104. Recent conferences have been funded by the Visiting Scholar Program in the Law and Psychology Program. Program of Excellence (UNL) award made to Richard L. Wiener (PI), Brian H. Bornstein, Robert F. Schopp, and Steve Willborn

(2005–8). The first symposium, entitled "Legal Decision Making in Everyday Life: Controversies in Social Consciousness," featured a three-day seminar in 2005 that brought together eminent psychological and legal authors in the areas of affirmative action, discrimination at work, racial profiling, and regulation of hate behavior and speech. See Richard L. Wiener, Brian H. Bornstein, Robert Schopp, Steven L. Wilborn, eds., *Social Consciousness in Legal Decision Making: Psychological and Legal Perspectives* (New York: Springer, 2007). The second symposium, held in 2006, covered a variety of issues related to civil juries and civil justice. See Brian H. Bornstein, Robert Schopp, and Richard L. Wiener, eds., *Civil Juries and Civil Justice: Psychological Perspectives* (New York: Springer, 2008). The third symposium, held in 2007, focused on mental health issues in criminal law. Other noteworthy conferences sponsored by the LPP have been mentioned throughout this article.

105. E.g., Tapp, "Psychology and the Law"; Bersoff, "Preparing for Two Cultures."

106. Richard L. Wiener, "Psychology and Law: Research Experiences for Undergraduates at the University of Nebraska-Lincoln," *National Science Foundation* (grant proposal, 2005–8), n.p., on file with the author.

TEN

Mark R. Scherer

NEBRASKA NATIVE AMERICAN LEGAL HISTORY

An Overview

Nebraska holds a prominent position in the field of Native American legal history. Over the past two centuries, the state's native inhabitants have been at the center of many sweeping developments in federal Indian policy. On dozens of legal issues—treaty making, land dispossession, removal policy, allotment, forced acculturation, civil rights, criminal jurisdiction, land claims, water and mineral rights, and gaming conflicts—Nebraska's Native American nations have shaped and been shaped by broad-based evolutionary shifts in the exceedingly complex pathways of federal Indian law.

The resulting historical legacy is just as complex. Nebraska Indian legal history is replete with stories of failure and success, triumph and heartache, hope and misery—but those qualities have not always been present in equal measures. Nebraska's aboriginal inhabitants have endured more than their fair share of suffering and hardship, yet they remain today a vibrant and significant force in the state's social, cultural, and political milieu. Their modern status is largely the result of legal developments that have become obscured by the passage of time. It is a legal history that deserves to be remembered.[1]

Nebraska today is the home of four Native American nations. The Omaha Tribe, headquartered in Macy, Nebraska, controls a reservation of some 180,000 acres that comprises the southern half of Thurston County along the Missouri River in the northeastern corner of the state. Immediately adjacent to the Omaha, the Winnebago Tribe occupies a reservation of approximately 120,000 acres that makes up the northern half of Thurston County, with tribal headquarters located at the village of Winnebago. In the north-central part of the state, the Santee Sioux occupy a reservation in Knox County near the confluence of the Niobrara and Missouri rivers along the South Dakota border. The fourth modern Nebraska tribe, the Northern Ponca, was restored to federally recognized status in 1990. Although the Ponca do not have a reservation in the state, they maintain tribal headquarters in the town of Niobrara just west of the Santee Reservation and are striving to rebuild a land base and cultural community in their ancestral homelands in that area of the state. Although these groups are the only Indian nations with a physical tribal presence in modern Nebraska, they are certainly not the only Native American nations with historical connections to the state. (In fact, compared to some other tribes, several modern Nebraska Indian groups are relative newcomers to the region.)

In the centuries before Lewis and Clark made the first formal American contact with the area that later became the state of Nebraska, the region was the permanent home to thousands of Native Americans. The Omaha, Otoe-Missouria, Pawnee, and Ponca nations were well-established in what is now the eastern half of the state and probably comprised more than fifteen thousand inhabitants living in dozens of small villages scattered along the region's principal waterways.[2] In the western and northern portions of modern Nebraska, nomadic Sioux, Cheyenne, and Arapahoe bands lived and roamed, epitomizing the classic Plains Indian lifestyles that became part of the iconic imagery of the nineteenth-century American Wild West. Those western bands never established a permanent or sedentary occupation in the region, and by the late nineteenth century, even their nomadic roaming in the area had been terminated by a combination of resource depletion, military conquest, and forcible displacement. Accordingly, the discussion that follows will be directed primarily to those Indian groups that once did or still do maintain a permanent presence in Nebraska.[3]

On August 3, 1804, Lewis and Clark conducted their first parley with American Indians on a bluff overlooking the Missouri River, at a site located about twenty miles north of present-day Omaha. At that first meeting, the federal representatives sought to convince six Otoe-Missouria headmen that their new Great Father in Washington, D.C., would protect them from their enemies and engage with them in a mutually profitable fur trade, provided that they directed their allegiance to the American government and rejected the continuing overtures of the French, Spanish, and English traders who had been operating in the area for many years.[4] Gifts were exchanged, mutual promises were made, and the Corps of Discovery proceeded up the Missouri, to repeat the process with other Native American nations. In the aftermath of that initial contact, the lives and destinies of the Nebraska Indians were profoundly changed. In those fateful changes for the Nebraska Indians may be found a microcosmic case study in the broader themes and patterns of Native American legal history.

Omaha

Having lent their name to the state's largest city and possessing one of the largest and most visible populations among Indian groups in the state today, the Omaha Tribe is arguably the most prominent and identifiable modern manifestation of the long Native American presence in Nebraska. The Omahas' legal history, like that of the other Nebraska tribes, provides a prototypical example of the way in which broad-based shifts in federal Indian policy have trickled down to the grassroots level of individual Indian nations, often with devastating effect. At the same time, the continuing and dynamic presence of the Omaha in Nebraska today serves as a powerful illustration of the resiliency and perseverance of Indian nations throughout the United States. Often, that tenacity has taken the form of legal struggles, as Indian nations have sought to avail themselves of judicial and legislative remedies for years of hardship and deprivation. Many times, the Omaha and the other Nebraska Indian nations have led the way in forging this unique and complex legal legacy.[5]

The people who ultimately came to be called the Omaha Tribe of Nebraska arrived on the Great Plains several hundred years ago, migrating westward with their close relatives the Ponca from a "wooded country near a great body of water."[6] By 1775, the Omaha had separated from the Ponca and had established a home territory in what is today northeastern Nebraska, centered on their settlement at Large Village along Omaha Creek. The eighteenth-century Omaha practiced a seminomadic Plains Indian lifestyle, spending about three months of each year in their earth-lodge villages cultivating corn, beans, pumpkins, and squash and ranging far out onto the plains on both sides of the Missouri River for their semiannual bison hunts—generally held in the early summer after planting and again in the late fall after the harvest.[7]

The Omahas' spiritual life centered on Umon'hon'ti, the Sacred Pole, also known as the Venerable Man. According to tribal history, the pole was "a gift from Wakon'da," the Great Spirit, cut from a luminous burning tree whose fire could be seen only at night. Umon'hon'ti served as a deeply powerful symbol of tribal identity, unity, and authority, and it was preserved through the years by a succession of honored priests, or "keepers."[8] As tribal fortunes declined through the nineteenth century, the Sacred Pole ultimately found its way to the Peabody Museum at Harvard University, where it was housed as an obscure ethnocultural relic until 1989, when it was returned to the tribe after a long and emotional campaign by the Omaha and their non-Indian supporters. The story of the Sacred Pole and its return to the Omaha has been the subject of substantial academic and popular attention.[9]

Although the first white contact with the Omaha is difficult to pinpoint, the tribe was known to French fur traders as early as 1724. Through the 1700s, the tribe generally prospered, becoming increasingly enmeshed in the burgeoning and lucrative European fur trade along the Middle Missouri River. From about 1780 to 1800 were the glory years for the Omaha. Under the leadership of their enigmatic and controversial chief, Black Bird, the well-armed Omaha were able to force traders coming upriver to stop, unload their wares, and bargain for safe passage. So powerful was Black Bird's presence that French, Spanish, and English traders could not hope to succeed without gaining and keeping the great chief's favor. When trader James Mackay constructed a cabin and trading post near the Omahas' Large Village in 1795, he advised his company that Black Bird was "more despotic than any European prince" and instructed them to ensure that the chief received a suitably prestigious annual gift.[10]

The Omahas' golden age did not last long. Like so many of their brethren across the country, they were brought down not by Europeans' guns but by their germs. A smallpox epidemic swept through the tribe in the winter of 1800–1801, killing Chief Black Bird and reducing the tribe's population by as much as one-half. Their longtime enemies, the Sioux, quickly took advantage of the Omahas' weakened condition and unsettled leadership, sweeping down from the north in the years immediately after the epidemic to ravage the tribe in bloody raids. By 1810, the once-powerful Omaha had lost control of their northeastern Nebraska territory to the Sioux. Reduced to near starvation and nomadic wandering, the tribe attempted to regroup farther to the south along the Elkhorn River, but Sioux attacks continued. By 1815, some whites thought the Omaha to be teetering on the brink of extinction.

It was at this low ebb in its history that the tribe first entered into a formal relationship with the young American government. On July 20, 1815, several Omaha chiefs and warriors executed a "treaty of peace and friendship" by which the tribe purported to place itself under the exclusive protection of the United States. This ostensibly innocuous Portage des Sioux Treaty of 1815 proved to have far-reaching consequences for the tribe—a fateful first step in what became a long series of disastrous treaties with the U.S. government. Cumulatively and inexorably, those agreements resulted in massive land cessions that culminated in the tribe's 1854 treaty, wherein it relinquished all of its traditional homeland in return for a 300,000-acre reservation in the Blackbird Hills of northeastern Nebraska.

Tribal fortunes continued to decline after the Omaha moved onto their new reservation in the 1850s. Depredations by the Sioux continued, despite treaty assurances to the Omaha that they would be protected by the United States. White settlers and land speculators, dissatisfied with Indian control of the fertile and picturesque Blackbird Hills area, crowded the reservation from all sides. Promised annuities of foodstuffs and other provisions were chronically late in arriving and often of inferior quality. As white homesteaders pushed farther onto the Nebraska plains, the bison became increasingly scarce, until eventually that "pillar of the Omahas' traditional life" was eliminated as well. Through it all, however, the Omahas' agricultural fields continued to produce excellent yields, and their population actually increased slightly during the 1860s to a total of 1,020 by 1870.[11]

Ironically, the perceived success of the Omaha on their reservation during the 1860s and 1870s led to further government attempts to deconstruct their tribal identity through assimilationist reforms. Beginning in the 1870s and continuing virtually to this day, the Omaha have borne more than their fair share of the burden of shifting government policies. Indeed, since the establishment of their reservation in 1854, the Omaha have served as involuntary guinea pigs in the laboratory of federal Indian policy, whose every new program contributed, until recently, to a cumulatively devastating impact on the tribe's culture and economy.

The Omaha suffered particularly grievous consequences from the assimilationist initiatives pushed through Congress in the late nineteenth century by various eastern reform groups that came to be known collectively as the "Friends of the Indian." The centerpiece of the reformers' program was a move toward detribalization through the allotment of reservation lands to individual Indians. In 1882, the Omaha became one of the first tribes in the nation to undergo the allotment process, pursuant to a statute enacted largely at the behest of the tribe's most renowned white benefactor, Alice Fletcher. Fletcher's role in the story of the Omahas' ultimate dispossession is both critical and complex. She unquestionably possessed a sincere and deeply held interest in the tribe's well-being and no doubt believed that her actions would help the Omaha to survive and to thrive. Indeed, her vigorous campaign for allotment on the Omaha Reservation was supported by many influential tribal members who believed, as she did, that individual ownership of the land would protect the Omaha from removal to Indian Territory in Oklahoma and would provide a valuable and secure legacy for their children. Despite those good intentions, allotment proved disastrous to the tribe in every conceivable way—economic, social, and cultural. Wracked by pervasive poverty, alcoholism, and other social ills, many Omaha leased their allotments to white farmers or speculators. Even more sold their lands outright. By 1910, 50,000 acres of Omaha land had been lost, and forty-five years later, that figure had risen to more than 107,000 acres, leaving only about 28,000 acres of the tribe's formerly vast homeland in Omaha hands.[12]

Despite the pernicious effect of the 1882 allotment proceedings on tribal landholdings, government bureaucrats and assimilation advocates touted the Omaha experiment as a success, paving the way for the landmark 1887 Dawes Severalty Act, which extended the allotment program nationwide. As historian Michael Tate has observed, the net effect of the allotment programs first instituted on the Omaha Reservation was "the impoverishment of Indians everywhere, the loss of more than ninety million acres of land once guaranteed by treaty, and the total assault upon Indian culture in the name of pragmatic assimilation."[13]

During much of the twentieth century, the Omaha continued to play the role of sacrificial pawns in the chess game of Indian policy making. As Bureau of Indian Affairs commissioner John Collier's relatively enlightened Indian New Deal of the 1930s gave way to the misguided postwar swing toward termination, the Omaha Reservation once again became the proving ground for a new direction in Indian policy. The passage of Public Law 280 in 1953 transferred civil and criminal jurisdiction over reservations in five selected states, including Nebraska, from the federal government to state and local governments.[14] As developments on the Omaha Reservation subsequently proved, almost no one at the federal, state, or local level had accurately envisioned the potential impact of that action on the designated reservations. Indeed, many Nebraska state officials proved to be woefully ignorant of the meaning and effect of PL 280, even years after its passage and despite the state's ostensible prior consent to its provisions.

Like the allotment experiments seventy years earlier, the transfer of federal criminal jurisdiction over the Omaha Reservation to the state of Nebraska produced catastrophic results. Law enforcement on the Omaha reservation had been minimal at best even before the transfer, but the shift of jurisdiction to the state made an already bad situation significantly worse. A combination of inadequate state funding and racial tension between the Omaha and their white neighbors in Thurston County brought additional lawlessness and jurisdictional chaos to the reservation. Thus, the Omaha again attained unwanted national prominence, this time as the unfortunate victims of the bureaucratic folly inherent in PL 280.[15]

In part because of the jurisdictional debacle on the Omaha Reservation, Congress amended PL 280 in 1968 to allow states to retrocede Indian jurisdiction to the federal government.[16] The state of Nebraska, seeing an opportunity to rid itself of an expensive bureaucratic headache—but again not clearly understanding what it was doing—initially offered to return jurisdiction to the federal government. Its offer was accepted. Although the state later changed its mind and attempted to rescind its offer of retrocession, the federal courts negated that effort. The Omaha then became the first Indian tribe in the PL 280 group to escape state criminal jurisdiction. After retrocession, the tribe created its own police force and tribal court system, but conflicts between the Omaha and local law enforcement authorities concerning jurisdictional uncertainties continue to plague the county to this day.[17]

The postwar years also saw a shift in federal policy regarding the legal resolution of Indian grievances stemming from two hundred years of broken treaties. When Congress created the Indian Claims Commission (ICC) in 1946, it sought to provide a forum for the final resolution of all lingering Native American legal claims, as a precursor to the eventual termination of tribal existence and the full assimilation of Indians into white society. Like almost every other tribe in the country, the Omaha took advantage of this new avenue of redress, filing two separate claims before the commission.[18]

Just as the Omahas' experience with PL 280 and retrocession offers an instructive case study for the localized impact of those policies, so the tribe's experience before the ICC provides valuable insights into both the merits and the flaws of the commission's operations. Ultimately, the Omaha came to negotiated agreements with the government for the compromise and resolution of both claims. In reaching those results, the Omaha achieved another nationally significant first, as their pathbreaking compromise with the government forged the commission's so-called Omaha Rule for the processing of similar settlements in dozens of other cases.[19] In 1960, the tribe received an award of $2.9 million in settlement of grievances arising out of the inadequate compensation paid for their Nebraska homelands pursuant to the 1854 treaty.[20] Four years later, they received a second award of $1.75 million in settlement of their claims arising from the loss of aboriginal lands located east of the Missouri River, in modern-day Iowa.[21]

Although those ICC awards provided a much-needed infusion of funds into tribal coffers, the Omahas' experience before the ICC, like that of virtually every other Indian nation that sought relief there, cannot be considered a perfect, or even a complete, resolution of tribal claims. In the first place, the judgments were obtained only after nearly twenty years of tedious and complex litigation that sorely taxed tribal patience and resources. In addition, the awards were diminished by the payment of hundreds of thousands of dollars in attorneys fees, expert witness expenses, and various other setoffs mandated by ICC procedures. Most significantly, the ICC's remedial powers were constrained—fatally so—by the fact that it was not authorized to award interest to Indian claimants on amounts due them. By failing to take into account the time value of the money owed to the Indians, the ICC judgments received by all the Indian claimants, including the Omaha, fell substantially short of making the tribes whole for the injustices they had suffered. Finally, and in some ways most disturbingly, the Omahas' receipt of the ICC judgment funds resulted in the development of troubling intratribal factionalism over the distribution of proceeds. Controversies centering on the use of tribal funds still occasionally plague the tribe to this day, generally pitting tribal members who live in urban areas against those who live on the reservation.

In the 1970s and 1980s, the Omaha retained their prominence as legal warriors, waging a prolonged and exceedingly complex judicial battle in which they sought to regain possession of more than 11,000 acres situated east of the Missouri River. The tribe claimed that the land had been a part of its reservation before changes in the river channel moved it to the Iowa side, where it was occupied over time by white farmers.[22] The story of the Blackbird Bend litigation exposes several recurring and important aspects of modern Indian relations.[23] Among those themes are issues relating to Indian political and legal activism, racial tensions between tribes and their white neighbors, and the often controversial role of the federal government as the continuing trustee of Indian lands. The Blackbird Bend litigation is particularly noteworthy on the latter issue because the Omaha spent nearly as much energy fighting against the United States' representation of the tribe as they did battling the white claimants in Iowa. Ultimately, the Omaha won an imperfect victory at Blackbird Bend, regaining a small portion of the land they sought, which has become the site of their current tribal gaming operation, Casino Omaha.

Pawnee

Whereas the Omaha maintain one of the most prominent and identifiable Indian presences in Nebraska today, the Pawnee Nation claims the longest and most deeply embedded historical roots in the state. According to tribal oral tradition, the Pawnee migrated into central Nebraska and northern Kansas from the southwestern plains, probably during the sixteenth and seventeenth centuries.[24] The Pawnee Nation is composed of four distinct bands. The Skidi—Wolf, or Loup Pawnee—were the first to arrive on the central plains, establishing their villages in the Loup River watershed of east-central Nebraska by the early 1700s. In later years, the Grand, Republican, and Toppage Pawnee bands followed the Skidi northward, settling along the Platte River, which bisects the state of Nebraska on an east-west axis, and the Republican River, which meanders along the border between Nebraska and Kansas.[25] During these generations of movement onto the central plains, the Pawnee began to acquire horses from the Spanish. Over time, they accumulated huge herds, both through raids on neighboring tribes and through successful breeding and husbandry practices, and they became remarkably adept horse warriors. The Pawnee maintained extensive and generally lucrative trade relationships with a wide range of partners, including other Nebraska tribes like the Omaha and the Ponca, as well as the Arikara to the north and the Wichita to the south. They even dispatched trade expeditions to points as far south as the Spanish outposts in and around Santa Fe.

During the late seventeenth and much of the eighteenth centuries, the Spanish and French vied for imperial and commercial control over the Nebraska plains. Both European interests sought to ally themselves with the powerful Pawnee. The Pawnees' tilt toward the French culminated in 1720, when a Pawnee military force attacked and nearly annihilated a Spanish force commanded by Don Pedro de Villasur at the confluence of the Loup and Platte rivers near present-day Columbus, Nebraska. The Villasur Massacre, as the battle became known in Spanish accounts, represented a high-water mark for Pawnee economic and military prowess in the region and ushered in a period of some eighty years during which the Pawnee were generally able to dictate the terms and the scope of their relationships with the European powers. In 1800, Spain transferred its claims in the area to France, which in turn transferred its interests to the Americans in the 1803 Louisiana Purchase. Change loomed on the horizon.

For nearly thirty years after the purported American acquisition of the Pawnees' territory, the tribe maintained its formidable strength and prominent presence along the Platte. By the 1820s and 1830s, however, a complex confluence of catalytic forces had begun to coalesce in such a way as to dramatically diminish their power and prestige. By far the most damaging of those forces was disease. Epidemics of smallpox, influenza, and whooping cough swept through the Pawnee villages, killing perhaps half of the total population during the 1830s. At the same time, Christian missionaries seeking—as they saw it—to civilize the Pawnee met with varying degrees of acceptance among tribal members, further sapping the tribe's spiritual strength and unity. Even more significantly, raiding activity by the Pawnees' traditional adversaries, including most notably the Sioux, became ever more frequent and damaging. The tribe's demographic and military strength dissipated.

Sick, hungry, and increasingly susceptible to Sioux depredations, the Pawnee in 1833 entered into the first of several treaties with the American government. In return for small payments of food and supplies and an even smaller promised annuity, the Pawnee relinquished to the American government some 13 million acres of their territory located south of the Platte River. Fifteen years later, as thousands of Americans followed the Oregon, California, and Mormon trails across Pawnee lands, the tribe gave up a sixty-mile-long strip of land along the Platte River near present-day Grand Island, Nebraska, the bounty of which the government used to provision its nearby military post, Fort Kearny.

In 1854, Congress passed the Kansas-Nebraska Act, officially organizing and opening the Nebraska Territory to white settlement. The ensuing rush of American settlers into the area placed additional pressure on Pawnee resources, and the tribe entered into the Table Creek Treaty in 1857, their seminal agreement with the U.S. government. Under its terms, the Pawnee relinquished all of their remaining lands north of the Platte River in exchange for a 288,000-acre reservation along the Loup River. As was common in almost all treaties of that era, the U.S. government agreed to provide the Pawnee with food supplies, farming and blacksmith equipment, annuities and annual provisions, and, most important from the Pawnee perspective, protection from raids and hostilities initiated by their enemies, most notably the Sioux. As was also common during the era, the U.S. government failed to meet most of those obligations.

The years on the Loup River reservation (modern Nance County, Nebraska) were bleak ones for the Pawnee. Continuing white population pressure, decimation of the bison, incessant raids by the Sioux, and a series of bad harvests resulting from drought and grasshopper infestations combined to reduce the total Pawnee population to fewer than two thousand by the early 1870s. The most devastating blow came on August 5, 1873, when a force of almost a thousand Brulé and Oglala warriors slaughtered more than seventy Pawnee men, women, and children engaged in a bison hunt in southwestern Nebraska, at a site the Pawnee still refer to as Massacre Canyon.

Despite their increasingly beleaguered condition in the mid-nineteenth century, the Pawnee remained loyal to the federal government. Indeed, a significant cause of continuing hostility between the Pawnee and the Sioux was the existence and the activities of the Pawnee Scouts. Beginning in the 1860s, Pawnee warriors served in the U.S. Army under the command of Major Frank North and other white officers in campaigns against other Plains Indian tribes, including the Sioux. Although their primary duties involved scouting and reconnaissance for regular army units, the Pawnee also served as guards for Union Pacific Railroad construction crews. Those activities, combined with the fierce competition among all the Plains Indian tribes for diminishing resources, contributed to an atmosphere of intense intertribal hostility that hastened the Pawnees' already precipitous decline in power and prestige.[26]

The Pawnees' hemmed-in position and increasingly tenuous hold on their land were dramatically illustrated in a notorious legal proceeding that began in 1869. A white settler was murdered under mysterious circumstances near the Pawnee reservation in central Nebraska. Naturally, the murder exacerbated the tension that already existed between the Pawnee and the surrounding white community. Federal authorities arrested and charged several Pawnee men for the crime, including Yellow Sun, Horse Driver, and Little Wolf. Those arrests initiated litigation that one legal scholar has called "Nebraska's most important legal case to date involving Indians."[27] Yellow Sun and the other defendants initially were tried by federal prosecutors in the courtroom of U.S. district court judge Elmer Dundy in early November 1869.[28] After several days of testimony that might be described most charitably as dubious, an all-white jury convicted the Indian defendants and sentenced them to death. Ultimately, however, Dundy suspended that judgment pending the resolution of a jurisdictional issue that had arisen during the litigation: Did the federal court have jurisdiction over a crime committed by an Indian against a white man on state land?

In the spring of 1870, Dundy and Judge John F. Dillon, sitting together as the U.S. circuit court, held that the federal courts did not have jurisdiction over such cases.[29] Dillon and Dundy reasoned that no treaties or statutes granted jurisdiction over such cases to the federal government and that, therefore, criminal jurisdiction over Indians for murder and other crimes remained solely in the hands of state and local authorities. In the wake of that ruling, state officials took control of the proceedings. Yellow Sun and the other Pawnee defendants were indicted again for the murder in November 1870, this time by a state grand jury. As these proceedings plodded through the court system, the Pawnee defendants languished miserably in jail, suffering from hunger and illness. At least three of the four accused men attempted suicide during their ordeal. Finally, after almost two full years of confinement, they were freed from jail on a writ of habeas corpus without a second trial. Later, a state court judge ended the long saga by dismissing the case from his docket.[30] All four of the accused Pawnee men died within months of their release.

The *Yellow Sun* litigation brought more misery to the Pawnee. By effectively abandoning the tribe to state jurisdiction, the federal court's decision emboldened local white settlers to step up their depredations on the Pawnee reservation. Thefts of timber and horses from reservation lands increased, and when the Pawnee sought to prevent the thievery and drive whites out of their lands, anti-Indian animosity in the area was further inflamed.[31]

By the fall of 1873, the Pawnees' condition had deteriorated to the point that many tribal members had become convinced that they could no longer remain in their traditional Nebraska homeland. Lakota raids and white animosity had taken their toll. In October, a group of 485 Pawnee led by Big Spotted Horse left Nebraska and migrated southward into Indian Territory (modern Oklahoma), where they moved onto the reservation held by their friends, the Wichita. Over the next two years, the remainder of the demoralized and destitute Pawnee followed Big Spotted Horse's group out of Nebraska. The government formalized the Pawnee exodus in an agreement executed with tribal leaders in the fall of 1874. In that treaty, the tribe relinquished its reservation in Nebraska in exchange for a new 300-

square-mile reserve in Indian Territory. By 1876, the Pawnee were completely gone from Nebraska. They had been paid, on average, about ten cents per acre for their once-vast ancestral landholdings in the state.

Although the migration to Oklahoma in the 1870s ended the Pawnees' presence in Nebraska, it did not end their suffering. Disease and deprivation, caused largely by hostile environmental conditions, plagued the tribe in its new home, and the Pawnee population declined to a nadir of 650 by 1906. Meanwhile, their new Oklahoma reservation was allotted to tribal members in individually held parcels in the 1890s, and the remainder of the reservation was sold away to non-Indian settlers and investors. The result was a net loss of more than 170,000 additional acres of tribal land.

In the 1950s and 1960s, the Pawnee, like the Omaha and almost every other Native American nation, filed a petition with the Indian Claims Commission seeking fair compensation for the Nebraska lands they had sold under duress to the government a century before. After a typically prolonged legal battle, the ICC ultimately awarded the tribe a net judgment of about $6.4 million in 1962.[32] The Pawnees' ICC award, of course, shared all the same flaws discussed with regard to the Omaha claims, including the failure to include interest on the amount received. (In fact, it was in an appeal brought by the Pawnee that the U.S. Court of Claims confirmed and reiterated the principle that interest would not be paid on ICC awards.)[33] Also like the Omaha, the Pawnee became internally divided over the method for distributing and using the judgment fund. Ultimately, the money was disbursed in per capita payments of about $3,530 to each enrolled tribal member.[34]

The 1980s brought a new and particularly poignant chapter in Pawnee legal history, as the tribe began a campaign to stop the disturbance and desecration of Pawnee grave sites in Kansas and Nebraska and to recover and reinter the skeletal remains of Pawnee dead held and sometimes displayed by various public and private entities, most notably the Nebraska State Historical Society (NSHS). With financial support and legal representation provided by the Native American Rights Fund (NARF), the Pawnee engaged in an emotional, well-publicized, and often acrimonious struggle for the return of thousands of Pawnee bones and grave artifacts held by the NSHS. In 1989, the controversy culminated in the Nebraska Legislature's enactment of LB 340, the Unmarked Human Burial Sites and Skeletal Remains Protection Act.[35] The law—the first of its kind in the United States—required the return of remains to the tribes to which they belonged and the protection of unmarked Indian burial sites wherever they might be found throughout the state. In September 1990, the NSHS formally relinquished control of more than four hundred Pawnee skeletons to tribal representatives, who then ceremoniously reinterred the remains at a site in Genoa, Nebraska, on ground that had been part of the nineteenth-century Pawnee reservation.[36]

Otoe-Missouria

Until the late eighteenth century, the Otoe and the Missouria were two distinct groups, both of which were driven into the Midwest by population pressures and dwindling resources in their ancestral homelands in the Great Lakes region. By the early 1700s, the Otoe had established a permanent presence in eastern Nebraska on the Salt Creek tributary of the Platte River near present-day Ashland. By the late 1700s, they had been joined in that area by their relatives the Missouria, who had been forced out of their previous location in northwestern Missouri by the aggressions of the Sauk and Fox nations.[37] From that point forward, the two groups were identified and dealt with as a single unit by the federal government.

In many ways, the legal history of the Otoe-Missouria in the nineteenth century is depressingly similar to that of the Omaha and the Pawnee. Faced with many of the same pressures that affected the other Nebraska tribes, the Otoe-Missourias' traditional semisedentary earth-lodge lifestyle, combining agriculture with semiannual bison hunting expeditions, began to succumb to increased reliance on manufactured goods. Never as populous or as strong as their Omaha and Pawnee neighbors, the Otoe-Missouria were particularly vulnerable to the aggression of other tribes. Even more disastrously, they found themselves decimated by famine and disease. A smallpox epidemic swept through the area in the early 1800s, and by the time Lewis and Clark encountered the Otoe-Missouria and conferred with them at the now famous Council Bluffs parley in 1804, the tribe's total population had been reduced to less than eight hundred. When fur traders established the first permanent white settlement in Nebraska at Bellevue in the 1820s, the proximity of that outpost to the Otoe-Missourias' villages accelerated the tribe's decline. Alcohol and other divisive factors wreaked havoc with the Indians' spiritual and cultural unity. By the 1830s, the tribe was at low ebb, mired in poverty and plagued by malnutrition. The stage was set for the familiar process of dispossession.

The Otoe-Missourias' first sale of land to the U.S. government occurred under the 1830 Treaty of Prairie du Chien. In that agreement, the tribe relinquished its territorial claims east of the Missouri River, in modern Iowa, and sold off a chunk of land in southeastern Nebraska that became known as the Half-Breed Tract. (So called because it was originally used as a reservation for mixed-bloods from all the Indian groups in the region). Three years later, the tribe sold off another one million acres of their Nebraska territory in exchange for payments, provisions, and annuities that totaled only about four cents per acre. The opening of Nebraska to white settlement in 1854 placed tremendous additional pressure on the Otoe-Missouria, just as it had on the Omaha and Pawnee. They sold all their remaining land in the southeastern portion of Nebraska Territory to the government, retaining for themselves only a reservation of about 160,000 acres along the Kansas-Nebraska border. But like the Pawnee, the Otoe-Missouria could not gain refuge even within their reservation. In 1876 and 1881, the tribe gave up its Nebraska reservation and was removed to Indian Territory. There they remain today, on a reservation in what is now Noble County, Oklahoma.

In 1955, the Otoe-Missouria became the first of the aboriginal Nebraska Indian nations to win a claim before the ICC. Finding that the compensation that the tribe had received for its land cessions in 1833 and 1854 had been "unconscionably low," the ICC awarded the tribe a judgment for $1,156,035. When the government appealed, the Court of Claims affirmed, issuing an opinion that historian David Wishart has appropriately called a landmark ruling that "made it easier for the other Nebraska Indians to prove title to their ancestral lands" in Nebraska and other parts of the Midwest.[38] Nine years later, the tribe received a second ICC judgment, this one in the amount of $1,750,000, for lands east of the Missouri River taken from them pursuant to the 1830 Treaty of Prairie du Chien.[39] Other Otoe-Missouria claims challenging the fairness of the final sales of their Nebraska lands in 1876 and 1881 were dismissed by the ICC. In those cases, the commission essentially ruled that the tribe either had been adequately compensated or had already compromised and resolved the grievances involved.[40]

Although the Otoe-Missouria no longer maintain a physical home in Nebraska, the tribe has recently taken steps to reconnect with its ancestral Nebraska lands. As events commemorating the bicentennial of the Lewis and Clark expedition got under way in eastern Nebraska during the summer of 2004, more than seventy Otoe-Missouria tribal members traveled north from Oklahoma to take part in the ceremonies. The result was a poignantly emotional homecoming, as the participants experienced a renewed awakening of their Nebraska heritage. As one tribal member noted, "You know that your ancestors lived there. They made their homes there. They're buried there. Our grandpas and grandmas are there, and we know they always looked out for us—even future generations."[41] The events also served as a reminder to white Nebraskans of the Otoe-Missourias' history in the state and of the tribe's continuing vitality in Oklahoma. As one tribal member put it, "Originally, we're Cornhuskers, but we want to let people know that we're still alive and well down in Oklahoma. We're still strong and vibrant as a tribal community and sovereign government."[42]

Ponca

No episode in Nebraska Indian legal history is more familiar and celebrated than that of Standing Bear and the Ponca.[43] But Standing Bear's famous litigation most certainly did not mark the end of the Poncas' tribal legal history in the state. In 1881, the federal government returned some 26,000 acres in modern Knox County, Nebraska, to the Ponca. About half of the tribe moved back north from Oklahoma to reoccupy that traditional homeland, becoming the Northern Ponca Tribe. The remainder of the tribe in Oklahoma became known as the Southern Ponca. As on the other Nebraska reservations, the allotment process of the late 1880s and 1890s wreaked havoc on the Poncas' Nebraska land base and seriously weakened the tribe's cultural unity, coherence, and structure. Poverty and disease took their toll on the Ponca through the first half of the twentieth century, and by the 1950s and 1960s, they had become a particularly vulnerable target for the federal government's emerging termination policy. In 1966, the tribe was formally terminated, and its 442 remaining members were detribalized. The remaining 834 acres of tribal land in Nebraska and all other tribal resources and assets were liquidated and apportioned to the former members in severalty. As far as the federal government was concerned, the Northern Ponca no longer existed.

Over the next two decades, the Ponca undertook a long and emotional struggle for the restoration of their tribal status. The restoration initiative gained strength and momentum in 1987 with the creation of the Northern Ponca Restoration Committee, Inc., a nonprofit coalition of various pantribal Native American interest groups dedicated to the goal of Ponca restoration. The following year, the Nebraska Legislature lent its support to the effort, passing LB 128, which gave state recognition to the Ponca. In

1989, Nebraska's U.S. senators James J. Exon and Robert Kerry introduced the Ponca Restoration Bill, which passed through Congress the following summer and was signed into law by President George H. W. Bush on October 31, 1990.[44]

Although the restoration of tribal status did create a new reservation in Nebraska, the Ponca tribe has reestablished itself as a sovereign governmental entity and is striving to rebuild its land base, tribal identity, and physical presence in its traditional home territory around the confluence of the Niobrara and Missouri rivers in north-central Nebraska. As a nonresident tribe, the Ponca tribal government provides services and resources to a designated area that spans more than a dozen counties in Nebraska, Iowa, and South Dakota. Headquartered in Niobrara, Nebraska, the tribe also maintains offices in Norfolk, Omaha, and Lincoln, as well as in Sioux City, Iowa.

Even as the Ponca were undergoing the trauma of termination, the tribe sought and received compensation from the federal government for their wrongful displacement from their ancestral Nebraska lands in the nineteenth century. In ICC Case No. 322, the Ponca won a judgment for $1,878,500, the amount they should have received for their first cession of their traditional hunting grounds in the Nebraska Territory in 1858.[45] In a second ICC claim, Case No. 323, the Ponca sought additional compensation for their 1877 displacement from their Niobrara reservation and forced exodus to Oklahoma (the tragic Ponca exile and trail of tears that led to the Standing Bear litigation). In that case, the commission took the unusual step of granting the tribe interest on the judgment it received, resulting in a final award of $1,013,425.[46]

Winnebago

The Winnebago Tribe of Nebraska did not establish a permanent residence in Nebraska until the mid-1860s, when the federal government persuaded the Omaha to yield the northern half of their reservation in northeastern Nebraska to the Winnebago. During the generations prior to their arrival in Nebraska, the tribe had endured a prototypical odyssey of displacement and continual forced relocation.[47] In 1837, they were pushed off of their traditional homelands in Wisconsin and moved to a reservation in northeastern Iowa. In 1846, they were moved from Iowa to a new reservation in central Minnesota. Nine years later, they were moved to a different reservation in southern Minnesota. In 1863, they were pushed westward once again, this time landing in Crow Creek, South Dakota. There the Winnebago endured several more years of particularly severe hunger, deprivation, and misery. In the years following their arrival at Crow Creek, the Winnebago began to trickle southward along the Missouri River in small groups, finding refuge with the Omaha. In March 1865, the Omaha agreed to sell about 100,000 acres off the north side of their reservation, which the government then used to create a reservation for the Winnebago. There the tribe remains today.

In the late nineteenth century, the Winnebago Reservation was subjected to many of the same pressures and problems that beset the Omaha. Pursuant to the 1887 Dawes Severalty Act, the reservation was divided into parcels and allotted to individual tribal members and families. The nonallotted lands were sold or leased away to non-Indians. The net result was the loss of almost two-thirds of the total reservation acreage by 1913.

The Winnebagos' twentieth-century legal history has paralleled that of their neighbors, the Omaha. Through the 1950s and 1960s, the tribe prosecuted a claim before the ICC that ultimately produced a judgment of $4.6 million in 1975.[48] The ICC funds were used to initiate tribal land acquisition programs, as well as housing and medical service programs that have been continued to the present day. Like the Omaha, the Winnebago also took legal action to recover former reservation lands in Iowa—land that subsequently became the site of the tribe's WinnaVegas Casino in 1992. Although the casino operations were immediately successful and profitable for the Winnebago, increased gaming competition in the Council Bluffs and Omaha metropolitan areas seventy miles to the south have diminished those profits considerably in recent years. The Winnebago have responded by diversifying their tribal economic initiatives through Ho-Chunk, Inc.—a tribally owned corporation that has raised and invested millions of dollars in various innovative and nationally recognized entrepreneurial initiatives on the reservation over the past several years.[49]

Santee Sioux

Like the Winnebago, the Santee Sioux—the fourth modern Nebraska Indian group—are relative newcomers to the state and, like the odyssey of the Winnebago, their movement here was not voluntary. Established in 1869 by order of President Andrew Johnson, the Santee Reservation today lies along the Nebraska–South Dakota border, about 110 miles west of Sioux City, Iowa. The reservation was created for the Santee after their displacement from their traditional homeland in Minnesota in the aftermath of the notorious Santee Uprising in 1862. In that brief but tragic episode, Santee warriors, frustrated by the failure of the government to make good on previous promises of supplies and annuities, lashed out in a violent uprising that resulted in the deaths of more than 500 white settlers in central and southern Minnesota. After federal forces subdued the rebellion, more than 1,800 Santee were imprisoned, and 303 Santee men and boys were convicted of various capital crimes and sentenced to death. President Abraham Lincoln subsequently commuted all but thirty-eight of the death sentences, and five others were later granted reprieves. On December 26, 1862, the remaining thirty-three Santee defendants were executed in a mass hanging at Mankato, Minnesota. The event remains the largest formally sanctioned mass execution in American history.[50]

Following the rebellion, the federal government unilaterally abrogated all of its existing treaties and agreements with the Santee. The tribe was exiled from its Minnesota homelands, and an all-too-familiar story of forced displacement began to play itself out. In 1863, the tribe was dispatched to Crow Creek, South Dakota, where hundreds died from disease, exposure, and malnutrition within months of their arrival. Recognizing that Crow Creek could not sustain the Santee indefinitely, the government sought alternate locations for a permanent reservation. Ultimately, the current site in north-central Nebraska was chosen, and the tribe moved again. The original reservation comprised four townships in what is now Knox County. The allotment process of the late nineteenth and early twentieth centuries dramatically reduced the reservation from its original 115,000 acres. Today the Santee Tribe controls only about 7,900 acres; the rest of the reservation land is held privately either by tribal members or by non-Indians, in the familiar checkerboard pattern of land ownership that is today common to virtually all Indian reservations on the Great Plains.

Like the other Nebraska Indian tribes, the Santee have not been reluctant to use the legal system to assert, maintain, and perpetuate their rights as a sovereign people. In February 2005, the tribe concluded a decade-long legal battle with the federal government over the legality of a small on-reservation gaming operation, the Ohiya Casino. When the Santee opened the establishment in 1996, the federal government quickly filed a lawsuit to shut it down, claiming that it violated state and federal gaming regulations. The Santee argued that the casino complied with federal and state statutes, inasmuch as it offered gaming devices that were substantially similar to those already allowed by the state of Nebraska. The litigation dragged on for nine years, involving three separate appeals to the 8th Circuit Court of Appeals and two petitions for review by the U.S. Supreme Court. Early in the proceedings, the federal district court ordered the Santee to shut down the casino operation, but the tribe refused to comply. The courts then imposed a $6,000-per-day fine for the tribe's contempt of court. Over time, the levied fines accumulated to a total of more than $4 million, and the federal government took steps to seize approximately $265,000 from tribal assets and bank deposits. The litigation turned in the Santees' favor in December 2001, when U.S. district court judge Joseph Bataillon held that the video pull tab machines that the Santee were then utilizing in their casino were legal, inasmuch as they were substantially similar to the so-called pickle card machines operating legally at thousands of locations across the state. Over the next four years, Bataillon's ruling was upheld by higher courts, leading to a final settlement of the litigation in early 2005. Under that settlement, the tribe continues its gaming operation and is relieved of any further liability for the $4 million in accumulated fines.[51] With the rather modest proceeds from their small gaming operation, the Santee have been able to provide financial support for various service programs on the reservation, including a youth center, a nutrition center, and Head Start programming for youth education and training.[52]

Even more recently, the Santee achieved success in a five-year legal effort to regain jurisdiction over nonmajor criminal offenses committed by tribal members against other tribal members through the same process of retrocession accomplished by the Omaha in 1969 and by the Winnebago in 1986. Under the new arrangements, the Santee are building their own police force and tribal court system, while clearing away much of the jurisdictional confusion that has long plagued the reservation. As tribal chairman Roger Trudell recently noted, the retrocession agreement "serves as an affirmation of the tribe's inherent sovereignty and jurisdiction over its reservation lands."[53]

Trudell's words are strikingly applicable to all of the legal struggles waged by each of the Nebraska Indian nations in the last two hundred years. Through their legal efforts and through many imperfect victories, the state's aboriginal inhabitants have created and continue to maintain a rich and impressive historical legacy. That legal history provides a solid foundation for an increasingly optimistic and confident future for all of Nebraska's Native American groups.

Notes

1. This chapter is a work of synthesis, collecting, collating, and summarizing the previous research efforts of many exemplary scholars, including most notably David Wishart, Michael Tate, and Judith Boughter. David Wishart's *An Unspeakable Sadness: The Dispossession of the Nebraska Indians* (Lincoln: University of Nebraska Press, 1994), which traces the history of all the Nebraska Indian tribes from the late eighteenth through the twentieth centuries, is an indispensable starting point for any analysis of Native American legal history in the state. Tate and Boughter, among their many other scholarly accomplishments, have created annotated research bibliographies of two of the largest and most significant Nebraska tribes—the Omaha and the Pawnee, respectively. See Michael L. Tate, *The Upstream People: An Annotated Research Bibliography of the Omaha Tribe* (Metuchen, N.J.: Scarecrow, 1991), and Judith Boughter, *The Pawnee Nation: An Annotated Research Bibliography* (Lanham, Md.: Scarecrow, 2004). Both of these award-winning volumes are exceedingly valuable research tools.

2. Wishart, *Unspeakable Sadness,* xiii.

3. For a map of Indian land cessions, see James C. Olson and Ronald C. Naugle, *History of Nebraska* (Lincoln: University of Nebraska Press, 1997), 118.

4. Ibid., 3.

5. For an assessment of the Omahas' legal history, with particular emphasis on twentieth-century developments, see Mark R. Scherer, *Imperfect Victories: The Legal Tenacity of the Omaha Tribe, 1945–1995* (Lincoln: University of Nebraska Press, 1999). The Omaha content of this chapter is drawn largely from the author's previous work therein.

6. See Judith Boughter, *Betraying the Omaha Nation, 1790–1916* (Norman: University of Oklahoma Press, 1998), which provides a remarkably comprehensive examination of the tribe's origins and evolution, with particular emphasis on nineteenth- and early twentieth-century developments. The classic presentation of the Omahas' ethnohistorical and anthropological history is Alice C. Fletcher and Francis La Flesche, *The Omaha Tribe* (Lincoln: University of Nebraska Press, 1972), 1:70–71.

7. Boughter, *Betraying the Omaha Nation,* 13–14.

8. Wishart, *Unspeakable Sadness,* 23–25; Boughter, *Betraying the Omaha Nation,* 16–17.

9. The most thorough telling of the story is presented in Robin Ridington and Dennis Hastings, *Blessing for a Long Time: The Sacred Pole of the Omaha Tribe* (Lincoln: University of Nebraska Press, 1997).

10. Boughter, *Betraying the Omaha Nation,* 22.

Mackay was a Scot who traded with the Indians initially for the British but who eventually became manager of the Spanish trading operations along the Missouri and Platte rivers. Olson and Naugle, *History of Nebraska,* 34–35.

11. Wishart, *Unspeakable Sadness,* 153–54.

12. Ibid., 238.

13. Tate, *Upstream People,* vii.

14. 67 Stat. 588 (1953).

15. For more on the effects of PL 280 on and around the Omaha Reservation, see Scherer, *Imperfect Victories,* chaps. 1–2.

16. 82 Stat. 77 (1968), codified at 25 U.S.C. § 1323.

17. See, for example, Paul Hammel, "Confusion before the Law on Omaha Reservation," *Omaha World-Herald,* August 10, 2005, 1, describing the "crazy world of law enforcement across the Omaha Reservation" as tribal, state, and federal officials "wrangled over who had the legal right to file charges" against a hit-and-run driver on the reservation. Recently, state and tribal authorities have sought to resolve at least some of the jurisdictional confusion by agreeing to cross-deputize tribal police officers, but the issue remains highly controversial on and around the reservation. See Paul Hammel, "County Opposes Joint Policing Plan," *Omaha World-Herald,* July 27, 2005, 5B.

18. For details of the Omahas' experiences before the ICC, see Scherer, *Imperfect Victories,* chaps. 3–4.

19. The Omaha Rule imposed rather elaborate procedures to ensure full and open disclosure of all the terms and conditions of proposed settlements of ICC claims, including evidentiary hearings requiring the presence of tribal officials and the introduction into evidence of tribal resolutions specifically authorizing the settlement. See Scherer, *Imperfect Victories,* 61–63.

20. The claim based on the 1854 treaty was docketed as ICC Case No. 225, 8 Ind. Cl. Com. 407 (1960).

21. The claim based on the Omahas' Iowa lands was docketed as ICC Case No. 138, 13 Ind. Cl. Com. 289 (1964).

22. For details of the Blackbird Bend litigation, see Scherer, *Imperfect Victories,* chap. 5.

23. Wilson v. Omaha Indian Tribe, 442 U.S. 653 (1979).

24. Boughter, *Pawnee Nation,* xv.

25. Ibid.

26. For more on the Pawnee Scouts, see Thomas Dunlay, *Wolves for the Blue Soldiers: Indian Scouts and Auxiliaries with the United States Army, 1860–90* (Lincoln: University of Nebraska Press, 1982), and Ken Bauc, "Pawnee Scouts: Guardians of the Union Pacific," *NEBRASKAland* 59 (April 1981): 20–23, 45–48.

27. James Riding In, "*The United States v. Yellow Sun et al. (The Pawnee People):* A Case Study of Institutional and Societal Racism and U.S. Justice in Nebraska from the 1850s to 1870s," *Wicazo Sa Review* 17, no. 1 (2002): 13–41. Riding In, a Pawnee legal historian, is stridently critical of the state and federal authorities' handling of the *Yellow Sun* case, contending that the litigation had "cataclysmic consequences" for the tribe and resulted in the "unbearable pressure" that ultimately caused the tribe to seek refuge in Indian Territory.

28. The same Judge Dundy, ten years later, famously declared Ponca leader Standing Bear to be a "person" under federal habeas corpus law. See chapter 11, *infra.*

29. United States v. Sa-Coo-Da-Cot [Yellow Sun], 27 Fed. Cas. 923 (C.C.D. Neb. 1870) (No. 16,212).

30. The specific grounds for the state court's final dismissal of the case remain unclear. See Riding In, "*United States v. Yellow Sun et al.,*" 32.

31. Ibid., 34–35.

32. For an excellent overview of the Pawnees' claims before the ICC, see David Wishart, "The Pawnee Claims Case, 1947–64," in *Irredeemable America,* ed. Imre Sutton (Albuquerque: University of New Mexico Press, 1985), 157–86.

33. Pawnee Indian Tribe of Oklahoma v. United States, 157 Ct. Cl. 134, 301 F.2d 667 (1962).

34. Boughter, *Pawnee Nation,* xx, citing Wishart, "Pawnee Claims Case," 183–84.

35. 1989 Laws of Nebraska LB 340.

36. For a short summary of the repatriation controversy and abundant citations to the extensive newspaper coverage of the story, see Boughter, "Nebraska Legislative Bills (LB) 612 and 340," in *Pawnee Nation,* 227–48. For extensive detail and analysis of the struggle over the Nebraska legislation, see Robert M. Peregroy, "Nebraska's Landmark Repatriation Law: A Study of Cross-Cultural Conflict and Resolution," *American Indian Culture and Research Journal* 16, no. 2 (1992): 139–95, and idem, "The Legal Basis, Legislative History, and Implementation of Nebraska's Landmark Reburial Legislation," *Arizona State Law Journal* 24, no. 1 (1992): 329–89.

37. Wishart, *Unspeakable Sadness,* 5–6. See also Olson and Naugle, *History of Nebraska,* 22–25.

38. Wishart, *Unspeakable Sadness,* 241. The original Otoe-Missouria claim was docketed as ICC Case No. 11. The Court of Claims' opinion is at 131 Ct. Cl. 593 (1955).

39. 13 ICC 289 (1964).

40. Wishart, *Unspeakable Sadness,* 242. The ICC opinion is at 13 Ind. Cl. Com. 272 (1964).

41. David Hendee, "Relive the Journey for the Otoe-Missouria," *Omaha World-Herald,* July 25, 2004, supp., 1.

42. Ibid.

43. Because that story is well told by Charles E. Wright elsewhere in this volume, no further comment on the case will be made here. See chapter 11, *infra.*

44. 25 U.S.C. § 983.

45. 26 Ind. Cl. Com. 217 (1971).

46. 28 Ind. Cl. Com. 350 (1972). The commission was empowered to award interest in the case because it found that the government's taking of the Ponca reservation in the 1877 case was wholly without the tribe's consent.

47. See generally Wishart, *Unspeakable Sadness,* 159–61.

48. The Winnebago claims were docketed as ICC Case Nos. 243, 244, and 245. Their compromise settlement with the government is at 23 Ind. Cl. Com. 482 (1970). Funds to satisfy the judgment were appropriated by PL 91-665, approved January 8, 1971 (84 Stat. 1981). After further proceedings related to setoffs, expenses, and attorneys fees, the tribe received its award in 1975. See 37 Ind. Cl. Com. 96 (1975).

49. For more on the Winnebagos' ongoing economic development initiatives and the activities of Ho-Chunk, Inc., see Bradford McKee, "A New-Style Indian Village Rises from the Dust," *New York Times,* September 30, 2004, F1.

50. For details on Santee history, the Santee uprising in Minnesota, and the subsequent criminal trials and executions, see Roy W. Meyers, *History of the Santee*

Sioux: United States Indian Policy on Trial (Lincoln: University of Nebraska Press, 1967), and Dee Brown, *Bury My Heart at Wounded Knee* (New York: Holt, Rinehart, 1970).

51. The full details of this lengthy and complex litigation are beyond the scope of this chapter. The critical and ultimately dispositive opinion by Judge Bataillon, which includes citations to the earlier relevant holdings, is at *United States v. Santee Sioux Tribe of Nebraska,* 174 F. Supp. 2d 1001 (D. Neb. 2001), *aff'd,* 324 F.3d 607 (8th Cir. 2003), *cert denied,* 540 U.S. 1229 (2004).

52. See Amanda Stone, "Most See Santee Casino as Winner, but Others Cite Problems," *Lincoln Journal-Star,* August 13, 2005, A6.

53. "Santee Given Criminal Jurisdiction on the Reservation," *Sioux City Journal,* February 17, 2006, A1.

ELEVEN

Charles E. Wright

STANDING BEAR

A Long Walk for Liberty, A Firm Step for Justice

What would an obscure habeas corpus hearing that took place in 1879 have to do with the Battle of the Little Big Horn, which occurred some thirty-four months earlier? Well, if you believe in the rule of law and that the United States is a nation of laws, what happened to Ponca chief Standing Bear has much to do with what took place on the western frontier during the middle six months of 1876.

The Ponca were a small tribe of fewer than a thousand souls living near the mouth of the Niobrara River in northeastern Nebraska during the early part of the nineteenth century when they were visited by two members of the Lewis and Clark expedition. One of their chiefs, named Smoke (Shoo-de-ga-cha, whose portrait was painted by Catlin), was signatory to an early treaty between the United States and the Ponca dated June 9, 1825.[1] As was typical of the early Indian treaties, the Ponca admitted that they resided within the territorial limits of the United States, acknowledged its supremacy, and claimed its protection, also admitting the right of the United States to regulate all trade and intercourse with them. The United States in turn agreed to receive the Ponca into their friendship and under their protection and to extend to them, from time to time, such benefits and acts of kindness as may be convenient and seem just and proper to the president of the United States. None but American citizens duly authorized by the United States were permitted to trade or to hold intercourse with the Ponca. The Ponca agreed to behave themselves and to protect the property of traders and persons legally employed in their territory and to apprehend any foreigners coming into their territory for the purposes of trade. (At this point in its brief history, the United States was intent on stamping out the English, French, and Spanish traders who at various times operated within the area of the Louisiana Purchase.) Misconduct on the part of individual Indians was to be the responsibility of the governing body of the Ponca, and misconduct by individual Americans was to be the responsibility of the United States. The Ponca agreed that their tribe would never supply any nation or tribe of Indians unfriendly with the United States with guns and ammunition or other implements of war.

During the eighteenth and nineteenth centuries, the United States entered into numerous treaties with various Indian tribes, including the Sioux. In May 1858, the Ponca ceded a large portion of their land to the United States, reserving a small tract as their future home. They intended to replace hunting with farming. This agreement had the effect of dispossessing the Ponca of their traditional homeland, much of which was located in the state of Nebraska. The Ponca were probably the most obedient and well-behaved tribe ever encountered by the United States during the settlement of the Louisiana Purchase. They immediately honored the treaty (although it had not been ratified by the Senate) and moved into the newer and smaller area reserved for them, where it was difficult if not impossible for them to subsist. Game was soon extirpated by the neighboring Sioux, who were not friendly or helpful. Although they were starving and in a pitiful state, the Ponca did not beg from others and kept the promises that were made in the treaty. They suffered also from random acts of violence perpetrated by cowardly thugs of the 7th Iowa Cavalry (not to be mistaken for the 7th U.S. Cavalry Regiment)[2] as well as other unfriendly Indians.

Because the Ponca were not doing well on their 1858 reservation, a new treaty was enacted in 1865 by which the Ponca traded their 1858 reservation for a new reservation of approximately 96,000 acres north of the Niobrara River in what is now South Dakota. This resulted in more favorable living conditions for the Ponca. The ink was barely dry on Senate ratification of the 1865 treaty, however, when the United States entered into the Treaty of Fort Laramie (1868), ceding to the Sioux all of the Ponca reservation north of the Niobrara River. The United States, because of its prior cession of this land to the Ponca, lacked any legal ability to transfer these 96,000 acres to the Sioux. This was all that remained of the Poncas' traditional lands in South Dakota, Iowa, and Nebraska. Because they were a very small tribe and disdained the use of violence to protect their very existence, they were easy prey for the United States and its representatives in the military and the Office of Indian Affairs who were responsible for the welfare of the peaceful tribes under their jurisdiction.

The Ponca attempted to survive on their own but had no ability to protect themselves from the neighboring Brulé Sioux. They sought refuge in Nebraska with their close neighbors, the Omaha. One of the Ponca chiefs, Standing Bear, was signatory to an agreement pursuant to which the Ponca offered to purchase part of the Omaha reservation. He also participated in discussions between the Ponca and the federal government, which wanted to remove the Ponca to Indian Territory (now Oklahoma) in 1874 and 1875.

In 1877, the federal government ordered the Ponca to relocate to Indian Territory. Standing Bear, the most prominent of their chiefs, participated in efforts to disapprove of the move prior to its occurrence, and many Ponca passively resisted the relocation. It was accomplished, however—unwillingly but without violence—in May 1877 when the Ponca were forced to walk southward from Nebraska ("toward the heat") to Indian Territory. The Indians were beset with bad weather and disease. They arrived sick and exhausted. Many children, including a daughter of Standing Bear, died before they reached the southern boundaries of Nebraska. Standing Bear's daughter (Prairie Flower) was given a Christian burial near the small village of Milford, Nebraska. Of the 581 Indians who commenced the trek, 158 died within the year, and others were sick and disabled.

When the Ponca arrived in Indian Territory, they found that no arrangements had been made for their subsistence. Potable water and food were not available. No land was set aside for them to occupy. No funds had been appropriated for their support. They were extremely dissatisfied with the Indian Territory and its living conditions, and the climate was not agreeable to them. Indian agent E. A. Howard, in charge of matters involving relocation of the Ponca, was at a loss to explain to them how this occurred.

In November 1877, Standing Bear, along with Ponca chiefs White Eagle, Standing Buffalo, and Big Chief, journeyed to Washington to carry their protest to the president. Rutherford B. Hayes gave them each a limp handshake, promising to consider the matter and "let you know the result."[3] The result was no change, and the situation deteriorated over time. On January 2, 1879, Standing Bear and a band of twenty-nine male followers broke away from Indian Territory and walked back to Nebraska. The trip, undertaken in the dead of winter, lasted ten weeks. The fugitives had started with twenty dollars between them, and it cost a dollar each day for provisions. Thereafter they were fed by sympathetic whites encountered along the way. They arrived in Nebraska on March 4, 1879, where Chief Iron Eye provided them with sanctuary on the reservation of the Omaha Indians.[4] Brigadier General George Crook (commander of the Department of the Platte) was ordered to arrest Standing Bear and his followers and to hold them until they could be returned to Indian Territory. They were incarcerated at Fort Omaha.

Then entered the humanitarian, Thomas Henry Tibbles, who took up the cudgel on behalf of Standing Bear and the Ponca. Before the Civil War Tibbles had fought to assist runaway slaves and to support the abolitionist movement. He had taken on William Clarke "Charlie" Quantrill and his band of raiders. He had attended Mount Union College in Ohio, married an English lady, Amelia Owen, and worked as a local and later a traveling preacher. He had championed the cause of Nebraska farmers when he went east to raise funds during the famine brought on by the grasshopper plague in 1874.

When Standing Bear returned to Nebraska, Tibbles was an assistant editor of the *Omaha Daily Herald* and a friend of Crook. Although Crook had led the army against the Indians several times, he was a man of honor who refused to lie to them. Both Crook and Tibbles were later honored by initiation into the Indians' Soldier Lodge, "which gave a unique understanding and appreciation of Indian life and culture." Crook stated to Tibbles:

> During the quarter century that I've been on the plains in government service . . . I've been forced many times by orders from Washington to do most inhuman things in dealing with the Indians, but now I'm ordered to do a more cruel thing than ever before. I would resign my commission, if that would prevent the order from being executed—but it would not. Another officer would be assigned to fill my place. I've come to ask if you will not take up the matter. It's no use for me to protest. Washington always orders the very opposite of what I recommend.[5]

Tibbles visited Standing Bear and his cohorts at Fort Omaha on March 30, 1879. At that meeting, the Indians asked the following questions of Tibbles:

> Why were they imprisoned when they had committed no crime?

> Why were they not free to live where they willed?
>
> Why did not the same laws apply to Indians as applied to whites?
>
> Why would it not be better for the United States to permit the Ponca to farm and raise their own food instead of providing rations for their subsistence?[6]

On March 31, Crook met with the prisoners and Tibbles, accompanied by his aide, Captain John G. Bourke, who recorded his observations about Standing Bear:

> Standing Bear, the head man, was a noble-looking Indian, tall and commanding in presence, dignified in manner and very elegantly dressed in the costume of his tribe. He wore a shirt made of blue flannel, having collar and cuffs of red cloth, ornamented with brass buttons, leggings of blue flannel, moccasins [*sic*] of deerskin, and over his shoulders was draped a beautiful blanket, one-half red, the other half blue . . . The most striking feature in his attire was a necklace of claws of the grizzly bear, of which he appeared highly proud.[7]

Tibbles notified other newspapers of Standing Bear's plight. Local church members, who were acquainted with Secretary of the Interior Carl Schurz, requested that he discontinue his efforts to return Standing Bear and the others to Indian Territory.

Tibbles was not unlettered in the law, having previously studied the Constitution and read the law in an Iowa law office. He enlisted the assistance of Omaha lawyers John Lee Webster and A. J. Poppleton (chief attorney for the Union Pacific Railway) to advise the Ponca. Both agreed to serve without a fee. Webster and Poppleton promptly filed an application for a writ of habeas corpus in the U.S. Circuit Court for the District of Nebraska. Habeas corpus is an action in which a person under detention is brought before a judge to test the legality of the detention. The hearing on the petition for habeas corpus was held before U.S. district court judge Elmer Dundy on May 1, 1879. The petition for the writ of habeas corpus was directed against Crook because he was the officer holding Standing Bear and the other Ponca against their will. Standing Bear, who had a magnificent gift of eloquence, was allowed to testify on his own behalf. His testimony was provided to the court through an interpreter on each individual sentence. James A. Lake described the testimony of Standing Bear as follows:

> The Chief rose, extended his hand toward the bench, and for an embarrassingly long time stood in that posture, and then, according to Tibbles, spoke:
>
> "That hand is not the color of yours; but if I pierce it, I shall feel pain. If you pierce your hand, you also feel pain. The blood that will flow from mine will be the same color as yours. I am a man. God made us both."
>
> Standing Bear then described his desire to return to their traditional Ponca home on the Swift Running Water (the Niobrara), and said:
>
> "[A] man bars the passage . . . I . . . must obey his orders. If he says that I cannot pass, I cannot. A long struggle will have been in vain."
>
> After a long pause, the Chief looked at Judge Dundy and concluded:
>
> "You are that man."
>
> Tibbles reported that General Crook leaned forward, covered his eyes with his hands; women spectators sobbed and tears appeared on the judge's face; then the entire assemblage shouted approval of the speech. General Crook, followed by the entire audience, shook Standing Bear's hand.[8]

Indicating his own sympathy and the sympathy of the respondent, Crook, and most of the spectators in the court, Dundy opened his opinion with the following prelude:

> During the fifteen years in which I have been engaged in administering the laws of my country, I have never been called upon to hear or decide a case that appealed so strongly to my sympathy as the one now under consideration. On the one side, we have a few of the remnants of a once numerous and powerful, but now weak, insignificant, unlettered, and generally despised race; on the other, we have the representative of one of the most powerful, most enlightened, and most Christianized nations of modern times. On the one side, we have the representatives of this wasted race coming into this national tribunal of ours, asking for justice and liberty

> to enable them to adopt our boasted civilization, and to pursue the arts of peace, which have made us great and happy as a nation; on the other side, we have this magnificent, if not magnanimous, government, resisting this application with the determination of sending these people back to the country which is to them less desirable than perpetual imprisonment in their own native land. But I think it is creditable to the heart and mind of the brave and distinguished officer who is made respondent herein to say that he has no sort of sympathy in the business in which he is forced by his position to bear a part so conspicuous; and, so far as I am individually concerned, I think it not improper to say that, if the strongest possible sympathy could give the relators title to freedom, they would have been restored to liberty the moment the arguments in their behalf were closed. No examination or further thought would then have been necessary or expedient. But in a country where liberty is regulated by law, something more satisfactory and enduring than mere sympathy must furnish and constitute the rule and basis of judicial action. It follows that this case must be examined and decided on principles of law, and that unless the relators are entitled to their discharge under the constitution or laws of the United States, or some treaty made pursuant thereto, they must be remanded to the custody of the officer who caused their arrest, to be returned to the Indian Territory, which they left without the consent of the government.[9]

The U.S. attorney, Genio Lambertson, argued strenuously that the right to seek a writ of habeas corpus was available in the U.S. district court only to "subjects of the kingdom," or the parent country, the right of habeas corpus having originated under the laws of Great Britain. By analogy, he claimed that none but American citizens were entitled to seek the writ. Using reason and logic, Dundy turned the government's argument against it:

> I have not examined the English laws regulating the suing out of the writ, nor have I thought it necessary so to do. Of this I will only observe that if the laws of England are as they are claimed to be, they will appear at a disadvantage when compared with our own. This only proves that the laws of a limited monarchy are sometimes less wise and humane than the laws of our own republic—that whilst the parliament of Great Britain was

> legislating in behalf of the favored few, the congress of the United States was legislating in behalf of all mankind who come within our jurisdiction.[10]

On the question of the standing of the Ponca to seek the writ of habeas corpus in a U.S. district court, Dundy held:

> Now, it must be borne in mind that the habeas corpus act describes applicants for the writ as "persons," or "parties," who may be entitled thereto. It nowhere describes them as "citizens," nor is citizenship in any way or place made a qualification for suing out the writ, and, in the absence of express provision or necessary implication which would require the interpretation contended for by the district attorney, I should not feel justified in giving the words "person" and "party" such a narrow construction. The most natural, and therefore most reasonable, way is to attach the same meaning to words and phrases when found in a statute that is attached to them when and where found in general use. If we do so in this instance, then the question cannot be open to serious doubt. Webster describes a person as "a living soul; a self-conscious being; a moral agent; especially a living human being; a man, woman, or child; an individual of the human race." This is comprehensive enough, it would seem, to include even an Indian. . . . It is said, however, that this is the first instance on record in which an Indian has been permitted to sue out and maintain a writ of habeas corpus in a federal court, and therefore the court must be without jurisdiction in the premises. This is a non sequitur. I confess I do not know of another instance where this has been done, but I can also say that the occasion for it perhaps has never before been so great. It may be that the Indians think it wiser and better, in the end, to resort to this peaceful process than it would be to undertake the hopeless task of redressing their own alleged wrongs by force of arms. Returning reason, and the sad experience of others similarly situated, have taught them the folly and madness of the arbitrament of the sword. They can readily see that any serious resistance on their part would be the signal for their utter extermination. Have they not, then, chosen the wiser part by resorting to the very tribunal erected by those they claim have wronged and oppressed them?[11]

Dundy then went on to recite the history of U.S. relations with the Ponca. He noted that they had made treaties with the United States on March 12, 1858, and March 10, 1865, giving the Ponca land in South Dakota, which subsequently was taken from them by the April 29, 1868, Treaty of Fort Laramie (to which the Ponca Nation was not a party). This treaty effectively dispossessed the Ponca of their land in Iowa, South Dakota, and Nebraska.

Standing Bear's party had arrived in Nebraska in bad condition, Dundy noted:

> The land from which they fled in fear has no attractions for them. The bones of the dead son of Standing Bear were not to repose in the land they hoped to be leaving forever, but were carefully preserved and protected, and formed a part of what was to them a melancholy procession homeward. Such instances of parental affection, and such love of home and native land, may be heathen in origin, but it seems to me that they are not unlike Christian in principle.[12]

Whereas most historians have focused on the standing issue ("the Indian is truly a person"), the most significant aspect of the court's holding relates to the legality of the army's detention of Standing Bear and the remedy:

> I have searched in vain for the semblance of any authority justifying the commissioner in attempting to remove by force any Indians, whether belonging to a tribe or not, to any place, or for any other purpose than what has been stated. Certainly, without some specific authority found in an act of congress, or in a treaty with the Ponca tribe of Indians, he could not lawfully force the relators [Standing Bear and his cohorts] back to the Indian Territory, to remain and die in that country, against their will. *In the absence of all treaty stipulations or laws of the United States authorizing such removal, I must conclude that no such arbitrary authority exists.* It is true, if the relators are to be regarded as a part of the great nation of Ponca Indians, the government might, in time of war, remove them to any place of safety so long as the war should last, but perhaps no longer, unless they were charged with the commission of some crime. This is a war power merely, and exists in time of war

> only. Every nation exercises the right to arrest and detain an alien enemy during the existence of a war, and all subjects or citizens of the hostile nations are subject to be dealt with under this rule. [italics supplied]
>
> But it is not claimed that the Ponca tribe of Indians are at war with the United States, so that this war power might be used against them; in fact, they are amongst the most peaceable and friendly of all the Indian tribes, and have at times received from the government unmistakable and substantial recognition of their long-continued friendship for the whites. In time of peace the war power remains in abeyance, and must be subservient to the civil authority of the government until something occurs to justify its exercise. No fact exists, and nothing has occurred, so far as the relators are concerned, to make it necessary or lawful to exercise such an authority over them. If they could be removed to the Indian Territory by force, and kept there in the same way, I can see no good reason why they might not be taken and kept by force in the penitentiary at Lincoln, or Leavenworth, or Jefferson City, or any other place which the commander of the forces might, in his judgment, see proper to designate. I cannot think that any such arbitrary authority exists in this country.[13]

In ordering that Standing Bear and his followers be released from custody, Dundy also held:

> 2. That General George Crook, the respondent, being commander of the military department of the Platte, has the custody of the relators, under color of authority of the United States, and in violation of the laws thereof.
>
> 3. That no rightful authority exists for removing by force any of the relators to the Indian Territory, as the respondent has been directed to do.
>
> 4. That the Indians possess the inherent right of expatriation, as well as the more fortunate white race, and have the inalienable right to life, liberty, and the pursuit of happiness, so long as they obey the laws and do not trespass on forbidden ground.[14]

Secretary Schurz advised the attorney general not to pursue an appeal. The hearing and decision constitute a dramatic, resounding act of justice in the enforcement of the inalienable right to liberty of the individual human being. The hearing and the entire proceeding had everything for a good day in court:

> An outburst in the courtroom followed by a demonstration that was not squelched;
>
> A judge openly demonstrating sympathy for a litigant and expressing his sympathy in his opinion;
>
> An impoverished litigant seeking justice in a courtroom where he could communicate only through an interpreter;
>
> A litigant who spoke on his own behalf with an eloquence that would put Cicero to shame;
>
> An opinion that dispelled unreasonable contentions on the procedural issue of standing; and
>
> An opinion that provided an unequivocal remedy for an unfortunate group of individuals who had been grievously wronged.

The event not only brought honor and respect to Standing Bear and his followers, but was also a tribute to

> General George Crook, who had the decency and fortitude to challenge wrongdoing;
>
> Thomas Henry Tibbles, who mustered support for Standing Bear;
>
> Nebraska lawyers John Lee Webster and Andrew Jackson Poppleton, each an outstanding example of what a lawyer ought to be, who successfully represented the petitioners without thought of remuneration; and
>
> U.S. district court judge Elmer Dundy, who was equal to the contest before him.

Dundy's ruling needs to be considered in light of the conditions that existed at the time of the Battle of the Little Big Horn. In December 1875, the commissioner of Indian affairs directed his agents on the various reservations to notify members of the Cheyenne and Sioux tribes that they must return to their reservations by January 31, 1876, or be treated as hostiles subject to action by the army of the United States, which would be directed at every man, woman, and child who refused to comply. The United States was not at war with the Sioux or Cheyenne. Only Congress can declare war. If the secretary of the interior, who exercised jurisdiction over the Ponca in this instance, had no authority to force Standing Bear to return to Indian Territory, then President Ulysses S. Grant and Secretary of

War William W. Belknap, in 1876, acting through Generals William T. Sherman, Philip H. Sheridan, and Alfred H. Terry and Lt. Colonel George A. Custer, were without any authority to force the Sioux, Cheyenne, and Arapaho, who were engaged in hunting buffalo at the Little Big Horn River, to return to their reservations against their will. Dundy's opinion held, in essence, that Indians possessed the inalienable right to life, liberty, and the pursuit of happiness, so long as they obeyed the laws and did not trespass on forbidden ground. They had the right to be free from restraint of liberty under color of authority in violation of the laws of the United States. Accordingly, the attack without provocation against the Sioux and Cheyenne by the 7th U.S. Cavalry Regiment, on June 25, 1876, in an attempt to force them to return to their reservations was, among other things, against the law.

Following the court proceedings, the secretary of war ordered the release of Standing Bear, who went to Poppleton's residence and presented him with a "magnificent headdress," telling him: "If I had to pay you I could never get enough to do it."[15]

In 1880, the Ponca Tribe of Indians filed an action against Chief Red Cloud "in his own behalf and in behalf of the Sioux Nation of Indians."[16] The United States did not intervene, and the matter was heard before Dundy. The judge found that the Ponca had a legal estate in their old reservation (given by the United States to the Sioux in 1868) and that the Ponca were entitled to possession of all their lands in Nebraska and other parts of the disputed reservation.

Tibbles and others remained concerned about the plight of the remaining Ponca in Indian Territory. Bright Eyes and Iron Eye visited the tribe and reported back to Tibbles. Support was rallied from the governor of Nebraska, General Crook, and church leaders. Tibbles, Standing Bear, Bright Eyes, and her brother, Frank La Flesche, headed east to engender support for their cause. They made many friends for themselves and for the Indians, including Henry Wadsworth Longfellow, Edward Everett Hale, the writer Helen Hunt Jackson, Massachusetts governor John D. Long, and Boston mayor Frederick O. Prince. As a result of their efforts and the efforts of other interested citizens, Congress passed the Dawes Severalty Act (or General Allotment Act) on February 8, 1887, which allowed reservation lands to be allotted in severalty to individual Indians, and made Indians who received allotments citizens of the United States.[17] This was a mixed blessing because many tracts of allotment land were promptly sold to alleviate temporary financial crises.

The issue remained in a state of flux while congressional committees sought a solution. By this time, the Ponca Tribe was divided into two geographical groups—northern (Nebraska) and southern (Indian Territory). In February 1881, Congress appropriated funds to the Southern Ponca (605 members) to purchase land in Indian Territory from the Cherokee and funded per capita lump-sum payments to its members. For the Northern Ponca (217 members),[18] there was a per capita stipend, lump-sum amounts for dwellings, schools, and livestock, and an endowed fund of $70,000 to yield 5 percent annually for the benefit of all.[19] The question of the Northern Ponca land title was resolved in an 1881 agreement between the Ponca and the Sioux pursuant to which each Ponca head of family received 320 acres, each orphan under eighteen and each single person over eighteen received 160 acres, and every other member received 80 acres. This agreement was not implemented until 1890.

In subsequent years, the Southern and Northern Ponca went their separate ways. At one time, Standing Bear wanted to go back to Indian Territory but relented and returned to Nebraska, where he died in 1908. In 1962, Congress dissolved and terminated the tribal status of the Ponca Tribe in Nebraska.[20] Because their land had been allotted in severalty, there was no longer a reservation of the Northern Ponca. In 1990, however, the Ponca Restoration Act reconferred tribal status on "The Ponca Tribe of Nebraska"—with a proviso that they shall never establish a residential reservation in Nebraska.[21] The tribe and its government are active and well organized. They seem to be doing very well under the governance of their tribal council currently chaired by Mark Peniska.

Notes

1. Francis Paul Prucha, *Documents of the United States Indian Policy,* 3d ed. (Lincoln: University of Nebraska Press, 2000), 40.

2. Including the murder and forcible rape of women, looting and malicious destruction of a campsite, and shelling of an unprotected village with artillery. Dorothy Clarke Wilson, *Bright Eyes: The Story of Susette La Flesche, an Omaha Indian* (New York: McGraw-Hill, 1974), 75.

3. Ibid., 147.

4. Ibid., 161–62.

5. Ibid., 169.

6. James A. Lake, "Standing Bear! Who?" *Nebraska Law Review* 60, no. 3 (1981): 451, 472.

7. Ibid., 473.

8. Ibid., 476.

9. 25 F. Cas. 695 (C.C.D. Neb. 1879) (No. 14,891).

10. Ibid., 696.

11. Ibid., 697.

12. Ibid., 698–99.

13. Ibid., 700.

14. Ibid., 701.

15. Wilson, *Bright Eyes,* 200.

16. Lake, "Standing Bear," 482.

17. 24 Stat. 388 (1887).

18. Valerie Sherer Mathes and Richard Lowitt, *The Standing Bear Controversy: Prelude to Indian Reform* (Urbana: University of Illinois Press, 2003), 181.

19. 21 Stat. 422; see also Lake, "Standing Bear," 487.

20. 76 Stat. 429 (1962).

21. 104 Stat. 1167 (1990); the proviso prohibiting a residential reservation in Nebraska was inserted at the request of Congressman Doug Bereuter and would not survive judicial scrutiny under the equal protection clause of the Fourteenth Amendment of the U.S. Constitution.

TWELVE

Tim A. Garrison and Warren K. Urbom

WOUNDED KNEE

The Historical Background of the Wounded Knee Trials

TIM A. GARRISON

In the late 1950s and early 1960s, a number of young and persuasive American Indians, such as Clyde Warrior, Mel Thom, and Hank Adams, began urging native people to take pride in their heritage and to unite to address the problems that existed in their communities. Young Native Americans, many of them residing in urban areas, responded to their calls and organized Indian rights associations to bring national attention to indigenous issues. In particular, they condemned the failed federal policies of tribal termination and urban relocation, criticized the institutional corruption and incompetence of the Bureau of Indian Affairs (BIA), and demanded that the U.S. government allow the tribes to determine their own destiny. One of the groups that emerged, the American Indian Movement (AIM), organized in Minneapolis in 1968, became particularly adept at drawing media and government attention to Indian concerns.[1]

The activists publicized their causes with legal action, civil disobedience, and dramatic acts of resistance. Three protests, in particular, drew national interest. On November 20, 1969, a small group of Indians, most of whom resided in the San Francisco and Oakland areas, boated over and seized the island of Alcatraz. The protesters, who designated themselves the "Indians of All Tribes," were soon joined by natives from around North America. The Indians of All Tribes called for the return of unused federal properties to the former tribal owners and demanded that the island be transformed into an educational center for the study and protection of native culture. After an occupation of almost a year and a half, the federal government and the Indians of All Tribes negotiated a settlement and the protesters abandoned the island.[2]

After Alcatraz, Indian activists staged protests and sit-ins at several locations around the United States. In the fall of 1972, a large group of concerned natives traveled what they called the Trail of Broken Treaties to Washington, D.C., stopping at reservations along the way, to voice their grievances to federal policy makers. Frustrated because high federal officials refused to meet with them and unable to secure satisfactory accommodations, the protesters seized control of and ransacked the office of the Bureau of Indian Affairs.[3]

The third pivotal event in the Red Power movement, the occupation of Wounded Knee, began in February 1972, when an Oglala man named Raymond Yellow Thunder was murdered in Gordon, Nebraska. When the state court released the white assailants without bail, Severt Young Bear, a local leader, called on AIM to intervene. AIM members traveled to Gordon to protest. The local government responded by expanding the investigation and creating a council to improve relations between Indians and non-Indians in the area. Hostile relations around the Pine Ridge Reservation were renewed in January 1973, when a white man was accused of murdering Wesley Bad Heart Bull, a resident of Pine Ridge, in Custer, South Dakota. AIM members arrived in Custer to protest the fact that local officials had set a low bail for the assailant and charged him only with involuntary manslaughter. When negotiations between AIM and the local authorities deteriorated, a riot broke out. In the aftermath, several people were injured, thirty-seven Indians were under arrest, and the Custer courthouse was in flames.

At some point, the general protest against white law enforcement around the reservation also became conflated with political unrest at Pine Ridge. Many residents of the reservation were frustrated by the overbearing leadership of Richard Wilson, the recently elected tribal chairman, and they drew AIM into that conflict. Wilson's opponents denounced him as a corrupt accommodationist agent of the BIA, described him as a politician who cared little for the interests of the Indian residents of the reservation, and accused him of misappropriating tribal funds.

By February 1973, the intratribal conflict between the pro-Wilson and anti-Wilson factions among the Oglala and between whites and Indians in the area around the reservation had produced an extremely tense situation at Pine Ridge. On February 25, the U.S. Department of Justice sent fifty marshals to maintain order on the reservation. By this point, the federal government was targeting AIM as a dangerous group and conducting surveillance against its leaders and members. On February 27, Russell Means, Frank Fools Crow, and Pete Catches led a group of about two hundred Indians, many of them AIM members, to Wounded Knee on the Pine Ridge reservation. They seized control of the trading post, a museum, and several churches. In public statements and negotiation discussions, the occupiers called on Congress to conduct hearings "on treaties made with American Indian nations." They demanded that the United States recognize the property and political rights that federal treaty makers had acknowledged to the Sioux in the Treaty of Fort Laramie (1868), including the Sioux peoples' rights to the Black Hills. They also called for the abolition of Wilson's government, condemned corruption in the BIA, and bemoaned the living conditions of American Indians in general.[4]

AIM recognized that Wounded Knee was a powerful symbolic site for a protest. In the late 1880s, a Paiute man named Wovoka had experienced a series of prophetic visions. At this time, native people throughout the West had been demoralized by poverty, hunger, and the despair wrought by being penned up on reservations. Wovoka began to teach a message that synthesized native and Christian spiritual ideas. He promised that if native people remained morally upright and performed specific dances and ceremonies, then their game would be restored, their dead friends and ancestors resurrected, and non-Indians removed from their country. By 1889, Wovoka's Ghost Dance, a circle dance in which participants entered a dreamlike state, had spread to Indian communities throughout the West, including the reservations in the Dakota Territory. Although Wovoka encouraged his followers to avoid conflict, relations between the Sioux peoples and U.S. government officials were particularly acrimonious, and the ritualistic dancing, which went on for days on some reservations, unnerved Daniel F. Royer, the federal Indian agent at Pine Ridge. Royer believed that the dancers were preparing for war, and he telegraphed Washington for military assistance to suppress the Ghost Dance. In December 1890, U.S. Army troops under the command of General Nelson A. Miles arrived in the area to put down the resistance.[5]

Lakota police, dispatched to arrest Sitting Bull, killed the great chief instead. After hearing of the killing of Sitting Bull, who had supported the Ghost Dance movement and was considered by federal officials to be one of its leaders, a group of Miniconjou Sioux, led by a chief named Big Foot, abandoned their reservation at Cheyenne River and headed south. Miles ordered the notorious 7th U.S. Cavalry, under the authority of Colonel James W. Forsyth, to intercept the band. The federal troops directed the

Indians to Wounded Knee Creek on the Pine Ridge Reservation. The army surrounded the Wounded Knee encampment, emplaced Hotchkiss guns, and ordered the Indians to disarm. On the cold and snowy morning of December 29, 1890, a brief skirmish broke out when some of the Miniconjou men refused to surrender their weapons. The U.S. forces turned their artillery on the Indians, including the women, children, and elderly, encamped at the creek. In just a few minutes the U.S. forces had massacred at least 150 and perhaps as many as 300 of the Miniconjous. Twenty-five American soldiers also died in the fighting.[6]

Wounded Knee became symbolic of all the atrocities that native people had suffered at the hands of the government, and AIM understood that the seizure of the impoverished town would concentrate public attention on the plight of contemporary Indians. The federal government, however, refused to cede Wounded Knee to the occupiers. A well-armed force that included FBI agents, U.S. marshals, and U.S. Army troop carriers quickly surrounded the town and attempted to seal it off from outside contact and resupply. Richard Wilson assembled his auxiliary police force (referred to by his critics as "the goon squad") to enforce order on the reservation. Surrounded and cut off, the activists announced that Wounded Knee would be the birth site of a new "Independent Oglala Nation," and they dug defensive trenches and bunkers around the village. For more than seventy days, the forces of AIM and its sympathizers refused to surrender. The two camps frequently fired shots at each other from their entrenched positions; during the occupation and siege, two Indian protesters were killed, and one FBI agent was seriously wounded. Finally, on May 8, 1973, after long and often bitter negotiations, the standoff ended, and the protesters vacated Wounded Knee.[7]

During and after the Wounded Knee episode, state and federal authorities arrested 562 people, many of whom were AIM members. The U.S. Department of Justice issued 185 indictments, charging the defendants with crimes ranging from minor property violations to complicated conspiracy counts. During the standoff, supporters of AIM and the Oglala had created the Wounded Knee Legal Defense / Offense Committee (WKLDOC) to fund legal representation for any who might be arrested, and AIM leaders and their attorneys used the trials to publicize Indian concerns. Russell Means and Dennis Banks, two of the more prominent leaders of AIM, were tried in St. Paul, Minnesota. Although their trial became a media circus to some extent, it did reveal to the public that federal authorities had used illegal and heavy-handed tactics against the movement. After an eight-month trial, federal judge Fred Nichol dismissed all charges when the U.S. attorney refused to allow an eleven-member jury (one of the jurors had fallen ill near the end of the trial and the prosecutors had objected to the alternates) to reach a verdict.[8] The trials of other defendants, which were held in state and federal courtrooms throughout the Midwest, continued for more than two years. According to one study, the U.S. government secured only fifteen convictions (eleven for felonies) out of 185 original indictments. The government was not the only loser in the episode. Attorneys fees to defend their members drained the AIM treasury, and the group never again achieved the prominence it had acquired at Alcatraz, the Trail of Broken Treaties, and Wounded Knee. At the same time, however, the public had been put on notice that American Indians expected to have their individual and tribal rights respected and that native people possessed the will to solve their difficulties if the national and state governments respected the sovereignty of the tribal nations and dealt with them in a fair manner.[9]

Animosities between AIM, on one side, and the FBI and Wilson and his allies, on the other, continued long after the Wounded Knee occupation had ended. AIM spokesman Russell Means tried to unseat Wilson as tribal chief in the 1974 election, and Wilson continued to use his personal security force to intimidate his opponents. The WKLDOC claimed that somewhere between sixty-one and sixty-nine Indians died or disappeared during this period, and it accused the FBI of being complicit in their demise.[10] In one notorious episode, in June 1975, two FBI agents and an AIM member were killed in a gun battle at Pine Ridge. The government arrested four Indian activists and tried three of them for the deaths of the agents. Two of the defendants were acquitted; the other, Leonard Peltier, remains in prison as of the time of this writing, despite years of protest by his allies that his arrest was politically motivated and his trial marred by government misconduct.[11]

Judge Warren K. Urbom[12] presided at several of the Wounded Knee cases in Sioux Falls, South Dakota, and Lincoln, Nebraska. In this piece, originally presented as an address to the International Society of Barristers, Urbom reflected on the unconventional manner that he adopted to deal with these special cases during this unique time.[13]

You Can Bury My Heart at Wounded Knee

WARREN K. URBOM

A few days after Christmas 1890, 350 men, women, and children of the Sioux Nation trudged across the prairie, trying to reach the last of the great chiefs, Red Cloud, at Pine Ridge. They were led by Big Foot, so ill with pneumonia that he traveled lying in a wagon. The 7th U.S. Cavalry overtook them, and the white flag was immediately hoisted over Big Foot's wagon. When the disarming of the Indian men was almost finished, shooting broke out. At least half of the Indian men, women, and children and twenty-five soldiers were killed. It was the symbolic end, at least, of the armed resistance by American Indians. The place was Wounded Knee.[14]

I had occasion to summarize the broader historical context this way:

It cannot be denied that official policy of the United States until at least the late nineteenth century was impelled by a resolute will to control substantial territory for its westward-moving people. Whatever obstructed the movement, including the Indians, was to be—and was—shoved aside, dominated, or destroyed. Wars, disease, treaties pocked by duplicity, and decimation of the buffalo by whites drove the Sioux to reservations, shriveled their population and disemboweled their corporate body. They were left a people unwillingly dependent upon the United States.

It is an ugly history. White Americans may retch at the recollection of it.[15] American Indians retched too, and remembered. In February 1973, perhaps two hundred of them drove to Wounded Knee, now a tiny village on the Pine Ridge Reservation in western South Dakota, to protest what one of them called a "boot on our neck." In 1934, Congress had passed the Indian Reorganization Act, authorizing a degree of self-government of the tribes. Dick Wilson was the current tribal council president, elected under that act on that reservation. He was viewed by a substantial number on the reservation as running an autocratic, oppressive, and corrupt administration, knowingly supported by the Bureau of Indian Affairs of the Department of the Interior. The boot was a coagulation of factors and events, and it was personified in Dick Wilson. The reservation was boiling with unrest.

The Indians, led by members of the American Indian Movement, AIM, occupied Wounded Knee for seventy-one days, holding out against the police, the FBI, and the U.S. Marshal Service, who ringed the tiny settlement. Criminal charges were leveled against perhaps 150 people—Indians and whites—who were in or trying to get into the beleaguered village. The charges ranged from assault with a dangerous weapon to cattle rustling to burglary to interfering with a federal officer.

I was the lucky judge chosen to try most of them.

It had not been planned that way. A series of federal judges was to conduct a series of trials, two at a time, at different cities in South Dakota. The first trial was to last a week, and I was glad to leave Nebraska to get my stint out of the way early. That didn't work out. I stayed with the cases for a year. At the end of a long suppression hearing in that first trial, the defense team suggested and the prosecutors agreed that a great saving of time and money could result (a) if one judge would hear all the cases (except the trial of six leaders, including Russell Means and Dennis Banks, which was going on in St. Paul, Minnesota, simultaneously); (b) if most of the trials would be nonjury; and (c) if the judge could hear only once the massive amounts of testimony that was applicable to many cases.

The prosecutors and defense team declared that if I would assent to be the judge, I could expect a good many waivers of jury trials and stipulations to allow me to take into account evidence I had previously heard on common issues. I could also expect, they said, a number of pleas of guilty and a number of voluntary dismissals. The reckoning was that under that arrangement, the cases could be finished in a year; otherwise it would take three or four years.

I succumbed, and I am glad I did. There are three reasons: the Native Americans, the lawyers, and the issues.

First, the Native Americans

When I went to Sioux Falls, South Dakota, where the trials began, I was warned by the U.S. marshals that the defendants were itching for further confrontations: only by getting publicity could the AIM's purposes be furthered, and quietness would not bring publicity. Tight security was already in place in and about the courthouse. On the first day, some of the Indians—defendants and spectators—failed to stand when court opened. I did not notice it at first, but even when I did, I did not know what to do about it. On about the second day, a young Indian woman named Madonna Gilbert, who was to be a defendant in a later trial, came to my office to tell me that she and others were not standing because they thought standing would mean they respected the prosecution—and they did not respect the prosecution. I realized that I did not—and I still do not—know why people are expected to stand when a judge comes into a courtroom, and it occurred to me that if we are going to ask people to do a symbolic act without telling them what it symbolizes, we in fairness must leave it to each of them to decide. So I told her that if standing symbolized to her something she could not accept, then she ought to remain seated.

The marshals earnestly counseled me that I was making a grievous mistake. The Indians, they advised, would come next with hats on and shirts off and would do whatever else it took to make me draw the line for confrontation. And, they argued, I might as well draw it early. I chose not to draw it. If any effort was made to make me draw it, I never knew it. In fact, when we moved the trials to Lincoln, Nebraska, four months after they began, we so eased security that there was virtually no sign of it, because there appeared to be no need.

That's not to say that there was no publicity or planned publicity. People of instant recognition, such as Marlon Brando, Buffy St. Marie, and Angela Davis came, but only for a moment. And the press dutifully and responsibly reported it all.

I feel fortunate about the no-standing matter, because in another courtroom in the same city a few weeks later a judge took a different tack in another case involving Indians but not arising from Wounded Knee. He insisted that everybody stand at the opening of court, and the result was a riot. Ten people were hospitalized, and the courtroom became a shambles.

There were some unusual happenings at our trials, of course, but the Indian spokesman or a defense attorney always told me openly about them before they occurred, and we were able to work things out. For example, on the first day of the trials in Lincoln, the Indians planned a ceremonial worship service—to be held in the courtroom. It was to be in the three languages of the three tribes that would participate from around the country. It was to take an hour and a half. I agreed but told them to be finished in time to open court at nine o'clock. They were.

Another time, one of the defendants wanted to deliver his own opening statement and wanted to ask the jury to stand and pray with him. I said that he might pray and that I would tell the jury that they were free to pray or not to pray but to stay seated. He said okay, and everything went without a hitch.[16]

Many of the Indian witnesses chose to take their oaths on the sacred pipe. My law clerks could find no authority of any kind on the subject, except a Middle District of Pennsylvania case, as I recall, having to do with strange ways of taking oaths. I puzzled about the matter, until I reasoned that an oath should be designed to impress the oath taker with the burden of his or her own conscience and that such an outcome would be more likely if the oath were taken on something sacred to him or her. So I approved the pipe request.

On one occasion we had a jury box full of Indian leaders—traditional chiefs and headmen. We were having a two-week nonjury hearing on the validity of the 1868 treaty between the United States and the Great Sioux Nation, and the Indian leaders had come to testify to their people's oral history of that treaty. The courtroom was full, so we had these special people sit in the jury box. I have an indelible picture in my mind of those deeply lined faces coming one by one to take the oath on the sacred pipe and testifying in the Lakota language about their proud and disconsolate heritage. A book about that treaty hearing got its name from that scene. Roxanne Dunbar Ortiz in the introduction says: "The court room there in Lincoln, Nebraska, felt more like a holy place than an American court of law. Since the proceedings did not require the presence of a jury, the traditional leaders sat in the jury box, sitting in judgment on America."

The title of the book was *The Great Sioux Nation: Sitting in Judgement on America.*

Second, the Lawyers

The prosecution was under the guidance of William Clayton, U.S. attorney for the District of South Dakota. About ten attorneys at one time or another served as assistant U.S. attorneys or special prosecutors in the trials before me in Sioux Falls and Lincoln. At least three of them, Carleton R. Hoy, Joseph M. Butler, and Ronald W. Banks, had never before been on the prosecution side of the table. I applauded them privately then and I applaud them publicly now for what they did for the judicial system. Edward C. Carpenter, of Rapid City, and Duane Nelson, of Lincoln, carried the bulk of the trial work for the prosecution.

The prosecutors were in an extraordinarily difficult position. The reports were voluminous, scattered, and hopelessly indexed. Witnesses were uncooperative or hard to find. Scarcely a person who had been inside Wounded Knee was willing to testify to anything that anybody did there. Almost all prosecutions, therefore, had to be of persons who were arrested for something they did at the perimeter while trying to get either into or out of Wounded Knee.

Carleton Hoy has passed on this recital of the plight of one defendant: He was a man who heard about the action at Wounded Knee and decided to be a part of it; he boarded a bus in Chicago and got as far as Valentine, Nebraska, before running out of money; he hitchhiked from place to place and was let out on the road going north from the town of Pine Ridge, where he started to walk; he walked most of the night or day, became too tired to go on, and crawled into a lean-to to sleep—and there an FBI agent saw him sleeping and arrested him for something or other. As Hoy says, "Like so many chapters of our lives, his war was over before he ever found the battlegrounds." That story is not an isolated one.

Joe Butler, after the Wounded Knee chapter was closed, told Hoy that he had no inner drive to become totally involved in bar or other activities because he had given a significant portion of his lifeblood for the cause. Of that, Hoy says, "I understood." I, too, understand.

The defense team efforts were coordinated by the Wounded Knee Defense/Offense Committee, presided over by Joseph Beeler, of Milwaukee, now of Miami, and Kenneth Tilson, of St. Paul, Minnesota. Forty or so lawyers appeared for the defense at various times. Most of the trial work was by members of the National Association of Criminal Defense Lawyers or the National Lawyers Guild. Robert Heeney, now deceased, of Rockville, Maryland, organized volunteers from the national association. I say "volunteers" accurately. The appointed defense counsel received no fee; I allowed twenty-five dollars a day for expenses and one round-trip plane ticket. Their terms of service varied from a few days to several months, and I am sure that Joe Beeler, at least, spent more than a year, full-time, with no Criminal Justice Act fee.

Heavyweights and featherweights came—cause lawyers and noncause lawyers, brilliant and fumbling, experienced and inexperienced, pugnacious and gentle—a dazzling display of the assortment that is the American trial bar. I loved it.

The defendants' lawyers came from everywhere—Boston, New York, Chicago, Minneapolis, Milwaukee, Denver, San Jose, San Francisco, Hollywood. Their styles and attitudes were a continent apart, too.

John Thorne was the first one I met, I think. I had just arrived in the judge's chambers in Sioux Falls when a call came from a marshal, asking me to come to the front door of the courthouse. There was colorful John Thorne—full-bearded, clothed in a denim jacket, beads, and a sea captain's cap—unable to get past the security guards because he refused to let his briefcase be searched. I let him in and changed the rule to exempt counsel from search requirements.

John Thorne had long been, and still is, an avid civil rights defender in "movement cases," such as the sit-in trials in San Francisco, the courthouse raid trial of Reies Tijerina in New Mexico, and litigation against the war in Vietnam. He gave at least nine months to the Wounded Knee trials, all the time ebullient, persistent, in tune with his client's cause, and thoroughly respectful. James and Gilda Shellow were of similar background, having defended civil rights workers in the South in the 1960s and Father James Groppi in Milwaukee.

Clyde Christopher Henning, of Rockville, Maryland, on the other hand, was not a cause lawyer, unless a firm belief in the Sixth Amendment means automatically that he was.

Albert J. Krieger, of New York City, now of Miami, was something else. Sleek of build, smooth of dome, and impeccable in attire, he could swagger even when he was sitting still. His mind was expansive, his speech was powerful, and his attitude was irreproachable. He was a complete trial lawyer.

One of the prosecuting attorneys later said that one incident arising from the Wounded Knee trials that stuck most vividly in his mind was his first meeting with Al Krieger, whom, he said, "I regard to be one of the finest lawyers I have ever been privileged to meet and watch. Mr. Krieger's abilities that were demonstrated at the trial took second place only to his sense of professionalism." Another of those prosecutors has written, "Al stands above all of them." When your opposition likes you, you are either very bad or very good.

Michael Kennedy, a young redheaded Irishman from San Francisco, tried one Wounded Knee case. It was a jury trial of a misdemeanor charge of assault by the defendant's running the wheel of a car over the toe of an FBI agent's boot—not the toe of his foot, but the toe of the boot. We tried the case for eight full days. Kennedy stood between the counsel table and the witness box and questioned the witnesses without notes, very straight, very poised, very controlled. At one point the prosecutor, Alan Kirshen, of Sioux City, Iowa, now of Omaha, asked a witness about an incident at the BIA Building in Washington, D.C. Kennedy moved for a mistrial, arguing that there was an innuendo that the defendant had participated in violence:

> MR. KENNEDY: . . . [A]nd the prosecutor knows it is a lie, your Honor . . .
>
> MR. KIRSHEN: I am getting tired of this, Mr. Kennedy—
>
> MR. KENNEDY: Don't you address me or I'll lay you on the floor.

Kirshen didn't and Kennedy didn't.

Kirshen was reported to me during another trial as probably carrying a gun in the courtroom. I asked him about it. He declared that he needed it to protect himself from threats he had received. I directed him not to carry it in the courthouse and assured him of a security guard if he wanted one. He did not ask for a guard, and I have no reason to think that he did not follow my directive.

Toward the end of 1974, Kirshen negotiated a dismissal of a criminal charge, conditioned upon the defendant's saying nothing to the press about the fact of dismissal. I was not aware of the condition until Kenneth Tilson of the defense team wrote to me and to the Justice Department to protest. I replied only that if a motion were filed, I would rule on it. A few days later, the Justice Department informed me that Kirshen would no longer be involved in the trials. I do not know whether there was a connection.

Do you wonder why all these lawyers made sacrifices for the trials? Some have told me. For Clyde Henning, "It was simply . . . the right to counsel." For Ronald Banks, it was to repay the profession which had been good to him. For Elliot Taikeff, of New York, it was sympathy for the cause of the Native Americans. As far as I can tell, there was not a selfish or mean reason in the bunch.

Third, the Issues

Rarely does anyone get to wrestle with issues as fundamentally different as those that inhered in the Wounded Knee trials. Most of the law had emerged from its own peculiar background. I became intimate with what theretofore had been strange to me: the Major Crimes Act, the Fort Laramie Treaty of 1868, the doctrine of posse comitatus, and the reliance upon oral history.

Hovering over every trial was this defense: that under the treaty of 1868 the United States had no jurisdiction over acts committed on the land of which Wounded Knee was a part. A two-week hearing turned on the proposition that the law, which had been pronounced by Chief Justice John Marshall at least as early as 1821 and often reiterated since, that the Indian nations are not sovereign and that treaties with them may be altered or abrogated unilaterally by the United States, is unjust and immoral because it is based upon the false premise that the Indians were and are uncivilized savages.

The evidence from anthropologists, historians, and traditional Indians strongly indicated that the Indians were not uncivilized or savages—at least when compared with their white contemporaries. In the closing arguments, this colloquy occurred between John Thorne and me:

> THE COURT: [If I conclude that the facts show a lack of basis for the rule of law and that the law is therefore immoral and unjust,] [w]hat shall I do with my oath to uphold the law when the United States Supreme Court has declared what the law is?
>
> MR. THORNE: What would you do, Judge, if the Congress passed a law and said every third child born to a family shall be put to death, if the issue came before you?
>
> THE COURT: I might resign, Mr. Thorne. That is different from saying that I will not obey what the Supreme Court has said is the law. . . .
>
> MR. THORNE: As you put the question, Judge, in this case your duty is to resign if you honestly do not think that the defendants' position is legally sound, when you know what the facts are. . . .

I decided against the defendants' position and did not resign. But I hoped that an adequate record had been made to enable the Supreme Court to reassess the law, if it chose to do so. It chose not to do so. I also hoped that the Indian people could never again say that they had never been fully and fairly heard. There was one great disappointment in the Wounded Knee scenario.

In the early weeks, just after I had granted a motion to suppress, the prosecution team proposed a settlement. If the five defendants whose convictions were most wanted by the prosecution would plead guilty, the other hundred-plus indictments would be dismissed. The defense team gathered the five and got their consent. All was set, except approval of the Justice Department in Washington. It never came.

So there followed a year of trials. In that time, five defendants were convicted, only two of crimes serious enough to draw a term in jail.

What of it all?

These are comments of some of the counsel.

Clyde Henning, defense counsel: "Even for those of us who played only a small part, there is a feeling that we recognized our responsibility to our system of law and to the traditions of the bar and did our best."

John Thorne, defense counsel: "Since those trials . . . I am doing all I can to get out of the law practice because I find it so discouraging."

Albert Krieger, defense counsel: "[T]he Wounded Knee trials are excellent examples of the best that we have to offer and some of the worst."

Carleton Hoy, prosecutor: "I have a profound respect for the people that make the system work."

Joe Butler, prosecutor: "The most significant memory I have of the trials was the manner in which the Department of Justice handled the problem. Many of the cases . . . should never have been in court. . . . When you say you can bury your heart at Wounded Knee, you can also put mine alongside."

Ed Carpenter, prosecutor: "I wonder if . . . I go home tonight and discover someone occupying my home, would I have any recourse?"

Elliot Taikeff, defense counsel: "I don't know if the Barristers would appreciate a caveat, but at least some might want to be cautious about involvement in political trials, lest they significantly alter their lives."

I close with this. Lewis Gurwitz, a young bear from Boston, came to my office upon his arrival as a defense counsel. There was a chip on his shoulder. He let me know at once that he had been in courtroom brawls before and was ready for another now. He looked at me squarely and said, "I don't take crap from anybody." When the trial was over, he came in again. He held out his hand and said, "I don't understand you." That said worlds to me. The chip was still there, maybe, but its edges were a little smoother now.

And that's my perception of the Wounded Knee trials.

Notes

1. Paul Chaat Smith and Robert Allen Warrior, *Like a Hurricane: The Indian Movement from Alcatraz to Wounded Knee* (New York: New Press, 1996), 36–59.

2. Ibid., 1–5, 26–30, 73–111; Troy R. Johnson, *The Occupation of Alcatraz Island: Self-Determination and the Rise of Indian Activism* (Urbana: University of Illinois Press, 1996).

3. Smith and Warrior, *Like a Hurricane,* 141–77.

4. John William Sayer, *Ghost Dancing the Law: The Wounded Knee Trials* (Cambridge, Mass.: Harvard University Press, 1997), 29–30, 31–32; Smith and Warrior, *Like a Hurricane,* 177–93.

5. Robert M. Utley, *The Lance and the Shield: The Life and Times of Sitting Bull* (New York: Henry Holt, 1993), 281–307; Colin G. Calloway, ed., *Our Hearts Fell to the Ground: Plains Indian Views of How the West Was Lost* (Boston: Bedford-St. Martin's, 1996), 196–99.

6. Francis Paul Prucha, *The Great Father: The United States Government and the American Indians,* 2 vols. (Lincoln: University of Nebraska Press, 1984), 2:726–29; Calloway, *Our Hearts Fell to the Ground,* 199–204. The reported number of casualties at Wounded Knee varies dramatically relative to the source.

7. Sayer, *Ghost Dancing the Law,* 32–35; Smith and Warrior, *Like a Hurricane,* 194–268.

8. For a thorough discussion of the Means and Banks case, see Sayer, *Ghost Dancing the Law.*

9. Ibid., 2–5, 228.

10. For the varying reports on the disputed number of deaths, see ibid., 297n124.

11. Smith and Warrior, *Like a Hurricane,* 269–78.

12. Then chief judge, now senior judge, U.S. District Court for the District of Nebraska.

13. Address delivered at the Annual Convention of the International Society of Barristers, Phoenix, Arizona, March 1982, originally published in *International Society of Barristers Quarterly* 17, no. 2 (1982): 259–66, reprinted with permission (notes renumbered and minor stylistic changes made to keep the style of this volume consistent).

14. This is essentially the view of Dee Brown's *Bury My Heart at Wounded Knee.*

15. United States v. Consolidated Wounded Knee Cases, 389 F. Supp. 235, 238 (D. Neb. and D. S. Dak. 1975).

16. This was Roger Iron Cloud's prayer: "O Great Spirit, we pray to you at this time to help us and guide us throughout this court, and give guidance to these jurors and their deliberations, their quest for the truth and justice."

THIRTEEN

Susan I. Strong

THE FIRST WOMEN OF NEBRASKA LAW

> Counsel intimates with a curl on his lip that I am called the lady lawyer. I am sorry I cannot return the compliment, but I cannot. I never heard anybody call him any kind of a lawyer at all.
>
> —*Clara Shortridge Foltz*

The Women's Rights Movement in the United States: The Early Years

Most people think of the 1960s and 1970s when they hear someone talk about feminists or the women's rights movement. Thoughts turn to Gloria Steinem, the controversy over the Equal Rights Amendment, and *Roe v. Wade,*[1] the U.S. Supreme Court decision giving women the right to an abortion. In truth, the fight for women's rights began hundreds of years before this time.[2]

The involvement of women and the law in America dates back to colonial times, before this country even began. From the beginning, women fought for the rights to own land, to vote, and to be recognized as equals by their male counterparts. Within the greater movement to attain these rights, women found themselves also fighting for the right to enter the legal profession. Interestingly enough, women gained the right to practice law long before they were allowed to vote in most states.

During the colonial period, women became increasingly involved in the legal system in this country. Although women had not yet formally entered the rolls of the state bars, some were, in effect, practicing law. In 1797, Lucy

Terry Prince, of Vermont—born in Africa, enslaved in the United States, and freed by her husband—according to local legend presented an oral argument before the U.S. Supreme Court concerning her farmland and won.[3] If the legend were true, she would have been the first woman and possibly the first African American to have argued before the Supreme Court, although not as a licensed attorney. But the legend does not comport with reality. Lucy Terry Prince did appear a number of times before local Vermont courts, arguing on behalf of her husband, children, and herself, and eventually before the Vermont Supreme Court, but she never appeared before the U.S. Supreme Court or before Justice Samuel Chase sitting in circuit.[4]

Women's entry into the legal system is inextricably linked with the woman suffrage movement, the fight for women's right to own property, and the abolitionist movement. Women began speaking about these issues in public forums, perhaps for the first time, in the early to mid-1800s. In 1831, Maria W. Miller Stewart, abolitionist, feminist, and African American, went on one of the first public speaking tours to talk about abolition, the education and history of women, and civil rights for African Americans.[5] In 1839, several states, the first of which was Mississippi, began passing married women's property acts, providing women some security in their own property.[6]

The Declaration of Sentiments, often credited as the impetus of the women's rights movement, was published at the first women's convention, held at Seneca Falls, New York, in 1848.[7] The declaration, authored by Elizabeth Cady Stanton and modeled after the Declaration of Independence, demanded equal treatment for women and men under the law, including the right to vote: "The history of mankind is a history of repeated injuries and usurpations on the part of man toward woman, having in direct object the establishment of an absolute tyranny over her. To prove this, let facts be submitted to a candid world."[8] In 1851, Sojourner Truth, a former slave, delivered her famous "Ain't I a Woman" speech at a women's rights convention in Akron, Ohio, calling for equal rights for women as well as for African Americans.[9] In 1868, Myra Bradwell established the *Chicago Legal News* and began writing a column called "Law Relating to Women," calling for suffrage and reporting on women practicing law before any had been formally admitted to the bar.[10]

As disappointed as women had been with their legal status after the Revolutionary War, they were even more disappointed after the Civil War. When the Union victory was at hand, many women abolitionists assumed that their hard work would result in suffrage for women as well as for African Americans, but the Fourteenth and Fifteenth amendments to the Constitution, adopted in 1868 and 1870 respectively, granted citizenship and suffrage only to male African Americans, not to women.[11]

Thus, 1869 was an important year in the battle for women's rights in the legal profession, and the charge was led by women in the Midwest.[12] In that year, Belle A. Mansfield passed the state bar examination in Iowa after informal study, becoming the first woman in the United States to be admitted to a licensed bar.[13] Also in 1869, Lemma Barkaloo became the first woman law student in the nation; after one year of study, she passed the Missouri bar examination and began practicing.[14] Women in other states endured a more difficult course. Myra Bradwell's application to the Illinois bar in 1869 was rejected on the ground that she was a woman, and in *Bradwell v. Illinois,* the U.S. Supreme Court held that states may statutorily deny women the right to practice law.[15]

The Contributions of Nebraska Women

Nebraska did not deny women the right to practice law by statute as a territory or as a state, although no women sought admission during the territorial period.[16] Nebraska statutes provided for the admission of "persons" or "citizens," without words of limitation.[17] And whereas many other states with similar statutes waited for the passage of legislation specifically requiring the admission of women, the Nebraska bar readily admitted women on their first application.[18] Nebraska women were formally admitted to practice law as early as 1883, and three of the first twenty women admitted to practice before the U.S. Supreme Court were from Nebraska.[19]

First Lawyer—Ada Matilda Cole Bittenbender

Without question, the person who had the single largest impact on Nebraska women in the legal profession was Ada M. Bittenbender, who not only blazed a trail for other Nebraskans but set an example for women lawyers across the nation. On August 17, 1883, Bittenbender became the first woman admitted to practice before the Nebraska Supreme Court, and, on October 15, 1888, she became only the third woman admitted to practice before the U.S. Supreme Court.[20]

Ada M. Bittenbender was born Ada Matilda Cole in Asylum, Bradford County, Pennsylvania, on August 3, 1848.[21] Her ancestors were from New England, and her father died from illness as a Union soldier.[22] She graduated in 1869 from Binghamton (N.Y.) Commercial College and in 1875 from the Pennsylvania State Normal School.[23] She taught for one year and then attended the Froebel Normal Institute, from which she graduated in 1877.[24] She took a job as principal at a school in Pennsylvania but resigned because of the heavy workload.[25] On August 9, 1878, she married Henry Clay Bittenbender, a young lawyer from Bloomsburg, Pennsylvania, and a graduate of Princeton College.[26]

Soon after their marriage, Henry and Ada moved to Osceola, Nebraska, where Henry purchased a newspaper and Ada became its editor.[27] She began studying law with her husband while editing the *Record,* the first Farmers' Alliance paper established in the state.[28] The paper was devoted to temperance, good morals, and Republican politics.[29] Ada also served as secretary of the Polk County Agricultural Association and became the first delegate ever received by the State Board of Agriculture.[30] In 1881, she was elected recording secretary of the Nebraska Woman's Suffrage Association and was eventually elected president at a subsequent convention.[31]

In 1882, she applied for and was granted admission to the bar in Nebraska.[32] She and her husband became law partners in the firm of H. C. & Ada M. Bittenbender and moved to Lincoln in December 1882.[33]

Many early women attorneys took care of office duties while their husbands went to court, but Ada Bittenbender preferred the courtroom.[34] In 1893, it was written of her: "Unlike many other lawyers of her sex, she prefers court practice to office work. She is a successful lawyer, and is said to have lost but one case that has been brought by her. She has won several cases before the Supreme Court, and has been admitted to the United States District and Circuit Courts of Nebraska."[35]

In addition to practicing law, Bittenbender continued to lobby for the causes that were near and dear to her heart. She secured the passage of the scientific temperance instruction bill, a bill prohibiting the sale of tobacco to minors, and a law giving the mother guardianship of her children equally with the father.[36] Bittenbender also authored bills establishing a home for penitent women and girls and an industrial school, which the Nebraska Legislature enacted in 1887 and 1891 respectively.[37]

She traveled to Washington, D.C., in 1888 to give a speech titled "Women in the Law" at the International Council of Women.[38] She then became active in representing the Woman's Christian Temperance Union movement, eventually as its national attorney, and remained in Washington during several sessions of Congress to draft and advocate the passage of legislation for the advancement and protection of women.[39]

On October 15, 1888, Bittenbender became the third woman to be admitted to practice before the U.S. Supreme Court. The motion for admission was made by Senator Henry Blair, of New Hampshire, with whom she had worked in passing certain legislation concerning the protection of women.[40]

Of the first twenty women attorneys admitted to the Supreme Court bar, only four actually litigated in the court—Bittenbender was one of them.[41] She and her husband filed a brief on their own behalf in *Nebraska ex rel. Bittenbender v. Excise Board*[42] during the Court's 1916 term.[43] At issue was whether an 1858 act of the Nebraska Territorial Legislature had repealed an 1855 act prohibiting the manufacture and sale of intoxicating liquor. The Bittenbenders argued that it had not, and they sought a writ of mandamus directing the excise board to perform its duties in regulating the manufacture and sale of intoxicating liquor.[44] On May 21, 1917, the Supreme Court dismissed their appeal for want of jurisdiction.[45]

In 1890, Ada Bittenbender added another first by moving for the admission of another woman to the U.S. Supreme Court.[46] Emma Gillett, the seventh woman member of the Supreme Court bar, returned the favor and moved for the admission of Marilla Ricker, the ninth woman member, in 1891.[47] These examples set off a series of motions by women for women—more than twenty-five between 1890 and 1920.[48] Bittenbender was truly a pioneer of women's networking in the legal profession.

In September 1891, Bittenbender was nominated by the Prohibition Party for judge of the Supreme Court of Nebraska, and she received the largest number of votes ever cast for the head of the Prohibition ticket.[49] She was again nominated for the same position in August 1893, but once more failed to win enough votes.[50]

Women as Jurors and Jurists in the United States

During the nineteenth and twentieth centuries, women's advancement in society resembled a tug of war between the legal system and political arena, each resisting until pulled by the other in the direction of recognizing women's rights.[51] While the courts were allowing women to become members of the bar and even judges, the legislatures were refusing to allow them to participate on juries, holding to the notion that women belonged in the home taking care of the family.

Following the common law, most states initially viewed women as ineligible for jury service, and in 1880, the U.S. Supreme Court upheld the states' right under the Fourteenth Amendment to confine jury service to males.[52]

Utah broke the barrier in 1898, and eventually all other states followed, although most gave women only limited access to the jury box.[53]

As late as 1961, although a majority of states by then allowed women to serve as jurors, the Supreme Court continued to hold that state laws that effectively excluded women from jury pools were not invidious discrimination but an "inoffensive" attempt to accommodate the "special responsibilities" of women.[54] It was not until 1975 that the Supreme Court reversed its earlier position and held that the Sixth Amendment rights of criminal defendants render the exclusion of women from juries impermissible.[55] Just six years later, President Ronald Reagan nominated Sandra Day O'Connor to serve as the first woman on the U.S. Supreme Court.

Women as Jurors in Nebraska

Not until 1943 were women allowed to sit on juries in Nebraska.[56] The shortage of males available for jury duty during World War II prompted James H. Anderson, of Scottsbluff, to introduce a bill to change the maximum age of jurors from sixty-five to seventy and to remove the requirement that jurors be "good and lawful men."[57] The bill was approved on March 31, 1943, and became effective immediately.[58]

The new statute, however, contained a section requiring the presiding judge in a district to determine whether the accommodations and facilities of the courthouse permitted the service of women as jurors and provided that women could be excused from service if requested in writing and if good cause was found by the presiding judge of the court.[59] Those two sections of the statute effectively prohibited women from serving as jurors in some districts, and they were not repealed until 1977 and 1967, respectively.[60]

Today's statute still provides that a nursing mother who requests to be excused shall be excused from jury service for good cause.[61] And, although the U.S. Supreme Court held in 1986 that it is unconstitutional to use peremptory challenges to exclude persons from jury panels on account of their race,[62] many state courts, including those of Nebraska, have refused to extend the decision to include discrimination on the basis of sex.[63] Finally, in 1994, the U.S. Supreme Court held that the equal protection clause prohibits sex discrimination in the exercise of peremptory challenges.[64]

Women in the Federal Judiciary

Soon after women began gaining admission to state bars, they also began serving in the judiciary.[65] For instance, the first woman judge on record was a justice of the peace in the Territory of Wyoming in 1870, and the first woman elected to a state supreme court was Florence Ellinwood Allen, of Ohio, in 1922.[66] But the ascension of women into the ranks of the federal judiciary would not be as "easy."

In 1934, President Franklin Delano Roosevelt appointed Judge Allen to the U.S. Court of Appeals for the Sixth Circuit.[67] After serving on the Ohio Supreme Court for eleven years, unsuccessfully running for the U.S. Senate in 1926 and the U.S. House of Representatives in 1930, Allen became the first woman in the nation appointed to an Article III federal court.[68] One of her colleagues on the Sixth Circuit was so distressed that he reportedly took to his sickbed for two days following her appointment.[69]

After Allen's appointment, no woman was appointed to the federal bench for another fifteen years. It wasn't until 1949 that President Harry Truman appointed Burnita Shelton Matthews to the U.S. District Court for the District of Columbia.[70] She was the first female Article III federal trial court judge in the country. Again, after Matthews's appointment, several years went by before any women were appointed at the federal level. The Kennedy and Johnson administrations appointed four women to the federal bench, and the Nixon and Ford administrations named just two.[71] The logjam finally broke during the Carter administration in the 1970s. President Carter appointed forty women to the federal bench during his one term in office, from 1976 through 1980.[72]

Presidents Ronald Reagan (1980–88), George Bush (1988–92), Bill Clinton (1992–2000) and George W. Bush (2000) have continued the trend and have appointed women in significant numbers.[73] In 1981, Sandra Day O'Connor became the first woman to serve on the highest court in the country. Ruth Bader Ginsburg became the second woman on the U.S. Supreme Court when appointed by Clinton in 1992. The retirement of Sandra Day O'Connor in 2005 left the High Court once again with only one woman justice.

Women in the Nebraska Judiciary

Although Ada Bittenbender was admitted to the bar in 1883,[74] it wasn't until 1971 that a Nebraska governor appointed the first female judge in the state, nearly ninety years after the first woman was admitted to the Nebraska bar.[75]

First Judge—Elizabeth Davis Pittman

On April 8, 1971, Governor J. James Exon broke not only the sex barrier but the racial barrier as well when he appointed forty-nine-year-old

Elizabeth Davis Pittman as municipal judge for the city of Omaha.[76] Pittman proved to be worthy of the appointment.[77]

Pittman was born on June 3, 1921, in Council Bluffs, Iowa. Her parents moved to Omaha when she was young, and she graduated from North High School in 1938. She attended the University of Nebraska for two years and, in 1942, married Dr. A. B. Pittman, a veterinarian.[78] She earned her B.A. and LL.B degrees from Creighton University in 1948.[79] The first African American to graduate from Creighton University Law School, she was admitted to the bar in 1949.[80]

In 1950, there were twenty-eight women lawyers in Nebraska, and only one of them—Pittman—was African American.[81] Pittman had always been interested in becoming a lawyer. Her love for the law was inspired by her father, Charles Franklin Davis, a lawyer and political activist. Pittman joined her father's law office and became one of the few women to enter private practice at that time.[82] After her father died, she continued the firm as a sole practitioner.[83]

Like her father, Pittman was politically active and became the first African American elected to the Omaha School Board in 1950.[84] Unfortunately, shortly after her election she became ill and was hospitalized, suffering from "nervous exhaustion."[85] She resigned a year later, possibly because of health concerns, although an explanation was never given.[86] In 1964, she achieved another first—she was the first woman appointed to the deputy county attorney's office in Douglas County.[87] In 1970, she applied for a seat on the municipal court in the city of Omaha.

The appointment of Pittman was a bold and courageous move by Exon, heralded by many but not appreciated by all in the legal community. Undaunted by the mixed reviews she received in her ratings by members of the Omaha Bar Association, Pittman remained true to her stated goal of dispensing justice equally to all.[88] In response to the ratings, she once said: "I've been called a lenient judge and I've been called a hard judge. I try to be a fair and impartial judge. If I'm successful in that, I'll be perfectly satisfied."[89]

She did her share of speaking in the community, advocating the importance of women in society and the contributions they could make, if given the opportunity.[90] She was outspoken against the use of drugs by youth and urged parents to take responsibility for their children.[91] With the exception of drug pushers, Pittman believed in rehabilitation of criminals rather than punishment by incarceration, and she opposed capital punishment because she felt it was contrary to the principles of a civilized nation.[92] This was in keeping with her philosophy that freedom, which she viewed as one of the most important things in the world, was a right, not a privilege.[93]

Pittman served fifteen distinguished years on the bench. Only two of her decisions were ever reviewed by the Nebraska Supreme Court, and only one resulted in a finding of error on the part of the municipal court.[94] She retired on October 1, 1986, and died on April 8, 1998, at the age of seventy-six.[95] In appreciation for her years of service, on October 3, 1998, Creighton University dedicated the Elizabeth Davis Pittman Building on its Omaha campus.[96]

Other Judicial Appointments

J. James Exon[97] served two four-year terms as governor from 1971 through 1979 and appointed a total of four women to the bench, including the first female district court judge.[98] On September 1, 1972, he appointed Betty Peterson Sharp district judge for the Second Judicial District.[99] Also appointed by Exon were Colleen R. Buckley, in 1973, to the Douglas County Juvenile Court, and Janice Gradwohl, in 1974, to the municipal court in Lincoln. All four women were former prosecutors, and Sharp had been elected county attorney for Otoe County for three terms.[100] Sadly, there was an eleven-year gap between Gradwohl's appointment and that of the next woman named to a judicial position.[101]

First Appellate Judge—Lindsey Miller-Lerman

Lindsey Miller-Lerman has the distinctive honor of being not only the first female judge on the Nebraska Court of Appeals but the first woman on the Nebraska Supreme Court, as well. On December 12, 1991, Miller-Lerman was appointed by Governor Ben Nelson as one of the six original members of the Nebraska Court of Appeals. Miller-Lerman was the first woman in Nebraska to serve on an appellate court and, at the time of her appointment, was the only woman serving on a court higher than the county or juvenile court.[102]

Miller-Lerman graduated from Wellesley College in 1968 and received her law degree from Columbia University in 1973, where she was a member of the law review. She clerked for two years for Judge Constance Baker Motley, U.S. district court judge for the Southern District of New York. She then worked in private practice in Omaha at the Kutak Rock law firm from 1975 through 1992.

In 1996, Miller-Lerman was chosen as chief judge of the Nebraska Court of Appeals and served in that capacity until her appointment to the Nebraska Supreme Court in 1998. Miller-Lerman was the first woman to serve on that court, assuming office on September 1, 1998. Prior to her appointment, Nebraska was one of only four states which had never had a woman on its highest court.[103] To this day, Miller-Lerman remains the only woman ever appointed to the Nebraska Supreme Court.

In 2000, Governor Mike Johanns appointed Frankie Moore, a North Platte attorney, to the Nebraska Court of Appeals. A graduate of Nebraska Wesleyan University and the University of Nebraska College of Law, she practiced at McCarthy, Gale, Moore and Hall and served as a judge on the Commission of Industrial Relations prior to her appointment.[104] She is the second and only other woman to serve on Nebraska's appellate courts.

Out of a current total of 144 judges in the Nebraska state judicial system, only 27 of them are women. Of these, there are ten district court judges, eleven county court judges, three juvenile court judges, one workers' compensation court judge, one judge on the court of appeals, and one on the Nebraska Supreme Court.[105]

First Federal Judge—Laurie Smith Camp

Although Kathleen Jaudzemis became a federal magistrate judge in 1992,[106] it was not until 2001 that Nebraska saw its first female U.S. district court judge.[107] Laurie Smith Camp was nominated by George W. Bush to the U.S. District Court for the District of Nebraska in 2001. The Senate confirmed her nomination by a vote of 100 to 0, and she took office on November 2, 2001.[108]

Judge Smith Camp graduated with distinction from Stanford University in 1974 and from the University of Nebraska College of Law in 1977, where she served as editor in chief of the law review. Her distinguished career included private practice from 1977 to 1980, serving as general counsel to the Nebraska Department of Corrections from 1980 to 1991, heading the Nebraska attorney general's civil rights section from 1991 to 1995, and acting as chief deputy attorney general for criminal matters from 1995 to 2001. During her years at the attorney general's office, she made significant contributions to the passage of federal and state legislation in the areas of prosecution, sentencing, criminal records management, inmate litigation, and inmate work programs.

Prior to her appointment, Smith Camp was very active in the legal community as a former chair of the Nebraska Federal Practice Committee, past president of the Robert Van Pelt American Inn of Court and former director of the Nebraska County Attorneys Association and Nebraska Coalition for Victims of Crime. In addition, from 1982 until her appointment to the federal bench in 2001, Smith Camp and three partners initiated and sustained the development of Lincoln's historic Haymarket district.

Smith Camp, widely known for her high professional standards as a litigator, has brought those same standards and qualities to the federal bench. As Judge Janice Gradwohl wrote of her, "There could be no better role model for all in the legal profession."[109]

Women's Role in Nebraska's Legal Organizations

In recent years, women have accounted for close to one-half of the law student enrollment at both Creighton University School of Law and the University of Nebraska College of Law, the only two accredited law schools in Nebraska. It was not until the mid-1970s, however, that women began graduating in double digits from both law schools.[110] The Nebraska State Bar Association currently has 8,907 licensed members, 2,355 of whom are women.[111]

First NSBA President—Amy Longo

In 1929, at a meeting of the Nebraska State Bar Association, Irene Courtney Buell stated, "I just wish to remind our fellow lawyers, that hereafter when you are electing officers, we want to submit that the women should be recognized, too."[112] No one heeded Buell's remarks, however. It was not until 2000 that the Nebraska State Bar Association had a woman as its president.

Amy Longo was elected as president of the Nebraska State Bar Association and served her term in 2000–2001. She is a partner in the Omaha law firm of Ellick, Jones, Buelt, Blazek, and Longo. She also served as chair of the NSBA House of Delegates and as a member of the board of directors of the Nebraska State Bar Foundation.

The second woman to serve as president of the Nebraska State Bar Association was Linda Crump, who was elected in 2004 and began serving her term in 2006. Linda is the first African American and the first person of color to hold this position. In 2000–2001, Linda also became the first African American and first person of color to serve as chair in the House of Delegates.

Nebraska Women's Organizations

Women learned early that to advance their cause they had to stick together. The earliest of these networking groups revolved around woman suffrage.[113] Later, when women began entering the practice of law in significant numbers, they began their own organizations to advance their status in the legal profession. In Nebraska, there are currently two organizations devoted to the promotion and advancement of women in the profession.

Women and the Law Section

The Women and the Law Section of the Nebraska State Bar Association was founded in 1982, approximately one hundred years after the first woman attorney was admitted in Nebraska. Some members of the bar objected to a separate section for women attorneys and expressed concern over the objective of such an organization. Well-meaning attorneys opined that such an organization would create a "separate but equal" group within the bar. Some simply failed to see the necessity of having a separate section for women attorneys, because bar sections or committees had traditionally represented a particular type of practice such as bankruptcy or family law. The only thing that these women had in common was their interest in promoting women within the legal profession.

Several determined women, however, continued to push for a separate section for women attorneys, and on October 21, 1982, they held an organizational meeting at the Red Lion Inn in Omaha. Betty Holcomb Keller acted as the temporary chairperson, and she appointed Eleanor Knoll Swanson secretary pro tempore. The first year was spent drafting the bylaws and discussing the purpose and direction of the organization.

The stated purpose of the section is to promote the study of the legal system and its effect on women, to enhance professional skill and competence, to increase general awareness and understanding in substantive areas as they affect women, to promote consistency and fairness in the judicial forum and legislative arena with regard to substantive areas as they affect women, and to encourage the integration and active participation of women in the Nebraska system of justice as lawyers, judges, and scholars.

In October 1983, thirty-six women attended a meeting to elect officers and further discuss the direction of the organization. Pam Mattson was elected chairperson, Joan Hopkins was elected vice chair, Lynn Robertson was chosen to serve as the secretary, and Judy Hoffman became the treasurer. Patty Zieg and Marsha Fangmeyer were also elected as executive committee members. The Women and the Law Section hoped to provide networking opportunities to women engaged in the practice of law, to promote women lawyers within the hierarchy of the bar association, and to advocate for more women judges in the state judiciary.

Today, the section averages approximately two hundred members and actively participates in the annual bar association meeting as well as its own events during the year. At the 2004 meeting of the Nebraska State Bar Association, the Women and the Law Section presented the first annual Outstanding Contributor to Women in Law award to the Honorable Janice Gradwohl. The award recognizes an individual who has directly contributed to advancing the rights of women in law by advocating for women's issues, being a pioneering woman in the law, acting as a mentor or role model for women in the law, or advancing gender equality in the justice system. Gradwohl was chosen as the first award recipient because, as the fourth woman judge in the state of Nebraska, a bar member of fifty years' standing, and a founding member of the section, she has excelled in each and every criterion of the award.[114]

As one of the most active sections of the bar association, the Women and the Law Section continues to inspire and encourage both men and women to promote and advance the rights of women in law. Although the section emphasizes networking among women attorneys and advancing women's rights, it is open to male members as well.

Nebraska Women's Bar Association

Shortly after the formation of the Women and the Law Section, its members found that the organization's functions were limited by its tie to the Nebraska State Bar Association. As a division of the state bar, the Women and the Law Section was unable to take official positions on political matters or to advocate for women judicial candidates.

As a result, in 1997, a small group of progressive, committed women formed the first women's bar association in Nebraska. The organization was called the Nebraska Lawyer's Club (NLC) after a similar organization in San Diego. The first officers were Tracy Grinstead-Everly, president; Anna Bednar, vice president; Barbara Pratt Alf, secretary; and Karen Bates-Crouch, treasurer.

Like the Women and the Law Section, the new organization sought to advance the status of women in the law, to support and improve the administration of justice, and to promote equality of the sexes in society. Unlike the Women and the Law Section, however, the Nebraska Lawyer's Club could provide a unified voice for women who wanted to support or to oppose legislation affecting women's rights and to become active in overcoming barriers to equal representation on the bench.

The NLC provided support and encouragement for women applying for a judgeship and sponsored specialized forums to familiarize potential candidates with the process. One member with vast experience in this area created a packet of information to advise women on the procedure of judicial application. Officers also met with the governor regarding the importance of appointing more women to the bench. NLC members monitored and lobbied for legislation affecting the mission of the organization. To that end, they provided testimony on several key pieces of legislation before legislative committees.

Another primary reason for forming the organization was to ensure implementation of the recommendations of the Nebraska Supreme Court Task Force on Gender Fairness. One of the first major achievements of the NLC was the writing and passage of the revised Nebraska Code of Professional Responsibility Disciplinary Rule 1-102(A)(5), which prohibits discrimination on the basis of race, national origin, gender, or religion. One of the members who wrote this rule was also instrumental in including the additional categories of disability, age, sexual orientation, and socioeconomic class in Rule 8.4(d) to the Nebraska Rules of Professional Conduct adopted in 2005.

Eventually, the name of the organization was changed to the Nebraska Women's Bar Association (NWBA). The name change better reflected the purpose of the organization and the fact that strides had been made in organizational recognition and respect. Members no longer had to be concerned with avoiding controversy or appearing adversarial but could instead focus on their past achievements and those to come. Today, the NWBA has approximately fifty members and continues to uphold the original mission and work for implementation of the sex equity the members know, with hard work and dedication, can become a reality.

The first women of Nebraska law had a lot in common. Their courage and determination blazed the way for women who later entered the legal profession as a matter of right, without even realizing the sacrifices that had been made earlier. If "being first is success itself,"[115] you'd never know it by studying these women. They were not content with merely being the first. They went beyond their first achievements and strove to be the best in their profession, not merely the best women in their profession. Without question, these women were role models not only for other women but for all in the legal profession. And although Nebraska women have already accomplished many firsts, there are many more yet to come.

Table 13.1. The First 105 Women Lawyers in Nebraska by Date of Admission

1. Ada Bittenbender 8/17/1883
2. Mary Baird Bryan 11/23/1888
3. Winona S. Sawyer 11/23/1888
4. Addie M. Billings 10/28/1890
5. Fannie O'Linn 2/12/1891
6. Nellis Moore Richardson 9/1/1891
7. Zara A. Wilson 9/29/1891
8. Alice A. Minick 5/17/1892
9. Arnasa Cobb Kamplain 6/29/1893
10. Thea Elliott 2/21/1894
11. Kate M. Hall 11/22/1894
12. Mae C. Wood 5/21/1895
13. Maud Marston Burrows 4/7/1896
14. Vesta Gray 5/5/1896
15. Ettella Mae Davisson 6/11/1896
16. Helen M. Goff 6/10/1897
17. Emma Madeen 6/10/1897
18. Alpha Morgan 6/171897
19. Ethel A. Robbins 6/17/1897
20. Elfleda E. Wright 5/3/1899
21. Anna D. Grimison Dworak 5/3/1899
22. Bertha B. Stull 6/15/1899
23. May Chaddock Orcutt 6/15/1899
24. Julia H. Batterson 6/13/1901
25. Mary T. Brennan 11/20/1901
26. Olive Gillmor Failor 6/11/1902
27. Grace M. Ballard 7/1/1914
28. Stella B. Wilson 9/20/1915
29. Bertha I. Winterton Schick 4/29/1916
30. Effie Cover Sullivan 6/17/1916
31. Florence E. Maple 6/20/1916
32. Theodosia Trehearne Urbach 6/20/1916
33. Irene Cox-Buell 12/11/1916
34. Josephine M. Wild 11/21/1917
35. Mona Helene Cowell Finn 6/1/1918
36. Gladys J. Shamp 6/1/1918
37. Elisabeth Parsons 11/20/1918
38. Margaret Jane Carns 6/2/1919
39. Lorene Lindburg Knudsen 6/9/1920
40. Irene Huffington 11/24/1920
41. Penelope Hamilton Anderson 6/21/1921
42. Jeanette M. Regan Duffie 6/21/1921
43. Mathilde J. Kinneberg Long 6/21/1921
44. Millie Blihovde 9/19/1921
45. Florence Zeiser 6/19/1923
46. Helen McGerr 11/27/1923
47. Bessie James 11/27/1923
48. Beatrice Montgomery Sattler (Nix?) 6/2/1924
49. Mary Agnes Mullen 6/2/1924
50. Ruth Comstock Van Auken 6/7/1924
51. Grace M. McGerr 6/7/1924
52. Ada O'Brien 6/17/1924
53. Clara Ruth Mozzer 2/13/1925
54. Phoebe J. O'Donnell 6/16/1925
55. Edith Beckman 11/28/1925
56. Margaret Gettys Hall 6/5/1926
57. Lillian Margolin Mirviss 6/5/1926
58. Magdeline Craft Radke 7/2/1926
59. Lyda Hafer 7/2/1926
60. Margaret E. Goos 7/2/1926
61. Emmeline E. Ferris Haack 6/4/1927
62. Verda Vallier Johnson 6/15/1927
63. Leona I. Latham 6/15/1927
64. Carlyn G. Wolfe 1/3/1927
65. Eva E. Hannan 6/13/1928
66. Dora Nelson Miller 7/13/1928
67. Mary J. Leamy 7/13/1928
68. Zanzye H. Hill 6/8/1929
69. Eva I. Watts Spencer 6/20/1929
70. Margaret Ruth Fisher 6/20/1929
71. Iva G. Baker Chace 1/7/1929
72. Leola Marie Groth Jensen 7/1/1930
73. Alice M. Holeman 7/1/1930
74. Sara Mullin Baldwin 11/19/1930
75. Helena M. Gebuhr 11/19/1930
76. Florence Marion Holbein-Whitaker 1/6/1930
77. Agnes C. Killian 6/5/1931
78. Marie Herney 6/6/1931
79. Jessie P. Grandy 6/30/1931
80. Grace Genevieve Allen 6/30/1931
81. Lucille C. Regan 6/30/1931
82. Dorothy J. Exon 6/16/1932
83. Vera H. Chamberlin 11/17/1932
84. Margaret Alice Getscher 6/16/1932
85. Audrey Mae Gregory 6/5/1933
86. Lilyan Marie Pospichal 6/24/1933
87. Joyce E. Rodgers Tyler 6/4/1934
88. Virginia Mancuso Potter 6/8/1934
89. Elizabeth G. Byron 6/27/1934
90. Pearl Demary 11/27/1934
91. Imogene M. Steinmeier 2/2/1935
92. Helen M. McFarland Sherman 6/4/1935
93. Mary Kahler Cate 6/7/1935
94. RoseMarie O'Donnell 6/7/1935
95. Zelma D. Derry Barrow 6/26/1935
96. Josephine Rucker 11/21/1935
97. Myrtle H. Skaggs 11/21/1935
98. Grace H. Simpson 11/21/1935
99. Bernice Frances Peterson 11/21/1935
100. Grace Florence Grosvenor (Dellinger?) 1/31/1936
101. Mary K. Quigley Harrison 6/8/1936
102. Evelyn M. Smith 6/11/1936
103. Eva Graham 11/19/1936
104. Edna M. Lovewell 11/19/1936
105. Martha B. Miesner 11/19/1936

Source: Adapted from *A Celebration of Legal Pioneers: The First 100 Women Lawyers in Nebraska* (Lincoln: Nebraska State Bar Association, 2000), n.p. Reprinted by permission of the Nebraska State Bar Association.

Table 13.2. Women Judges in the State of Nebraska, Past and Present

STATE COURT JUDGES

Name	*Type/District*	*Appointed By*	*Dates of Service*
Elizabeth Pittman	County-Douglas	Exon	1971–86
Betty Peterson Sharp	District-Otoe	Exon	1972–76
Colleen Buckley	Juvenile-Douglas	Exon	1973–94
Janice Gradwohl	County-Lancaster	Exon	1974–90
Jane H. Prochaska	County-Douglas	Kerrey	1985–2006
Lyn V. White	County-Douglas	Kerrey	1987–
Kristine Cecava	County-Keith	Orr	1987–99
	District-Keith	Johanns	1999–
Toni G. Thorson	Juvenile-Lancaster	Orr	1989–
Mary L. Doyle	County-Lancaster	Orr	1990–
Edna Atkins	County-Douglas	Nelson	1992–
Lindsey Miller-Lerman	Appeals-2nd Dist	Nelson	1992–98 (Chief 1996–98)
	Supreme-2nd Dist	Nelson	1998–
Mary Gilbride	County-Saunders	Nelson	1992–98
	District-Saunders	Nelson	1998–
Mary G. Likes	District-Douglas	Nelson	1992–2002
Laureen Van Norman	Work Comp-State	Nelson	1993–
Teresa K.Luther	District-Hall	Nelson	1994–
Elizabeth Crnkovich	Juvenile-Douglas	Nelson	1995–
Laurie Yardley	County-Lancaster	Nelson	1995–
Karen B. Flowers	District-Lancaster	Nelson	1996–
Patricia Lamberty	District-Douglas	Nelson	1998–
Marcena Hendrix	County-Douglas	Nelson	1998–
Jean Lovell	County-Lancaster	Nelson	1999–
Sandra Dougherty	District-Douglas	Nelson	1999–
Linda S. Porter	Juvenile-Lancaster	Johanns	1999–
Terri S. Harder	District-Kearney	Johanns	1999–
Frankie J. Moore	Appeals-6th Dist	Johanns	2000–
Donna F. Taylor	County-Antelope	Johanns	2001–
Vicky L. Johnson	District-Saline	Johanns	2004–
Linda Caster Senff	County-Merrick	Heineman	2005–
Jodi A. Nelson	District-Lancaster	Heineman	2006–
Karin Noakes	District-Howard	Heineman	2006–
Susan Strong	County-Lancaster	Heineman	2006–
Susan Bazis	County-Douglas	Heineman	2007–
Anne Paine	County-11th Dist	Heineman	2007–

FEDERAL COURT JUDGES (GENERAL JURISDICTION)

Name	*Type*	*Appointed By*	*Dates of Service*
Kathleen Jaudzemis	U.S. magistrate	judges' panel	1991–2003
Laurie Smith Camp	U.S. district	George W. Bush	2001–

Source: Adapted from *A Celebration of Legal Pioneers: The First 100 Women Lawyers in Nebraska* (Lincoln: Nebraska State Bar Association, 2000), n.p. Reprinted by permission of the Nebraska State Bar Association.

Table 13.3. J.D.s Issued by Creighton and University of Nebraska through 2005

	University of Nebraska Graduates		Creighton University Graduates			University of Nebraska Graduates		Creighton University Graduates	
Year	*Men*	*Women*	*Men*	*Women*	*Year*	*Men*	*Women*	*Men*	*Women*
1891	3				1949	52		47	1
1892	12	1			1950	66		64	1
1893	23				1951	41	3	78	
1894	24	1			1952	65	2	56	1
1895	41				1953	29		19	1
1896	39	1			1954	34	3	30	1
1897	33	2			1955	34		19	
1898	39				1956	30		15	
1899	52	2			1957	30		27	1
1900	66				1958	41		17	2
1901	79	1			1959	30	3	34	
1902	60	1			1960	31		40	1
1903	83				1961	37	1	26	
1904	61				1962	33		36	1
1905	13				1963	35		29	
1906	35		6		1964	49		25	
1907	33		7		1965	42		37	3
1908	41		10		1966	55		35	1
1909	30		6		1967	51	1	45	
1910	35		23		1968	73		57	
1911	51		11		1969	84		61	1
1912	37		19		1970	84	5	60	2
1913	54		25		1971	75	3	59	3
1914	40		20		1972	131		91	5
1915	52		28		1973	139	4	118	2
1916	43	1	35	1	1974	133	7	149	9
1917	35		9		1975	112	20	137	16
1918	14		14	2	1976	117	33	171	26
1919	16	1	12		1977	117	30	139	28
1920	32		12		1978	118	36	128	33
1921	34	1	14		1979	105	44	141	30
1922	56		18		1980	98	45	128	42
1923	66		26		1981	111	36	124	41
1924	51	2	24	2	1982	114	45	115	52
1925	29		15		1983	105	43	114	60
1926	50	2	33		1984	101	43	112	57
1927	48	1	38		1985	82	51	105	38
1928	34		34		1986	88	53	121	43
1929	39	1	36		1987	85	54	112	47
1930	48		41		1988	75	40	102	56
1931	36	1	48	1	1989	96	42	120	48
1932	36		30		1990	73	48	97	48
1933	35	1	35		1991	75	53	97	65
1934	40	1	39	1	1992	90	46	95	73
1935	42	1	31	3	1993	84	60	132	75
1936	41	2	35		1994	97	53	118	78
1937	46	1	48	1	1995	75	72	101	69
1938	40	5	50		1996	84	64	94	78
1939	55	2	47	1	1997	82	48	91	71
1940	49		34	1	1998	64	45	76	60
1941	44	1	24	1	1999	59	59	84	57
1942	25	1	17		2000	77	44	88	51
1943	10		2	2	2001	70	49	70	59
1944		2		1	2002	66	50	77	61
1945			6		2003	71	51	80	67
1946	17		5		2004	64	68	104	64
1947	18		22		2005	74	65	87	65
1948	45		75						

Source: Adapted from *A Celebration of Legal Pioneers: The First 100 Women Lawyers in Nebraska* (Lincoln: Nebraska State Bar Association, 2000), n.p. Reprinted by permission of the Nebraska State Bar Association.

Notes

The exchange in the epigraph was quoted in Barbara Allen Babcock, "Clara Shortridge Foltz: 'First Woman,'" *Valparaiso University Law Review* 28, no. 4 (1994): 1232. In 1878, Foltz became the first woman lawyer admitted to practice in the state of California.

1. 410 U.S. 113 (1973).

2. In 2000, the Nebraska State Bar Association celebrated its hundredth anniversary, and on July 28, 2000, the bar honored the first one hundred women lawyers in the state of Nebraska. In preparation, the executive committee of the Women and the Law Section of the bar association dug through the handwritten rolls of the Nebraska Supreme Court and the bar association to compile a list of the first one hundred women lawyers. In an article describing the endeavor, Tara Muir admitted, "During one meeting, we wagered a guess that we would not have 100 women attorneys on record until the mid-1970's. . . . Our guess was not even close. . . . The provisional list following this article includes more than 100 [women attorneys], and the 100th woman was admitted in 1936!" Tara L. Muir, "From Petticoats to Petitions: The First 100 Women Attorneys of Nebraska," in *A Celebration of Legal Pioneers: The First 100 Women Lawyers in Nebraska* (Lincoln: Nebraska State Bar Association, 2000), n.p.

3. Professor Cunnea and Lisa Small, "A Timeline of Women's Legal History in the United States," http://womenslegalhistory.stanford.edu/articles.html.

4. Gretchen Holbrook Grezina, *Mr. and Mrs. Prince: How an Extraordinary Eighteenth-Century Family Moved out of Slavery and into Legend* (New York: HarperCollins, 2008), 154–88.

5. Cunnea and Small, "Timeline of Women's Legal History."

6. Ibid.

7. Bonnie Eisenberg and Mary Ruthsdotter, "Living the Legacy: The Women's Rights Movement 1848–1998," *National Women's History Project,* http://www.legacy98.org/move-hist.html (1998).

8. Ibid. The declaration went on to enumerate many grievances, and, at the convention, resolutions were adopted calling for equal treatment of women and men under the law, including the right to vote.

9. Cunnea and Small, "Timeline of Women's Legal History."

10. Ibid.

11. "Women's History in America," *Women's International Center,* http://www.wic.org/misc/history.htm, excerpted from Compton's Interactive Encyclopedia (Compton's NewMedia, Inc., 1995).

12. Cunnea and Small, "Timeline of Women's Legal History." During this same year, Elizabeth Cady Stanton and Susan B. Anthony founded the National Woman Suffrage Association, and Lucy Stone founded the American Woman Suffrage Association. The Wyoming Territory granted suffrage to women, followed by the Utah Territory in 1870, Colorado in 1893, Idaho in 1896, and other western states between 1910 and 1912. Ibid.

13. Ibid. Belle Mansfield, at the age of twenty-three, became the first officially recognized woman lawyer in the United States. After an apprenticeship at her brother's law firm, she formally applied for admission to the Iowa bar despite statutory

provisions limiting admission to "white males." She was permitted to take the examination, passed, and was formally admitted to the bar in 1869. Carolyn Sleeth, "First Women Lawyers in the United States," http://www.law.stanford.edu/library/wlhbp/papers/sleeth.pdf.

Ada M. Bittenbender once wrote:

> The statute under which she was admitted provided only for the admission of "any white male person," but there was also a section which allowed "words importing the masculine gender only may be extended to females." And Mrs. Mansfield writes me that the presiding judge said very significantly that when any of those restrictive words did a manifest injustice to individuals, the court was justified in construing statutes as extending to others not expressly included in them.

Quoted in Inez Haynes Irwin, *Angels and Amazons: A Hundred Years of American Women* (Garden City, N.Y.: Doubleday, Doran, 1933), 172.

14. Cunnea and Small, "Timeline of Women's Legal History."

15. 83 U.S. 1 (6 Wall.) 130 (1873). While the Bradwell case was pending in the U.S. Supreme Court, Illinois passed legislation prohibiting the exclusion of women from any occupation, and Bradwell was finally licensed in 1890 when the Illinois Supreme Court, on its own motion, reconsidered her 1869 application. Cunnea and Small, "Timeline of Women's Legal History."

16. See table 13.1 listing of the first 105 women attorneys in Nebraska. Reprinted with permission from the Nebraska State Bar Association.

17. Catharine Waite, "Admission of Women to the Bar," *Chicago Law Times* 1 (Chicago: C.V. Waite, 1887): 86–87.

18. Ibid.

19. Ada Bittenbender, of Lincoln, was the third woman admitted; Fannie O'Linn, of Chadron, was the eleventh woman admitted; and Alice Minick, of Lincoln, was the fourteenth woman admitted to practice before the U.S. Supreme Court. Mary L. Clark, "The First Women Members of the Supreme Court Bar, 1879–1900," *San Diego Law Review* 36, no. 1 (1999): 92–93.

20. "Ada M. Bittenbender," Women at the Bar, *Law Student's Helper* 1, no. 10 (1893): 303, http://womenslegalhistory.stanford.edu/profiles/BittenbenderAda.html.

21. Ibid.

22. Ibid.

23. Ibid.

24. Ibid.

25. Ibid.

26. Ibid.

27. Ibid.

28. Ibid.

29. Ibid.

30. Ibid.

31. Ibid.

32. Ibid.

33. Ibid.

34. The second and third women to be admitted to practice in Nebraska were Mary Elizabeth Baird Bryan and Winona S. Branch Sawyer. Both were admitted in 1888, but neither actually practiced law. Mary Bryan undertook the study of law to assist her husband, William Jennings Bryan, and Winona Sawyer used her legal skills to further her business ventures with her husband. "The Biographies of Nebraska's First 100 Women Lawyers," in *Celebration of Legal Pioneers.* See also *Woman's Journal,* July 12, 1890, 218, col. 1–2.

35. "Ada M. Bittenbender."

36. Ibid. On August 17, 1883, the day she was admitted to practice before the Supreme Court of Nebraska, Ada Bittenbender applied to that court for a writ of mandamus to compel a town board to hear remonstrances before granting saloon licenses under the Slocumb law. She won the argument, and the precedent was well followed. *Woman's Journal.*

37. 1887 Laws of Nebraska 466 (home for penitent women and girls) and 1891 Laws of Nebraska 293 (girls' industrial school).

38. Ibid.

39. Ibid.; Sleeth, "First Women Lawyers in the United States." In 1893, it was said that "she drafted the bill to accompany the great petition for the protection of women offered by Senator Blair, and it was mainly through her efforts that Congress passed it." "Ada M. Bittenbender."

40. Ibid.

41. Clark, "First Women Members of the Supreme Court Bar," 94.

42. 244 U.S. 645 (1917).

43. Ibid.

44. Ibid.

45. Ibid. The Nebraska Supreme Court had affirmed the district court's ruling against their cause.

46. Clark, "First Women Members of the Supreme Court Bar," 94.

47. Ibid.

48. Ibid. Belva Lockwood, the first woman admitted to practice before the U.S. Supreme Court moved the admission of Alice A. Minick from Lincoln, Nebraska, in 1897. Ibid., 95. Fannie O'Linn, from Chadron, Nebraska, was moved by William Jennings Bryan, a congressman from Nebraska, in 1893. Ibid.

49. "Ada M. Bittenbender." She was the author of several prohibition manuals.

50. Ibid.

51. During the 1900s, women were finally given the opportunity to take part in the political process in the United States. In 1916, Jeanette Pickering Rankin, of Montana, was the first woman elected to the U.S. House of Representatives; in 1920, the Nineteenth Amendment was ratified, giving women the right to vote; and in 1933, Hattie Wyatt Caraway, of Arkansas, became the first woman elected to the U.S. Senate, and Frances Perkins became the first female cabinet member as secretary of labor under President Franklin Delano Roosevelt. In the 1960s, the Equal Pay Act (77 Stat. 56 [1963]; 19 U.S.C. § 206[d]) and Civil Rights Act (78 Stat. 241 [1964]; 42 U.S.C. §§ 2000e et seq.) were passed, giving women equal opportunities in employ-

ment and wages. In 1972, Title IX (the Educational Amendments Act, 86 Stat. 235 [1972]; 20 U.S.C. § 1681) was passed, giving women equal access to academic and athletic resources, and in that same year, Congresswoman Shirley Chisholm became the first woman and first African American to run for a major party's nomination for the presidency. Cunnea and Small, "Timeline of Women's Legal History in the United States."

52. Strauder v. West Virginia, 100 U.S. 303 (1880).

53. C. Herman Pritchett, *The American Constitution,* 3d ed. (New York: McGraw-Hill, 1977), 464–65.

54. Cunnea and Small, "Timeline of Women's Legal History in the United States." See Hoyt v. Florida, 368 U.S. 57 (1961).

55. Cunnea and Small, "Timeline of Women's Legal History in the United States." See Taylor v. Louisiana, 419 U.S. 522 (1975).

56. In 1873, however, the Nebraska Supreme Court held that no one may be denied the right to sit on a jury because of race. Brittle v. People, 2 Neb. 198 (1873).

57. 1943 Laws of Nebraska 191.

58. Ibid., § 6, 197. The new statutes replaced the words "all male citizens" with "all citizens" and "good and lawful men" with "good and lawful persons." See Neb. Rev. Stat. §§ 21-903, 22-903, 25-1601, 29-2004 (1943).

59. Neb. Rev. Stat. § 25-1601 (1943). See also Neb. Rev. Stat. § 29-2004 (1943).

60. 1977 Laws of Nebraska, LB 283, § 4; 1967 Laws of Nebraska, ch. 149, § 1.

61. Neb. Rev. Stat. § 25-1601 (2003).

62. Batson v. Kentucky, 476 U.S. 79 (1986).

63. See State v. Culver, 233 Neb. 228, 232, 444 N.W.2d 662 (1989).

64. J. E. B. v. Alabama ex rel. T. B., 511 U.S. 127 (1994). Justice Harry Blackmun, writing for the majority, stated: "Intentional discrimination on the basis of gender by state actors violates the Equal Protection Clause, particularly where, as here, the discrimination serves to ratify and perpetuate invidious, archaic, and overbroad stereotypes about the relative abilities of men and women." Ibid., 130–31.

65. Sleeth, "First Women Lawyers in the United States," table 1. In Wyoming (still a territory at that time), however, Esther Morris was appointed a justice of the peace, even though the first woman listed as an attorney was a "Miss Heberd" in 1899. Ibid.

66. Ibid.

67. Ruth Bader Ginsburg and Laura W. Brill, "Women in the Federal Judiciary: Three Way Pavers and the Exhilarating Change President Carter Wrought," *Fordham Law Review* 64, no. 2 (1995): 283.

68. Ibid.

69. Ibid.

70. Ibid., 284.

71. Ibid., 286–88.

72. Ibid., 287.

73. Ibid., 288.

74. See table 13.2 for a listing of the current women judges in Nebraska.

75. Nebraska's first and only female governor to date, Kay Orr, was elected in 1986.

76. Janice L. Gradwohl, "Inching through the Glass Ceiling: The History of the Selection of Women Judges in Nebraska," in *Celebration of Legal Pioneers,* n.p. On December 10, 1991, Judge Edna Atkins became the only other African American woman appointed to the bench as of this date. Also a graduate of Creighton University School of law, she had considerable courtroom experience and was appointed to the Douglas County Court by Governor Ben Nelson.

77. J. Clay Smith Jr., "Elizabeth D. Pittman: Black Legal Pioneer in the Midlands," *Creighton Law Review* 32, no. 2 (1998): 511–30.

78. Ibid., 514. A. B. Pittman was the only black licensed veterinarian in Nebraska. They had one child together, Antoinette, and divorced after thirteen years of marriage.

79. Ibid.

80. Ibid.

81. Ibid., 515.

82. Ibid., 516–17.

83. Ibid.

84. Ibid., 517.

85. Ibid., 518.

86. Ibid.

87. Ibid.

88. Ibid.

89. Ibid., 522.

90. Ibid., 523–24.

91. Ibid., 522.

92. Ibid., 523.

93. Ibid., 525.

94. The two cases reviewed were *State v. Davis,* 203 Neb. 284, 278 N.W. 351 (1979), and *State v. Nielsen,* 199 Neb. 597, 260 N.W.2d 321 (1977). In *Nielsen,* the Nebraska Supreme Court held that Judge Pittman had committed an error in allowing a defendant to file a motion for jury trial beyond the requisite time period. 199 Neb. at 601, 260 N.W.2d at 323.

95. Smith, "Elizabeth D. Pittman," 525–26.

96. Ibid., 528–29.

97. Exon went on to serve as a U.S. senator for three terms between 1979 and 1997. He died of cancer at the age of eighty-three in Lincoln, Nebraska, on June 10, 2005.

98. Gradwohl, "Inching through the Glass Ceiling."

99. The next female district court judge to be appointed was Mary G. Likes, in 1992, to the Douglas County District Court. Ibid.

100. Ibid.

101. Ibid. No woman was appointed during the tenure of Governor Charles Thone. Governor Robert Kerrey appointed Jane H. Prochaska to the County Court of Douglas County on August 15, 1985.

102. Ibid.

103. Ibid.

104. Ibid.

105. This does not include five women judges who have retired from the bench (Colleen Buckley, now deceased; Janice Gradwohl; Mary Likes; Elizabeth Pittman, now deceased; and Jane Prochaska) and one who died while still in office (Betty Peterson Sharp). The current ten women district court judges are Kristine Cecava, Sandra Dougherty, Karen Flowers, Mary Gilbride, Terri Harder, Vicky Johnson, Patricia Lamberty, Teresa Luther, Jodi Nelson, and Karin Noakes; serving as county court judges are Edna Atkins, Mary Doyle, Marcena Hendrix, Jean Lovell, Linda Caster Senff, Susan Strong, Donna Taylor, Lyn White, Laurie Yardley; Elizabeth Crnkovich, Linda Porter, and Toni Thorson are juvenile court judges; Laureen Van Norman is a workers' compensation court judge; Frankie Moore serves on the Nebraska Court of Appeals; and Lindsey Miller-Lerman is on the Nebraska Supreme Court.

106. Kathleen Jaudzemis was chosen by a three-judge panel from a field of forty-nine applicants in October 1991. She received her undergraduate degree with distinction from the University of Nebraska and, after teaching in Nebraska's public high schools for a number of years, returned to earn her master's degree. Jaudzemis eventually received her law degree from the University of Nebraska College of Law, where she was elected to the Order of the Coif and served as editor of the law review. Before her appointment, she was the first female law partner at Cline, Williams, Wright, Johnson and Oldfather, one of Lincoln's premier law firms. According to chief district court judge Richard Kopf, Jaudzemis "was possessed of an uncanny and unyielding sense of what was right. Her fellow judges marveled at her discipline and her skills." Kopf, Resolution, Retirement of the Honorable Kathleen A. Jaudzemis, United States Magistrate Judge, District of Nebraska. Jaudzemis retired on May 2, 2003.

107. In 1990, Emily Cameron Shattil became the first woman administrative law judge for the Social Security Administration; in 1997, she became chief judge of the court. She received her undergraduate degree from the University of Nebraska–Lincoln and her law degree from the University of Kansas Law School. She was counsel for the Department of Public Institutions before being appointed to the bench. She also served as a special assistant attorney general with the Kansas Department of Health and Environment, and as an assistant attorney general for the state of South Dakota. Gradwohl, "Inching through the Glass Ceiling."

108. Although many of President Bush's appointments met with difficulty during the confirmation process, Laurie Smith Camp's impeccable background made her an exceptional candidate.

109. Jan Gradwohl, "Federal Judges Camp, Riley Bring High Standards to the Bench," *Nebraska Transcript* 36, no. 1 (2003): 36–38.

110. See table 13.3.

111. *NSBA Directory* (Lincoln: Nebraska State Bar Association, 2005), 48.

112. Muir, "From Petticoats to Petitions."

113. In 1848, the first women's rights convention was held in Seneca Falls, New York, and published its Declaration of Sentiments. In 1869, Elizabeth Cady Stanton and Susan B. Anthony founded the National Woman Suffrage Association and Lucy Stone formed the American Woman Suffrage Association. Cunnea and Small, "A Timeline of Women's Legal History."

114. As the fourth woman judge in Nebraska and first woman judge in Lancaster County, Gradwohl served with great distinction, receiving numerous national awards and recognitions during her tenure on the bench (1974 through 1990). Now retired from the bench, as an adjunct faculty member at the University of Nebraska College of Law, Gradwohl has written numerous articles to promote and recognize the achievements of women in law, some of which are cited within this chapter. She continues to serve as a role model and mentor, providing encouragement to all generations of female law students, lawyers, and judges. As U.S. district court judge Laurie Smith Camp remarked when nominating Gradwohl for the Outstanding Contributor to Women in Law award, "Judge Gradwohl's own personal and professional achievements in Nebraska, nation-wide, and abroad, merit celebration." In 2005, Smith Camp became the second recipient of the Outstanding Contributor to Women in Law Award. Eleanor Knoll Swanson, a private practice attorney in Omaha for more than fifty years, became the third recipient in 2006. In 2007, attorney Roberta Stick, also of Omaha, received the award.

115. Babcock, "Clara Shortridge Foltz," 1285. In concluding her article about the first woman lawyer in California, Babcock wrote: "As lonely as it is to be first, as much as it draws attack, it has one towering advantage. There is no standard for comparison, and thus no room for failure. Being first is success itself."

FOURTEEN

William G. Ross

MEYER V. NEBRASKA

Meyer v. Nebraska,[1] a case involving a teacher in a one-room rural Nebraska schoolhouse, changed the course of American constitutional doctrine and is one of the cornerstones of civil liberties law. Although the ethnic and cultural conflicts that spawned the case have long since disappeared and are nearly forgotten, the U.S. Supreme Court's decision remains at the heart of modern controversies involving parental rights, privacy law, abortion, and the regulation of sexual conduct.

The Court in *Meyer* invalidated Nebraska, Ohio, and Iowa statutes that curtailed the teaching of foreign languages in elementary schools. Similar laws were promulgated in at least sixteen other states during and shortly after the First World War in an effort to promote Americanism and to ensure the assimilation of ethnic enclaves, particularly the large and often insular German American communities that existed in many parts of the nation, especially the Midwest.[2]

Although the tenacity with which the German American community retained its ethnic identity had generated tensions even before the First World War, Anglo-Americans generally admired German Americans for their high cultural and intellectual standards and their work ethic. This model minority, however, suddenly became the object of widespread suspicion and overt hostility when the United States declared war on Germany in April 1917. Prejudices were fanned by the U.S. government's Committee on Public Information, which churned out massive amounts of propaganda derogating all aspects of German culture in order to inspire support for a war that many Americans initially had opposed.[3] Meanwhile, voluntary patriotic societies, particularly the National Security League and the American Defense Society, denounced German American institutions and expressed hostility toward the use of the German language in the United States.[4] German Americans, who constituted the nation's largest and most visible ethnic group at the start of the war, quickly shed many markers of their identity in an effort to avoid the wrath of advocates of 100 percent Americanism.

Animus against German Americans was particularly pronounced in Nebraska, where the German American community was large enough to attract resentment but often too weak to resist assaults caused by wartime frenzy. Nebraska's German Americans were especially vulnerable to nativist attacks because many resided in isolated and essentially closed enclaves.[5] Moreover, Nebraska, like other Great Plains states, had a high concentration of German emigrants from Russia, who were even more tenacious than other German groups in retaining their ethnic heritage[6] and who suffered the double stigma of German and Russian heritage in the wake of the First World War and the Bolshevik revolution.[7] Hostility toward German Americans and other ethnic groups also may have been more intense in the Great Plains because the elites in this frontier region were less secure in their social status than were their counterparts in the East and the South.[8]

Shortly after the war began, Nebraska's Council of Defense, a state agency that coordinated war efforts, alleged that many Lutheran clergy were insufficiently patriotic and that a large number of parochial schools operated by German American Lutherans were failing to instill American values in their students. Although most of the more than two hundred German Lutheran parochial schools in Nebraska used English as the language of instruction, virtually all taught German, as well, to enable children to prepare for their confirmations and to participate in German-language religious services. In December 1917, the council requested that all public and private schools refrain from teaching foreign languages.[9] Meanwhile, many Nebraskans urged the state to close all German parochial schools.[10] In 1918, the legislature repealed a 1913 statute, the Mockett Law, which had required schools to offer foreign-language instruction for at least five hours per week if fifty or more students requested it.[11]

The council also pressured churches to eliminate foreign-language services, even though many parishioners of Bohemian, German, Polish, and Scandinavian congregations could not speak English. At the council's behest, the legislature in 1918 enacted a statute requiring alien teachers and preachers to obtain a court license.[12] County councils of defense, the local arms of the state council, were even more aggressive. In May 1918, for example, the Cedar County Council of Defense commanded a Roman Catholic priest immediately to desist from any use of a foreign language in instruction or public worship, except for the Latin Mass.[13] Other local officials interrupted Swedish-language funeral services,[14] and the state council rebuked a Lutheran minister for delivering a short German-language sermon at a soldier's funeral even though the liturgy was conducted in English.[15] Much of the animus against the use of foreign languages in religious services arose out of the suspicion with which many Nebraskans regarded the Lutheran and Roman Catholic churches, whose elaborate liturgies, richly decorated sanctuaries, and highly intellectual doctrines often seemed alien to Anglo-American Protestants.

Finally, on June 8, 1918, the state council issued a proclamation calling for the exclusive use of English in all public places in Nebraska, including church services and telephone communications.[16] Although the council acknowledged that it had no legal authority to enforce this proclamation, it relied on voluntary compliance generated by the threat of vigilante action.[17] The council sometimes granted special dispensations in order to prevent hardship.

In several other states, the councils of defense, public officials, and private citizens similarly harassed ethnic Americans. In Iowa, for example, the governor banned the use of German in all public places, including churches,[18] declaring that "God is listening only to the English tongue."[19] Although these measures were vulnerable to constitutional challenge, German Americans generally refrained from initiating lawsuits in the face of a rising tide of physical assaults on their fellow ethnics and vandalism and arson of German schools and churches.[20] Although many acquiesced in these language restrictions, others ignored them or remonstrated with state officials.[21]

Organized efforts to hasten the assimilation of ethnic communities continued in Nebraska and in most other states even after the armistice in November 1918. These efforts at Americanization were stoked by a resurgent nativism, which directed much of its animus against Roman Catholics. In 1919, the Nebraska house approved a measure that would have required all children to attend public schools, but the bill failed by one vote in the senate. The legislature instead approved a measure that obligated parochial school teachers to obtain state certification and required parochial schools to comply with state standards for attendance, equipment, and supplies and to offer courses in American history and government.[22]

On April 9, 1919, the legislature also enacted the Siman Act, which prohibited instruction in any foreign language in any public, private, or parochial school except for foreign languages taught as academic subjects to students who had passed the eighth grade. The penalty for each offense was a fine of between twenty-five and one hundred dollars or confinement in jail for not more than one hundred days.[23] The Nebraska attorney general later issued an opinion stating that the Siman Act did not prohibit the teaching of German in weekend religious classes,[24] even though the legislature had explicitly rejected an amendment that embodied this interpretation and even though this reading contravened the language of the statute.[25]

Lutherans and Roman Catholics commenced litigation to enjoin the Siman Act five weeks after its enactment. They believed that time was of the essence, fearing that parents would withdraw their children from parochial schools if they no longer taught foreign languages and that the schools would be very difficult to reopen once they had closed.[26] They also feared that acquiescence in the Siman Act would revive support for a compulsory public education law. As Carl Frederick Brommer, pastor of Zion Lutheran Church near Hampton, Nebraska, explained to a prominent Lutheran scholar, this was "a battle of life or death" because opponents of German-language instruction were attempting "to kill our schools."[27] Although a trial court issued a temporary injunction against enforcement of the statute in June 1919, the court dissolved the injunction after further consideration of the case.[28] The plaintiffs, who included parents of Bohemian, Danish, German, and Polish extraction, took an appeal to the state supreme court. The plaintiffs argued that the Siman Act violated property rights under the due process clause of the Fourteenth Amendment to the U.S. Constitution by diminishing the value of parochial schools and interfering with the vocations of teachers. They also emphasized that the statute interfered with their religious liberty. Although they claimed that this, too, violated due process under the federal Constitution, they relied primarily on the religious liberty clause of the Nebraska constitution because the U.S. Supreme Court had not yet held that the First Amendment—or any other part of the Bill of Rights—was binding on the states.[29]

In a decision issued during the last week of 1919, the Nebraska Supreme Court affirmed the lower court's denial of an injunction but gave the statute a narrow interpretation. Like the attorney general, the court read the statute to permit foreign-language instruction during such times that did not interfere with instruction under the state's mandatory education law. Although the court concluded that the state had a compelling interest in enacting measures to facilitate an understanding of the English language and to encourage patriotism, the justices explained that any sweeping prohibition on any foreign-language instruction would constitute an unreasonable exercise of the police power and would unduly interfere with personal liberty.[30] This strained interpretation of the statute hints that the court would have invalidated the act if the justices had not feared that nativists would retaliate against them at the next judicial election.[31]

The strengths and weaknesses of nativist forces were apparent at the constitutional convention held between December 1919 and March 1920, during which the status of parochial education and foreign-language instruction was a source of much controversy. Critics of foreign-language instruction tried to write the major provisions of the Siman Act into the state constitution.[32] They failed in that effort, but did succeed in having English declared the official language of the state, mandating the use of English in all official documents and proceedings, and requiring the teaching of all basic subjects in English in private, parochial, and public schools.[33]

In response to the state supreme court's decision, parochial schools throughout Nebraska began to offer foreign-language instruction during recess periods, although many advocates of the Siman Act denounced this as a subterfuge. In particular, the two schools operated by Zion extended their midday recess period by a half hour and offered German-language instruction during this time.[34] In an apparent expression of outrage over the continuation of these German lessons, vandals blasted out the windows of one of the schools with shotguns and destroyed all German-language books except the Bible.[35] Because Zion's schools continued to open at nine o'clock and close at four o'clock, county officials contended that schools were evading the Siman Act. On May 25, 1920, the county attorney, Frank E. Edgerton, visited both of Zion's schools in order to make certain that they no longer were teaching German. The teachers knew that the county attorney did not wish to provoke trouble with the otherwise law-abiding and politically influential German Americans and that the state would not prosecute them if he did not catch them in the act of teaching German.[36] One of the teachers therefore omitted his German lesson during the county attorney's visit.[37]

The other teacher, Robert T. Meyer, was braver. When Edgerton entered his classroom during the German lesson, Meyer, a mild-mannered forty-two-year-old father of six, continued to speak in German. As he later explained, "I had my choice. I knew that, if I changed into English, he would say nothing. If I went on in German, he would arrest me. I told myself that I must not flinch. And I did not flinch. I went on in German. . . . It was my duty to uphold my religion by teaching the children the religion of their parents in the language of their parents."[38] Edgerton asked Raymond Parpart, an eleven-year-old fifth-grader, to read a few sentences from a book of German-language Bible stories and to explain in English what he had read. Edgerton then seized the book and turned to Meyer, with whom he had a whispered conversation. Meyer admitted that he taught German each day from one o'clock until one thirty by order of Zion's school board. Meyer then resumed the lesson in German. Edgerton listened for a while and then departed.[39]

Meyer was charged in the Hamilton County Court, convicted of violating the statute, and fined twenty-five dollars—the equivalent of a month's salary—by Hamilton County judge Fred Jeffers. Although members of Meyer's congregation offered to pay the fine, Meyer insisted on appealing his conviction. "This is a question of principle," Meyer declared. "If I go to jail, I shall not compromise what I know is not right."[40] Raymond Parpart's father posted bond to keep Meyer out of jail. Covered with animal furs to keep warm, Meyer traveled by carriage eleven miles through the snow shortly before Thanksgiving in the company of Raymond and Zion's pastor, Brommer, to testify before the district court in Aurora in a de novo jury trial over which district court judge E. E. Good presided.[41] During the hearing, Brommer testified that "the ultimate and only object we had in view in teaching German" was to enable children to worship at home and at church with their German-speaking parents.[42] The court upheld the conviction and the fine.[43]

During the pendency of Meyer's appeal, the Nebraska Legislature repealed the Siman Act and replaced it with the Norval Act, which explicitly closed the loophole that the Nebraska Supreme Court had created in its 1919 decision.[44] In an apparent effort to appease German Americans, however, the law explicitly stated that a parent could offer foreign-language instruction to a child at home.[45] Like the Siman Act, the Norval Act generated considerable opposition. Novelist Willa Cather complained that "no Nebraska child now growing up will ever have a mastery of a foreign language, because your legislature has made it a crime to teach a foreign language to a child in its early years, the only period when it can really lay a foundation for a thorough understanding of a foreign language."[46] The German Evangelical Lutheran Synod of Missouri, Ohio, and Other States (known today as the Lutheran Church–Missouri Synod), the Lutheran denomination with which Zion was affiliated, wasted no time in challenging the Norval Act's constitutionality on the ground that it interfered with religious education. John Siedlik, the father of four children who attended a Roman Catholic school that taught the Polish language, joined the action in an apparent effort to demonstrate that the law offended not only German American Lutherans but other groups, as well.[47] The district court enjoined enforcement of the Norval Act, and the state appealed to the Nebraska Supreme Court during the pendency of Meyer's appeal.[48]

The Missouri Synod argued that the statute was clearly unconstitutional because the state supreme court already had held that the Siman Act would be unconstitutional if it prohibited the teaching of foreign languages outside of regular school hours. Although the synod maintained that the Norval Act unconstitutionally deprived them of both property and religious liberty, it placed less emphasis on religious liberty than it had in its original challenge to the Siman Act. The synod argued that the statute jeopardized its investment of more than one million dollars in its schools and that the law interfered with the right of teachers to pursue their vocation.[49] The state, in turn, responded that the synod had failed to demonstrate that the law diminished the value of their schools or interfered with religious worship, and that the statute was needed to facilitate assimilation.[50] As the American Legion declared in an amicus brief, "We must eliminate every influence that tends to perpetuate foreign ideals and foreign influences."[51]

The Nebraska Supreme Court ruled in favor of the state by a vote of 4 to 2 in the *Meyer* case in February 1922.[52] As in its 1919 decision upholding the Siman Act, the court declared that the legislature could reasonably have concluded that there was a compelling need to ensure that the children of immigrants not learn any foreign language until thoroughly grounded in the English language and American values. Even though the parties had not emphasized the religious issue, the court concluded that religion was the central issue in the case: it found, however, that there was no interference with religious freedom because religious doctrines could be taught in English. Recognizing that its decision upholding the state's position was at odds with its interpretation of the Siman Act three years earlier, the court expressly conceded that its earlier decision should be modified to the extent that it had interpreted the Siman Act to apply only to regular school hours. Because neither the Siman Act nor the compulsory public education law defined the scope of a regular school day, the court reasoned that the legislature had intended the Siman Act to prohibit instruction in foreign languages whenever pupils attended school for the purpose of receiving instruction. The court's decision, which made no reference to the subsequent enactment of the Norval Act, also concluded that Zion had altered its schedule in an effort to evade the Siman Act. In a dissent, Justice Charles B. Letton argued that the legislature could not "interfere with the fundamental right of every American parent to control, in a degree not harmful to the state, the education of his child." Letton asserted that the Siman Act "was the result of crowd psychology; that it is a product of passions engendered by the World War, which had not had time to cool."[53]

The court's affirmation of the constitutionality of the Siman Act ensured that the court would sustain the constitutionality of the Norval Act. In a 5-to-1 decision issued two months after its *Meyer* opinion, the Nebraska Supreme Court declared the Norval Act "a reasonable exercise of the police power" that did not abridge any constitutional liberty.[54] Meanwhile, in February 1921, the Iowa Supreme Court by a 4-to-3 vote upheld the conviction of Lutheran parochial school teacher August Bartels for violating a 1919 statute that was very similar to Nebraska's Siman and Norval acts.[55] Four months later, the Supreme Court of Ohio unanimously affirmed the convictions of a teacher and a trustee of a Lutheran school near Cleveland for violating a 1919 statute that prohibited the teaching of German in any elementary school.[56]

Undaunted by their defeats in the state courts, the opponents of the language laws carried their battle to the U.S. Supreme Court, which simultaneously considered the two Nebraska cases, the two Ohio cases, and the Iowa case. Meyer's attorney in his appeal to the Supreme Court was Arthur F. Mullen, a prominent Roman Catholic layman who understood that the language laws threatened the very existence of parochial education because they could serve as a legal wedge for garnering judicial approval of the compulsory public education laws that anti-Catholic nativist groups were promoting in many states.[57]

In their arguments before the Supreme Court, the opponents of the language laws acknowledged that states had a legitimate need to ensure that their citizens were fluent in the English language; the statutes were overly broad, however, because prohibiting foreign language instruction in elementary schools did not facilitate the stated legislative purpose of ameliorating ignorance of English.[58] Because the U.S. Supreme Court at this time was inclined to protect property rights more than personal liberties, Mullen and the other attorneys based the appeals largely upon the economic arguments that the prohibition on the teaching of German would destroy the value of the schools and that parochial schools and parents had the right to enter into contracts for the education of their children without undue interference from the state. The states, in turn, argued that the statutes were valid under the doctrine of the so-called police power, which permits a state to enact legislation for the protection of public health, safety, welfare, and morals. According to the states, the statutes constituted appropriate exercises of the police power because they ensured that children were assimilated into American values and that they were protected from the poison of the German values against which the nation had fought during the war.[59]

The appellants also argued that the statutes violated certain fundamental personal rights, including the right of parents to supervise the education of their children, the right of citizens to acquire knowledge, and the right of teachers to pursue their vocation. Most of the appellants largely ignored the issue of religious liberty, probably because the provisions of the First Amendment had not yet been incorporated into federal constitutional restrictions on state action.[60] In his brief for the Missouri Synod and in his oral argument before the Court, however, Mullen advanced the novel argument that the Fourteenth Amendment protected religious liberty.[61]

In two separate 7-to-2 decisions in June 1923, the Supreme Court held that the Nebraska, Iowa, and Ohio statutes were unconstitutional because they deprived parents and teachers of liberty and property without due process of law, in violation of the Fourteenth Amendment to the U.S. Constitution.[62] Both opinions were written by Justice James C. McReynolds, who read them aloud in a sarcastic tone that appeared to ridicule those legislators who attempted to deprive citizens of fundamental rights.[63] Although the Court in *Meyer* expressed sympathy with the legislative motivation to "foster a homogeneous people with American ideals," these statutes exceeded the power of the states because "[m]ere knowledge of the German language cannot reasonably be regarded as harmful." Because German American Lutheran parochial schools already taught basic curricular subjects in the English language, the Court found that the Nebraska, Ohio, and Iowa statutes did not promote the states' interest in encouraging patriotism and the use of a common language.

Although the Court based its decisions partly upon a theory of economic rights, particularly the right of teachers to follow their vocation and the right of parents to hire foreign-language teachers, it also suggested that the law interfered with the right of students to acquire knowledge and with the right of parents to supervise the education of their children.

Although the Court acknowledged in its *Meyer* decision that "the state may do much . . . in order to improve the quality of its citizens," it also declared that "the individual has certain fundamental rights which must be respected."[64] In sweeping language, the Court held that the Fourteenth Amendment "denotes not merely freedom from bodily restraint but also the right of the individual to contract, to engage in any of the common occupations of life, to acquire useful knowledge, to marry, establish a home and bring up children, to worship God according to the dictates of his own conscience, and generally to enjoy those privileges long recognized at common law as essential to the orderly pursuit of happiness by free men."[65]

In a dissent joined by Justice George Sutherland, Justice Oliver Wendell Holmes Jr. wrote that the Court ought to have deferred to the legislatures' determination that the statutes were necessary for the protection of public welfare. Although Holmes acknowledged that he dissented "with hesitation and unwillingness," he explained that "youth is the time when familiarity with a language is established and if there are sections in the State where a child would hear only Polish or French or German spoken at home I am not prepared to say that it is unreasonable to provide that in his early years he shall hear and speak only English at school."[66]

It may seem strange that the dissent was written by Holmes, who is widely revered as a great civil libertarian, whereas the Court's expansive decision was authored by the archconservative McReynolds, who is widely execrated for his hostility toward social reform legislation and his bigotry against Jews, African Americans, and women. This is not so surprising, however, because Holmes in *Meyer* espoused the same ideal of judicial restraint that he propounded in many decisions involving economic regulation, while McReynolds exercised judicial review in the same expansive manner that he often employed in denying the constitutionality of legislative efforts to ameliorate social and economic injustice.

Although proponents of parochial education regarded *Meyer* as a victory for religious freedom, the Court's decision did not rely upon the First Amendment's free exercise clause or any other specific provision of the Bill of Rights, which the Court had not yet applied to state actors. *Meyer*'s emphasis on personal liberties, however, presaged the Court's gradual application of the various provisions of the Bill of Rights to the states, beginning later in the 1920s.

The *Meyer* decision was also significant because it was the first case in which the Court invoked the Fourteenth Amendment to protect noneconomic rights against intrusion by the states. Until *Meyer,* the Court generally had struck down state statutes only when they unreasonably interfered with economic activities. In suggesting that the statute unconstitutionally infringed both economic rights and noneconomic rights, *Meyer* marked the start of the Court's modern role as a guardian of personal liberties. In his famous *Carolene Products* footnote in 1938, Justice Harlan Fiske Stone cited *Meyer* in support of his suggestion that the Court might exercise a higher level of scrutiny in reviewing statutes directed at particular national groups than it does in reviewing economic legislation.[67]

Indeed, the Court may have grounded its decision partly on personal liberties and included its magisterial dictum about the rights of free men in order to deflect a rising tide of criticism engendered by its decisions striking down economic regulatory legislation and limiting the rights of organized labor. In the wake of the Court's increasing conservatism under the leadership of Chief Justice William Howard Taft, critics proposed various measures to curtail judicial power. Hostility toward the Court had reached a crescendo two months before *Meyer,* when the Court invalidated a federal law providing a minimum wage for women workers in the District of Columbia.[68]

Regardless of what the justices may have intended, *Meyer* provided grist for conservatives who had been arguing that the Court could use its power of judicial review to protect personal rights as well as property rights, and the decision appears to have ameliorated hostility toward the Court. During the 1924 presidential campaign, Republicans skillfully used *Meyer* to win Lutherans and Roman Catholics away from Robert La Follette's third-party bid for the presidency, which was attracting such widespread support among ethnic voters in the Midwest that it threatened to throw the election into the House of Representatives. Republicans argued that La Follette's proposal to curtail the Court's power to review the constitutionality of legislation would leave ethnic and religious minorities vulnerable to majoritarian tyranny.[69]

Meyer also was well-timed because it was decided just as the assault on parochial education was reaching its zenith in campaigns for compulsory public education. Gaining momentum even as hostility toward German Americans was waning, the movement to eliminate parochial education enjoyed the active support of the newly resurgent Ku Klux Klan, which attracted millions of members throughout the nation during the early 1920s and exercised political clout far beyond the South. The movement also attracted support from otherwise respectable sources, including many political progressives, Masonic organizations, and prominent educators, who believed that compulsory public education would promote social harmony by ameliorating racial, class, and religious prejudices and antagonisms.[70]

Although Michigan voters defeated compulsory public education referenda in 1920 and 1924 and Washington state voters rejected a similar measure in 1924,[71] Oregonians approved a compulsory education law in 1922.[72] A coalition of religious groups, including Roman Catholics, Lutherans, and Jews, organized a vigorous legal challenge to the Oregon law.[73] Mullen believed that the Court in deciding *Meyer* had considered the larger issue of compulsory public education[74] and that his declaration during oral argument that the state had no power to require children to attend public schools had won over a previously hostile McReynolds, at least insofar as Mullen had convinced him that the language laws could generate the same tyranny that pervaded the Soviet Union.[75] On the day that the Court heard arguments on the Oregon school law, Chief Justice Taft remarked to the attorney for the Roman Catholic Church that "[i]n principle, this case is simply the Meyer case over again."[76]

In its unanimous decision in *Pierce v. Society of Sisters*[77] in June 1925, the U.S. Supreme Court held that the statute unconstitutionally interfered with the property rights of private schools and with the right of parents to direct the education of their children. Amplifying *Meyer,* the Court declared that "[t]he child is not the mere creature of the State; those who nurture him and direct his destiny have the right, coupled with the high duty, to recognize and prepare him for additional obligations."[78] Although *Pierce* added little to what the Court had said in *Meyer, Pierce* is the better-known decision because its immediate impact was more sweeping: it conclusively terminated the national movement for compulsory public education. Because the cases involved similar issues, the names *Meyer* and *Pierce* are often linked in discussions of constitutional law. The Court further reaffirmed these principles in a 1927 decision, *Farrington v. Tokushige,* which invalidated a Hawaiian statute that restricted the teaching of Asian languages.[79]

The significance of *Meyer* has outlasted the political and cultural turmoil of its era. Seventy years after he read German in Meyer's classroom during the visit of the county attorney, Raymond Parpart remarked that the *Meyer* decision demonstrated that legislatures "can't just make up laws to tell people that they can't do what they want to do. It shows how valuable the Constitution really is."[80] But although the basic principles of *Meyer* and *Pierce* appear to constitute settled legal doctrine, the opinions themselves are among the most delphic in the Court's history. They have meant many different things to different people at different times.

Although most civil liberties decisions after *Meyer* and *Pierce* have been grounded in specific provisions of the Bill of Rights, *Meyer* remains a precedent for the proposition that there are some constitutional rights that are not found in specific provisions of the Constitution. Although the Supreme Court shortly after the *Pierce* decision began to decide personal liberties cases by applying to state law the specific liberties of the Bill of Rights rather than relying on the general language of the Fourteenth Amendment, *Meyer* and *Pierce* acquired renewed importance during the 1960s when the Court began to protect liberties not spelled out in the Bill of Rights.

In particular, *Meyer* has served as a cornerstone for the development of the right of privacy. In 1965, the Court invoked *Meyer* in its decision in *Griswold v. Connecticut,* overturning the conviction of a physician and Planned Parenthood official who had violated Connecticut law by recommending the use of contraceptives to married persons.[81] Unable to find any specific provision in the Constitution that protected the dissemination of birth control information, Justice William O. Douglas cited *Meyer* in support of his proposition that a state may not restrict the spectrum of available knowledge. Similarly, the Court cited *Meyer* in support of its 1977 decision limiting restrictions on the sale and advertising of contraceptives.[82]

In its landmark decision in *Roe v. Wade,* which held that a state could not prohibit abortion before fetal viability, the Court likewise relied upon *Meyer* in support of its proposition that a right to privacy may be inferred from the concept of liberty as guaranteed by the Fourteenth Amendment.[83] In reaffirming the right to abortion in their opinion for the Court in *Planned Parenthood of Southeastern Pennsylvania v. Casey* in 1992, Justices Sandra Day O'Connor, Anthony M. Kennedy, and David H. Souter cited *Meyer* and *Pierce* in support of the principle that "the Constitution places limits on a State's right to interfere with a person's most basic decisions about family and parenthood."[84] Four dissenting justices in *Casey* wrote, however, that *Roe* had "reached too far" in analogizing abortion to the rights involved in *Meyer* and *Pierce,*[85] a sentiment echoed by many opponents of legalized abortion. As one scholar has observed, "*Meyer* and its progeny, properly understood, support the destruction, rather than the recognition, of abortion and autonomy rights" insofar as those decisions were based on natural law, embodied in common law, that acknowledged "the primacy of the family in relation to the state."[86]

Meyer likewise remains at the center of controversies involving parental rights, particularly school vouchers and homeschooling.[87] The ambiguity of *Meyer* and *Pierce* was acutely demonstrated in the U.S. Supreme Court's 2000 decision in *Troxel v. Granville,* which invalidated a statute that permitted courts to allow grandparents and other persons to visit children even over the objection of parents. In an opinion for the Court joined by three other justices, O'Connor cited with approval *Meyer*'s statements that the "liberty" protected by the due process clause includes the right of parents to "establish a home and bring up children" and "to control the education of their own."[88] Justice Souter cited the same language in his concurring opinion and argued that "*Meyer*'s repeatedly recognized right of upbringing would be a sham if it failed to encompass the right to be free of judicially compelled visitation by 'any party' at 'any time' a judge believed he 'could make a "better" decision' than the objecting parent had done."[89] Justice Antonin Scalia, however, asserted that "the theory of unenumerated parental rights" underlying *Meyer* and *Pierce* had "small claim to *stare decisis* protection."[90] Similarly, Justice Kennedy urged that "courts must use considerable restraint" in applying the broad formulations of these cases.[91]

In its 2003 decision invoking due process to strike down state laws that prohibit consensual homosexual conduct, the Court referred to the "broad statements" in *Meyer* and *Pierce* concerning "the substantive reach of liberty under the Due Process Clause," although the Court found that *Griswold* was "the most pertinent beginning point."[92] In his dissent, Scalia rejected *Meyer* as a relevant precedent because *Meyer* stated only that due process protects "those privileges long recognized at common law."[93]

Critics of *Meyer* and *Pierce* have complained that their reliance upon rights that are not specifically spelled out in the Constitution invites undue judicial activism. In contrast to Mullen, who hailed *Meyer* for its vision of a "fenceless land of liberty,"[94] many critics of *Meyer* and *Pierce* would prefer a liberty confined by at least some fences, particularly if the Supreme Court is to be the ultimate surveyor of liberty's terrain. Moreover, some feminist scholars and advocates of the rights of children have criticized *Meyer* and *Pierce* for aggrandizing private rights at the expense of community values and for "constitutionalizing a patriarchal notion of parental rights" that "interrupted the trend of family law moving toward children's rights."[95]

Although the scope of the liberties recognized by *Meyer* is likely to continue to cause controversy, its ruling that "the individual has certain fundamental rights which must be respected" is likely to endure as long as the nation has citizens who are as willing to fight for their rights as courageously as did a Nebraska schoolmaster nearly a century ago.

Notes

1. 262 U.S. 390 (1923).

2. William G. Ross, *Forging New Freedoms: Nativism, Education, and the Constitution, 1917–1927* (Lincoln: University of Nebraska Press, 1994), 61.

3. See James R. Mock and Cedric Larson, *Words That Won the War: The Story of the Committee on Public Information, 1917–1919* (Princeton, N.J.: Princeton University Press, 1939); Stephen L. Vaughan, *Holding Fast the Inner Lines: Democracy, Nationalism, and the Committee on Public Information* (Chapel Hill: University of North Carolina Press, 1980).

4. Frederick C. Luebke, *Bonds of Loyalty: German Americans and the First World War* (DeKalb: University of Illinois Press, 1974), 215–16.

5. Ross, *Forging New Freedoms,* 74.

6. Klaus Wust and Norbert Muehlen, *The Story of German Involvement in the Founding and Development of America* (Philadelphia: National Carl Schurz Association, 1976), 47.

7. Frederick C. Luebke, "Ethnic Group Settlement on the Great Plains," *Western Historical Quarterly* 8, no. 4 (1977): 413–15.

8. Ross, *Forging New Freedoms,* 43.

9. "Statement by Nebraska Council of Defense," December 11, 1917, RG 23, box 31, Nebraska State Historical Society (NSHS), Lincoln. See also "Report on German Private Schools in Nebraska," (undated), box 31, ibid. The council, however, did not object to weekend instruction in foreign languages for students enrolled in public schools. Sarka Hbrokova to C. V. Svoboda, February 8, 1918, ibid.

10. Ross, *Forging New Freedoms,* 81.

11. Ibid., 79–80.

12. Ibid., 84–85.

13. Writ from Cedar County Council of Defense to Ferd. Schuettgen, May 31, 1918, and reply from Fr. Schuettgen, RG 23, box 12, NSHS.

14. *Lincoln Daily Star,* December 17, 1918, 1.

15. Ross, *Forging New Freedoms,* 85.

16. Proclamation sent by Nebraska State Council of Defense to county chairmen, June 10, 1918, RG 23, box 15, NSHS; *Lincoln Daily Star,* June 8, 1918, 1.

17. Ross, *Forging New Freedoms,* 81–82.

18. "A Proclamation," H. J. Metcalf Papers, box 10, State Historical Society of Iowa, Iowa City.

19. Nancy Derr, "The Babel Proclamation," *Palimpsest* 60 (July–August 1979): 114.

20. For a general discussion of the wave of hostility against German Americans during the First World War, see Luebke, "Ethnic Group Settlement on the Great Plains." See also Ross, *Forging New Freedoms,* 47–50.

21. Ross, *Forging New Freedoms,* 82, 85–86.

22. Ibid., 93–94.

23. 1919 Laws of Nebraska 1019.

24. Report of the Attorney General of the State of Nebraska, 1919–20 (Lincoln: Attorney General's Office, 1920), 228–30.

25. Ross, *Forging New Freedoms,* 97.

26. Ibid., 98.

27. C. F. Brommer to Theodore Graebner, May 14, 1919, box 40, Theodore Graebner Papers, Concordia Historical Institute, Clayton, Missouri.

28. Arthur F. Mullen, unpublished history of the language laws, 4–5, Arthur F. Mullen Papers, Creighton University, Omaha, Nebraska.

29. Ross, *Forging New Freedoms,* 100.

30. Nebraska District of Evangelical Lutheran Synod of Missouri, Ohio, and Other States v. McKelvie, 104 Neb. 93, 175 N.W.2d 531 (1919).

31. Ross, *Forging New Freedoms,* 101–2.

32. Clyde H. Barnard, ed., *Journal of the Constitutional Convention of* 1919–20 (Lincoln, Neb.: Kline, 1921), 1:962.

33. Ibid., 2:2647.

34. Meyer v. Nebraska, record, Hamilton County District Court, 19–20, 33 (testimony of C.F. Brommer), and 24–25 (testimony of Raymond Parpart); Zion Lutheran Church Records, 1875–1976, series 3, *Minutes,* 1876–1969, 2:78, RG 4373, Nebraska State Historical Society (minutes of church council meeting of January 5, 1920).

35. Author interview with Clarence Heiden, Hampton, Nebraska, June 27, 1990.

36. Ross, *Forging New Freedoms,* 3.

37. Heiden interview.

38. Arthur F. Mullen, *Western Democrat* (New York: W. Funk, 1940), 218. Mullen quotes these statements in his autobiography, written nearly two decades after his interview with Meyer. Although Mullen placed Meyer's statements in quotation marks, the words are probably not literally accurate.

39. Author interview with Raymond Parpart, Hampton, Nebraska, June 27, 1990; Meyer v. Nebraska, record, 30 (testimony of Frank E. Edgerton); *Grand Island Independent,* January 3, 1988.

40. Mullen, *Western Democrat,* 38.

41. Ross, *Forging New Freedoms,* 4.

42. Meyer v. Nebraska, record, 33 (testimony of C. F. Brommer).

43. Ross, *Forging New Freedoms,* 4.

44. 1921 Laws of Nebraska 244–45.

45. Ibid., 244.

46. Brief of Joseph T. Votava, as amicus curiae, Nebraska District of Evangelical Lutheran Synod et al. v. McKelvie et al. (No. 22422), 16 (quoting *Omaha World-Herald,* October 30, 1921), State Law Library, Lincoln. See 843 Nebraska Briefs 753, 772 (1922).

47. Ross, *Forging New Freedoms,* 106.

48. Ibid., 106–7.

49. Brief of appellees, Nebraska District of Evangelical Lutheran Synod et al. v. McKelvie et al., 17–18, 27–28, 30–34, 5–6, 21, 10–14, 21–30, 10–11, 22, 25, 27–28.

50. Brief of appellants, ibid., 31–35, 66, 67–68.

51. Brief of the American Legion, Department of Nebraska, as amicus curiae, ibid., 25.

52. Meyer v. State, 107 Neb. 657, 187 N.W. 100 (1922).

53. Ibid., 107 Neb. at 667 and 669, 187 N.W. at 104 (Letton, J., dissenting).

54. Nebraska District of Evangelical Lutheran Synod v. McKelvie, 108 Neb. 448, 187 N.W. 927 (1922).

55. Bartels v. State, 191 Iowa 1060, 181 N.W. 508 (1921).

56. Bohning v. State and Pohl v. State, 102 Ohio St. 474, 132 N.E. 20 (1921).

57. Ross, *Forging New Freedoms,* 4–5, 69.

58. Ibid., 116, citing briefs of various parties to the case.

59. Ibid., 120–23, citing briefs.

60. Ibid., 118.

61. Brief of Evangelical Lutheran Church of Missouri, Ohio, and other states, *Nebraska District of Evangelical Lutheran Synod v. McKelvie,* 262 U.S. 404 (1923) (No. 440), 38; Oral argument of Arthur F. Mullen, in behalf of plaintiffs-in-error, *Meyer v. Nebraska,* 262 U.S. 404 (1923) (No. 325). For a discussion of the doctrinal significance of these arguments, see Ross, *Forging New Freedoms,* 118–19.

62. Meyer v. Nebraska; Bartels v. Iowa; Bohning v. Ohio and Pohl v. Ohio; Nebraska District of Evangelical Lutheran Synod v. McKelvie, 262 U.S. 404 (1923).

63. Arthur F. Mullen to John J. Burke, June 14, 1923, box 9, Records of the United States Catholic Conference, Department of Archives and Manuscripts, Catholic University of America, Washington, D.C.

64. 262 U.S. at 401.

65. Ibid., 399.

66. Ibid., 412.

67. United States v. Carolene Products Co., 304 U.S. 144, 152n4 (1938).

68. Ross, *Forging New Freedoms,* 193–94.

69. William G. Ross, *A Muted Fury: Populists, Progressives, and Labor Unions Confront the Courts,* 1890–1937 (Princeton, N.J.: Princeton University Press, 1994), 265, 267, 275, 277, 279. See also Ross, *Forging New Freedoms,* 194–95.

70. Ross, *Forging New Freedoms,* 142–43, 150–52.

71. Ibid., 134–47.

72. Ibid., 148–58.

73. Ibid., 160–71.

74. Arthur F. Mullen to F. X. McMenany, March 17, 1923, box 9, USCC Records.

75. Mullen, *Western Democrat,* 224–25.

76. John J. Burke to Thomas F. O'Mara, March 25, 1925, box 14, USCC Records.

77. 268 U.S. 510 (1925).

78. Ibid., 535.

79. 273 U.S. 284 (1927).

80. Parpart interview.

81. 381 U.S. 479 (1965).

82. Carey v. Population Services, 431 U.S. 678, 684–85 (1977).

83. 410 U.S. 113, 152–53 (1973).

84. Planned Parenthood of Southeastern Pennsylvania v. Casey, 505 U.S. 717, 849 (1992).

85. Ibid., 953 (Rehnquist, C.J., dissenting).

86. David M. Smolin, "The Jurisprudence of Privacy in a Splintered Supreme Court," *Marquette Law Review* 75, no. 4 (1992): 1064 and 1052.

87. See William G. Ross, "The Contemporary Significance of *Meyer* and *Pierce*

for Parental Rights Issues Involving Education," *Akron Law Review* 34, no. 1 (2000): 194–207.

88. Troxel v. Granville, 530 U.S. 57, 65 (2000).

89. Ibid., 77–78.

90. Ibid., 92.

91. Ibid., 95–96.

92. Lawrence v. Texas, 539 U.S. 558, 564 (2003).

93. Ibid., 593.

94. Mullen, *Western Democrat*, 226.

95. Barbara Bennett Woodhouse, "Who Owns the Child?: *Meyer* and *Pierce* and the Child as Property," *William and Mary Law Review* 33, no. 4 (1992): 1113.

FIFTEEN

Richard E. Shugrue and Alan G. Gless

ROSCOE POUND

Arguably Nebraska's Single Greatest Contribution to American Legal History

Nathan Roscoe Pound was born in Lincoln, Nebraska, on October 27, 1870, when both the city and the state were only three years old and the University of Nebraska only one. In his nearly ninety-four years, he earned a Ph.D. in botany and later practiced and taught that science; studied and practiced law; served as an appellate judge; taught law in one undergraduate program and five law schools; served as dean of two of those five law schools; served on numerous national and international private and governmental commissions; worked as a consultant to the Chinese government of Chiang Kai-Shek; and published more than 1,073 books, articles, and essays on jurisprudence, law, and legal history. He also published more than 200 additional books, articles, and essays on other subjects, including botany and general history, as well as 255 Nebraska Supreme Court opinions.[1] This listing only begins to describe Pound's activities; he worked seventeen-plus-hour days until his mideighties.

Richard E. Shugrue's article, reprinted here as the first part of this two-part chapter, briefly describes Roscoe Pound's life in Lincoln and discusses the extent to which Pound's service as a Nebraska Supreme Court commissioner may have contributed to the legal philosophy he eventually developed.[2] The second part, written by Alan G. Gless, examines the accomplishments that made Pound arguably Nebraska's single greatest contribution to American legal history.

Roscoe Pound, Commissioner

RICHARD E. SHUGRUE

When Roscoe Pound was a thirty-year-old lawyer in Lincoln, he was appointed to the Nebraska Supreme Court Commission. Pound was the youngest of nine men named to the body, authorized by the legislature after prodding by bar, political, and legal officials to provide some relief to the growing case load and backlog on the high court.

Pound had graduated from the University of Nebraska at age eighteen in 1888 and begun reading law in the firm of his father, Stephen Pound, who had left the district court bench the previous year after having served four terms as a district court judge in Lancaster County. In the fall, however, the young graduate returned to the university to study botany. He left for Cambridge, at his father's behest, the following autumn, to begin legal studies at the Harvard Law School.

The young scholar returned from Harvard in the summer of 1890, following only one year of legal studies. Despite his earlier experience reading the law and his year of formal legal training, he was not listed among the lawyers licensed in the state until volume 34 of the Nebraska Reports, published in 1892. Pound began practicing with his father's firm and served as stenographer to an eminent Lincoln attorney, L. C. Burr.

A Highly Active Decade

Roscoe Pound by no means devoted his entire attention to the practice of law during that decade following his return from Harvard. He was deeply involved in scientific research at the University of Nebraska, having been a founder of the Botanical Survey of Nebraska. During his second year back in Lincoln he devoted huge amounts of time to that work, including two months in the summer of 1892, when he tramped through the state's vast sand hills and made meticulous notes about Nebraska's vegetation. He also took the time [t]o complete his studies and dissertation for the doctor of philosophy degree, which was awarded in 1897. His joint dissertation, with Frederick Clements, *The Phytogeography of Nebraska,* was published in 1898.

Another great Nebraskan, Willa Cather, was at the university during the 1890s, having begun her collegiate studies in 1891. There she met and befriended Louise Pound, Roscoe's sister. Cather was often a guest in the home of Judge Stephen Pound. This relationship ended abruptly after

Cather, who was the editor and mainstay of the college literary magazine, *The Hesperian,* published a satirical piece describing a character whom, though fictional, the entire community knew to be Roscoe Pound. This lampoon appeared in the March 1894 issue of the magazine. She wrote:

> [He] is pompous, stuffy, conceited, and impressed with his own importance. He stands around the halls buttonholing old acquaintances and showing the University to them . . . He belongs to the botany seminar and calls everything by its longest and most Latin name. In his earliest youth he was a notorious bully, and little boys of the neighborhood used to be afraid to go past his house. [He now loves to] browbeat [students], argue them down, Latin them into a corner and botany them into a shapeless mass.

Cather concluded by noting that the target of her lampoon likes to hang around the university "in order that people may ask who he is and be told what fine marks he used to get in his classes."

Pound also spent considerable time during the 1896 political campaign working on behalf of the Republican ticket and against his fellow Lincoln attorney William Jennings Bryan, the Democratic presidential candidate. A Republican judge of the supreme court, Frank Irvine, congratulated Pound on the persuasive campaign literature he had written on behalf of the McKinley ticket. In October of that same year, Pound was chosen a member of the commission appointed by the supreme court for the purpose of examining candidates for admission to the bar.

Continuing his activity chairing the Republican party in Lancaster County, Pound also found himself on the Committee on Organization for the new Nebraska State Bar Association. In July 1900, when the constitution of the NSBA was adopted, Pound was named secretary. He held that position both throughout his service on the Supreme Court Commission and at the College of Law.

The 1890s were, indeed, busy years for the young scholar: his legal career had begun in earnest, he undertook a monumental and rigorous doctoral program at the university, he engaged in the heated presidential campaign of 1896, and he was serving the supreme court as a bar examiner.

The Origins of the Supreme Court Commission

Nebraska's constitution of 1875 provided for a three-member supreme court. No attempt to expand the number of judges had succeeded, and no intermediate appellate tribunal had been created since then. Once before, in 1893, the legislature had created a commission to assist with the growing case load, but its authority expired in 1899. The supreme court decided a case in 1893 that held the commission form of decision making was not a violation of the state constitution. This earlier commission had only three members. The group to which Pound was named in 1901 had nine commissioners, who sat in panels of three. Nebraska continued to use commissioners to assist the high court long after Pound left the bench for a career in the academic world. Some of his original colleagues had gone on to other positions prior to 1903, the year Pound assumed the deanship at the University of Nebraska College of Law. Although the original life of the "Pound Commission" was a brief two years, it was reauthorized by the legislature and lasted until 1909. One commissioner, Edward Duffie, was continuously reappointed until that date.

Yet another commission was created in 1915, and this body and its successors were utilized until 1931. In all, over the thirty-eight years in which various commission-form tribunals were employed by Nebraska, thirty-seven men served as judges.

The 1901 legislation authorizing the nine-member body was, doubtless, the most aggressive attempt to move cases along in the appellate process because of the sheer numbers of judicial officers involved. Although the legislation provided for some stenographic assistance to the commissioners, there is no record that the state made any physical accommodation for them. Judges of the supreme court were not required to live in and work at the capital city in those days.

The requirement of residency in Lincoln was not added to the constitution until 1908, when the size of the court was expanded to seven. The legislation creating the 1901 commission was silent as to any provision for offices. The law specifically forbade commissioners to engage in the practice of law during their terms of office; it did not prohibit engaging in other forms of compensated work, however, such as teaching.

Pound's Work on the Commission

Pound's biographers have debated the impact of the judicial years on the man who was to become a giant in the world of legal education and a pioneer in the field of modern jurisprudence. The workload of the commission was heavy. The supreme court determined which cases were to be referred to the commission, and the high court reserved the most interesting cases to itself. Routine appeals dealing with mortgages, taxes, civil procedure, property, and banking matters constituted the bulk of the commission's case load. A small number of criminal matters were assigned to the commission, and, for the most part, constitutional questions were the exclusive reserve of the supreme court.

Whatever may be the correct answer to the question of how the court years shaped the young scholar, most biographers have erred in conducting their research on these years in one significant respect. With the exception of Paul Sayre, the author of the 1948 book *The Life of Roscoe Pound,* each was mistaken as to the number of opinions Pound wrote as a commissioner.[3] At best, these mistaken biographers saw only a portion of the work the prolific young jurist produced in his tenure as a judge.

One author, Lewis C. Cassidy, stated in the *New York University Law Review* that Pound wrote 99 opinions.[4] He said of Pound's work, "Lawyers who have long admired the cogency and lucidity of the style of Mr. Justice Holmes and of Lord Shaw of Dunfermline, will discover here opinions which are models of form and substance, of comprehensiveness and brevity."

In January 1942, Harold Gill Reuschlein, then a professor of law at Georgetown, wrote a biographical essay on Pound's experience on the commission.[5] He claimed that Pound wrote 103 opinions. He seemed to take pleasure in revealing that Cassidy had erroneously reported the number of opinions.

Reuschlein wrote that Pound's opinions yielded an understanding of how the young jurist "took problems as they came before him for adjudication and in their solution experimented with techniques of weighing and evaluating interests, of subordinating procedure to substance, of assessing the conflicting demands for rule and discretion, for certainty and flux in the legal order, of taking cognizance of social and economic conditions, of utilizing the good in other legal systems and of drawing upon the resources of history." Reuschlein added that the judicial years "served as an experimental laboratory for the philosophy, the method and the dynamic which he was later to recommend to all who follow the lawyer's craft."

In 1965, a year after Pound's death, Sheldon Glueck edited a book on the great scholar's contributions to the American criminal justice system.[6] Glueck misstated the number of opinions written by Pound, claiming there were only 103. Of those cases that he read dealing with criminal justice, Glueck maintained that they reflect "a so[r]t of dynamic triad of history, philosophy, and science, organically interrelated and skillfully focused on practical day-to-day issues of law in an ever changing society."

The finest biography of Pound was written by David Wigdor in 1974.[7] He characterized the court as a congenial setting for Pound's intellectual endeavors. The cases addressed by the commission were mundane, Wigdor wrote, and yet Pound's contributions "revealed the direction of his emerging legal philosophy." The biographer claimed that the judicial work evidenced an "unresolved dualism" in Pound.

His intellectual loyalties, divided between competing themes, were at once instrumental and organic, catholic and parochial, venturesome and defensive. Clad in the robes he had earlier celebrated, Pound displayed a passion for common-law fundamentals. At the same time, his opinions showed movement toward some advanced positions, and there were suggestions of the sociological jurisprudence to come.

Wigdor's book examined a total of nineteen cases in which, he believed, Pound's approach to and philosophy of law are revealed. All of these opinions are found in the Official Reports. Wigdor was convinced that Pound's work on the court did not result in his development of an internally cohesive legal theory. This intellectual defect, Wigdor concluded, "would haunt him in the future."

In truth, Pound wrote 25[5] opinions while serving on the commission. The error that some of his biographers made may be attributed to their failure to discover the Unofficial Reports of the Nebraska Supreme Court. These five volumes were intended to cover the work of the commission formed by the 1901 legislation. They reported the tribunal's work beginning with the January 1901 term, through the January 1904 term, that is, to a time almost a year after Pound had left the commission. The first volume of the Unofficial Reports contains the language of the statute authorizing the creation of the commission. That law was rushed through the legislature in the early months of 1901.

The work of the commission was not completed when Pound left in the late summer of 1903 for the law college, despite a claim to that effect by the president of the Nebraska State Bar Association to the annual meeting of the new lawyers' group and Pound's own recollection in an interview by Robert Manley six decades later.

The Meaning of the Commission Years

In 1997, N[atalie] E. H. Hull explored the contributions of Pound and Karl Llewellyn, the chief drafter of the Uniform Commercial Code, to the development of American jurisprudence.[8] Hull sifted through the vast collection of Pound's papers to determine what forces drove the great teacher in shaping his approach to the law. [S]he examined Pound's early years in Lincoln, his brief sojourn to Harvard Law School as a student, his return to Lincoln, the years of service on the commission, and his tenure at the law college.

Hull reveals that Pound was unhappy in Lincoln as a young lawyer. Pound felt during the early 1890s that he was tied to his father and his father's practice, and he was driven to return to his first love, botany. The author describes a Pound restless in his practice, ambitious in his pedagogic career, and eager to be released from the mundaneness of Lincoln, a frontier community far removed from the art, opera, and ideas he had found in Cambridge and Boston.

While Hull generally glosses over the years on the commission, [s]he does make two important observations about Pound's judicial experience. First, Hull maintains, one prime reason for Pound's abandoning the commission for academe was that he did not possess a judicial temperament. In a letter to a close friend before his appointment to the bench he wrote, "I hope I may never be a judge! The strain of being fair is a fearful one to a man naturally partisan—bitterly and uncompromisingly partisan, as you know." Second, Hull declares that more than being a professor or college administrator, Pound wanted to change the law.

Pound's court years, Reuschlein wrote in the 1940s, "served as an experimental laboratory for the philosophy, the method and the dynamic which he was later to recommend to all who follow the lawyer's craft." David Wigdor echoed this observation, stating that Pound's "most advanced theme" was "his denial that the law is a fixed body of immutable rules to be applied regardless of the social consequences."

In the sixty years following his judicial service, Commissioner Pound was to become a giant of the law, revered throughout the world for his vast learning, great scholarship, and immense contributions to the rule of law. His three years spent deciding relatively uncomplicated cases about the life and commerce of the plains undeniably contributed to his mastery of procedure and his understanding of the human condition.

Pound's Accomplishments

ALAN G. GLESS

Pound accomplished so much that only a very brief sketch can be presented here. As the third dean of the Nebraska College of Law, he led a major restructuring of the college's curriculum and approach to teaching, introducing the Socratic and case law methods he had learned at Harvard Law School. As Harvard Law School's dean from 1916 to 1936—through World

War I and the deepest years of the Great Depression—Pound created a graduate-level legal education program for the purpose of teaching law professors how and what to teach law students (although he left the regular law curriculum untouched), doubled the size of the student body, quadrupled the number of faculty, expanded and renovated the physical facility, increased the endowment sixfold, and further solidified the law school's standing as a premier institution of legal education in the United States.[9] His professional stature as Harvard Law School dean allowed him to exert a major influence on other legal education programs nationwide. His legal education reforms and his enhancements to the Harvard program—even either one of those accomplishments—would have sufficed to earn Pound a permanent place in American legal history. He also avidly sought reforms of the American court systems, legal procedure, and criminal law administration. But all those accomplishments still take a backseat to his work in legal philosophy.

As Wigdor noted: "American jurisprudence still stands in [Pound's] shadow."[10] Even within this single field of endeavor, constraints of time and space will limit the discussion to only two of his philosophical contributions. Pound was a prolific author. He delivered many, if not most, of his books and articles as lectures and later put them in print. Pound's legal philosophy, while generally consistent throughout his academic life, remained a work in progress until after he reached about ninety years of age. Many of his later jurisprudential publications reworked, elaborated, and refined his earlier efforts, frequently under the same or similar titles. A number of his later publications represented elaborations of ideas and themes introduced, but not fully developed, in earlier works.[11] A few, however, explored topics new to Pound's thought,[12] and others responded to the recent work of other legal philosophers or to changed conditions and developments in the legal world.

Pound became the primary developer and promoter of a movement he named sociological jurisprudence. The rise of this school of thought effectively led to the demise of the nineteenth-century focus on maximization of free individual self-assertion without regard for social consequences. In one of his earliest descriptions, he explained, "The sociological movement in jurisprudence is a movement for pragmatism as a philosophy of law; for the adjustment of principles and doctrines to the human conditions they are to govern rather than to assumed first principles; for putting the human factor in the central place and relegating logic to its true position as an instrument."[13]

When Pound wrote "Mechanical Jurisprudence," he was only beginning his journey into the science of law; he had not yet worked out his theory of principles, for he exhorted his readers to "[l]et the principles be formulated by whom or from whence you will."[14] In line with his early description of sociological jurisprudence, Pound envisioned "the task of the judge [as being] to make a principle living, not by deducing it from rules . . . but by achieving thoroughly the less ambitious but more useful labor of giving a fresh illustration of the intelligent application of the principle to a concrete cause, producing a workable and a just result."[15]

By the 1930s, Pound's attention had turned away from sociological jurisprudence and toward other philosophical work. He felt free to pursue other philosophical matters for at least three reasons. Sociological jurisprudence had accomplished its goal of releasing American legal philosophy from the grip of nineteenth-century formalism. Sociology itself had turned away from assisting in the development of law and toward its own internal methodological concerns and a desire to reestablish itself as an independent discipline. Finally, a number of Pound's disciples had gone beyond theoretical foundation he had laid, creating what came to be called legal realism and causing far more philosophical mischief than Pound could tolerate.

Whereas Pound may be recognized by most American lawyers as the primary architect and promoter of sociological jurisprudence, he influenced American legal philosophy far beyond that. Obviously, Pound was a legal pragmatist. Law, in all of its possible meanings, remained for him a practical matter. Generally, he claimed that he stuck to a descriptive or diagnostic legal philosophy, seldom venturing into the realm of prescriptive work. But he was unable totally to avoid prescriptive philosophy. As outlined below, he built his theory of interests on a prescriptive foundation.[16]

He did not construct his philosophy from hypotheticals or abstractions. His was primarily a practical philosophy based on the study of the actual cases brought before courts throughout legal history. His ability in both modern and classical languages allowed him to infuse his own philosophy with insights gleaned from ancient Greek, Roman, and Germanic law and legal philosophies as well as from modern Continental legal philosophies, a feat no other American jurisprudent had accomplished.

Pound built his thought on a foundational belief that both law and legal philosophy must remain flexible and responsive to the actual conditions and needs of different times and places. Pound firmly believed there were and could be no final answers to legal and jurisprudential questions. Time and place not only changed the answers but sometimes changed the questions as well.

His preface to the 1954 revised edition of his 1921 classic, *Introduction to Legal Philosophy,* illustrates this belief:

> Problems of philosophy of law have arisen in the generation since the first edition which have required rethinking of some of the things I said in 1921–22. Likewise discussions and recent theories of legal liability and some features of the law of property and of the law of contract, which have been developed throughout the world in recent decades, have called not only for rewriting of no little but also for considerable additions to the original text.[17]

Pound's ability to go back to the ancient Greek and Roman sources of the legal philosophical propositions undergirding the Western legal canon and to work his way to the present through both Continental and common-law sources allowed him to actualize his basic methodological belief that

> [a] philosopher, troubled by some vexing problem of his time and place, works out some reasoned solution. His disciples take it up and develop it as a universal theory good for all men in all times in all places. In order to understand it we must go back to the problem for which it was originally devised and must compare that problem with those of the times in which it comes to be applied as a universal solution.[18]

When he performed that very exercise, he found the legal philosophies of his predecessors generally lacking because of the change in circumstances between his present and the present of the earlier philosophers. But he also uncovered the permanent contributions of earlier legal philosophers, such as the Roman concept that judges and jurists should measure all situations by an idealized form of the social order of the time and place and so shape the law as to maintain and further this ideal of the social status quo.[19] According to Pound, this idealized form of the social order of the time and place forms the ideal element in law, that is, a body of received ideals regarding the end (purpose) of law and what a society's legal precepts should be and how they should be applied.

He also isolated juristic principles, or ideal elements, that had remained valid from the earliest times to his present. In ancient legal systems, Pound located as the first ideal of the legal order the simple concept of keeping the peace. Then he found in Greek legal philosophy that the ideal of the legal order became the maintenance of the social status quo. In the Dark Ages, the ideal reverted to keeping the peace. The Middle Ages saw the readoption of the ideal of maintaining the social status quo. The ideal that developed and prevailed in the seventeenth through the nineteenth centuries was located in the post-Reformation Kantian goal of creating a maximum of free individual self-assertion as the greatest good. Pound's conception of the various stages of the history of law embodies the gradual refocusing of law.[20]

Pound, himself, sought the displacement of the ideal of maximum free individual self-assertion and free competition with an ideal of cooperation and with the reconception of law in terms of social engineering. Pound's law-as-social-engineering concept carried none of the negative connotations current in the early twenty-first century.

When Pound described law as social engineering, he envisioned law and its administration as a part of a much wider process of social ordering, one functioning through courts and administrative agencies with the aid of legal precepts as partial guides. His perceived task of social ordering presupposed a sincere effort to avoid or, at least, to reduce the number and severity of collisions resulting from the conflict of interests.

Pound believed that all the activities of the legal order—the efforts of courts, administrators, legislatures, and jurists—should be directed toward the adjustment of relations, the compromise of conflicting claims, the securing of interests by determining boundaries within which each interest may be asserted with a minimum of friction, and the finding of means whereby a greater number of claims may be satisfied with a sacrifice of fewer. In Pound's understanding of social engineering, law's purpose lay in the satisfaction of all demands and the securing of all interests with a minimum of conflict so that the means of satisfaction may have the widest possible distribution.[21]

Pound's comparisons of the activities of courts over the course of history led him to his theory of interests. This theory became a bedrock feature of his philosophy and probably its most lasting contribution to American law. He believed that the vindication of rights—what late nineteenth- and early twentieth-century American courts claimed they were doing—should be dropped as the focus of litigation.

Instead, when resolving disputes, courts should interpret the applicable legal doctrines and the bases of the claims seeking legal recognition in terms of the social interests secured by the application of legal doctrines and recognition of claims. In other words, adjudication requires that adjudicators identify, weigh, and balance the competing interests involved in disputes submitted for resolution. For purposes of his theory of interests, Pound defined an interest as:

> a demand or desire which human beings either individually or in groups or in associations or in relations, seek to satisfy, of which, therefore, the ordering of human relations must take account. . . . It is not group demands or desires, but the strivings of men in (or perhaps one should say through) groups and associations and relations to satisfy certain demands or desires. The legal order or the law does not create these interests. There is this much truth in the old idea of a state of nature and theory of natural rights, namely, that interests in this sense would exist if there were no legal order but were some other form of social control, and no body of authoritative guides to conduct or decision. Conflicts or competition between interests arise because of the competition of individuals with each other, the competition of groups or societies of men with each other, and the competition of individuals with such groups or societies, in the endeavor to satisfy human wants. The law, then, does not create these interests. But it classifies them and recognizes a larger or smaller number. Also it defines the extent to which it will give effect to these interests which it recognizes. It may do this in view of other interests. These other interests may be directly recognized and limited or secured . . . . Or the extent to which it will give effect to recognized interests may be limited in view of other interests which get only indirect recognition through limitations imposed on expressly recognized interests . . . . Or the extent to which legally recognized interests are given effect may be limited in view of the possibilities of effectively securing them through the legal order. Next, the legal order devises means for securing interests when recognized and within the defined limits.[22]

Pound developed,[23] and redeveloped,[24] as times and needs changed during his lifetime, six broad categories of social interests by studying as many actual litigated cases as he could and by isolating the claims pressed upon the courts in those cases, as supplemented by his studies of earlier legal systems. He then categorized the interests. He identified a social interest in general security, which comprised public health, protection against crime and foreign aggression, and security of contracts and property. His social interest in the security of social institutions encompassed protection of religion, domestic relations, political freedoms, and the economy. The social interest in general morals related to the problems of obscenity and other violations of community moral standards. His social interest in the conservation of social resources included both physical and human resources. His final category included social interests in general progress and in the individual life.[25] Pound's placement of an interest in one category did not preclude it from membership in another category as well. After reworking these categories over time, he came to believe that the social interest in the individual life might very well have become one of the most important.[26]

Pound designed his categorical scheme to promote thorough and systematic analysis of legal problems, but he did not consider his catalogue of interests complete or unchanging. He framed flexible, expansive categories that could accommodate new demands. The primary interests were social rather than individual and suggested clusters of interrelated problems. Furthermore, they were not a priori values. Social interests were constructs that emerged from the operation of society itself, and the balancing of those interests gave society its basic character and unity.[27]

Pound also described the tasks required by his theory of interests:

> [I]n determining the scope and subject matter of the legal system we have to consider five things: (1) we must take an inventory of the interests which press for recognition and must generalize them and classify them; (2) we must select and determine the interests which the law should recognize and seek to secure; (3) we must fix the limits of securing the interests so selected . . . ; (4) we must consider the means by which the law may secure interests when recognized and delimited, that is, we must take account of the limitations upon effective legal action which may preclude complete recognition or complete securing of interests which otherwise we seek to secure . . . ; (5) in order to do these things we must work out principles of valuation of interests. The chief importance of these principles is in determining what interests to recognize, or, in other words, in selection of interests to be recognized. But we must use these principles also in fixing the limits of securing recognized interests, and fixing upon the means of securing interests, and in judging of the weight to be accorded in any given case to the practical limitations upon effective legal action.[28]

Consistently with his perceived need for flexibility to fit valuation criteria to the time and the place, Pound declined to identify criteria for the weight to be given the interests so that they can be balanced. Instead, he advised:

> In practice interests are recognized and secured and legal precepts are interpreted and applied with reference to ideals of the end of law and ultimately of the ideal relation among men. While philosophers argue as to an absolute measure of values, received ideals of the purpose of the legal order and of justice as the ideal relation among men, received traditionally in the time and place, have to serve.[29]

Pound did caution that when "weighing or valuing [interests] with respect to other [interests], we must be careful to compare them on the same plane."[30] That is, one must compare a social interest with another social interest. Comparing an individual interest with a social interest decides the question by the way one poses the comparison without ever reaching the comparative underlying values. Pound also observed:

> [T]he practical process of the legal order does not stop at finding by experience what will serve to adjust conflicting and overlapping interests. Reason has its part as well as experience . . . . Jurists work out the jural postulates, the presuppositions as to relations and conduct, of civilized society in the time and place, and arrive in this way at starting points for judicial reasoning. Experience is developed by reason on this basis, and reason is tested by experience.[31]

Pound's theory of interests is probably his philosophy's most lasting contribution to American law, because it has described for generations of law students an approach to the resolution of legal disputes through court and administrative agency action. Whether they realized it or not, as lawyers and judges, those generations of law students have used (and continue to use) Pound's theory of interests almost as a matter of second nature in arguing and deciding cases. When properly applied, Pound's theory of interests works and will continue to work as a theory of advocacy and adjudication. Thus, one reasonably can argue that Roscoe Pound was Nebraska's single greatest contribution to the history of American law.

Notes

The title of this chapter was inspired by Paul Finkelman.

1. George A. Strait, *A Bibliography of the Writings of Roscoe Pound, 1940–1960*, (Cambridge, Mass.: Harvard Law School Library, 1960); Franklin C. Setaro, *A Bibli-*

ography of the Writings of Roscoe Pound, Harvard Series of Legal Bibliographies 3 (Cambridge, Mass.: Harvard University Press, 1942). Strait and Setaro credit Pound with 1,056 law-related publications. Pound's 1959 major publication, *Jurisprudence,* earned him credit from Strait for only one major book publication, but *Jurisprudence* was five volumes long. Between Strait's 1960 cutoff date and Pound's 1964 death, Pound published sixteen more articles. His seventeenth and last article, published posthumously, appeared as "The Case for Law," *Valparaiso University Law Review* 1, no. 2 (1967): 201.

2. Originally published in *Nebraska Lawyer* (August 2000): 18–22 (citations added and minor stylistic changes made to keep the style of this volume consistent), reprinted with permission from the Nebraska State Bar Association.

3. Paul Sayre, *The Life of Roscoe Pound* (Iowa City: College of Law Committee, State University of Iowa, 1948).

4. Lewis C. Cassidy, "Dean Pound: The Scope of His Life and Work," *New York University Law Quarterly Review* 7, no. 4 (1930): 897–940.

5. Harold Gill Reuschlein, "Roscoe Pound—The Judge," *University of Pennsylvania Law Review* 90, no. 3 (1942): 292–329.

6. Sheldon Glueck, ed., *Roscoe Pound and Criminal Justice* (Dobbs Ferry, N.Y. : Published for National Council on Crime and Delinquency by Oceana Publications, 1965).

7. David Wigdor, *Roscoe Pound: Philosopher of Law* (Westport, Conn.: Greenwood, 1974).

8. N. E. H. Hull, *Roscoe Pound and Karl Llewellyn: Searching for an American Jurisprudence* (Chicago: University of Chicago Press, 1997).

9. Wigdor, *Roscoe Pound,* 248.

10. Wigdor, *Roscoe Pound,* 287.

11. For example, Roscoe Pound, *The Spirit of the Common Law* (Boston: Marshall Jones, 1921), slightly revised and heavily elaborated upon ideas initially presented in Roscoe Pound, "The Spirit of the Common Law," *Green Bag* 18 (January 1906): 17–25. Roscoe Pound, "A Survey of Social Interests," *Harvard Law Review* 57, no. 1 (1943): 1–39, completely revised and rewrote Roscoe Pound, "A Theory of Social Interests," *Publications of the American Sociological Society* 15 (May 1921): 16–45. Many other examples could be cited; these two suffice.

12. For example, Roscoe Pound, "Natural Natural Law and Positive Natural Law," *Law Quarterly Review* 68 (July 1952): 330–36.

13. Roscoe Pound, "Mechanical Jurisprudence," *Columbia Law Review* 8, no. 8 (1908): 609–10.

14. Ibid., 623.

15. Ibid., 622.

16. I thank Edward B. McLean for this observation shared with me in the course of reviewing this chapter.

17. Roscoe Pound, *An Introduction to the Philosophy of Law,* rev. ed. (New Haven, Conn.: Yale University Press, 1954), ix.

18. Pound, "Natural Natural Law and Positive Natural Law," 333. This position on legal philosophy is reminiscent of his much earlier position on the flexibility of the meaning of the "common law of England" as used in Nebraska's common-law

adoption statute. In *Williams v. Miles,* 68 Neb. 463, 469–71, 94 N.W. 705, 708 (1903), Commissioner Pound wrote: "The theory of our system is that the law consists, not in the actual rules enforced by decisions of the courts at any one time, but the principles from which those rules flow; that old principles are applied to new cases, and the rules resulting from such application are modified from time to time as changed conditions and new states of fact require." Thus, as early as 1903, Pound had begun to abandon the idea of law as a body of fixed and immutable rules to be applied no matter what might be the social result. His idea that legal rules must respond to social change was already coming to the fore in his thought. Cf. Wigdor, *Roscoe Pound,* 84.

19. Pound, *Introduction to the Philosophy of Law,* 12.

20. I also owe Edward B. McLean for this observation.

21. Roscoe Pound, *Interpretations of Legal History* (New York: Macmillan, 1923), 151–65.

22. Roscoe Pound, "My Philosophy of Law," in *The Great Legal Philosophers: Selected Readings in Jurisprudence,* ed. Clarence Morris (Philadelphia: University of Pennsylvania Press, 1959), 536–37. Originally published as Roscoe Pound, "My Philosophy of Law," in *Credos of Sixteen American Scholars* (Boston: Julius Rosenthal Foundation, 1941), 249–62, of which WorldCat reports only two libraries worldwide have a copy.

23. Pound, "Theory of Social Interests," 16–45.

24. See, e.g., Roscoe Pound, *The Ideal Element in Law* (Indianapolis, Ind.: Liberty Fund, 2002): 109–39; *Introduction to the Philosophy of Law,* 42–47; "My Philosophy of Law," 532–37; "Survey of Social Interests," 1–39.

25. I have adapted this compressed restatement of Pound's social interests from Wigdor, *Roscoe Pound,* 213.

26. See, e.g., Pound, "Survey of Social Interests," 1–39. Pound distilled far more than his category of social interests from the cases. His other categories included individual interests and public interests. For condensed descriptions of the full gamut of Pound's categories of interests, see Edward B. McLean, *Law and Civilization: The Legal Thought of Roscoe Pound* (Lanham, Md.: University Press of America, 1992), 215–47.

27. Wigdor, *Roscoe Pound,* 213–14.

28. Pound, "My Philosophy of Law," 536–37.

29. Pound, *Ideal Element in Law,* 139. The Liberty Fund's 2002 publication was the first time *The Ideal Element in Law* was published in the United States. The 1948 Tagore Law Lectures were published for the first time only in 1958 as Roscoe Pound, *The Ideal Element in Law* (Calcutta: University of Calcutta, 1958).

Pound delivered the lectures comprising *The Ideal Element in Law* at the University of Calcutta, India, in 1948, according to Stephen Presser's introduction to the Liberty Fund edition (ibid., viii). Presser also gave Pound's year of birth incorrectly as 1872 (ibid., vii). Presser claimed, "The [Tagore] lectures were delivered in 1948, six years *before Brown v. Board of Education* 1954 (citation in original omitted), and they are blessedly free of the arrogance of the kind of imperative legal theory that began with that case," and used the occasion to launch an attack on the Supreme Court's jurisprudence in the years after *Brown*. Ibid., xii–xiii.

Strait gave the date of Pound's Tagore lectures as 1948, but said that they were delivered in 1953. Strait, *Bibliography of the Writings of Roscoe Pound, 1940–1960,* 6.

McLean said that the lectures were delivered in 1956. McLean, *Law and Civilization,* xviii.

In response to my inquiry, the Law Library of Congress's online reference law librarian found in the Library of Congress's Manuscript Division microfilm copies of Pound's papers, the originals of which were deposited with Harvard University. Reels 50 and 51 concerned the Tagore lectures. "From correspondence on these reels between Professor Pound and the University of Calcutta, it is clear that Professor Pound delivered the Tagore Law Lectures in August/September 1953." E-mail, Law Library of Congress, Public Services Division, to Alan G. Gless, February 21, 2007.

30. Pound, *Ideal Element in Law,* 114.

31. Ibid., 124.

CONTRIBUTORS

J. DAVID AIKEN, a native Nebraskan, graduated from Hastings College and received his law degree from George Washington University in Washington, D.C. After law school, Aiken joined the staff of the University of Nebraska Department of Agricultural Economics in 1975. Aiken is a member of the Nebraska Bar Association and is past chairman of the Natural Resources Section of the Nebraska State Bar Association. He has published more than a hundred technical and popular works dealing with water rights, environmental law, and agricultural law.

BRIAN H. BORNSTEIN is professor of psychology and law at the University of Nebraska–Lincoln, where he is associate director of the Law-Psychology Program. He received his Ph.D. in psychology from the University of Pennsylvania and his master of legal studies from the University of Nebraska–Lincoln. Prior to joining the UNL faculty in 2000, he taught at Louisiana State University. His primary research interests are jury decision making, eyewitness testimony, and justice.

THOMAS H. COX is assistant professor of history at Sam Houston State University in Huntsville, Texas. A native of Shreveport, Louisiana, Cox received his Ph.D. in history from the State University of New York at Buffalo. He is also a graduate of Birmingham-Southern College in Birmingham, Alabama. His monograph on *Gibbons v. Ogden* and the transformation of commerce in the early republic is forthcoming from Ohio University Press.

MARK R. ELLIS is associate professor of history at the University of Nebraska–Kearney. He is a specialist in the legal history of the American West and has published articles in *Western Historical Quarterly, Nebraska History,* and *South Dakota History.* His book, *Law and Order in Buffalo Bill's Country: Legal Culture and Community in the Great Plains,* will be published by the University of Nebraska Press.

TIM A. GARRISON is associate professor of history and director of Native American studies at Portland State University. He is the author of *The Legal Ideology of Removal: The Southern Judiciary and the Sovereignty of Native American Nations.*

ALAN G. GLESS, district court judge for the Fifth Judicial District of Nebraska, earned his bachelor's and law degrees at the University of Nebraska–Lincoln. Gless is now in his twenty-eighth year as a state trial court judge, and his previous writings have dealt primarily with criminal procedure, criminal law, evidence, and American legal history in such publications as the *Nebraska Law Review, Justice System Journal, The Green Bag 2d, Behavioral Science and Law,* and the *American Journal of Legal History.*

JOHN M. GRADWOHL is Judge Harry A. Spencer Professor of Law at the University of Nebraska College of Law. He holds B.S. and J.D. degrees from the University of Nebraska and an LL.M. from Harvard Law School.

JAMES W. HEWITT has earned a B.S., M.A., J.D., and Ph.D., all from the University of Nebraska. He was admitted to the Nebraska bar in 1956. He has served as the president of the Nebraska State Bar Association (1985–86), a member of the board of governors of the American Bar Association (1980–83), chair of the fellows of the American Bar Foundation (1995), president of the Nebraska State Historical Society Foundation (1999–2003), and adjunct professor of history at Nebraska Wesleyan University (2001 to date).

PETER J. LONGO, professor of political science at the University of Nebraska–Kearney, holds a B.A. in history from Creighton University, a J.D. (barely) from the University of Nebraska–Lincoln, and a Ph.D. in political science from the University of Nebraska–Lincoln. Longo coauthored with the late Robert Miewald *The Nebraska State Constitution,* coedited a water policy book, and has written a number of articles.

EVELYN M. MAEDER is a graduate student in the Law-Psychology Program at the University of Nebraska–Lincoln. She is currently pursuing her Ph.D. in social psychology as well as a master of legal studies (M.L.S). Evelyn studies jury decision making, including death penalty research, sexual harassment research, generic prejudice, and the effects of race.

WILLIAM G. ROSS is professor of law at Cumberland School of Law at Samford University in Birmingham, Alabama, where he has taught since 1988. His courses include legal history, constitutional law, and legal ethics. A graduate of Stanford and Harvard Law School, he practiced law in New York City for nine years. His books include a history of the *Meyer* case, *Forging New Freedoms: Nativism, Education, and Constitution, 1917–1927; A Muted Fury: Populists, Progressives, and Labor Unions Confront the Courts, 1890–1937;* and

The Chief Justiceship of Charles Evans Hughes. He is also the author of *The Honest Hour: The Ethics of Time-Based Billing by Attorneys.*

MARK R. SCHERER is associate professor of history at the University of Nebraska–Omaha. He holds a Ph.D. from the University of Nebraska and a J.D. from the Ohio State University Moritz College of Law. His areas of specialization include U.S. legal and constitutional history as well as the history of Nebraska and the Great Plains. His research agenda has devoted special attention to Native American legal themes. Along with numerous journal articles and other publications, he is the author of *Imperfect Victories: The Legal Tenacity of the Omaha Tribe, 1945–1995.*

ANTHONY B. SCHUTZ is assistant professor at the University of Nebraska College of Law. Schutz is a 2003 graduate of the College of Law and joined the faculty in 2006. During law school, he worked for Cline, Williams, Wright, Johnson, and Oldfather in Lincoln, Nebraska, and was the editor in chief of the *Nebraska Law Review.* Schutz then clerked for the Honorable C. Arlen Beam of the U.S. Court of Appeals for the Eighth Circuit until 2005. During the 2004–5 academic year, he also taught legal research and writing at the College of Law as an adjunct instructor. During the 2005–6 academic year, he was a visiting lecturer in the Lawyering Program at Cornell Law School.

RICHARD E. SHUGRUE is professor of law at Creighton University in Omaha (retired). Shugrue earned his bachelor's, law, and doctoral degrees from the University of Nebraska–Lincoln. He has taught at the University of Nebraska–Lincoln, the University of Nebraska–Omaha, Nebraska Wesleyan University, and was a faculty member at Creighton for more than thirty-five years. Shugrue is a former chair of the Nebraska State Bar Association's house of delegates.

SUSAN I. STRONG graduated with a B.A. from the University of Nebraska in 1981 and received a J.D. (cum laude) from Pepperdine University School of Law, where she was a literary editor of the *Pepperdine Law Review,* in 1985. She clerked for the Honorable Richard P. Matsch, judge of the U.S. District Court for the District of Colorado, before becoming an associate at Sherman and Howard (1986–90) and at Kobayashi and Associates (1990–94) in Denver, Colorado. In 1994, she returned to Lincoln, Nebraska, where she practiced litigation with Plessman Law Offices (1994–2006), after which she joined the Public Protection Bureau of the Attorney General's Office. She is a past chair and current member of the executive committee for the

Women and the Law Section of the Nebraska State Bar Association, as well as past vice chair and former member of the District One Disciplinary Committee on Inquiry of the Nebraska Supreme Court. She is also a member of the Lincoln, Nebraska, Colorado, and American bar associations, Nebraska Association of Trial Attorneys, and Robert Van Pelt American Inn of Court. Also in 2006, she was appointed a county court judge serving the Third Judicial District.

WARREN K. URBOM practiced law in Lincoln, Nebraska, from 1953 until he was appointed judge of the U.S. District Court for the District of Nebraska by President Richard Nixon in 1970. He moved into senior status at the end of 1990 and has continued to try cases in Nebraska and elsewhere as need beckons.

RICHARD L. WIENER received his Ph.D. from the University of Houston and his master in legal studies at UNL. He was professor of psychology at Saint Louis University (1982–2000), chair of the Department of Psychology at Baruch College, City University of New York (2000–2002), and now directs the Law and Psychology Program at the University of Nebraska. He was editor of *Law and Human Behavior* for nine years, until December 2005. Wiener's research applies theories of social cognition to problems in legal decision making. He has published articles and book chapters on perceptions of sexual harassment, judgments of medical malpractice, and sociolegal jurisprudence. Wiener teaches courses at UNL on behavioral sciences and the law and legal decision making.

CHARLES E. WRIGHT earned a B.S.L. from the University of Nebraska in 1954 and an LL.B. in 1958. He is a member of the Lincoln and Nebraska bar associations, past president of the Great Plains Federal Tax Institute, Nebraska Continuing Education, Inc., and fellow of the Nebraska and American bar associations. He has served in various capacities with the University of Nebraska Foundation, Nebraska Game and Parks Commission, and the Museum of Nebraska Art. Wright is also the author of the forthcoming *Horses, Rifles and Reconnaissance.*

INDEX